RESEARCH
ESSENTIALS

RESEARCH
ESSENTIALS

AN INTRODUCTION
TO DESIGNS AND PRACTICES

STEPHEN D. LAPAN
MARYLYNN T. QUARTAROLI

EDITORS

JOSSEY-BASS
A Wiley Imprint
www.josseybass.com

Published by Jossey-Bass
A Wiley Imprint
989 Market Street, San Francisco, CA 94103-1741—www.josseybass.com

Jossey-Bass books and products are available through most bookstores. To contact Jossey-Bass directly call our Customer Care Department within the U.S. at 800-956-7739, outside the U.S. at 317-572-3986, or fax 317-572-4002.

Jossey-Bass also publishes its books in a variety of electronic formats. Some content that appears in print may not be available in electronic books.

Library of Congress Cataloging-in-Publication Data

Research essentials : an introduction to designs and practices / Stephen D. Lapan, Marylynn T. Quartaroli, editors.
   p.cm.
 Includes bibliographical references and index.
 ISBN 978-0-470-18109-6 (pbk.)
 1. Research—Methodology—Textbooks. 2. Education—Research—Methodology—Textbooks. 3. Social sciences—Research—Methodology—Textbooks. I. Lapan, Stephen D. II. Quartaroli, Marylynn T., 1950-

 Q180.55.M4R458 2009
 001.4′2—dc22

                  2008038209

Printed in the United States of America
FIRST EDITION

PB Printing   10 9 8 7 6 5 4 3 2 1

To my wife and closest friend, Pat Hays, who supports or, when necessary, tolerates my dozens of projects like this one.

—SDL

To Richard D. Quartaroli, my husband and dearest companion, for his continuous supply of interest, encouragement, and delicious meals as I venture out into yet another enterprise.

—MLQ

.

.

CONTENTS

TABLES, FIGURES, AND EXHIBITS

TABLES

FIGURES

EXHIBITS

PREFACE

This beginning textbook, *Research Essentials: An Introduction to Design and Practices*, is designed specifically for students taking their first and possibly only research course. Writing a text for students in education and the social sciences, we set out to serve three main purposes:

1. Provide a broad spectrum of research approaches, ranging from traditional experiments to practitioner self-study (action research)

2. Detail the basic purposes and processes of research approaches, explaining in each case how they are planned, conducted, and reported

3. Offer explanations and examples of how educational and social scientific research study results can be interpreted, evaluated, and applied across many professions

This book can also serve as an introductory source for students who plan to pursue advanced study and conduct their own research, but its primary aim is to offer readable, accessible content for the practitioner-consumer.

TO THE INSTRUCTOR

> *[T]he scientific approach is a logical method of inquiry, not a body of knowledge. It is not tied to particular fields of study,*
> *to laboratory situations, or to men and women in white coats developing complex theories.*
> —McMillan, 2004, p. 5

This introductory research text is intended as a guide for your students, who are most likely to be consumers but not producers of research. While the book might serve as a primer for fledgling researchers, the overarching goal is to support your efforts in teaching students to become more intelligent readers and interpreters of research conducted by others.

The specific audiences are students in upper-level undergraduate and beginning graduate research courses who are *not* likely to pursue additional research course work on their own. Thus, no prior experience or prerequisite course work would be required before using this text.

The book is structured to support your instructional endeavors in encouraging students to recognize important distinctions between research-based work and alternative sources of knowledge, to be able to understand the language and procedures normally encountered in different types of research studies, and to make practical sense of such studies in translating findings for use in everyday practice. Instructional objectives emphasized in this text include:

- Using, where possible, nontechnical language to explain research ideas
- Providing practical explanations of research approaches and the kinds of questions each answers
- Presenting clear-cut descriptions of most approaches used in educational and social scientific research
- Making clear distinctions between a wide array of research approaches
- Offering explanations for necessary technical terms needed to understand how research is reported
- Examining forms and criteria for planning and conducting research
- Showing how each approach can be critically evaluated and interpreted from a practitioner's perspective
- Identifying actual research studies to allow students to practice critical analysis

The book is organized for a college course format where one to two chapters may be assigned each week. And because each chapter can stand on its own, the instructor may use the sequence offered or select a sequence that suits unique instructional plans. Additional instructional features are:

- The inclusion of special chapters on ethics, reviewing literature, meta-analysis, quantitative and qualitative data analysis, and the potential influence of research on practice
- A writing style that makes ideas accessible to students new to the field
- A diverse and balanced perspective of a broad range of research methodologies
- A distribution of challenging questions throughout each chapter to aid in instructional planning
- The identification of key research ideas, concepts, and terms
- An annotated set of relevant readings and an array of journals, organizations, and Web sites as sources for assignments and class discussions at the end of each chapter
- Expert authors for each chapter

TO THE STUDENT

One of the most confusing things to the student of science is the special way the scientist uses ordinary words. To make matters worse, he (or she) invents new words.
—Kerlinger & Lee, 2000, p. 3

This text is presented to you based on the assumption that you have little or no background in how research is conducted in your field. Most who take a course of this kind will not major in research nor become researchers one day. They will need to know how to read, understand, and interpret research so that they may judge its worth and practical value.

Therefore, the material here is presented using nontechnical language whenever that is possible. When technical terms are needed, they are offered along with practical explanations to increase your understanding. Further, you are provided with a broad coverage of research approaches (sometimes called **methodologies**) ranging from traditional **survey research** (for example, "How do parents judge their local school programs?") to newer accepted research applications such as **program evaluation** (for example, "What are the strengths and shortcomings of the drug intervention program in our community?").

As a student, your objectives for a course using this text should include learning about how research is planned, carried out, and reported so that you, as a practitioner, might be able to read and interpret the results. Whether or not each research study's results should be used depends on your ability to judge if the studies are done well. To be effective readers and evaluators of research in education and the social sciences, a student should gain from this text the ability to

- Recognize and judge ethical issues in research

- See the relation between literature reviews and understanding research findings

- Comprehend the ideas and terms used to explain how each kind of research study is conducted

- Understand how each approach is organized and planned

- Recognize that practitioner questions may be answered differently depending on which research methodology is used

- Explain the similarities and differences found among research methodologies

- Know when specific data analysis approaches are appropriate

- Develop ways of evaluating actual research studies to determine whether or not findings can be trusted

- Gain insight into how or when research might be translated into policy and practice

Some Study Suggestions

Many students find the language and procedures associated with research to be frightening or at least foreign to their everyday world. The following suggestions may assist students in tackling this relatively new and unusual area of study:

- Read the textbook before the course begins, making margin notes

- Commit new terminology and definitions to memory along with at least two examples

- Use chapter questions to monitor understanding

- Rewrite class notes and compare to assigned readings

- Form a study group to test understanding "out loud"

- Talk with advanced students who have successfully completed the course for suggestions on content and study habits

ACKNOWLEDGMENTS

There are many who made significant contributions to the preparation of this textbook; most prominent among these are the chapter authors who worked diligently to adjust their individual writing styles to the rhythm and flow of the manuscript. We are grateful for their patience and considerable efforts on our behalf. We also want to acknowledge our doctoral students at Northern Arizona University who offered their continuous and timely suggestions for every chapter, and to Chris Cavert in particular, for his thorough literature review of case study methodology, saving us countless hours in the preparation of that chapter.

Finally, we are indebted to our editor, Andy Pasternack, who supported and advocated for our proposed text from the outset; to our assistant editor, Seth Schwartz, for his oversight of all the details; to our copyeditor, Donna Cohn, for her thorough and valuable feedback; and to Kelsey McGee for shepherding the book through to its publication.

INTRODUCTION

In this introductory text, **research** is defined as **disciplined inquiry**, that is, the organized and systematic study conducted in certain fields using each field's accepted procedures and rules. This disciplined inquiry includes applying standards recognized and set forth in each field or discipline that are considered necessary for producing trustworthy findings (**study validity**). The term "disciplined inquiry" refers to the idea that there are generally accepted principles and procedures that are expected to be followed as closely as possible by researchers. The study results are then reviewed by peers in the same field of study.

Generally accepted principles and procedures vary from one field or discipline to another, sometimes remarkably so. What counts as good research in psychology, for example, would be quite unlike the standards used in historical research. This text offers a wide spectrum of research methodologies ranging from **traditional** approaches that are much more laboratory-like (experimental, for example) to **naturalistic** methodologies that are characterized as more lifelike (case study, for example).

ROLE OF RESEARCH IN UNDERSTANDING

All of us do what we are able in making sense of and possibly controlling our environment, using whatever means we think are effective. *Personal experience* can assist in negotiating the world around us as we recall that ovens can be hot to the touch and busy streets may be dangerous to cross against the light. We also may depend on *tradition* or well-formed habits, often without reflecting on our reasons for using these rules of thumb. At yet other times, we apply our power of *reasoning* by weighing options in situations, choosing what logically appears to be the best course of action. Finally, there are circumstances where we depend on *experts* or authorities whose judgment we are likely to believe.

Many issues and problems that we confront are likely addressed, if not resolved, using any combination of experience, habit, logic, and authority. Our decisions about which school to attend or even choosing life partners are usually based on these **sources of knowledge**, sometimes effectively.

An alternative knowledge source, one likely to be more trustworthy, is what is known as **research-based knowledge** (empirical knowledge), information produced from careful observation and analysis by applying disciplined inquiry. These empirical investigations are carried out in fairly precise ways that involve well-defined samples, settings, and boundaries. One category of these empirical studies is called **scientific research**, conducted in highly controlled environments, often laboratories, where clearly defined causes are tested and manipulated to achieve desired effects. **Social scientific research** or **social inquiry**, by contrast, is more often characterized by the observation of real-life or natural events as they occur, with the goal of describing and explaining, rather than controlling and manipulating. Research studies conducted in education and the social sciences (social inquiry), the focus of this text, actually range in format from more or less laboratory-like studies such as experiments, comparing groups receiving different experiences, to studies that set out to observe and report natural accounts of an event or program, as case studies do. Social science research might, therefore, examine the effects of whole language versus phonics (treatments) on randomly sampled students or recount the essential functions of a conflict resolution program at a local prison. The language study is much closer to the scientific model, whereas the prison investigation is remarkably unlike laboratory research.

As a textbook focused on educational and social scientific research, the content outlined represents a full array of methodologies usually employed in (including but not limited to) the following social science fields:

- Anthropology
- Communication studies
- Criminal justice
- Economics
- Education
- Geography
- Health professions
- History
- Information science
- Linguistics
- Political science
- Psychology
- Sociobiology
- Sociology

A TOUR OF THIS TEXT

Research Essentials includes two chapters that introduce the reader to how social scientific research is planned, including ways study participants must be respected and protected (Chapter One), and how the inspection of past research literature contributes to the effective design of studies (Chapter Two). Chapters Three through Five (Experimental and Quasi-Experimental; Nonexperimental; and Survey Methods) contain explanations of more or less laboratory-like traditional methodologies emphasizing definitions, design options, typical data sought, and methods for producing valid findings. Experiments and quasi-experiments are usually designed to compare the effects of one experience to another, whereas nonexperimental studies often study the reasons behind effects that have already occurred, such as determining the causes behind high school dropout rates. Survey methods are used in obtaining broad-based data such as a region's corn crop production figures or the number and kind of special education programs in a state or country. Chapter Six offers guidance regarding specific statistical tests and procedures used to analyze data ordinarily collected in these traditional studies.

The reader is presented with a way to statistically summarize the results of many studies on the same topic in Chapter Seven. Here Gene V Glass, the inventor of the method called **meta-analysis**, outlines a practical framework for readers to use as they interpret meta-analytic reports. For example, practitioners can read summaries using meta-analysis to indicate whether or not the number of pupils in a classroom affects achievement.

Decidedly more **naturalistic**, nontraditional research methodologies are explained in Chapters Eight through Eleven. These include historical, case study, evaluation, and ethnographic studies presenting definitions, designs, data collection, and study validation frameworks for each approach. Historical research may focus on the reconstruction of the past related to a significant event, as one example, while case studies achieve the same objective for selected current phenomena. Evaluation studies examine programs and other entities to determine their quality and effectiveness; ethnographic research seeks to explain organizations or programs by studying patterns of beliefs and practices.

The special issues of feminist perspectives and the use of multimethods in research are addressed in Chapters Twelve and Thirteen, respectively. Feminist approaches recognize that, too often, studies emphasize white male and other dominant cultural beliefs when they are designed and analyzed, but can be reconsidered through other belief systems. Also, by using multimethod approaches researchers are taking advantage of both qualitative and quantitative data in planning their research to obtain richer detail in their findings.

Because nontraditional studies often emphasize the use of words (qualitative data) in their findings, a summary of how this data can be analyzed, summarized, and reported in meaningful ways is presented in Chapter Fourteen, explaining coding and other forms of classifying qualitative data.

Finally, the application of research to practice is framed in Chapters Fifteen and Sixteen. Chapter Fifteen explains how practitioners act as researchers (action research) using self-reflection to improve practice; and, in Chapter Sixteen, the author offers the challenge of whether or not research findings guide policy making or everyday practice.

A WORD ABOUT QUALITATIVE VERSUS QUANTITATIVE STUDIES

In educational and social scientific research, investigators must decide what kind of data or information they will obtain during their studies. Although this decision is driven primarily by the purposes served in a particular study design, it is generally expected that traditional research commonly employs numbers or quantitative data, most often test scores. Conversely, naturalistic designs more often emphasize words or qualitative data. These may be typical patterns but should not lead the reader to assume such data collection strategies are always in place. Indeed, many traditional researchers have planned their studies to include qualitative explanations of treatment choices and research settings, while naturalistic observers often summarize at least a portion of their findings quantitatively as a more precise way of presenting certain results.

In the world of social research, veterans commonly refer to traditional studies as "quantitative" and naturalistic research as "qualitative," but the reader should be cautious in assuming that these labels reveal the kind of data being used in every instance. While the terms conveniently classify these research designs, they can just as easily mislead. It is best to inspect the study design itself to determine exactly what kinds of information are being used in the investigation.

Stephen D. Lapan
MaryLynn T. Quartaroli
2008

THE EDITORS

STEPHEN D. LAPAN received a PhD in Educational Psychology from the University of Connecticut with emphases in research, measurement, and evaluation. He is currently a professor in the College of Education at Northern Arizona University (NAU) and directs the Curriculum and Instruction Doctoral Program. He has conducted various types of research including several program evaluations. He has developed and taught courses in statistics, tests and measurements, program evaluation, action research, introduction to research, paradigms for research, and currently teaches introductory and advanced research courses. Among his publications are two books, *Survival in the Classroom* (with E. House) and *Foundations for Research* (with K. deMarrais); a monograph, *The Meaning of Intelligence;* and several book chapters including *Evaluation Studies, The Defining Criteria for Excellence, and Policy, Productivity, and Teacher Evaluation* (with E. House). Recent awards include the Arizona Association for Gifted and Talented Honor Board Life Achievement Award, Northern Arizona University College of Education Distinguished Service Award for Research, and Northern Arizona University first campuswide Teaching Scholar award. Professor Lapan has served as editor for the *Excellence in Teaching* Journal, the NAU College of Education Monograph Series, and is past consulting editor for the *Journal of Research in Childhood Education*. E-mail: steve.lapan@nau.edu. Web site: www.nau.edu/ci-doc.

MARYLYNN T. QUARTAROLI has bachelor's degrees in theatre, history, and geology, a master's degree in geology, and her doctorate in curriculum and instruction. Her areas of specialization include research methodologies, evaluation and assessment, science education, and Native American and adult education, as illustrated in her dissertation, *An Evaluation of the American Indian Air Quality Training Program*. She is currently the project director of the NEXUS Math/Science NAU grant from Science Foundation Arizona. She is also evaluating programs funded by the U.S. Department of Education in projects as diverse as the Math Science Partnership and the Carol M. White Physical Education Program. She has twelve years of science and math teaching experience (grades 5–14) in public, private, charter, and reservation schools; she also taught curriculum and assessment courses to secondary education students for two years. She continues to teach the Paradigms for Research in Education and Advanced Curriculum Seminar classes for Northern Arizona University's Curriculum and Instruction Doctoral Program.

THE AUTHORS

ELPIDA AHTARIDOU works as a researcher at the Institute of Education, University of London. She was previously a lecturer of Education Studies at the University of Central Lancashire and prior to that a lecturer in Post-Compulsory Education and Training at the University of Plymouth.

SHADOW W. J. ARMFIELD earned an EdD in Curriculum and Instruction with a focus in Technology in Education from Northern Arizona University. He is currently assistant professor in the Educational Technology program at Northern Arizona University. His research agenda focuses on the utilization of technologies by teachers and students in the K–12 classroom and the preparation of pre-service educators for the integration of technology into the K–12 classroom. Past research includes *A Descriptive Case Study of Teaching and Learning in an Innovative Middle School Program,* "Meeting the Needs of Students, Administration, and NCATE: Redesigning an Undergraduate Educational Technology Course to Meet Changing Needs," and "Video Games, Learning, and Instruction in the Middle School Classroom." E-mail: Shadow.Armfield@nau.edu.

GABRIELLA BELLI is an associate professor in the Educational Research and Evaluation program of the School of Education at Virginia Tech. She holds a PhD in statistics and research design and an MA in measurement and evaluation from Michigan State University and a BS in mathematics from St. Bonaventure University. A former math teacher, she has taught graduate core courses in statistics and research methods and advanced courses in experimental design, survey research, regression, and multivariate statistics. Teaching and applied consulting projects sparked research interests in statistical consultancy and instruction, particularly as related to nontechnical audiences. She has worked with over ninety students on theses and dissertations in such diverse areas as adult learning, community college, computer science, counseling, curriculum and instruction, educational administration, educational research, engineering, marriage and family therapy, natural science, nutrition, and special education. Most of these were nonexperimental in nature. Helping students design the studies and interpret results correctly was an impetus for writing this chapter. A strong believer in the importance of statistical literacy and an understanding of basic research concepts, she hopes that readers of this book, and particularly of the nonexperimental chapter, will develop a basic appreciation for research and be motivated to learn more about research methods.

MARK BERENDS (PhD in Sociology, University of Wisconsin–Madison) is associate professor of public policy and education; director of the National Center on School Choice (www.vanderbilt.edu/schoolchoice), funded by the U.S. Department of Education's Institute of Education Sciences; and the vice president of the American Educational Research Association's Division L, Policy and Politics in Education. His areas of expertise are the sociology of education, research methods, school effects on student achievement, and educational equity. Throughout his research career, Berends has focused on how school organization and classroom instruction are related to student achievement, with special attention to disadvantaged students. Within this agenda, he has applied a variety of quantitative and qualitative methods to understanding the effect of school reforms on teachers and students. His latest books are *Examining Gaps in Mathematics Achievement Among Racial-Ethnic Groups, 1972–1992* (2005, RAND), *Charter School Outcomes* (2008, Lawrence Erlbaum Associates), *Leading with Data* (in press, Corwin), and *Handbook of Research on School Choice* (forthcoming, Lawrence Erlbaum Associates).

DAVID C. BERLINER is Regents' Professor of Education at Arizona State University. He has taught at the Universities of Arizona and Massachusetts, at Teachers College and Stanford University, as well as at universities in Australia, The Netherlands, Spain, and Switzerland. Berliner is a member of the National Academy of Education, a fellow of the Center for Advanced Study in the Behavioral Sciences, and a past president of both the American Educational Research Association (AERA) and the Division of Educational Psychology of the American Psychological Association (APA). He is the recipient of awards for distinguished contributions from APA, AERA, and the National Education Association (NEA). He is coauthor (with B. J. Biddle) of the best seller *The Manufactured Crisis,* coauthor (with Ursula Casanova) of *Putting Research to Work,* and coauthor (with N. L. Gage) of the textbook *Educational Psychology,* now in its sixth edition. He is coeditor of the first *Handbook of Educational Psychology* and the books *Talks to Teachers,* and *Perspectives on Instructional Time.* His newest book, *Collateral Damage* (with Sharon Nichols), is about the corruption of professional educators through high-stakes testing. Berliner has also authored more than two hundred published articles, technical reports, and book chapters.

KRISTA D. BRIDGMON received a PhD in Educational Psychology from Northern Arizona University with emphasis in counseling. She is an assistant professor of Psychology at Colorado State University–Pueblo. She has taught undergraduate courses in statistics, cognitive psychology, biology of psychology, history and systems of psychology, abnormal psychology, chemical dependency, and child/adolescent pathology. She has taught graduate courses in counseling, school counseling, development, and ethics. Her doctoral dissertation examined the stress that all-but-dissertation (ABD) students encounter in the disciplines of counselor education and supervision, counseling psychology, and clinical psychology. The study created an instrument using multivariate correlational methods to measure stress factors associated with being ABD, named the BASS (Bridgmon All-But-Dissertation Stress Survey).

CAROL BRANIGAN FELDERMAN is a doctoral student in Literacy Studies in the School of Education at Virginia Tech. She earned a bachelor's degree in English and Theatre Arts from Hollins University and a master's degree in Education from George Washington University. For seven years, she enthusiastically taught elementary school at Bailey's Elementary School for the Arts and Sciences in Fairfax County, Virginia. She currently serves as a member of the Northern Virginia Writing Project and recently published a paper about her teaching in the journal for that organization. She is currently collaborating with Vivian Vasquez on several projects that focus on critical literacy and technology for elementary children. She has presented her research at the annual meeting of the National Council of Teachers of English and the National Reading Conference.

ALISON FURLONG is currently a graduate student in the College of Arts and Letters at Northern Arizona University. She received her BSEd in English from Northern Arizona University in 2003, and then taught high school English at a rural school in northern Arizona. She is currently working on her MA in English.

GENE V GLASS has been a professor of education policy studies and professor of psychology in education at the Arizona State University College of Education since 1986. Trained originally in statistics, his interests broadened to include psychotherapy research, evaluation methodology, and policy analysis. He was twice (1968, 1970) honored with the Palmer O. Johnson award of the American Educational Research Association; and in 1984, he received the Paul Lazarsfeld Award of the American Evaluation Association. He is a recipient of the Cattell Award of the Society of Multivariate Experimental Psychology. His work on meta-analysis of psychotherapy outcomes (with M. L. Smith) was named as one of the Forty Studies that Changed Psychology in the book of the same name by Roger R. Hock (1999). His PhD was awarded by the University of Wisconsin–Madison in educational psychology, with a minor in statistics.

CAROL M. HADEN received an EdD in Curriculum and Instruction with an emphasis on educational program evaluation from Northern Arizona University. She is currently a senior research associate with Magnolia Consulting, an independent evaluation company offering expertise in K–12 education, adult education, school-based programs, and public outreach. Her particular area of expertise is in evaluation of science education programs. She has acted as evaluator on science education projects sponsored by the National Science Foundation, the William and Flora Hewlett Foundation, the Arizona Board of Regents, Goddard Space Flight Center, and the Arizona Department of Education. Through her work with Magnolia Consulting, she has expanded her expertise into evaluation of curriculum materials for English language learners.

LAURIE MOSES HINES earned her PhD in History of Education and American Studies from Indiana University–Bloomington. Before joining Kent State University, where she is currently an assistant professor, Hines worked for The College Board as lead developer and writer of an online public history project about The College Board's role in higher education. She was an assistant editor for the *History of Education Quarterly* and has published in that journal and *Education Next,* as well as in a number of edited texts. Her research focuses on the history of teachers, teacher education and higher education, and teacher professionalization. She currently is working on the historical dimensions of assessment of teacher dispositions for an edited volume on teacher assessment. Hines has presented research on historical topics and on teaching in higher education. She currently teaches courses in United States, world history, and cultural foundations of education at Kent State

University–Trumbull, where she was awarded a Kent State University teaching fellowship in 2003. She also is on the board of directors of Pi Lambda Theta, an educational honorary and professional association. She would like to thank the editors for their helpful comments.

DAVID HOPKINS is the inaugural HSBC Chair in International Leadership, where he supports the work of iNet, the international arm of the Specialist Schools Trust and the Leadership Centre at the Institute of Education, University of London. He is also a Professorial Fellow at the Faculty of Education, University of Melbourne. Between 2002 and 2005 he served three secretaries of state as the chief adviser on School Standards at the Department for Education and Skills. Previously, he was chair of the Leicester City Partnership Board and dean of the Faculty of Education at the University of Nottingham. Before that he was a tutor at the University of Cambridge, Institute of Education, a secondary school teacher, and Outward Bound instructor. Hopkins is also an international mountain guide who still climbs regularly in the Alps and Himalayas. Before becoming a civil servant he outlined his views on teaching quality, school improvement and large-scale reform in *School Improvement for Real* (Routledge/Falmer, 2001). His new book, *Every School a Great School,* has just been published by The Open University Press. E-mail: d.hopkins@ioe.ac.uk. Web site: www.davidhopkins.co.uk.

ROSARY LALIK is an associate professor of Literacy Studies in the School of Education at Virginia Tech, where she is a member of the Academy of Teaching Excellence. She serves as director of education programs for the Virginia Tech School of Education at the National Capital Region. She is a recipient of the Wine Award for Teaching Excellence and teaches courses and seminars and advises students at the masters and doctoral levels. Her research interests include literacy teacher education and critical literacy. She has presented her research at national and international research forums, and her work has been published in numerous scholarly outlets including the *Reading Research Quarterly,* the *Journal of Literacy Research,* and the *Journal of Curriculum Studies.* The book she coauthored with Kimberly Oliver, *Bodily Knowledge: Learning about Equity and Justice with Adolescent Girls,* makes use of numerous feminist principles.

KRISTIN LARSON earned an EdD in Educational Psychology with an emphasis in Counseling Psychology from Northern Arizona University. She is currently an assistant professor at Monmouth College in Monmouth, Illinois, and a licensed clinical psychologist. She is interested in ethics in both research and practice. She is the chair of the Human Subjects Review Board and serves on the Behavioral Intervention Committee and Human Rights Committee for a local social service agency. She has authored *Introduction to Research Ethics,* a guidebook for undergraduate capstone research courses. Her publications include the textbook chapters "Ethical Delivery of Creative Therapeutic Approaches" and "Ethical Guidelines for Creative Therapists in the Treatment of Sexual Abuse Survivors." E-mail: klarson@monm.edu. Web site: http://department.monm.edu/psychology/larson.htm.

WILLIAM E. MARTIN JR. is professor of Educational Psychology and senior scholar in the College of Education at Northern Arizona University. His areas of teaching are statistics, research methods, and psychodiagnostics. His research relates to person-environment psychology and psychosocial adaptation. Two of his books are titled *Person-Environment Psychology and Mental Health* and *Applied Ecological Psychology for Schools within Communities: Assessment and Intervention.* E-mail: William.Martin@nau.edu.

GRETCHEN McALLISTER is an associate professor of Teaching and Learning in the College of Education at Northern Arizona University, where she works with all levels of students. Her work involves teaching masters and doctoral students how to conduct and write research, as well as literature reviews. Her own area of research focuses on multicultural teacher education that examines how teachers develop multicultural beliefs, such as efficacy and the relationship of those beliefs to their teaching.

SHARON L. NICHOLS is an assistant professor in the Department of Counseling, Educational Psychology, and Adult and Higher Education at the University of Texas at San Antonio. She received a bachelor's in psychology from Bucknell University and her master's and doctorate degrees in educational psychology from the University of Arizona in Tucson. Her research interests focus on adolescent development, motivation, and the social contexts of learning. Her most current work focuses on how high-stakes testing pressure affects novice and veteran teachers and student motivation. She has coauthored two books, with David Berliner (*Collateral Damage: How High-Stakes Testing Corrupts America's Schools,* Harvard Education Press, 2007) and Tom Good (*America's Teenagers—Myths and Realities: Media Images, Schooling, and the Social Costs of Careless Indifference,* Erlbaum, 2004). Nichols is a consulting editor for the *Journal of Experimental Education,* and is on the editorial board for the journal *Education Policy Analysis Archives.*

FRANCES JULIA RIEMER received a PhD in Educational Anthropology from the University of Pennsylvania. She is currently an associate professor in the College of Education at Northern Arizona University and director of the university's Women and Gender Studies Program. Dr. Riemer is an ethnographer who has conducted both long and short-term ethnographic research in the United States, southern and eastern Africa, and Latin America. She has published a monograph, *Working at the Margins: Moving off Welfare in America,* based on a three-year ethnography of welfare-to-work transitions in the United States, and has published articles in *Anthropology and Education Quarterly, Practicing Anthropology, Research Methods: Current Social Work Applications, Action in Teacher Education,* and *Educational Technology and Society.* Riemer is currently working on *Becoming Literate, Being Human: Adult Literacy and Moral Reconstruction in Botswana,* based on ten years of ethnographic data collection in the southern African country of Botswana. She is the recipient of a Fulbright Scholar Award, a dissertation fellowship from the Spencer Foundation, a postdoctoral fellowship from the National Academy of Education/Spencer Foundation, and an Elva Knight research grant from the International Reading Association. Dr. Riemer has developed and taught courses in educational sociology, ethnographic research methods, qualitative data analysis, and women's studies research.

KELLY A. RODGERS, PhD, is an assistant professor of Educational Psychology in the Department of Counseling, Educational Psychology, and Adult and Higher Education at the University of Texas at San Antonio. She completed undergraduate studies at Westminster College in Missouri, receiving a dual bachelor's degree in mathematics and Spanish. She received her master's and doctorate degrees in educational psychology with an emphasis on learning and cognition from the University of Missouri. Rodgers's primary research area is in the psychosocial and motivational aspects involved in the social and academic experiences of minority college students. Her most recent work involves using motivational and self-systems constructs to explain retention patterns among African American and Hispanic undergraduate students. Rodgers is also interested in academic motivation and the socio-emotional aspects of giftedness, particularly as they apply to minority adolescents. She is an active member of the American Educational Research Association and American Psychological Association, and has published in several educational journals, including *Roeper Review* and *Educational Psychology Review.*

PAUL A. SCHUTZ is professor in the Department of Counseling, Educational Psychology, and Adult and Higher Education at the University of Texas at San Antonio. He earned his doctorate from the University of Texas at Austin in the Department of Educational Psychology. He currently teaches courses on classroom motivation and research methods. His research interests include motivation, emotion, and research methodologies. He has published in the journals *Educational Psychologist, Journal of Educational Psychology,* and *Contemporary Educational Psychology* and coedited a book with Reinhard Pekrun titled *Emotions in Education.* He was a coeditor for the *Educational Researcher: News and Comments* and has served on the editorial boards of several journals, including *Teacher College Record* and *Contemporary Educational Psychology.*

GENEVIEVE ZOTTOLA is a project manager at The National Center on School Choice, Vanderbilt University. She received her BS from Western Connecticut State University in Secondary Education. She taught middle school for four years and then completed a master's degree in Education from Vanderbilt University. She is particularly interested in parent involvement in choice schools and the impact it has on student achievement, and the effect of choice schools on academic rigor and students' sense of belonging. Currently, she is coauthoring two papers with the working titles, "How Social Capital Varies among Charter Schools: Examining Relationships to Academic Rigor from the Students' Perspective" and "Charter Schools and Parental Involvement: The Myth of the Structural Panacea."

RESEARCH ESSENTIALS

CHAPTER

RESEARCH ETHICS
AND THE USE
OF HUMAN PARTICIPANTS

KRISTIN LARSON

KEY IDEAS

- All research involves ethical considerations related to the well-being of the participants.

- Ethical research practices are represented by a continuum, balancing the rights of the research participant (the deontological approach) and the benefits of the research (the utilitarian approach).

- Current ethical guidelines are based on events in the history of scientific research.

- Federal and organizational ethical standards guide researchers in the decision-making process.

- Institutional review boards review research projects for their justification and ethical procedures.

- Ethical standards direct researchers to minimize potential risks for participants.

- An informed consent document informs participants about the nature of the research and their right to stop participation at any time.

- Much of the research in the social sciences involves some level of deception.

- It is the responsibility of the researcher to debrief the participants by informing them of the true nature of the research study.
- Confidentiality and anonymity are key ethical practices insuring the privacy of the participant.
- Ethics extend beyond the study to publication and presentation of research.
- High ethical standards not only positively impact the participant, but also maintain trust in the research community on a societal level.

EDUCATIONAL AND social research are generally undertaken with the hope that our new discoveries will, in some way, contribute to our knowledge of the human condition and will ultimately benefit humanity. Although researchers may not be thinking in such lofty terms when developing a project, it is an important focus that underscores the need for ethically developed and applied research practices. Ethical considerations are the foundation of quality research that contributes to the body of knowledge and protects the population that researchers are attempting to benefit. Moreover, high-quality research is the first requirement of ethical practice. The lower the quality of a social science research study, the less justified researchers are in involving human participants.

All research inherently involves ethical considerations, from the researchers and their motivations for conducting studies, extending to the well-being, freedom of choice, and dignity of the participants. Yet concern for the participant must often be balanced against the desire for progress through research.

Although the social science community generally accepts this balance, a philosophical debate exists between the **deontological approach**, which emphasizes respect for the autonomy and rights of the participant, and the **utilitarian approach**, which emphasizes weighing the benefits of the research against the risks for the participant (risks are defined in more detail later in this chapter). Researchers on the extreme end of the deontological continuum would suggest that it is never acceptable to deceive a participant in any form or cause any kind of discomfort, even if the outcome of the research is of significant value. This position is rare. Most researchers who lean this way recognize the need for deception at times and make every effort to avoid risk and discomfort to the participants. Researchers who fall into the utilitarian category believe it is acceptable to deceive participants as long as the extent of the deception is justified by the significant value of the research outcome. These researchers are usually comfortable with risk and discomfort as long as it is temporary. Researchers generally do not fall at the extreme end of the utilitarian approach, considering any level of physical or emotional pain as acceptable. In addition, research review boards, scholarly publishers, and the social science community do not condone harming research participants. Although this chapter does not attempt to resolve the differences between these approaches, it will assist the reader of research in understanding the ethical issues inherent in research studies by covering in some detail the following topics: ethical standards, minimizing risk to participants, publication, and the social impact of unethical research.

1. Which carries more weight for you, the rights of the participant or the benefits of the research?

2. To what degree can researchers accurately predict the potential impact of new knowledge through research?

3. At what point is the discomfort, deception, or embarrassment of a human participant unethical?

ETHICAL STANDARDS

Ethical standards are guidelines that attempt to provide direction for the decision-making processes and actions involved in conducting research. Typically government or professional organizations establish these standards. They are based on lessons learned through the history of research and on the experiences of professionals with the goal of minimizing risk to research participants. Ethical standards are the foundation for ethical decision making in research; wisdom and attention to detail complete the process.

The Genesis of Research Standards

The need for ethical guidelines in research was first acknowledged formally in response to biomedical experiments conducted on prisoners of war in Germany during World War II. The result was the **Nuremburg Code**, a set of ethical standards that emphasized that it is essential for researchers to have informed consent from their participants.

As a result of the Nuremburg Code, several professional organizations have developed ethical codes to guide research in the social sciences. The American Psychological Association (APA) first published the *Ethical Principles of Psychologists and Code of Conduct* in 1953. The code was revised in 1972, 1992, and most recently in 2002. In addition, the American Sociological Association (ASA) and the American Educational Research Association (AERA, 2000) have developed codes specifically to guide research in their respective fields. Although organizational codes of ethics are mandatory for their membership, they are also considered the standard by nonmembers doing research in related fields.

Ethical codes have to provide for an enormous breadth of subdisciplines, topics, and methods. The authors of these codes have chosen to take a broad, all-purpose approach as opposed to publishing exhaustive volumes of guidelines in order to cover every potential risk. Consequently, they only provide minimal guidance in the decision-making process, using general admonitions (Sieber, 1994) including "[researchers] take steps to protect the prospective participants from adverse consequences" (APA, 2002, paragraph 8.04). In addition, codes can be open to interpretation, need to be revised to meet new developments in the field, and often do not address rare or unique circumstances. For example, those conducting research in an educational setting must be sensitive to the rights of parents, the agenda of the teacher, the vulnerability of the student, the political context of the school, and the privacy of the family.

Not only can codes be vague, but a study can be consistent with all appropriate codes and still raise ethical concerns, as seen in the case of the Stanford Prison Experiment (SPE). In this landmark study of conformity, Zimbardo (1972) randomly placed participants in the roles of prisoner and guard in a realistic prison setting. The study had to be concluded prematurely due to harsh treatment by the "guards" and the psychological suffering of the "prisoners." Upon reflection of the study, Zimbardo described the SPE as ethical, because it was consistent with the guidelines of the American Psychological Association and the Human Subjects Review Board, which had given its approval (Zimbardo, Maslach, & Haney, 2000). Also, there was no deception, and no concern voiced by the many people outside of the study who witnessed the condition of the participants. Zimbardo went on to say it was *unethical* because "people suffered and others were allowed to inflict pain and humiliation on their fellows over an extended period of time" (p. 211). Ethically, the SPE study should have been terminated on the second day when one of the participants suffered a "severe stress disorder" (p. 211). According to Zimbardo, the study continued due to his dual role of principal investigator (responsible for ethical conduct) and prison superintendent, "thus, eager to maintain the integrity of [the] prison" (p. 212). The unanticipated behavior of the participants and the principal investigator illustrate that a study can adhere to the guidelines and still be ultimately unethical.

Federal Regulations for Ethical Research

In 1953, the **National Institutes of Health** (NIH), a United States government agency responsible for biomedical research, created the first U.S. federal policy for the protection of human subjects, based on the Nuremburg Code (Office of Human Subjects Research, 1991). Events in the 1970s (most notably the Tuskegee Syphilis Study, summarized later in this chapter) provoked new concern for the welfare of human participants and led to enactment of the **National Research Act of 1974**. This act required the Department of Health, Education and Welfare to make its policies into federal regulations in 1974 and resulted in the formation of the National Commission for the Protection of Human Subjects of Biomedical and Behavioral Research (The National Commission).

In order to determine what ethical problems existed in human research, this commission held hearings in the Belmont Conference Center of the Smithsonian Institution in Washington, DC, from 1974 to 1977. In 1979, the commission published **The Belmont Report**, a document that called attention to the need for respect for persons, protection of **autonomy**, **justice**, and **beneficence** (The National Commission, 1979). Autonomy ensures that each participant is given an informed choice to participate or decline at any point in the research process. Justice is a complex responsibility, as it stresses fair distribution of costs and benefits among persons and groups. As mentioned later in this chapter, not all cultural groups are fairly represented in current published research, despite researchers' efforts. Just as challenging is beneficence, the duty to demonstrate that the risk to participants can be justified by the potential benefits provided by new knowledge.

The Belmont Report then became the foundation for federal regulations, which are legally binding in institutions that receive grants for their research. Therefore, it is important to understand which federal ethical regulations would apply to each research project. Grants that originate in the **U.S. Department of Health and Human Services** (DHHS), a cabinet department of the United States government responsible for protecting the health of Americans, are regulated by two separate organizations. The Office of Human Research Protections (formerly the Office of Protection from Research Risks) oversees compliance with the Federal Policy for the Protection of Human Subjects, which applies to any research that is supported by any federal agency or any research conducted under the approval of an institutional review board (45 CFR part 46). The Office of Human Subjects Research refers to the same regulations for research funded by the NIH. Figure 1.1 describes the relative position of these organizations.

There are also federal regulations for research funded by the Department of Education (DOE), through the Family Policy Compliance Office. This office implemented two laws in 1974 that protect the rights of students and parents: The Family Educational Rights and Privacy Act (FERPA, 1974) (20 U.S.C. § 1232g; 34 CFR Part 99); and the Protection of Pupil Rights Amendment (PPRA, 1974) (20 U.S.C. § 1232h; 34 CFR Part 98). Specifics of these laws can be found at their Web sites, listed at the end of this chapter.

Institutional Review Boards

The National Research Act (1974) requires that institutions receiving federal grants for biomedical or behavioral research create an **institutional review board** (IRB), a committee that reviews research proposals for their justification and ethical concerns and upholds the standards of related ethics codes. Institutional review boards are made up of at least five members representing researchers and administrators. Not all educational institutions will have an IRB (sometimes referred to as a Human Subjects Review Board). In institutions with an IRB, it is a requirement to submit a proposal prior to gathering data. This is typically a standard form with questions regarding the investigators, the purpose of the research, the method of the study, any risks to participants, and

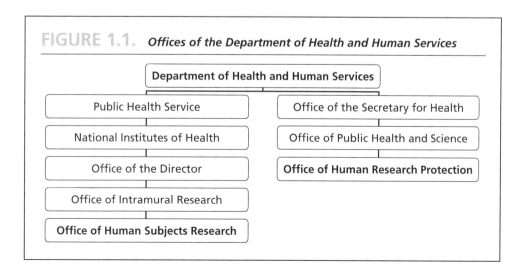

FIGURE 1.1. *Offices of the Department of Health and Human Services*

measures taken to minimize that risk. The board evaluates the proposal, weighing the benefits of the research against any risks and looking for undetected threats to participant well-being. In addition, researchers with an NIH grant are required to take an online tutorial on protecting human participants from research risks prior to submitting a proposal. Some academic institutions have adopted a similar requirement for all research regardless of the funding. The following lists experiences (though not exhaustive) that are potential risks for a research participant:

- A sense of obligation to participate in the project (for example, students in classes, children, employees in their work settings)
- Deception that leaves out information that may impact the participants' choice to participate
- Physical discomfort
- Situations resulting in stress
- A change in emotional state or mood
- A change in physiological functioning
- Potential loss of privacy, reputation, or dignity
- Distress from being induced into uncharacteristic or unexpected behavior
- Being a member of a vulnerable population, including children, the elderly, people with mental illness, people with a history of abuse, people with chronic or terminal medical illnesses, people who are incarcerated, and the homeless

The measures that researchers take to address these risks in a proposal can include (a) procedures that offset the effects of the risk, (b) a convincing argument that the risks do not exceed that which the participant might experience in daily living, or (c) a convincing argument that the benefits of the new knowledge justify the risk. The journal *IRB: A Review of Human Subjects Research* has a plethora of discussions that illustrate ethical dilemmas and resolutions.

MINIMIZING RISKS TO PARTICIPANTS

Organizations, ethics codes, and IRBs provide guidance for research, but ethical research is ultimately up to the researcher. Following the ethical guidelines related to informed consent, deception, debriefing, confidentiality, and anonymity can reduce the risks to participants in a study.

Informed Consent

An **informed consent** form is a document that notifies the participant about the nature of the study, the risks involved, and the participant's right to quit the study at any time. The participants' signatures on the form indicate their understanding of the requirements of the study and their rights. Informed consent is required by organizational and federal codes for all research except that which would not cause any anticipated distress and falls into the categories of observation of public behavior, surveys that require no identifying data, research using archived or previously collected data, activities that would normally take place in an educational setting, and activities that would normally take place in a work setting (APA, 2002). The purpose of informed consent is to ensure voluntary participation and to provide the participant with accurate information regarding her experience in the research project. The elements of a complete informed consent form are listed below:

- The names of the researchers
- The purpose of the study
- The expected length of participation and procedures the participants will encounter
- The participant's right to decline participation or withdraw once the study has begun, without prejudice
- The foreseeable consequences of declining or withdrawing
- The foreseeable factors that may influence their willingness to participate in the study (including discomfort or adverse effects)
- Any potential benefits of the research
- Limits to confidentiality (such as access to data by research assistants)
- Incentives for participation (for example, extra credit, money, or free psychological treatment)
- The name of someone to contact to ask questions regarding participation

The need for informed consent has been accepted as the standard since the Nuremburg Code, but the circumstances in which it is required continue to be debated. For example, Laud Humphreys conducted an observational study and survey of anonymous homosexual sex in public restrooms. His subsequent book, the *Tearoom Trade* (1975), described how Humphries took the role of observer-participant in order to watch the behavior of men in public restrooms, including one in a park. Humphries identified the men through casual conversation and by recording their license plate numbers. Although he disclosed his purpose to a few of the participants, he continued to deceive most of the participants when he later contacted them by phone and identified himself as conducting a local health survey. In this way, he was able to describe the marital status, sexual orientation, employment status, and other social factors of his population. Critics argue that sex in the confines of a restroom is private behavior, and that once Humphries identified the "participants" and contacted them, the study no longer qualified as an observational study and required informed consent. Humphries defended his study, stating that he maintained the confidentiality of the participants and that the social value of understanding in detail this otherwise unknown subculture has been significant. This utilitarian view of risk can be difficult to substantiate, and does not qualify for a waiver of informed consent as currently established by most ethical codes.

When a participant gives his or her informed consent, researchers are strongly encouraged to document it with a two-copy form that allows the researcher to obtain a signature and provide the participant with a copy of the signed form. Consent can also be given verbally, as in the case of a telephone survey. Mailed questionnaires can include a statement signifying that participants have given their consent by completing and returning it. Researchers must also inform participants and gain consent for recording their voices or images (unless it is behavior recorded during **naturalistic observation**, when a researcher unobtrusively observes behavior that naturally occurs in public and the individual cannot be identified or harmed by the recording).

If the study includes deception, permission to use the participant's data or recording must be obtained during debriefing (APA, 2002). In addition, the following generic statement can be included in the informed consent form prior to participation as a way of obtaining consent to be deceived: "Some research at this facility includes deception. The study that you are asked to participate in may or may not include a form of deception including, but not limited to, withholding the true nature of the study."

When developing an informed consent document, a researcher must consider the range of comprehension ability in the subject pool and write the consent form in language that can be clearly understood by every potential participant. For example, researchers investigating knowledge of research terms found that participants defined the term "confidentiality" as "no one sees you going in or out" and "the data will only be used in a positive manner" (Freimuth et al., 2001, p. 801). Many participants in the same study believed that signing a consent form equaled "signing away your rights" (p. 801). To minimize any misconceptions, researchers should explain the consent form and invite questions prior to having the participant read and sign the form.

Although informed consent provides participants with information, it is also intended to promote freedom of choice. Research within any kind of institution, whether it be academic, military, medical, correctional, or familial, carries the potential for real or imagined coercion. A common risk in using students or a participant pool in an academic setting is unintentional coercion. Although subjects read, understand, and sign an informed consent form, they still may believe that they will be disadvantaged in some way if they choose not to participate. Take into consideration a student in an introductory psychology class whose participation is part of a class requirement or who is offered extra credit for participation. Ethical guidelines require that investigators offer students an equitable activity if they choose not to participate (APA, 2002), but this guideline is often overlooked or purposely avoided for fear that the researcher will not get enough participants if an alternative is available. In addition, researchers should consider how the authoritative role in the research setting may "pressure potential subjects to participate against their will" (Sieber, 1996, p. 74).

Conducting research with participants who are unable to give consent to participate in research (for example, children under the age of eighteen or developmentally disabled adults) provides researchers with unique challenges. In 1983, the National Commission established federal regulations for research with children (45 CFR Part 46, Subpart D). These regulations require parents or legal guardians to give informed consent on behalf of the child. Therefore, in an academic setting, the consent does not lie with the teacher or administration, but with the parents of each participating child. Currently, the Department of Education and the Protection of Pupil Rights Amendment (PPRA) direct that children ages seven and older should assent, or indicate their own verbal or written agreement (providing the children with their own two-copy versions of an informed consent form written at their level of comprehension). Adolescents can assent to participation without the parent's consent in the case of abuse or neglect, according to DHHS guidelines. Although the PPRA applies only to Department of Education–funded research, it represents the highest standard of ethics and should be used as a guideline in any research with children.

Informed consent becomes more complex as researchers investigate issues related to the family, such as parent-child relations, parenting practices, family conflict, or abuse. Researchers often find that gaining consent is difficult when investigating sensitive topics and that the consent process can eliminate certain participants, biasing the sample.

Research involving any kind of psychological treatment requires some special consideration. Before participation has begun, the researcher must clarify several points about the treatment. The potential participant must understand the experimental nature of the treatment and that treatment may not be available if the method includes a control group. The researcher must also explain the way in which participation in the experimental and control groups will be determined, describe available alternatives if the individual chooses not to participate or decides to withdraw, and state the costs or compensation associated with participation (APA, 2002). Often, these issues are best explained by the researcher and in an informed consent form.

Finally, it is important that the inducement for participation not be so excessive or enticing that it unintentionally coerces participation. This guideline should be considered in relation to the population being studied. For example, it could be unintentionally coercive to offer access to free health care to potential participants of low socioeconomic status, or money to young children. If money is part of the inducement, participants who withdraw from a study should still be paid so that they can withdraw without penalty.

REFLECTION QUESTION

1. What are researchers able and not able to assume when parents or legal guardians give their consent that they are acting in the best interest of the child or impaired adult?

Deception

The term **deception** refers to research methodology that involves intentionally concealing aspects of a study from the participant. Deception can apply to a range of activities that includes withholding the full purpose of the research, lying to participants in order to manipulate their behavior, or observing participants' behavior without their knowledge. In addition, deception can include using **confederates**, or members of the research team who pose as one of the participants, in order to elicit specific behaviors. Social psychology, personality psychology, and memory studies often make use of deception in order to obtain valid results.

There is an ongoing controversy concerning deception that has fueled the deontological-utilitarian debate. Some believe that any deception, including leaving out small details that are not likely to influence the participants' willingness to participate, is an affront to the participant and therefore unethical (Ortmann & Hertwig, 1997). Others have openly debated this position, stating that researchers often withhold details that would not affect their willingness to participate, and this poses little risk to the participants' well-being (see Bröder, 1998; Kimmel, 1998; Korn, 1998).

Because the use of deception eliminates the acquisition of fully informed consent, it always carries with it the need for additional vigilance regarding participant welfare. The APA guidelines state that psychologists only use deception when all of the following criteria are met: (a) it is justified by the significant potential value of the research, (b) the deception does not involve aspects of the study that would affect the participants' willingness to be involved, (c) alternative methods that do not involve deception are not available, and (d) arrangements have been made to debrief participants immediately following the study (APA, 2002). In addition, participants must be given the option to withdraw their data once they have been made aware of the deception. Although it is not an ethical requirement, researchers may choose to offer another two-copy consent form during the debriefing following deceptive research so that the participants may intentionally give their consent to include their data in the study.

The use of deception has the potential of revealing to the participants unpleasant aspects of themselves and what they are capable of doing. Considering that the participants may not have been previously aware of their capacity to, for example, lie, steal, or cause harm to others, this realization has the potential of being very distressing. Stanley Milgram's study of obedience (1974) has often been criticized for just this kind of risk. This study, which is controversial to this day, allowed participants to believe they were giving painful electrical shocks to another participant who was in actuality a confederate. Sixty-five percent of the participants believed they had given the maximum level of shock, 450 volts, under the direction of the "authority" or principal investigator.

Although it is widely accepted that this study contributed to our understanding of obedience, it has also contributed to the field through the debate over its ethical issues. Critics of Milgram's study focused on the deception of participants through lying to them regarding the purpose of the study, the manipulation of participants' behavior, the level of discomfort for the participants during the study (as evidenced by sweating, twitching, and begging the "authority" to end the study) and the potential distress for many participants, realizing the level of harm they were capable of inflicting on another person (Baumrind, 1964). Milgram defended the study, citing the debriefing that revealed that many participants were glad that they had participated.

Ethical codes have generally prevented researchers from replicating Milgram's study using the original methodology. Recently, however, two modified replications have received attention. In 2006, a team of researchers developed a "virtual learner" and informed the participants that the learner was a computerized model of the learner role (Slater et al., 2006). In 2007, social psychologist Jerry Burger, from Santa Clara University, teamed up with the ABC News program *Primetime* (with approval from the APA) to replicate the study, stopping the participants at 150 volts (Borge, 2007). Both studies yielded similar results to Milgram's original study.

The history of social science research has many such examples in which deception caused participants emotional or physical distress. Bergin (1962) gave undergraduate students discrepant information regarding their masculinity and femininity based on mock assessments. Campbell, Sanderson, and Laverty (1964) gave participants in a conditioning study a drug that temporarily suppressed their respiration in order to induce trauma. The 2002 APA guidelines now prohibit the use of deception in research that may cause emotional or physical pain.

REFLECTION QUESTIONS

1. What types of deception do you consider to be acceptable? What is unacceptable?
2. Researchers can use deception when it does not involve aspects of the study that would affect the participants' willingness to be involved. What aspects of a study might influence a participants' willingness to be involved?

Debriefing

It is important for the researcher to consider that the experience of participating in a study has the potential to impact the participant's life. Participants might be changed minimally by learning something new, moderately by changing their self-perception, or substantially by being manipulated into unexpected behavior. It is the responsibility of the researcher to **debrief** participants following the data-gathering phase, giving the participants an opportunity to learn the true purpose of the research as soon as it is practical (at the conclusion of their participation or after all of the data has been collected), to ask any questions they might have, and to be made aware of the results and conclusions of the study, if available. The purpose of debriefing is to minimize the impact of participating in the study. The researcher has the additional responsibility of remedying any possible misconceptions that the participant may have. The APA code of ethics requires debriefing of participants following involvement in a research study (2002).

Often, the measures taken to offset the risks of participation are implemented during debriefing. For example, if a study involved physical exertion, the participants may be taken through a rest period during debriefing. Or, if participants were given alcohol as part of the study, the debriefing period might include testing the blood alcohol level until it returns to normal. If the study included deception, the researcher can take this opportunity to be forthright and fully explain the need for deception. For example, students who are given false failing grades after a mock quiz would need to be told first that the grades were false, have the reason for the deception explained, and be given a chance to ask questions.

REFLECTION QUESTIONS

1. What should be included in a debriefing for Zimbardo's prison study?
2. What are the ramifications that can stem from improperly debriefing or failing to debrief a participant?
3. Are there any situations in which debriefing might not be in the best interest of the participant?

Confidentiality and Anonymity

Participant welfare extends beyond the data-gathering phase of research, into the handling of data and documents. **Confidentiality** refers to keeping participant data or identifying information secure from exposure to any unauthorized person. This includes preventing theft of collected data (including interception of electronically transmitted data) and preventing inappropriate access by research assistants or others (Sieber, 1994). At its most basic form, confidentiality requires that collected data be kept locked up and that the researcher refrain from discussion of participant data in public areas.

An essential part of confidentiality is storing data securely, and long enough so that other researchers may review it. Ethical guidelines require that researchers not withhold their original data from other researchers who may want to verify their results and who intend to use the data only for that purpose (APA, 2002). If the data are requested, researchers must ensure that identifying data are kept separate or withheld, and that the request comes from a qualified researcher. Following the study, researchers should plan for the ultimate disposal of the written data through some form of shredding or burning. Computer data files require a thorough file erasure by a professional (placing a data file in the "recycling bin" or clicking the delete button is not sufficient). All data should be disposed of after about five years of secure storage.

Anonymity is different from confidentiality in that it involves concealing the identity of the participants by separating any identifying information from the participants' completed forms and assessments. In this way, participants' identities are hidden from the researcher, research assistants, potential publications, and anyone who requests to review the data. Participants' fear of disclosure can affect the honesty of their responses, particularly in relation to sensitive issues. Participants may not respond in an honest or genuine way for fear that their results may not remain private. The researcher must take this into consideration in both the wording of the informed consent and in the interpretation of the results. Taking measures to assure participants of anonymity may lessen this concern.

Researchers often employ the use of codes to match the findings from each participant to a separate form containing the identifying data. Coding is often implemented in the use of technology for gathering, analyzing, storing, and transmitting data in order to protect data from unauthorized access. These precautions are particularly important when researching areas that require sensitivity regarding the rights to privacy and confidentiality, including domestic violence, sexual abuse, sexual practices, and mental illness.

Confidentiality and anonymity may be challenged by legal requirements or concern for the welfare of the participant. Research with children and adolescents has the potential of uncovering mental health issues, self-harm, family problems, illegal activity, or behaviors that could compromise children's health (Fisher et al., 2002). To further complicate this matter, research indicates that adolescents often expect assistance in getting help when the aforementioned problems are revealed to the researcher during a study (Fisher, 2002). Before gathering data, researchers should determine what their ethical and legal responsibilities are and how such disclosures will be handled. In addition, the informed consent form should clearly state what steps will be taken if harm to self or others, or abuse is revealed.

REFLECTION QUESTION

1. What are the differences between confidentiality and anonymity? What are the potential consequences of not protecting participant privacy?

PUBLISHING RESEARCH

We often think of ethics in terms of how research participants are treated, but it also extends to how data are analyzed and published. For example, Joe is interested in surveying adolescents regarding their academic achievement and drug use, hypothesizing that a high grade point average (GPA) would be related to less drug use. Joe would create a list, typically in a database computer program, of the information gathered from the participants including demographics (such as age, race, and gender), GPA, and the results of a self-report of drug use. The challenge comes when some of this data is unavailable for some of the participants due to some error such as unreadable survey responses or lost records.

Clearly it would be an ethical violation to falsify data. Beyond creating data where none exists, the following describes four ethical mistakes that both new and experienced researchers may make.

1. **Fabrication of data** can be as subtle as making adjustments to the data set without documenting it in the manuscript or filling in missing data (for example, the school has lost the GPA of a participant who has never done drugs, so Joe is tempted to fill in the missing data with a perfect 4.0 GPA because it supports his hypothesis) assuming that no one will be the wiser. Ethically, Joe needs to survey a new participant. This is not to say that honest mistakes in data analysis do not get published. In this case, it is the researcher's responsibility to submit a correction or retraction for publication (APA, 2002; Miller, 2003).

2. Eliminating an **outlier**, or a participant whose data differs remarkably from the rest of the sample and therefore does not represent the general population, is a sound statistical procedure when one person's data influences the results in such a way that it leads a researcher to draw incorrect conclusions. For example, when Joe conducts a study to find the relationship between drug use and grade point average (GPA), his results include one participant who has a 4.0 GPA and reports using heroin and crack cocaine on a regular basis. Including this participant in the study is likely to cause Joe to conclude that drugs have little effect on GPA. If Joe eliminates the outlier, then his data is more likely to represent the general population and Joe will be able to draw valid conclusions. Yet, it is only ethical if Joe mentions it in his publication. **Data dropping** is considered unethical if Joe eliminates a participant's data without mentioning it because that participant's results contradict his hypothesis (Miller, 2003).

3. **Exploitation of data** occurs when overzealous authors make undue claims or overstate the significance of their findings (Miller, 2003). For example, when Joe finds that there is a relationship between listening to classical music and higher GPA, he may be tempted to state that listening to classical music *causes* higher GPA in order to garner more attention to his study. Although consumers see this type of exaggeration in media reports on a regular basis, scientific integrity requires that researchers accurately state their findings.

4. **Plagiarism** is defined as representing another author's work or data as your own by either failing to indicate direct quotes or failing to cite the source every time it is referenced (APA, 2002; Miller, 2003).

REFLECTION QUESTION

1. What harm is there in falsifying data if no one knows?

SOCIAL CONSEQUENCES OF UNETHICAL RESEARCH

Consistent with human behavior, the few unethical studies are better remembered and more widely known than the multitude of quality, ethical studies. The impact of unethical research reaches well beyond the mistreated participant. As corrupt or damaging studies are exposed, the willingness of voluntary participants diminishes, the results of even scrupulous studies are doubted, and the trust in the research community is weakened. Maintaining good relations with participants ensures the security and progress of continued research.

History has shown the damage to public relations leveled by unethical research practices. The Tuskegee Syphilis Study, conducted from 1932 to 1972 by the U.S. Public Health Service, is infamous in the medical community and among African Americans. This project involved following the progress of untreated syphilis in African American males. The participants were never told that they had the disease or offered treatment, even when antibiotics were developed during the midpoint of the study, resulting in the needless deaths of many men (Freimuth et al., 2001). Moreover, the U.S. Health Service conducted a midpoint review of the study and gave its approval for continuation (Adair, 2001). Consequent studies indicate that familiarity with this study greatly contributes to African Americans' reluctance to participate in research and to the resulting racial imbalance in the populations represented by current research (Freimuth et al., 2001). This creates a challenge for researchers as interest in minority populations grows and the National Institutes of Health mandate inclusion of minorities in its funded research (Gamble, 1977).

In one of the first widely publicized scandals in psychology, Sir Cyril Burt falsified data in a study of twins that received national attention, resulting in the distribution of misinformation and damage to the credibility of the entire field of psychology (Koocher & Keith-Spiegel, 1998). In spite of the overwhelming majority of ethical research studies, cases of falsification in both medical and other research (see Broad, 1982; Holden, 1987; Lafollette, 1992) have understandably caused the public to approach research findings with mistrust.

1. As a consumer of research, what is the impact on you when you read published research such as the Stanford Prison Experiment, the Tearoom Trade, or the Tuskegee Syphilis Study?

READING AND EVALUATING STUDIES

As readers of research, consumers will find little discussion of ethical issues in published studies. It is assumed that published research has been reviewed by an IRB and that measures have been taken in the study to protect the participants' welfare. In addition, publication editors provide limited space for describing a study, which does not allow for a description of potential ethical issues and how they were addressed. Yet valid ethical questions can still be considered when reading published studies: What kind of deception is being used? Is the protection of participants evident in the report? Is there any other way the researchers could have obtained the same information without exposing the participants to discomfort or risk? Do the potential benefits of the research outweigh the discomfort or risk to the participants?

SUMMARY

The knowledge gained from high-quality, ethical research serves both social science and the general population. Consumers of social science research will find an abundance of ethical studies in current scholarly publications. The ethical standards of organizations guide researchers in minimizing risks to participants, obtaining informed consent, using deception, debriefing, and maintaining confidentiality and anonymity. Knowledge of these standards contributes to a reader's understanding of the nature of quality research practices. As understanding of the participant's experience grows, the assurance of ethical practice in research continues to be an important undertaking that requires both diligence and creativity.

KEY TERMS

anonymity
autonomy
the Belmont Report
beneficence
confederates
confidentiality
data dropping
debrief
deception
deontological approach
ethical standards
exploitation of data
fabrication of data

informed consent
institutional review board (IRB)
justice
National Institutes of Health
National Research Act of 1974
naturalistic observation
Nuremburg Code
outlier
plagiarism
U.S. Department of Health and Human
    Services
utilitarian approach

FURTHER READINGS AND RESOURCES

Suggested Article to Read

Zimbardo, P. G. (1972). The pathology of imprisonment. *Society*, 6(4), 6–8.

Can also be found in: Heslin, J. M. (2007). *Down to earth sociology: Introductory readings* (14th ed.). New York: Free Press.

Questions for Discussion

1. Which ethical standards were violated during the course of the Zimbardo study?
2. Which, if any, ethical concerns could have been identified prior to the study?
3. What caused Dr. Zimbardo to terminate the study?
4. How could the study be conducted differently so as to eliminate the ethical concerns?

Related Publications

Israel, M., & Hay, I. (2006). *Research ethics for social scientists*. Thousand Oaks, CA: Sage.

Sales, B. D., & Folkman, S. (Eds.) (2000). *Ethics in research with human participants*. Washington, DC: American Psychological Association.

Associations and Web Sites

American Educational Research Association (AERA) Ethical Principles

www.aera.net/uploadedFiles/About_AERA/Ethical_Standards/EthicalStandards.pdf

The ethical standards of the AERA.

Amoeba Web

www.vanguard.edu/faculty/ddegelman/amoebaweb

The Amoeba Web from Vanguard University offers many links to research ethics subjects including the Tuskegee Syphilis Study, the Belmont Report, the Nuremburg Code, and online tutorials.

American Psychological Association (APA) Ethical Principles

www.apa.org/ethics/code2002.html

The 2002 APA ethical principles of psychologists and code of conduct.

National Institutes of Health (NIH) Resources

www.niehs.nih.gov/research/resources/bioethics/nih.cfm

http://ohsr.od.nih.gov/guidelines/index.html

Resources and guidelines for the Conduct of Research Involving Human Subjects at the National Institutes of Health, including the Office of Human Subjects Research, for guidelines and regulations with links to the Belmont Report and the Nuremburg Code.

Stanley Milgram

www.stanleymilgram.com/milgram.php

All about Milgram, hosted by T. Blass from the University of Maryland.

Tearoom Trade

www.angelfire.com/or3/tss/tearoom.html

A summary of the *Tearoom Trade* by Laud Humphreys.

United States Department of Education (DOE)

www.ed.gov

www.ed.gov/offices/OII/fpco

Family Policy Compliance Office; includes links to FERPA and PPRA.

United States Department of Health and Human Services (DHHS), Office of Human Research Protections

www.hhs.gov/ohrp

Home page of the Office of Human Research Protections: links to information on IRB, informed consent, and additional educational materials.

Journals

IRB: Ethics & Human Research. Publisher: The Hastings Center. ISSN: 01937758.

The Journal of Empirical Research on Human Research Ethics. Publisher: University of California Press. ISSN: 1556–2646.

Professional Psychology Research and Practice. Publisher: American Psychological Association. ISSN: 0735–7028.

Research Ethics Review. Publisher: The Association of Research Ethics Committees. ASIN: B000FUG63A.

CHAPTER

UNDERSTANDING LITERATURE REVIEWS

GRETCHEN MCALLISTER AND ALISON FURLONG

KEY IDEAS

- Literature reviews differ from term and research papers in that they examine and speak to a body of literature.

- Literature reviews can include a variety of sources, such as peer-reviewed articles, reports, and books.

- Literature reviews can be organized chronologically, historically, thematically, methodologically, and theoretically.

- Literature reviews can vary in the level of rigor or level and depth of analysis, which can affect their reliability.

- Most literature reviews consist of a purpose, rationale, analysis, conclusion, and recommendations.

IN TODAY'S world, anyone wanting to know information about a topic or an answer to a question is faced with a volume of research, opinion pieces, and general information. This is the same for the social sciences. How do you take in all that information? How do you know what information is worthwhile and valid? This is especially important in an environment of accountability where schools, agencies, and policy makers are looking at research to inform their decisions (Andrews & Harlen, 2006). As consumers of research, you want to be sure that you know how to evaluate and interpret research. But how can we consume such volumes and decide on what is good information? Literature reviews are one tool that can assist us in understanding a body of research. A **literature review** is a systematic synthesis and evaluation of a body of information that can provide an efficient overview of the information on a particular topic.

A literature review can save the reader a lot of time, in that the author identifies, reads, summarizes, synthesizes, and evaluates the research. Such reviews can often be more up-to-date than a textbook and provide a broad perspective on a topic in an efficient manner. In addition, they can identify gaps in the research, solicit thinking about a topic, and encourage discussion.

As a consumer of research, it is of utmost importance to be able to read and analyze a **body of research** or literature focused on a specific topic or research question. This chapter will provide an overview of the basic types of literature reviews, how to read and assess a literature review, and how to write one.

WHAT IS A LITERATURE REVIEW?

Students can be confused between a term paper, research paper, and a literature review. A term paper or research paper is a **summary** or an overview of information found on a particular topic or research question that often supports your argument. The term paper and research paper often end at the level of presentation. The literature review takes it to the next level of analysis and synthesis, as the focus shifts to the ideas and arguments of others. A reviewer will analyze particular literature in various ways, such as thematically or historically, and then synthesize those analyses. The **synthesis** may provide a new interpretation or reconceptualization of a body of research or trace the scholarly progression of the field, and address major arguments or debates on the subject. It will illustrate the strengths and weaknesses in a line of research as well as provide a general picture of what we know on a topic. Rather than focus on specific research data, as is done in a term or research paper, the literature *is* the data (Green, Johnson, & Adams, 2001). For example, when writing a term paper or research paper on high school dropouts, you would research the topic, summarize what the research says, and then make some conclusions. When writing a literature review, you would cull the research and look for articles, according to predetermined categories or criteria, called **parameters**, analyze and evaluate the content of the sources, and then synthesize that information to create a different perspective about that research on dropouts. The focus shifts in the literature review to the research itself, rather than just the data from the research.

Literature reviews are found in many places, such as the introduction to a report, an article providing a backdrop on what we already know about a topic, or they can exist as articles themselves. For example, there are journals, such as the *Review of Educational Research*, that are collections of **peer-reviewed** literature reviews. These journal articles are comprehensive, systematic reviews and consist of sources that have been critiqued and evaluated by a group of peers, or professionals in that particular field, such as education or sociology, which monitors the quality of the review. A **blind review**, where the reviewer does not know the author, provides a more rigorous and objective peer review. Reviews can also include sources that do not undergo any or little review, such as reports, unpublished articles, conference proceedings (papers presented at a conference), as well as published books. Literature reviews can also be found in most research articles as a short review that outlines and discusses the other studies and analyses that have been conducted in a specific research area. The next section will point out some basic elements that are often found in literature reviews.

REFLECTION QUESTIONS

1. How does a literature review differ from a research or term paper?
2. What can a literature review provide to researchers, practitioners, and policy makers?

Basic Elements of a Literature Review

Though the analysis of the literature and the subsequent organization of that analysis may vary from one literature review to the next, there are some basic elements found in most literature reviews. These include a **purpose** that identifies the focus of the literature review. Some authors will state the purpose very directly, such as "The purpose of this literature review is to examine the role of gender in teaching." Or authors will use other terminology, such as "This article aims to provide insight into contemporary theoretical gender perspectives. It also intends to connect these with empirical research that takes teacher gender into account" (Sabbe & Aelterman, 2007, p. 521). The purpose is usually found early in the article, in the first page or two. Often prior to or just after the purpose is stated, there is the **justification** for the review. Essentially the author tries to answer the question: Why should this review be done? Authors may allude to the need to understand a problem through the research, to examine new research, to update past literature reviews on a particular topic, or to identify changes in the context of the discipline.

The next important element is a description of the **methodology** or the decisions that the author made in conducting the literature review. This will include the **parameters** or **rules of inclusion**. The parameters identify what type of literature will be included in the review. This could include quantitative studies that use experiments to examine a hypothesis, qualitative studies that use various approaches to interpret a problem or phenomenon, unpublished reports, or peer-reviewed articles that have been evaluated by researchers for quality. In addition to a description of the various types of literature that are included in the review, the author will identify the range of the publication dates to be included; for example, a range of ten years from the current year is usually an adequate span of time. Often you will find literature reviews that do not explicitly tell you how an author researched or made decisions on what to include. In a more rigorous approach, the author will tell you the parameters of literature, as well as the reasoning behind them.

The next section is the **body of the literature review**, where the author will present the analysis. Some typical ways to analyze the research include chronologically, historically, thematically, methodologically, and theoretically. These will be further described in the next part of the chapter. Authors then will conclude their review with **recommendations**. For example, they might point to needed research, critiques of current research, recommendations for policy, or other concluding remarks.

Types of Literature Reviews

There are many terms to describe literature reviews and various types depending on the discipline (Green, Johnson, & Adams, 2001). Often the type of literature review is defined by the method of analysis, such as chronologically, historically, thematically, methodologically, theoretically, and using meta-analysis. Another distinction among literature reviews is based on the rigor and strictness of the parameters used in conducting the review. The next sections will highlight the various types of analyses used to organize a review. A discussion of levels of rigor will follow.

Chronologically Organized Literature Reviews   These reviews present the findings in sequential order. To present the findings from the research, the author may choose to order the literature to be reviewed by publication date or (especially for humanities and social sciences) by the time periods or dates in which the research was conducted. For example, Cindy Sullivan Kerber's article *Problem and Pathological Gambling* (2005) presents the research data from the most recent to the least recent. The entries look much like an annotated bibliography, but correlate with the information presented in the introduction of the review. This type of review can show a historical progression in the development of the literature or with a specific issue, such as the topic of gambling among college athletes.

Historical Literature Reviews   Historical reviews provide an analysis of how theories and ideas on an issue or topic have developed with the passage of time, and as a means to predict or suggest where future research and topics may be needed. This method differs from chronologically organized literature reviews in that although the information is presented in a sequential order, its focus is on the development of historical trends and not the publication dates or the date of the research material. For example, Griffin and Ouellett's article *From Silence to Safety and Beyond: Historical Trends in Addressing Lesbian, Gay, Bisexual, Transgender Issues in K–12 Schools* (2003) provides a historical overview of how perspectives have changed on addressing lesbian, gay, bisexual, and transgender issues in public K–12 schools over the past eighty years. The authors divide their study into three historical eras: 1920–1979, 1980–1989, and 1990–2002. Within these eras they address the subtopics of prominent concern. The article also explains where the authors think that research and educational policy on these issues in schools might go in the future. This example shows how to summarize and analyze historical trends and use the historical views of the past to predict areas of research or perspective shifts for the future.

Thematic Literature Reviews In a thematic literature review the analysis points to various themes or topics that are common across the literature. These topics become the organizational structure for the body of the literature review. For example, in the review *Grandparents in Custodial Care of Their Grandchildren*, Carlini-Marlatt (2005) provides an example of a thematic organization. In the introduction the author states, "Articles focused on how to aid grandparents to raise healthy grandchildren can be divided into four main topics: a) treatment for grandchildren's behavioral disorders; b) grandparents' education and training; c) support groups; and d) social services and policy" (p. 11). Thematic reviews aid the author in examining contrasting perspectives, approaches, methodologies, and findings as well as analyzing the strengths and weaknesses of previous research or ideas. As in the Carlini-Marlatt literature review, the author discusses the literature focused on grandparents' education and training, both the positive and negative aspects of this research, and what it says in terms of support for grandparents.

Methodological Literature Reviews These reviews focus on the methodologies (processes, procedures, or approaches of conducting the studies in a research project) used by the researchers or writers. This type of review is very useful when looking at past or current methodologies in order to assess their effectiveness. For example, in the first chapter of Gemmell, Moran, Crowley, and Courtney's *Literature Review on the Relation between Drug Use, Impaired Driving and Traffic Accidents* (1999), the authors examine a variety of tests concerning drug use and impaired driving, and discuss the methodologies behind these tests. The authors compare and criticize the different methods used in these tests and then offer suggestions on how to improve testing methods.

Theoretical Literature Reviews Often researchers use a certain theory or reasoning to understand a problem or analyze a research question. A theoretical literature review provides an analysis of the various theories guiding a topic. The authors evaluate how an issue or topic is addressed within certain theoretical constructs or how theory shapes the research. This type of review is best to use when the literature comes from a broad range of theoretical perspectives, or when the authors want to analyze criticism of particular theoretical constructs, or use past theories to suggest directions for future research. For example, researchers have been trying to understand the achievement gap between children of different races. Some researchers will point to a culture of poverty while others may point to theories focused on teacher expectations. A literature review on this topic would analyze the various theories informing research on the achievement gap and then compare and contrast those theories. Such an analysis allows the reader to gain a deeper understanding of the various ways researchers examine an issue and its possible effects on future policy. The document describes the various theories, provides criticisms of those theories, analyzes implications of the theories, and ultimately presents ideas for future research.

Meta-Analysis   This technique seeks to statistically summarize results from other studies by asking a specific research question and using previous research from all studies available to answer this question (see Chapter Seven). This has been a useful technique to gain understanding of a body of quantitative research over time, especially if the studies have small sample sizes. An example of this approach is a meta-analysis by Waxman, Connell, and Gray (2002) to study the effects of teaching and learning with technology on student outcomes. They compared twenty research studies involving about forty-four hundred students total, and then in 2003, Waxman, Lin, and Michko (2003) extended to include data from forty-two studies representing approximately seven thousand students. By comparing so many smaller studies, the authors of the review were able to provide an even larger picture of the research that had been conducted from a broad range of perspectives, giving the readers of the analysis much more background on the subject as well as ideas on where further research could be conducted. It is a selective and highly rigorous process to create a truly reliable meta-analysis; authors need to be concerned with how closely the studies are related and be sure to include as much relevant data as possible.

Literature Reviews and Rigor

Literature reviews can vary in the level of rigor that is used in setting the parameters and rules of inclusion as well as in conducting the analysis; the more rigorous the review process, the more reliable the conclusions and recommendations. Reviews at the least rigorous level would be simply a summary of a collection of sources that would allow many different types of materials on a topic. At the other end of the spectrum are reviews that have explicit and clearly articulated parameters for the research, as well as a very systematic analysis of the literature. Well-researched topics, or more mature topics, often lend themselves to analysis that offers new interpretations, understandings, and connections for researchers (Torraco, 2005). Conversely, new areas of research, or emerging areas such as distance education, will not have a deep and long history of completed research. These emerging literature reviews will often present new models or ways to think about the literature, or suggest a framework of conceptualization. This is important to keep in mind when reading literature reviews—how deep and mature is the base from which the review is written.

 REFLECTION QUESTIONS

1. Describe at least three different types of reviews and why you might use them.

2. If you were to construct a literature review, what type would be most useful in your professional practice? Why?

HOW TO READ A LITERATURE REVIEW

As a consumer of research and literature reviews, it is imperative that you read with a discerning eye. Literature reviews are like statistics in that they can be shaped to support different biases and certain interests. They can also greatly inform policy. For example, in the case of the No Child Left Behind Act, a key literature review conducted by the National Reading Panel (2000), titled *Teaching Children to Read: An Evidence-Based Assessment of the Scientific Research Literature on Reading and Its Implications for Reading Instruction*, informed important policies on the focus of reading education in schools nationwide. Since the publication of that report, critics have questioned how rigorously the review was conducted, such as the meta-analysis (Garan, 2001) and the parameters for the review. For example, critics have questioned which studies were included and which were left out. This document became very important and influential as schools responded by basing reading programs on the recommendations. Unfortunately, it was found that the panel, due to time constraints, did not complete an **exhaustive review**, meaning that they left out studies that should have been included.

When you read a literature review you need to ask yourself various questions that will assist you in identifying its strengths and weaknesses as well as the validity of its results. The **validity** of the review refers to whether the content accurately reflects the intended purpose. For example, did the authors provide a purpose? A solid review will have a clear purpose, which is then supported by the review. Be sure this is clear; otherwise authors can pull in a disparate body of research that lessens the validity of the results. For example, a broad purpose, such as to examine the literature on adolescents in juvenile facilities, may include a very wide selection of literature. A more focused purpose, such as to examine the literature on adolescents in juvenile facilities who have qualified for special education, may assist in a more solid, focused review. The conclusion usually will come back to the purpose and connect any recommendations to it. In the case of examining the literature on adolescents in juvenile facilities who have qualified for special education, the conclusion, at a minimum, would address what the literature says about those students, and then make recommendations regarding them. Next, you will ask if they included a description of the methodology, such as the rules of inclusion. As you read through the review, you need to note what types of information were left out. Did the boundaries bias the review? For example, if only peer-reviewed articles were included, but much of the discussion on school reform may be found in reports, then only part of the story on school reform will be told.

How do you know if the literature review is reliable, meaning that it can be replicated, and valid, meaning that its content accurately reflects the intended purpose? To enhance **reliability**, the ability to replicate the review, authors should make transparent their methods, or rather the process that they used to identify and collect the literature to be reviewed. This is especially useful in today's world of electronic databases. The disclosure of the methods, including the search terms, databases used, as well as other sources, increases the reliability of the literature review. Essentially, if the process or search method is clear enough, a reader could conduct a similar review and produce similar results.

In the discussion of the methods, the authors may include a discussion of the various decisions they made. What are the parameters or rules of inclusion for the review and why were they set that way? For example, why did they choose to include articles that date back twenty years versus ten? What impact does twenty-year-old information have on the research question or purpose of the review? To enhance **validity**, to assess whether the content accurately reflects the intended purpose, you need to identify the purpose of the review. Once you have identified the purpose, ask yourself if the authors' methods, such as the parameters or included information, support the purpose. Also assess whether the literature reviewed falls within the stated parameters. If not, this can lead to confusion, as well as faulty conclusions. An author could state that only peer-reviewed articles within the last ten years will be included, but then in the analysis five articles from thirty years ago were included and used as points of comparison. This does not provide a fair comparison and confuses the reader. If the author deviates from the parameters, then that should be explained to the reader. At the end of the review, ask whether the author kept to the stated parameters, and if so, it could be considered a "complete" analysis; if not, ask what might have been left out or included that does not support the methods.

Author bias can emerge through various decisions, as discussed above, as well as through the choices they make in interpreting and writing up the synthesis. You will want to ask: Who are the authors? Have they published on the topic of the review or are they new to this area? This can be both good and bad; if they are new they may be either unaware of the field and miss important studies or information, or they may do the opposite and be very concerned about not missing any information. Does the author have a prejudice or point that seems to be pervasive and biases the evaluation and presentation of the articles? One way an author can balance the perspective is to share the literature or research that is contrary to other data and perspectives. Is the author's perspective even-handed or prejudicial? Is contrary data considered or is certain pertinent information ignored to prove the author's point? Which of the author's theses or arguments are most and least convincing? For example, a literature review on adolescents in juvenile detention facilities who qualify for special education would examine the various ways those populations are discussed and represented. To enhance this discussion, it is important to include different examples of literature that may conflict with one another, such as in findings and conclusions.

Author bias can emerge through the discussion of the literature; for example, in the weight of importance given to each of the studies, as well as the depiction of each, and the relationship among a set of literature (Bangert-Drowns & Rudner, 1991). The author may not identify all relations noted, but craft the narrative to support a predetermined point. Some issues of concern will be how the author addresses the **level of heterogeneity** (diversity) within the literature collection. When the studies are diverse in nature, such as in varying purposes and methodological approaches, synthesis and comparison can be problematic. For example, does the literature include quantitative and qualitative data? (For more information, see Chapter Six, "Quantitative Data Analysis," and Chapter Fourteen, "Qualitative Data Analysis".) How does the author compare, contrast, and synthesize these diverse pieces of literature? Though these both can be included in the review, one must be careful how to compare a pre-post test study with a study that examined a similar phenomenon using observations. Authors need to take into account differences between studies in various areas, as well as various methodologies (Green, Johnson, & Adams, 2001). If literature of differing methodologies and purposes are grouped and analyzed together, distinctions should be noted, and relationships drawn between similar findings from different methodologies noted as well. For example, an author will identify that five of the studies analyzed the experiences of the adolescents in juvenile facilities using surveys, while another study conducted interviews. Though the approaches varied, the authors agreed that the students reflected a level of frustration with their pre-detention school experiences. Such a comparison will allow the reader to note the connections across studies.

Value of the Studies

How does a review reflect the varying levels of quality of the literature and its varying levels of value? For example, some studies in the review focus on new innovations that have been examined using questionnaires with low return rates or generalized findings to groups not researched, such as using college students and then applying the results to high school students (Hargreaves, 1996, 1998), and this may not provide useful information. When low-quality or weaker research is discussed in the same way as more substantial, well-constructed studies, it is easy for all the research to be dismissed or to misinform a policy decision. An author can avoid such confusion by emphasizing those studies that are stronger in methodology and pointing out methodological weaknesses in other studies. For example, an author might say something like the following: "These five studies provided insights into understanding the attitudes of adolescents in juvenile detention, but the return rates on the surveys were low. On the other hand, the interview-based study provided more feedback and was conducted using rigorous procedures".

Readability

Readability refers to the quality of the review itself. The authors should make the review reader-friendly so that arguments can be followed. If not, then the power of their arguments will be lost. It is key that the authors represent other authors' work with integrity and accuracy. The analysis of the literature should be made clear and supported by evidence (for example, primary historical material, case studies, narratives, statistics, and recent scientific findings). The authors should help the reader to understand which are the key and important studies or literature and which are of lesser importance or influence. The authors must first define these important studies for themselves and rate the level of rigor in the way the studies are conducted. Is the study well constructed, reliable, and valid? Is the study generalizable? Do other researchers reference the study? Has it gone through a peer-review process? Does it make an important contribution or add new ideas for readers to ponder? Does it help the reader think differently about the topic? Once these questions are answered, they will organize the literature according to level of prominence or importance. Then in the writing of the narrative, the authors will illustrate the relationship between the various kinds of literature by giving the more important and salient studies more discussion and space in the literature review.

As you read the conclusion, ask yourself if you agree with it and whether there is enough information to come to the same conclusion as the authors. Finally, the work should contribute to a greater understanding of the subject.

In summary, answer this list of useful questions when reading a literature review:

- What is the purpose of the literature review, and why is the literature review needed? (Is it because there is contradictory evidence, changes in trends, new information that has emerged, is there a need for background on a topic, or is it to inform a policy?)
- What are the research questions?
- What are the parameters, boundaries, or rules of inclusion that the authors use?
- Is there a description of search terms and methods of locating materials (methodology)?
- How did the authors categorize the literature?
- What language do they use to critique the research? (Give examples.)
- What weaknesses do they identify in the literature? What strengths do they identify?
- What do the authors find out and recommend?

REFLECTION QUESTIONS

1. What are key questions to ask when reading through a literature review?
2. Why are these important?
3. How can a reader find the answers to these questions?
4. What can an author do to increase the reliability and validity of a literature review?

ACTIVITY

1. To help you become better acquainted with literature reviews, it will be useful to analyze a basic review. Find the following literature review in a database: McAllister, G., & Irvine, J. J. (2000). Cross cultural competency and multicultural teacher education. *Review of Educational Research, 70*, 3–25.

   Answer the following questions:

   - What is the purpose of the literature review? What are the research questions?
   - What sources did they use to find literature to address the research question?
   - What are the boundaries or rules of inclusion the authors use?
   - What are the ways that the authors introduce the literature review?
   - Where are examples of advance organizers?

- How did the authors categorize the literature?
- What language do they use to critique the research? (Give examples.)
- What weaknesses do they identify in the literature? What strengths do they identify?
- What is the story they tell?
- What do the authors find out?
- What do they recommend?

The next section shifts you from consumer to creator as we discuss how to write a literature review. The literature review can be exhaustive and serve as an article itself, or it simply can be a general examination of a small body of research to serve as the context of an empirical study or as supporting background for a grant proposal or report. No matter the purpose, the following methods will assist you in gathering the literature, analyzing, synthesizing, and writing up your findings.

WRITING A LITERATURE REVIEW

Literature reviews can be useful for informing decision making, as well as setting the context for an article or grant proposal. Writing a good literature review can be a challenging task. You want to represent authors' works with integrity, but at the same time you want to offer the reader insights into the body of literature. To assist with the process of writing the literature review, below is a suggested process, as well as key aspects to include.

Muck About

It is important that you **muck about** in the literature before refining your purpose or research question. This term essentially means to play around in the databases to see what is already out there on your potential topic. This process can assist you in refining your research question or topic so as not to duplicate reviews that have already been done. Go to a database and try out different search terms and different combinations of search terms. Look at what others have written and note the search terms they have used. Once you begin to find literature that is close to your research interest, explore that literature further. After you are clearer about your topic, refine your research topic or a research question that will focus the purpose of your review.

Set Your Parameters

Create a list of decisions that will define what information will be included in your literature review. The following questions will assist you with that process:

1. What time period will you set? Generally a ten-year span will keep your work current. Older research can be included if it greatly informs the review.
2. What types of studies will be included? From what disciplines? Databases? Peer-reviewed? Unpublished reports? Be sure to ask yourself and record why you

have made these decisions. For example, why ten years? Why only published, peer-reviewed articles? Will leaving out reports from various agencies leave out important information?

3. Once you have your parameters, you will then seek out sources that fit within that decision box.

Conduct Your Research

Now that you have your parameters, you will begin to identify research. As you embark on this process, keep note of the search terms you use as well as the databases. Some people will even record the history of their searches, which some databases do for you.

It is good to think ahead how you will organize the literature you find. Some reviews could consist of a hundred or more works, while others may have twenty. Some people prefer to print out the literature while others take notes using an electronic organizing library such as RefWorks (www.refworks.com) or Endnote (www.endnote.com), or you may do both. Keep in mind that the literature review process is recursive, not linear, in nature. As you conduct your research you will go back to your purpose, you will find sources, read them, and begin to analyze, then find more sources, read them, and expand your analysis, and so forth. Often researchers will become frustrated with this process, but the frustration actually identifies that you are conducting a strong search.

Analyze the Literature

Often the analysis process will take several reads through the literature. Depending on your purpose, you will decide on an analytical process. You may decide this beforehand, or as you are reading you may identify the most effective way to communicate to a reader the body of literature. For example, you read through the forty articles a couple times and begin to see themes emerge, which become your point of comparison. Or you realize that a chronological presentation of the literature may be the most useful. Given the many choices and ways to analyze a body of literature, a table may assist you. The table may include title, data published, methodology used, conclusions of the study, strengths, and weaknesses. You can also add other points as well. Table 2.1 is an example. You can add other columns depending on your interest and purpose.

Once you have identified your analysis, you will then write up what you have found.

TABLE 2.1. **Sample Literature Review Research Study Table**

Source, Article, and Author Names	Purpose	Methods	Findings	Strengths	Weaknesses

ACTIVITY

1. Identify a topic or research question, and then conduct a literature review of at least ten sources. Using the suggested table or another of your own making, analyze the various sources.

Focus on the Purpose of Your Literature Review

As you go through the process of writing your own literature review, remind yourself of the purpose for which you are writing it. A strong purpose carried through the literature review will strengthen your analysis and the narrative itself. The easiest way to construct a purpose is to use the phrase: *The purpose of this literature review is to . . .* A concrete example of this approach would be, "The purpose of this literature review is to examine the research on adolescents who qualified for special education and their experiences in juvenile detention." You can also construct the purpose using a question. For example, "What is the experience of adolescents who have qualified for special education in juvenile detention?" Whatever way you choose to write the purpose, keep it focused and clear to make your rules of inclusion easy to follow.

Write Up the Literature Review

Remember—it is a synthesis, not a "data dump" where you simply create a narrative filled with findings and statistics (Torraco, 2005) or a name-dropping process where every couple sentences start with some author's name and follow with what they said. It is an integrated discussion of the literature. Essentially you are weaving together a story or a discussion that will provide readers with an overview of the literature as well as its strengths, weaknesses, themes, and other points. An effective review will provide a new light or new conception of the body of research. This is a creative endeavor that if analyzed well will lead to new understandings of the body of research. Most important, keep in mind all the issues raised concerning author bias in the earlier sections of this chapter. You want to write a reliable and valid literature review.

The organization of the review is made clear through the use of appropriate headings to define sections of your paper. The placement and delineation of headings can be found in your discipline's style guidelines. At a minimum you should include such **headings** as introduction, purpose, organization of the literature review, theme names, and conclusion. In addition, you should include advance organizers throughout the paper. The **advance organizer** is a paragraph that tells the reader what she will find in the next section. Usually you place an advance organizer early in your paper to provide the reader with an overall layout of the structure of the literature review. Inside the literature review you will have additional advance organizers that serve as transitions. These are key to helping the reader follow your argument.

This process, summarized in Exhibit 2.1, provides a basic outline to writing a literature review. If you are interested in a more in-depth process such as a meta-analysis or narrative, you will want to read specifically on how to construct those literature reviews. You will find resources at the end of this chapter and a complete explanation of meta-analysis in Chapter Seven.

EXHIBIT 2.1.   **Overview of Writing a Literature Review**

1. Choose a topic.

2. Muck about with what have others written on your topic; examine the articles and the search terms.

3. Refine your question or topic.

4. Set up parameters and rules of inclusion.

5. Identify articles that fit within those parameters.

6. Take notes (for example, a table format with categories of information along the top and article details along the vertical).

7. Analyze the articles.

8. Identify your "story"—organize your analysis.

9. Write up your review.

SUMMARY

Literature reviews can assist policy makers, practitioners, and agencies with understanding a body of research in a concise and insightful manner. Though literature reviews can contribute to our understanding and even inform policy decisions, we must read them with a critical eye. They should be as objective, reliable, and valid as possible. Authors can share their biases by being transparent with the decisions they made in constructing the reviews. The reviews should assist a reader in understanding the body of literature, key studies, strengths and weaknesses, as well as what the literature tells us about a topic. Different types of literature reviews will synthesize, analyze, and present the information in specific ways. These types of reviews can also be models for you when you write a literature review of your own.

KEY TERMS

advance organizer
author bias
blind review
body of the literature review
body of research
exhaustive review
headings
justification
level of heterogeneity
literature review
methodology

muck about
objectivity
parameters
peer-reviewed
purpose
reliability
rules of inclusion
summary
synthesis
validity

FURTHER READINGS AND RESOURCES
Suggested Literature Review Article

McAllister, G., & Irvine, J. J. (2000). Cross cultural competency and multicultural teacher education. *Review of Educational Research*, *70*, 3–25.

> This is a very straightforward review that follows a lot of the suggestions in this chapter.

Web Sites and Journals

www.unc.edu/depts/wcweb/handouts/literature_review.html

The Writing Center of University of North Carolina at Chapel Hill provides this handout that explains what a literature review is and gives information on the form and construction of a literature review in the humanities, social sciences, and sciences.

http://ual.stanford.edu/pdf/uar_literaturereviewhandout.pdf

"What Can a Literature Review Do for Me?": How to Research, Write, and Survive a Literature Review. This is a useful site for writing a literature review. It provides insights into using and writing literature reviews in a very concise manner.

Review of Educational Research

Review of Educational Research (RER) publishes critical, integrative reviews of research literature bearing on education. *RER* encourages the submission of research relevant to education from any discipline, such as reviews of research in psychology, sociology, history, philosophy, political science, economics, computer science, statistics, anthropology, and biology, provided that the review bears on educational issues. Publisher: American Educational Research Association. ISSN: 00346543.

CHAPTER

ESSENTIAL ELEMENTS OF EXPERIMENTAL AND QUASI-EXPERIMENTAL RESEARCH

WILLIAM E. MARTIN JR. AND KRISTA D. BRIDGMON

KEY IDEAS

- Experimental research informs evidence-based practice using information obtained from randomized controlled trials.

- Experimental research involves formulating experimental conditions and procedures, reducing imprecision in measurement, and controlling extraneous experimental influences.

- Experimental research involves controlling threats to internal and external validity.

- Quasi-experimental research resembles experimental research in purpose and essential elements, but it embodies compromise designs.

EXPERIMENTAL RESEARCH TODAY

EXPERIMENTAL METHODS are essential in answering important questions about health, mental health, and educational issues. Experimental research provides evidence to answer questions such as: Does a particular medicine reduce the size of a cancerous tumor when compared to a substance having no pharmacological effect (**placebo**)? What counseling techniques are more effective in decreasing symptoms of depression in children when compared to children receiving no treatment (**control group**)? Is an individualized reading instruction program more effective in increasing reading comprehension among first-grade students when compared to a group-focused reading instruction program?

The experimental research results used to answer these questions lead to **evidence-based practice**, which promotes the use of effective practices in professional disciplines including medicine, psychology, and education. Evidence-based practice integrates the best available research with clinical expertise and the personal-contextual characteristics of the patient, client, or student (American Psychological Association, 2006; Institute of Medicine, 2001; United States Department of Education, 2003). Different research methods contribute to evidence-based practice, and each method is better suited to answer certain research questions (see APA, 2006).

The goal of experimental research is to make **generalized causal inferences**. In other words, a researcher wants to demonstrate that A causes B and that the causal relationship can be repeated consistently in additional studies. The standard for making generalized causal inferences about the effects of interventions is a **randomized controlled trial** (also called **clinical trial**). Research participants are randomly assigned (by chance alone) into groups to receive one of several interventions in a randomized controlled trial. At least one of the interventions is a control condition, which is often a standard practice, a placebo, or no intervention. For example, one group of participants may be administered a new medication, a second group receives a traditional medication, and a third group is given an inactive medication having no treatment value (placebo). The participants are assessed and compared on outcomes using valid and reliable measures.

Randomized controlled treatment trials include both **efficacy** and **effectiveness trials**. Efficacy trials are conducted in more "laboratory-like" conditions with more controls initially to see whether an intervention has scientific usefulness under optimal circumstances. This type of trial emphasizes the systematic and scientific evaluation of whether an intervention works. For example, a clinical trial was conducted with postmenopausal survivors of early-stage breast cancer who took the drug letrozole compared to women taking a placebo (National Cancer Institute, 2008). This was an efficacy trial because there was a determination of whether the drug produced expected results under more ideal circumstances.

Effectiveness trials are conducted in more "real-world" conditions with fewer controls. This type of trial provides evidence about the clinical utility of an intervention to a local setting (APA, 2006). For example, a randomized clinical trial was conducted within a community with ninety concerned significant others of treatment-refusing illicit drug users (Meyers, Miller, Smith, & Tonigan, 2002). This was an effectiveness trial because three different methods were evaluated for their effectiveness in getting drug users into treatment within "real-world" clinical settings. This combination of randomized controlled trials provides information about whether interventions are safe and effective under controlled conditions. The systematic delivery of randomized controlled trials is widespread. There are 48,983 trials currently reported in 50 states and 153 countries on a wide range of conditions (United States National Institutes of Health, 2008).

Experimental researchers strive to accurately and consistently measure whether changes in an outcome (**dependent variable**) can be attributed to a specified cause (**independent variable**). At the same time, rival causes must be ruled out as affecting an outcome by controlling **extraneous variables** that are unwanted and make it difficult to isolate the independent variable as the cause of changes in the dependent variable. For example, a study showed that individualized reading instruction produced higher reading comprehension in first-grade students when compared to group reading instruction. The extent that prior reading training by parents was more prominent in the students who received individualized reading instruction compared to those students receiving group reading instruction had to be ruled out as a reasonable alternative explanation for improved reading results (called a **rival hypothesis** or cause). In this chapter, the terms *intervention, treatment, independent variable*, and *cause* will be used synonymously. Likewise, *outcome, dependent measure*, and *dependent variable* will be used synonymously.

REFLECTION QUESTIONS

1. What other conditions are the focuses of clinical trials? Go online to clinicaltrials.gov and investigate the various conditions in which randomized clinical trials are being conducted.

2. Why are effectiveness trials so important in understanding the causes of social, psychological, and educational problems?

ESSENTIAL ELEMENTS OF EXPERIMENTAL RESEARCH

Experimental research involves an independent variable manipulated by the researcher, random assignment of participants to the conditions of the independent variable including a control or comparison group, and accurate measurement of the outcome to determine if there are changes to the dependent variable. The essential elements of experimental research are presented in relation to three processes of designing and conducting experimental research.

Processes of Designing and Conducting Experimental Research

There are three important processes in designing and conducting experimental research (Kerlinger & Lee, 2000). First, the experimental researcher wants to formulate the experimental conditions and procedures to assure that the independent variable shows clear and systematic effects on the dependent variable. A second process entails reducing the imprecision in measurement associated with sampling of participants, measurement of dependent variables, and experimental procedures. The third process is controlling extraneous experimental influences with the purpose of enhancing the plausibility of the independent variable as the cause for changes in the dependent variable.

Descriptive information about a published experimental study is presented next. It will be useful to obtain a copy of the article using an online search engine such as PsycARTICLES from a university library to refer to as you read about the essential elements of research. The citation of the article is:

Rohan, K. J., Roecklein, K. A., Lindsey, K. T., Johnson, L. G., Lippy, R. D., Lacy, T. J., & Barton, F. B. (2007). A randomized controlled trial of cognitive-behavioral therapy, light therapy, and their combination for seasonal affective disorder. *Journal of Consulting and Clinical Psychology*, *75*, 489–500.

The study description is followed by a discussion of essential elements of experimental research grouped under the three processes of designing and conducting experimental research. Then, the researchers' application of these essential elements in their study is analyzed.

Study Example: What Are Effective Treatments for Seasonal Affective Disorder (SAD)? A randomized controlled trial was conducted by Rohan et al. (2007) to see if a newly developed supplementary psychotherapy treatment would decrease depression severity of individuals diagnosed with seasonal affective disorder (SAD). SAD most often occurs when summer turns to fall and on to winter. Symptoms of this winter depression include hopelessness, anxiety, loss of energy, social withdrawal, oversleeping, loss of interest in activities, cravings for foods high in carbohydrates, weight gain, and difficulty processing (Mayo Foundation for Medical Education and Research, 2007). The Mayo Foundation describes a less common type of summer depression with symptoms of anxiety, insomnia, irritability, agitation, weight loss, poor appetite, and increased sex drive. SAD can be diagnosed by qualified mental health professionals using criteria specified in the *Diagnostic and Statistical Manual of Mental Disorders* for major depression, recurrent, with seasonal pattern (APA, 2000).

Although the causes for winter SAD are unknown, one possible explanation given is that there is a disruption of the natural body clock (circadian rhythm), which interferes with letting one know when to sleep or wake. Another explanation is that the body increases the production of melatonin during the long nights of winter. Melatonin is a sleep-related hormone that is linked to depression. Finally, the neurotransmitter serotonin, which affects mood in a positive way, may be decreased because of the lack of sunlight in the winter, possibly leading to depression (Mayo Foundation for Medical Education and Research, 2007).

Study Example: Research Purpose. The researchers wanted to find out whether cognitive-behavior therapy, light therapy, and a combination of cognitive-behavior therapy and light therapy would improve depression symptoms when compared to a control group receiving no therapy (treatment). They also wanted to assess the effectiveness of the newer treatment of cognitive-behavior therapy. In addition, they wanted to determine if a combined procedure of cognitive-behavior therapy added to the more conventional light therapy would produce more positive effects than light therapy alone.

Study Example: Independent Variables. Two independent variables in this study are treatment condition and time of treatment. The first independent variable is seasonal affective disorder (SAD) treatment with four conditions.

Condition 1: Cognitive-Behavioral Therapy (CBT). CBT has demonstrated in randomized controlled trials to be an effective psychotherapy for depression (Vittengl, Clark, Dunn, & Jarrett, 2007). The CBT for SAD was implemented as group counseling for groups of four to eight participants per group, two sessions per week, over six weeks. The three important therapeutic goals in cognitive-behavioral therapy are to help clients to (1) identify and correct inaccurate thoughts associated with SAD, (2) become involved in more enjoyable life activities, and (3) enhance their problem-solving skills to improve SAD symptoms and maintain the improvements they have achieved.

Condition 2: Light Therapy (LT). LT is a common treatment for SAD, although it has not yet been approved by the Food and Drug Administration because of a lack of definitive evidence from clinical trials as to its effectiveness (Mayo Foundation for Medical Education and Research, 2007). LT imitates outdoor light and purportedly results in a biochemical change in an individual's brain that lifts mood, thus relieving SAD symptoms. An audiotape instructional session covering information about the rationale for LT and providing instructions on how to use the light box was presented to each participant. The light box emits an ultraviolet light with shield that was to be administered by the participants in doses of forty-five minutes in the morning (between 6:00 AM and 9:00 AM) and evening (6:00 PM and 9:00 PM) over six weeks. After week one, the LT prescription was modified to each individual's specific needs by an outside LT expert who monitored and supervised the LT treatment.

Condition 3: Cognitive-Behavioral Therapy + Light Therapy (CBT + LT). In the CBT + LT condition, the participants received both treatments simultaneously over six weeks.

Condition 4: Minimal Contact–Delayed Treatment control (MCDT). The MCDT groups of participants were the control group not receiving any treatment during the six weeks of the experiment, but they did complete the pretest and posttest assessments. The participants were monitored weekly in person to ensure their well-being, and after the six weeks they were administered the LT treatment.

A second independent variable is the time of treatment effects on the dependent variables at pretreatment, posttreatment, and summer follow-up. The pretreatment participants were assessed on the dependent variables before the four treatment conditions were implemented. The participants were assessed again on the dependent variables after the six weeks of treatment (posttreatment) and a final time during June or July as part of the summer follow-up. Changes in the participants' scores on the dependent variables were analyzed at pretreatment, posttreatment, and summer follow-up.

Study Example: Dependent Variables. The following three dependent variables were used in the study:

1. *Current SAD Episode*. The Structured Interview Guide for the Hamilton Rating Scale for Depression and SAD subscale (SIGH-SAD) was used to assess for the existence of a current SAD episode. The twenty-nine items of the SIGH-SAD were administered in interviews of the participants by two trained raters. The raters had to demonstrate proficiency in a mock interview before they could participate in actual rating interviews. Moreover, **interrater reliability** (agreement among raters) was computed for the two raters at pretreatment assessment, post-treatment assessment, and summer follow-up to help assure the consistency of the rating procedure. The raters were **blind** to the treatment condition, meaning that they were unaware of which treatment condition each participant was assigned to while they were interviewing them. This blind procedure reduces the chance of tester bias entering the assessment process. For example, a rater may assess participants more favorably (bias) in the cognitive-behavioral therapy condition if she believes that it is a more effective therapy than light therapy.

2. *Depressive Symptom Severity*. The Beck Depression Inventory–Second Edition (BDI-II) has twenty-one items that are completed by participants. It is a self-report measure of depressive symptom severity.

3. *Expected Efficacy and Personal Preferences*. The Pretreatment Expectations Survey was used to ask the participants to rank the four treatment conditions on expected efficacy (most effective to least effective) and personal preferences (most preferred to least preferred) prior to being assigned to receive a treatment condition.

Study Example: Participants. Participants were recruited from a large metropolitan area in the United States using print and radio advertisement. Over three consecutive fall-winter seasons, 490 individuals responded. A total of 92 individuals were phone screened and asked to participate in clinical interviews. Following the clinical interview, 61 individuals were selected for the study and randomly assigned to treatment condition. The number of participants by condition was cognitive-behavioral therapy (15), light therapy (16), cognitive-behavioral therapy + light therapy (15), and minimal contact–delayed treatment control (15).

Inclusion and **exclusion criteria** are often used by researchers to identify appropriate participants and assure that the participants chosen for the study would be safe in the treatment conditions. The inclusion criteria used to select the participants were (1) eighteen years of age or older, (2) met *Diagnostic and Statistical Manual of Mental Disorders* (APA, 2000) criteria for major depression, recurrent, with seasonal pattern, (3) met SIGH-SAD criteria for a current SAD episode, and (4) completed the pretreatment assessment. Participants were excluded from the study based upon the following exclusion criteria: (1) current psychiatric treatment, (2) having another major psychiatric disorder, (3) planned absences during treatment period, and (4) having bipolar-type SAD.

Study Example: Design. The experimental research design used in the study was a randomized multiple treatments and control with pretest (see Table 3.1).

TABLE 3.1. **SAD Study Design: A Randomized Multiple Treatments and Control with Pretest**

Random Assignment	Pretest	Treatment	Posttest	Follow-up
$R_{andomize}$	$O_{Pretest}$	X_{CBT}	$O_{Postest}$	$O_{Follow-up\ assessment}$
$R_{andomize}$	$O_{Pretest}$	X_{LT}	$O_{Postest}$	$O_{Follow-up\ assessment}$
$R_{andomize}$	$O_{Pretest}$	X_{CBT+LT}	$O_{Postest}$	$O_{Follow-up\ assessment}$
$R_{andomize}$	$O_{Pretest}$	C_{MCDT}	$O_{Postest}$	$O_{Follow-up\ assessment}$

Note. CBT = cognitive-behavioral therapy; LT = light therapy, CBT + LT = cognitive-behavioral therapy + light therapy; and MCDT = minimal contact–delayed treatment control.

Each row in Table 3.1 represents a group of participants receiving a different treatment condition (cognitive-behavioral therapy, light therapy, cognitive-behavioral therapy + light therapy, and minimal contact–delayed treatment control). The R designates that the participants were randomly assigned to treatment conditions. All O's (observations) represent assessments of the dependent variables. An O before a treatment condition is a pretreatment assessment, an O after the treatment condition is a posttreatment assessment, and an O following the posttreatment assessment represents the summer follow-up assessment. An X stands for a treatment condition, and C symbolizes a control condition.

Analyses that the researchers wanted to conduct were to assess significant differences in average scores by treatment condition group (cognitive-behavioral therapy, light therapy, cognitive-behavioral therapy + light therapy, and minimal contact–delayed treatment control) on the dependent measures (SIGH-SAD and BDI-II) at posttreatment (each $O_{Postest}$ of the four groups) and summer follow-up (each $O_{Follow-up\ assessment}$ of the four groups). Moreover, they wanted to determine whether the participants' scores on the dependent variables changed (increased or decreased) over time from (1) before the participants received the treatment conditions ($O_{Pretest}$ of the four groups), to (2) after they received the treatment condition ($O_{Postest}$ of the four groups), to (3) at summer follow-up ($O_{Follow-up\ assessment}$). Finally, they wanted to determine if changes in average group scores from pretreatment to posttreatment to follow-up differed according to the treatment condition administered to the participants.

REFLECTION QUESTIONS

1. Why was treatment condition an independent variable in the study?
2. Why was depressive symptom severity as measured by the Beck Depression Inventory a dependent variable in the study?

Formulating Experimental Conditions and Procedures

Experimental research starts with clearly stated hypotheses showing the relations between independent and dependent variables and asserting that the relations can be **empirically tested**, which means that the results can be verified by observation or experience. Carefully and operationally defining the **construct** underlying the interventions and specifying the procedures for implementation of the independent variable to the participants (both treatment and control) are activities essential in formulating experimental conditions. A construct is a theoretical concept that is not directly observable, such as personality. **Operational definitions** provide detailed ways to understand and measure constructs and variables. For example, one operational definition of personality is found in the items and scales of the Sixteen Personality Factor Questionnaire.

Operational definitions also link constructs and variables to related research, current knowledge, and theory. Operationalism is a key to achieving **objectivity** (unbiased judgment), which is paramount to experimental research, "because its demand that observations must be public and replicable helps to put research activities outside of and apart from researchers and their predilections" (Kerlinger & Lee, 2000, p. 59). **Replication** refers to reproducing the findings of other researchers with the purpose to increase (or decrease) confidence in the findings.

It is important to ensure that the treatment and control conditions adhere to the researcher's specifications, called **treatment fidelity** (also called *treatment integrity*). Treatment fidelity can be assessed through three components of implementation: **treatment delivery**, **treatment receipt**, and **treatment adherence** (Shadish, Cook, & Campbell, 2002). **Treatment delivery** refers to whether or not the intervention was actually delivered. Was a complete treatment, as intended by the researchers, delivered to the participants? A **treatment protocol** is a highly recommended procedure used to assure treatment delivery as desired by the researcher. Treatment protocols (treatment manuals) **standardize** (systematize) the steps and procedures that individuals providing the treatment must follow when giving the treatment to participants. The use of protocols increases the likelihood that the same treatment is delivered to each participant. Treatment protocols are especially important to researchers who conduct a follow-up research study to determine if their results are similar to findings from a previous study. The treatment protocol helps assure that the treatment implementation is similar from one study to another. Experimental researchers want to know that results can be replicated (reproduced) from one study to another. It is important to train and supervise the treatment providers to make sure they know exactly how to use the treatment protocols. Treatment delivery can be enhanced by giving participants reminders to engage in the treatment when they have choices to participate or not. Treatment conditions sometimes are standardized by audio- or videotaping the treatment protocols.

Improving whether the participants actually receive the treatment (**treatment receipt**) can be accomplished by giving written directions to participants on how they are expected to participate in the treatment condition and by repeating directions associated with the treatment. The extent to which participants received the treatment can be assessed by questioning the participants about the treatment procedures that they experienced, and having the participants keep written logs of their participation activities.

When participants follow through as intended with treatment, there is **treatment adherence**. Treatment adherence can be improved by giving the participants paper and pencil, audio, video, or CD homework assignments and using significant others to encourage the participants to take part in the treatment. Researchers can measure adherence by interviewing participants and significant others, recording observations of participation, reviewing engagement logs, as well as by conducting biological assays (analytical procedures) used in medical research (for example, assessing drug toxicity in human blood or monitoring pollutants in the environment). Several strategies were used in this study to enhance the formulation of experimental conditions and procedures.

Study Example: Treatment Operational Definitions. The conditions of the independent variable, seasonal affective disorder (SAD) treatment, have both theory and previous research to justify their use. The researchers identified several studies that demonstrated the effectiveness and theoretical support for light therapy (LT). Additionally, there are clearly established procedures and apparatus available to successfully treat persons who experience SAD. Cognitive-behavioral therapy (CBT) has demonstrated consistent efficacy in treating persons with depression, and SAD has characteristics similar to more generalized depression, therefore the researchers were able to establish their rationale to use CBT. The researchers conducted a **feasibility study** (pilot study), which is a preliminary study to assess whether a larger study using the cognitive-behavioral therapy would be practical and successful. The authors developed a CBT protocol (detailed procedural plan) for SAD and conducted the feasibility study that demonstrated that cognitive-behavioral therapy did reduce SAD symptoms. The rationale for the combined cognitive-behavioral therapy with light therapy condition was to determine if there would be an added benefit in reducing SAD symptoms if CBT was added to the established light therapy. This combined treatment showed the highest remission rate (substantially decreased symptoms) in the feasibility study. The cognitive-behavioral therapy + light therapy condition was administered simultaneously to participants using the same procedures as when the treatment conditions were administered individually. Alternative explanations for changes in the dependent variables could be ruled out by comparing participants who received the light therapy, cognitive-behavioral therapy, and light therapy + cognitive-behavioral therapy conditions to a minimal contact–delayed treatment control (MCDT) condition. The control condition allowed the three treatment interventions to show their effects by highlighting differences in scores of participants measuring the dependent variables of participants in each condition, and comparing these measures to the results from the nontreatment control group.

Study Example: Treatment Delivery. The cognitive-behavioral therapy was administered by therapists using a protocol that specified how to implement the therapy tailored to reducing SAD symptoms, including information about the targeted number of sessions, length for sessions, format for sessions, and the content and techniques to be used in the therapy. The light therapy (LT) was introduced to participants with an audiotaped instructional session covering a rationale for LT, use of the light box, and how to fill out implementation forms. Moreover, an expert consultant was used to supervise the LT to help assure the fidelity of the intervention. The CBT + LT group participants received the interventions simultaneously following the protocols used for each intervention individually. The participants were asked not to reveal their treatment assignments to other participants with the purpose of reducing spillover effects (**diffusion**) across treatment conditions. Treatment diffusion might confound the clarity of changes in the dependent measures resulting from each treatment condition. For example, participants in the minimal contact–delayed treatment condition (MCDT) may talk to participants in the light therapy condition and think it would be beneficial to them to seek out light therapy. It would be impossible to determine whether light therapy is more effective than no treatment if MCDT participants did use light therapy. The minimal contact–delayed treatment control participants were the control group not receiving cognitive-behavioral therapy or light therapy until after the six-week trial was complete when they received light therapy. However, the minimal contact–delayed treatment control participants were monitored weekly to assess their well-being in the event that an intervention was warranted (see Chapter One for more about participant protection).

The researchers also measured protocol adherence by conducting a **manipulation check** to determine if the treatments were implemented in the intended fashion. They used a scale for two trained raters to observe a random sample of CBT and LT session audiotapes to assess whether the CBT and LT treatments were carried out as detailed in the treatment protocol. The researchers concluded that there was adherence between the treatment and the protocol content. As such, the manipulation check demonstrated that the CBT and LT treatments were implemented in the intended fashion.

Study Example: Treatment Receipt. The session attendance of participants taking part in the cognitive-behavioral therapy condition was recorded. A daily diary was completed by each participant engaging in the light therapy condition to document the extent of use of the treatment.

Study Example: Treatment Adherence. The researchers measured the number of sessions attended and the reported minutes per day (morning and evening) that the participants engaged in activities as part of their treatment condition.

REFLECTION QUESTIONS

1. Why was it important for the study example researchers to monitor the weekly progress of participants who were in the minimal contact–delayed treatment control condition?

2. Written treatment protocols ensure intended treatment delivery but also are important for replication studies. How does the notion of replication relate to the term *generalized causal inference*?

Reducing Imprecision in Measurement

Experimental research depends upon having accurate and reliable measurements of changes in dependent variables. Three major sources of imprecision in measurement are sampling error, error of measurement, and procedural irregularities. The term **error** used in this context is not a mistake but is best understood as imprecision in measurement of the dependent variable attributed to unknown sources but within the range of estimation.

In most experimental studies, changes in measurements on a dependent variable resulting from an independent variable are studied using a small group of participants known as a **sample**. Researchers want to discover new information from the sample that is important to a larger group known as a **population**. For example, a researcher may study changes in math achievement of a random sample of one hundred third-grade students who experienced a new math teaching curriculum. Most often, the researchers want the results to be applicable to a larger group such as all third graders in a school district.

An imprecision in measurement of the dependent variable, known as **sampling error**, occurs when inferences are made about a population from sample results. Sampling error is random error or variability due to chance that occurs when a random sample is drawn from a population and when sample statistics, such as a mean and standard deviation of a dependent variable, are computed to estimate the population parameter mean and standard deviation. A mean is the average score of a set of scores; a standard deviation measures the variability of scores from the mean (see Chapter Six for additional explanations). The means and standard deviations for each random sample most likely will have different values, and they will differ from the "true" population mean and standard deviation. "True" population means and standard deviations are for all members of a possibly infinite population; they are by nature theoretical (hypothetical). The estimated difference between the sample statistic and the hypothetical population parameter is not caused by a mistake in sampling. Instead, the difference is due to chance associated with selecting a particular sample that is more or less representative of the "true" population. These chance differences add to the impreciseness in measuring of the dependent variable.

Using **random selection** enables the researcher to apply sampling error theory to quantify sampling error. Random selection involves choosing a smaller group of persons entirely by chance so that each individual has an equal chance of being selected from a defined larger group of individuals. This is typically the best procedure to obtain a sample that accurately represents the larger defined group. However, random selection is often impractical. As such, it is important that the sample be carefully conceptualized to represent a particular population. Shadish, Cook, and Campbell (2002) state that **purposive sampling** strategies (also called **purposeful sampling**) are mostly used to make cause-and-effect conclusions that generalize to other participants and settings. Whereas purposive sampling selects participants using a deliberate approach, random sampling selects participants by chance. In purposive sampling, the researcher clearly defines the characteristics that depict the persons, settings, times, independent variables, and dependent variables for which the researcher wants to generalize. Then, study participants are selected to match the targeted characteristics. Researchers often use inclusion and exclusion criteria to select participants in the matching process. Examples of inclusion and exclusion criteria are gender, age, previous treatment, and the addition of other disorders. The purpose of inclusion and exclusion criteria is to identify appropriate participants and assure that the participants chosen would be safe in the treatment conditions (United States National Institutes of Health, 2007).

Another source of imprecision in measurement is **error of measurement**. Many techniques are used to measure the changes in a dependent variable, such as observations, self-reports, interviews, surveys, and so on. It is important that techniques measure the dependent variable well (validity) and consistently (reliability) so that one can correctly attribute changes in the dependent variable to the independent variable rather than to imprecision resulting from invalid and inconsistent measurement. As such, efforts are made to minimize the inevitable fluctuations in measurements of the dependent variable due to such sources as individual differences of participants, measurement tools, observers, and contextual factors that result from error of measurement. The origins of error of measurement can be attributed to both random error and systematic error. An example of a systematic error of measurement is a weight scale that always reads three pounds lighter then it should because it is faulty. The systematic error would be **biased** if a weight scale were sensitive to some irrelevant attribute such as gender and measured males accurately but females lighter. Random error would be present if an observer responsible for recording the weights of persons was using an accurate weight scale, but from time to time transposed digits in recording the weights.

Error of measurement can be minimized (not eliminated) in a research study by confirming that measuring tools or tests have demonstrated evidence of **test validity** and **test reliability**. Test validity focuses on what is being measured and how well (Anastasi & Urbina, 1997). There are several types of test validity. **Face validity** refers to whether the test looks valid to individuals who use and administer the test. The extent that test items are assessed as appropriate for inclusion in a test is **content validity**. Determining how well a test measures a theoretical construct relates to **construct validity**. The effectiveness of a test in predicting an existing criterion or future criterion relates to **concurrent validity** and **predictive validity**, respectively.

A measurement tool or test also needs to demonstrate **test reliability**, which is a consistency in producing similar results when used again and again under similar circumstances. Assessing how well test items measure the test content and construct is referred to as **internal consistency**, which also is used to provide support for construct validity. A test should demonstrate temporal consistency (**test-retest reliability**) by demonstrating similar results with the same participants over time. Moreover, similar (consistent) results should be produced by different raters who are used in a study to generate scores on the dependent variable (**interrater reliability**).

Imprecision in measurement is also associated with other unknown influences, such as **procedural irregularities** made by researchers. For example, two data collectors in the same study might differ procedurally in how they use a standardized observational form to record the frequency and duration of the anger behaviors of children during recess, thus resulting in imprecise measurement. In another study, a procedural difference in administering directions to participants in the same treatment condition group can create imprecision in measurement. An important role of an experimental researcher is to account for possible sources of imprecision in the measurement of variables used in experimental research.

Study Example: Sampling Error. The researchers carefully defined the characteristics that depicted the persons, settings, times, independent variables, and dependent variables for which they wanted to generalize their findings. They matched information about the sixty-one participants selected to the defined characteristics using inclusion and exclusion criteria.

Study Example: Error of Measurement. The researchers described how the SIGH-SAD, BDI-II, and the Pretreatment Expectation Survey were operationally defined including how cut-off scores were used to determine **clinical significance**, which represents a meaningful change in symptoms. They cited a reference that provides evidence of the test-retest and construct validity of the BDI-II.

Two raters were trained to become independent administrators of the SIGH-SAD. They practiced using audiotapes of participants from past studies until they reached proficiency. One rater conducted the SIGH-SAD interview live, and the other individual rated an audiotape of the CBT interview, counterbalanced across session number and study year. The interrater reliability coefficients were high at each phase of assessment: pretreatment ($r = .96$), posttreatment ($r = .98$), and summer follow-up ($r = .97$) showing measurement reliability. The r coefficient is a Pearson Product-Moment Correlation that ranges from -1.0 to $+1.0$. The interrater reliability r coefficients in this study are near $+1.0$, which indicates there was a very high consistency in rating the audiotape of the CBT interviews between the two raters.

Controlling Extraneous Experimental Influences

Extraneous variables are nuisance variables that confound a researcher's understanding of the causal relation between the independent and dependent variables. Extraneous variables need to be identified and controlled because they act like unwanted independent variables. For example, suppose a researcher wants to study the effects of two different instructional reading methods and a no-method control group on reading achievement. The average measured intelligence of one group of participants who were assigned to a reading method condition was significantly higher than the other two groups. It may be that higher intelligence of one group causes changes in reading achievement more than in the other two groups. As such, when the group with higher intelligence scores higher on reading achievement than the other two groups, this may be due to intelligence rather than the reading condition. In this example, "intelligence" is an extraneous variable acting like an independent variable (presumed cause) having a confounding effect on the dependent variable. In another example, a criminal justice researcher compared the effects of three different diversionary programs in reducing criminal offenses by repeat offenders. The researcher identified "type of past offenses" as an extraneous variable that needed to be controlled. Finally, a psychologist identified "parental alcoholism" as an extraneous variable in a study comparing the effectiveness of counseling interventions to reduce anger among adolescent boys.

Internal Validity. An experimental study is said to have **internal validity** when extraneous variables have been controlled and the observed effect can be attributed to the independent variable. Campbell and Stanley (1963); Shadish, Cook, and Campbell (2002); and Gall, Gall, and Borg (2003) have identified several key threats to internal validity. Thirteen of these threats are identified and defined in Table 3.2. The first letter of each threat is combined to form the acronym **THIS MESS DREAD**.

Methods of Control. There are several general ways to control for extraneous variables. One way is to try to eliminate the extraneous variable. For example, a researcher may only select participants who have an IQ score between 100 and 120. Another way to control an extraneous variable is to build the variable into the design. A researcher may expect that males and females will show different performances in reading achievement apart from the effects of the independent variable. The extraneous variable associated with gender can be mathematically extracted from the scores on the dependent variable. A third control is matching participants in conditions on one or more identified

TABLE 3.2. **Threats to Internal Validity: THIS MESS DREAD**

Testing effect	The treatment effect may be confounded when changes in posttest scores of participants are influenced by their experience from taking a pretest.
History	An external but concurrent event to the experiment, such as a hurricane, may affect scores on a dependent measure that are unrelated to the treatment.
Instrumentation	Pretest and posttest scores may change because of a faulty measurement instrument, irrespective of the treatment.
Selection (differential)	Differences in characteristics of participants assigned (usually not randomly) to treatment conditions that confound attributing the changes in the dependent variable to the treatment.
Maturation	Psychological and physical changes within participants may occur in an experiment, especially over time. These participant maturational changes may have an extraneous effect on the dependent measure.
Experimental mortality (attrition)	The loss of participants to treatment or measurement of the dependent variable can produce unbalanced attribution of the effects of the treatment on the dependent variable.
Statistical regression	The phenomenon that extremely high or low group scores on a variable tend to regress to the mean (get lower or higher) on a second measurement of the variable, confounding the treatment effect.
Selection-maturation interaction	This is a combination of two threats to internal validity. For example, some participants in one assigned treatment condition group have matured in math self-efficacy more than participants in another treatment condition group, and the purpose of the study is to increase math achievement. Additionally, other combinations of threats could interact to confound the treatment effect.
Diffusion of experimental effect	The treatment may "diffuse" to the control group over time because the control group may seek access to the more desirable treatment.
Rivalry (compensatory)	The control group participants may perform beyond their usual level because they perceive that they are in competition with the experimental group.
Equalization of treatments (compensatory)	A treatment group may receive experimental rewards that appear more desirable than those received by the control group participants. Efforts are made by individuals outside of the experiment to compensate the control group participants with similar "desirable" goods. This would obscure the results of the treatment.
Ambiguous temporal precedence	Researchers are unsure which variable occurred first, thus confusing cause and effect.
Demoralization (resentful)	Lower performance of control group participants on the dependent measures may result from their belief that the treatment group is receiving a desirable treatment.

extraneous variables to rule out (hold constant) their effects on the relations between the independent and dependent variables. For example, a female participant who is forty-two years old in one treatment condition would be matched to a participant with similar characteristics in the second treatment condition and the control condition. All other participants would be matched to conditions in a similar fashion. The researcher would expect that by using matching, gender and age would not act as extraneous variables. The effects of extraneous variables can be statistically controlled through such techniques as analysis of covariance and simultaneous multiple regression. Similar to building the variable into the design, the effects of extraneous variables can be statistically removed or held constant from the effects produced by the independent variable. The most important way to control extraneous variables is random assignment because it reduces the plausibility of rival explanations of the cause-and-effect findings in a study.

Experimental designs comparing groups in randomized controlled trials must have random assignment or the design is not experimental. **Random assignment** involves assigning participants to groups in a way that each individual is assigned wholly by chance. Researchers use computerized random number generators to plan for random assignments. For example, statistical programs including SPSS (SPSS.com) and SAS (SAS.com) have capabilities to produce series of random numbers. All participants in a sample are entered into a spreadsheet, random numbers are generated for the participants, and then the participants are selected by group. Once all participants are randomly assigned to groups, the conditions are randomly assigned to groups. If there are 150 participants in the study sample, 50 participants would be assigned randomly to each of three groups. Then, the two reading method conditions and the control condition would be randomly assigned to each group. Randomization assures no bias in how participants or conditions are assigned to groups. Random assignment is the best way to assure that the groups of participants are equal as possible on all extraneous variables, thus controlling their effects. Shadish et al. (2002) state that random assignment "reduces the plausibility of threats to validity by distributing them randomly over conditions" (p. 248).

There are other specific ways to control for extraneous variables (see Kirk, 1995). For example, when **single-blind procedures** are used, participants are uninformed about the treatment condition to which they have been assigned. Single-blind procedures help control for participant bias for or against the treatment. A **double-blind procedure** is used when neither the participants nor those who administer a treatment or assessment are informed about who is or is not receiving a particular treatment condition. For example, a researcher wants to know how effectively a particular drug reduces pain, as compared to other drugs and to a placebo condition. The drugs and placebo condition can be coded so that those administering and receiving the drugs and placebo condition are unaware of what condition is being used by which participant.

Deception can be used to control for appropriate, inappropriate, or expected responses by participants when they are aware of the purpose of the experiment. Deception is used to direct the attention of the participants away from the purpose by leaving out relevant details or by communicating a fake purpose of the experiment. For example, participants are instructed that the study is about assessing their abilities to complete cognitive tasks in a timed format, when in reality the researchers are investigating stress associated with completing tasks under time pressure. Clearly, the use of deception in research involves risks to participants; thus, the ethical standards of professional organizations must be examined carefully and followed closely. Moreover, researchers must work with institutional review board, which will assess, approve, and monitor their research. The Ethical Principles of Psychologists and Code of Conduct delineate that the use of deception in research must be justified, and explanations must be given why nondeceptive alternative procedures are not feasible. Participants should be informed as soon as possible about the use of deceit in the experiment. Deception should not be used if it may cause physical or severe emotional distress (APA, 2002). Further discussion of this topic is included in Chapter One of this text.

Study Example: General Control Method. The researchers used random assignment of participants to the three treatment conditions (CBT, LT, CBT + LT) and control condition (MCDT), providing the necessary elements to account for the threats to internal validity associated with THIS MESS. The threats to internal validity of DREAD were controlled by the researchers in several ways. They used different persons to implement treatment conditions and arranged the conditions to minimize contact between experimental and control group participants. The researchers used a single-blind procedure to remove rater bias. The treatment conditions were clearly defined, and the researchers used past research and theory to guide the evidence of an A-to-B causal relationship.

Study Example: Specific Control Methods. The SIGH-SAD raters assessing the existence of a current SAD episode were blind to the treatment condition, reducing potential experimenter bias. A total of seven participants dropped out of the study (experimental mortality or attrition) before the posttest assessment. The losses were reasonably dispersed across the treatment condition groups: CBT (2), LT (2), and CBT + LT (3).

 REFLECTION QUESTIONS

1. How many threats to internal validity can you recall and define from the acronym THIS MESS DREAD?

2. Ethical guidelines for using deception in research were discussed. What are other ethical guidelines that researchers must follow? Go to the Web site of one of the professional associations listed below and read the ethical guidelines related to research.

    American Sociological Association (www.asanet.org)

    American Psychological Association (www.apa.org)

    Academy of Criminal Justice Science (www.acjs.org)

    American Educational Research Association (www.aera.net)

EXPERIMENTAL DESIGNS

Experimental designs are used to execute experimental research. We will next discuss examples of experimental designs and include an explanation of controlling THIS MESS features. We will then discuss the last five threats (DREAD). We use several symbols in presenting the designs. Each row represents a group of participants receiving a different treatment condition. An R designates that the participants were randomly assigned to treatment condition. All Os (observations) represent assessments of the dependent variables. An O before a treatment condition is a pretreatment assessment; an O after the treatment condition is a posttreatment assessment. An X stands for a treatment condition, and C symbolizes a control condition.

Randomized Posttest Only Control Group Design

$$
\begin{array}{ccc}
R & X & O \\
R & C & O
\end{array}
$$

This is one of the most basic of experimental designs. Each row is a group, X (treatment condition), C (control condition), and O (measurement), and because the O follows the treatment and control conditions, it is a posttest. This design does control for the threats THIS MES but a concern arises with the last S (interaction of two threats). More participants may be lost (attrition) from one group differentially (selection) during the course of an experiment. If there were a pretest in the design, information could be derived to explain how the participants dropping out of the experiment affected changes in the dependent variable. The interaction effect of attrition and selection would not be an issue if there was no loss of participants using this design. Without a pretest, it is impossible to know the causal effects of the independent variable on the dependent variable because of the disproportionate loss of participants from one condition compared to the other condition.

Randomized Pretest-Posttest Control Group Design

$$
\begin{array}{cccc}
R & O & X & O \\
R & O & C & O
\end{array}
$$

By adding a pretest to the previous design, this design removes the concern about understanding the effects of interaction between attrition and selection, thus controlling for all of the threats associated with THIS MESS.

Randomized Multiple Treatments and Control with Pretest Design

$$
\begin{array}{cccc}
R & O & X_1 & O \\
R & O & X_2 & O \\
R & O & C & O
\end{array}
$$

This design adds a treatment condition group. The X_1 represents one treatment condition and X_2 represents a second different treatment condition. THIS MESS is controlled in this design. This was the design used in the study example.

Randomized Longitudinal Design

$$
\begin{array}{cccccccc}
R & O & O & O & X & O & O & O \\
R & O & O & O & C & O & O & O
\end{array}
$$

This design adds several pretreatment and posttest assessments. Longitudinal studies usually extend over several months or years. There are many practical problems that can challenge THIS MESS over lengthy studies. Attrition increases over time, long-term outcomes are difficult to measure, ethical issues arise when withholding treatment for long periods of time, and external events (history) interacting with other threats are more likely in a long-term study (Shadish, Cook, & Campbell, 2002).

Choosing effective experimental designs does assist in controlling for the threats to internal validity of THIS MESS. However, other experimental research procedures are often needed to control for the threats of DREAD, such as those listed in the parentheses below.

- Use different persons to implement each treatment condition (diffusion of experimental effect, rivalry, equalization of treatments, and demoralization).

- Arrange treatment conditions so that contact between experimental and control group participants is minimized (diffusion of experimental effect, rivalry, equalization of treatments, and demoralization).

- Use single-blind or double-blind procedures to remove participant or experimenter bias (diffusion of experimental effect, rivalry, equalization of treatments, and demoralization).

- Debrief participants using interviews to assess their experiences and expectation of the treatment conditions (diffusion of experimental effect, rivalry, equalization of treatments, and demoralization).

- Consider not using experimental rewards (equalization of treatments).

- Clearly define treatment conditions (ambiguous temporal precedence).

- Use past research and theory to guide the evidence of an A-to-B causal relationship (ambiguous temporal precedence).

EXTERNAL VALIDITY

Internal validity relates to designing and implementing an experimental study that allows causal relationships between an independent variable and dependent variable to emerge if they really exist. The extent to which the results of an experimental study can be **generalized** to other settings, people, independent variables, and dependent variables is the focus of **external validity**. Can a researcher who found evidence of a causal relationship in one study expect to obtain the same findings in another setting, with different participants, and using other researchers' interpretations of treatment implementation and outcome measurements? After all, many researchers want to know that the results of their studies have implications to a larger population and multiple settings. A researcher wants to make generalized causal inferences to demonstrate that A causes B and that the causal relationship can be repeated consistently in additional studies. Population validity and ecological validity are two subtypes of external validity identified by Bracht and Glass (as cited in Gall, Gall, & Borg, 2003).

Population validity is concerned with how well the results of a study using an experimental sample can generalize to a larger defined population. This concern is assisted greatly if random selection has been used in the study, but only infrequently is that the case. Random selection is a sampling procedure in which a smaller group is selected entirely by chance from a larger, defined population of individuals. For example, a researcher might select a random sample of 938 students to study from a target population of 6,000 third-grade students in a school district. Another researcher may randomly select 2,000 social workers from a state registry of 10,000 licensed social workers to conduct a survey study. If random selection is used correctly and the sample is large enough in reference to the defined population, the sample will be typically representative of the defined population, thus leading to more reliable generalizations.

Appropriate sample sizes to use in a study can be identified with the help of formulated tables, formulae, and computer programs (Gall, Gall, & Borg, 2003). Random selection has a similar theoretical rationale to random assignment, and they both use similar procedures, but the purpose for using each is different. Random assignment reduces the likelihood of threats to internal validity by distributing them randomly across treatment condition groups. Purposive sampling is more common than random sampling for selecting a sample for experimental research because of impracticalities associated with defining and sampling from populations. The representativeness of the sample is achieved, though not fully, by clearly defining the characteristics that depict the persons, settings, times, independent variables, and dependent variables for which the researcher wants to generalize. Causal inference is of utmost importance in experimental research, and it is enhanced by using random assignment of sample participants to treatment condition.

A study has low **ecological validity** if the results of a study can only be generated in a particular context with specific conditions and by the original researcher. Ecological validity relates to how well the results can be generalized to other environments based upon the experimental conditions established by the researcher. Clear operational definitions of variables and descriptions of experimental procedures will enhance ecological validity. Moreover, they will provide other researchers direction in replicating the study in other settings with different participants, which will provide evidence to support or refute ecological validity of the original study.

Study Example: External Validity. Inclusion and exclusion criteria used by the researchers ensure a homogeneous sample that is controlled for extraneous variables that might influence the dependent variable but limit population validity. In other words, if the characteristics associated with sample participants have been restricted, it will be more difficult to generalize findings to a broad population. The highly controlled experimental conditions of the study also may influence ecological validity. The primary purpose of the study is to draw causal inferences about the effects of interventions. The reliability and generalizability of the findings will be established through several phased trials that include both efficacy and effectiveness trials.

Study Example: General Findings. Rohan et al. (2007) found that all three treatment conditions (cognitive-behavioral therapy, light therapy, and cognitive-behavioral + light therapy) produced large, comparable improvements in SAD depression severity when compared to participants in the minimal contact–delayed treatment control. They identified the combination of cognitive-behavioral therapy + light therapy as the most optimal for achieving complete remission. They concluded that cognitive-behavioral therapy alone or as an adjunct to light therapy holds promise as an effective treatment of SAD and should be added to a clinician's therapeutic repertoire.

QUASI-EXPERIMENTAL RESEARCH

Quasi-experimental research resembles experimental research in purpose and essential elements, including the three processes for designing and conducting experimental research, but these are considered compromise designs. Quasi-experimental designs do not provide full control of extraneous variables because they lack one essential element of experimental designs: random assignment. Sometimes there may be settings in which random assignment of participants to a condition is not acceptable by persons in the setting. For example, administrators, teachers, and parents may not allow a researcher to randomly assign students to classes, or administrators may not allow persons to be randomly assigned to the caseloads of social workers.

Researchers using quasi-experimental designs must provide carefully detailed, logical arguments in ruling out alternative explanations (**rival hypotheses**) to account for their findings of a causal relationship between an independent variable and a dependent variable. The effects of unwanted extraneous variables on the dependent variable that are not controlled become an especially important focus of thorough analyses. Adding design elements such as more pretreatment measures and control groups is common in designing quasi-experimental research to reduce and explain threats to internal validity (Shadish, Cook, & Campbell, 2002). Representative examples of quasi-experimental designs are presented next.

Nonequivalent Control Group Design

$$
\begin{array}{cccc}
\text{NR} & \text{O} & \text{X} & \text{O} \\
\text{NR} & \text{O} & \text{C} & \text{O}
\end{array}
$$

This design resembles the experimental Randomized Pretest-Posttest Control Group design but lacks random assignment. Non-random assignment (NR) considerably reduces the ability of the researcher to rule out threats of THIS MESS. Interaction effects of threats with selection are especially prevalent in this design. However, the pretest will provide information to help explain the effects on the dependent variable when more participants drop out of one condition group compared to another condition group.

Untreated Control Group Design with Dependent Pretest and Posttest Samples Using a Double Pretest

$$
\begin{array}{ccccc}
\text{NR} & \text{O} & \text{O} & \text{X} & \text{O} \\
\text{NR} & \text{O} & \text{O} & \text{C} & \text{O}
\end{array}
$$

This design is similar to the previous design, but another pretest has been added, which improves the design. If a significant effect is found using this design, the treatment and control groups should have similar scores at the first and second pretests. The control group should have a similar posttest score to its two pretests, and the treatment group should have a substantially different score from its two pretest scores and the posttest score of the control group. This design assesses a selection-maturation threat by analyzing whether the rates between the first pretest and second pretest continue between the second pretest and posttest in the control group. The two pretests provide information about pre-treatment growth differences. For example, the design is used to study the effects of a treatment condition compared to a no-treatment control condition on decreasing adolescent anxiety. If the control group and not the treatment group showed a substantial decrease in anxiety at each of the two pretests and posttest, the changes might be attributed to psychological changes within the participants (maturation) during the experiment. It would be difficult to make causal inferences about the effectiveness of the treatment under these circumstances.

Multiple Time-Series Design

NR   O   O   O   X   O   O   O
NR   O   O   O   C   O   O   O

This design is an excellent quasi-experimental design that controls for most of the threats to internal validity, THIS MES. However, an interaction between selection and history may be a concern. It is possible that one group of participants is affected differently by external events (history) that influence their scores more on a dependent variable than the other group. For example, a treatment group of students is exposed to an educational seminar to increase their sensitivity toward fellow students who have serious mental health problems, while a control group of students receives no sensitivity training. Attitudes toward persons with mental illness are measured over three weeks for both groups. During the fourth week, the treatment group participates in an educational seminar. Then, the attitudes toward persons with mental illness are measured again for both groups over the next three weeks. The results show that the control group has similar overall attitudes toward persons with mental illness when compared to the treatment group during the last three weeks. It is discovered that several members of the control group participated in an educational program on mental illness at a church. This event was external but concurrent to the experiment (history) and affected the scores on a dependent measure. The additional pretests and posttests in this design provide valuable information to rule out threats to internal validity.

REFLECTION QUESTIONS

1. Select another experimental research study using an electronic search engine targeting a research article database, such as Academic Search Premier, PsycAR-TICLES, ERIC, PubMed, or ScienceDirect. It may be useful to use the words *randomized controlled trial* as your descriptors in the search. Select a study

article that is interesting to you. First, read it through generally. Then, identify how the researchers applied the essential elements of experimental research to their study.

2. Use one of the search engines mentioned above, but this time use the descriptor *quasi-experimental research*. Then, read the article and use the essential elements of research to analyze the article.

SUMMARY

Experimental research is a necessary methodology in answering questions that relate to drawing causal inferences about the effects of interventions in many professional fields. Results from experimental research using randomized controlled trials lead to evidence-based practice. As a result, many safe and effective professional practices are in use today. The essential elements that comprise experimental research were conceptualized within three processes of designing and conducting experimental research. A randomized controlled trial study was presented to demonstrate the application of the essential elements of experimental research. Quasi-experimental designs were discussed as having a similar purpose to experimental designs but compromised by lacking random assignment. Examples of commonly used experimental and quasi-experimental designs were presented. Experimental methods represent an important portion of the body of research in most disciplines. As such, it is important to understand key elements and applications in order to more fully understand and appreciate the impact that experimental research has in creating new knowledge.

KEY TERMS

biased
blind
clinical significance
clinical trial
concurrent validity
construct
construct validity
content validity
control group
deception
dependent variable
diffusion
double-blind procedure
ecological validity
effectiveness trials
efficacy trials
empirically tested

error
error of measurement
evidence-based practice
exclusion criteria
experimental design
experimental research
external validity
extraneous variable
face validity
feasibility study
generalized
generalized causal inferences
inclusion criteria
independent variable
internal consistency
internal validity
interrater reliability

manipulation check
objectivity
operational definitions
placebo
population
population validity
power
predictive validity
procedural irregularities
purposive (purposeful) sampling
quasi-experimental
random assignment
random selection
randomized controlled trial
replication

rival hypothesis
sample
sampling error
single-blind procedures
standardize
test reliability
test validity
test-retest reliability
THIS MESS DREAD
treatment adherence
treatment delivery
treatment fidelity
treatment protocol
treatment receipt

FURTHER READINGS AND RESOURCES

Suggested Readings

American Psychological Association. (2006). Evidence-based practice in psychology. *American Psychologist*, *61*, 271–285.

This article defines and discusses evidence-based practice in psychology integrating science and practice.

American Psychological Association. (2002). *The ethical principles of psychologists and code of conduct*. Retrieved October 13, 2007, from www.apa.org/ethics/code2002.html.

This publication provides the ethical guidelines used by mental health professionals in providing services and conducting research.

Shadish, W. R., Cook, T. D., & Campbell, D. T. (2002). *Experimental and quasi-experimental designs for generalized causal inference*. Boston: Houghton Mifflin.

This book covers four major topics in the field of experimental research: (1) theory, (2) quasi-experimental designs, (3) randomized research, and (4) generalized causal inference.

United States Department of Education. (2003, December 9). *Identifying and implementing educational practices supported by rigorous evidence: A user friendly guide*. Retrieved October 4, 2007, from www.ed.gov/rschstat/research/pubs/rigorousevid/index.html.

This guide provides educators with tools to evaluate educational practices that are supported by rigorous evidence.

United States National Institutes of Health. (2005, May 20). *Resource information*. Retrieved September 19, 2007, from http://clinicaltrials.gov/info/resources.

This Web site provides information about understanding clinical trials and includes a glossary of important terms.

Associations and Web Sites

Center Watch

www.CenterWatch.com

This Web site lists industry- and government-sponsored clinical trials and new drug therapies in research.

American Psychiatric Association (APA)

www.psych.org

This Web site has a wide array of resources related to scientific research in psychiatry.

The New England Journal of Medicine

http://content.nejm.org

This Web site provides free journal articles related to clinical medical trials.

ClinicalTrials.Gov

http://clinicaltrials.gov

This is a registry site for more than 52,000 federally and privately supported clinical trials with locations in 154 countries.

National Institutes of Health

www.nih.gov

There are twenty-seven institutes and centers in the National Institutes of Health. The research focus areas of the NIH include cancer, human genome, aging, alcoholism, drug abuse, and mental health.

CHAPTER

NONEXPERIMENTAL QUANTITATIVE RESEARCH

GABRIELLA BELLI

KEY IDEAS

- The distinction between experimental and nonexperimental research rests on the manipulation of treatments and on random assignment.

- Any quantitative study without manipulation of treatments or random assignment is a nonexperimental study.

- Nonexperimental research is used when variables of interest cannot be manipulated because they are naturally existing attributes or when random assignment of individuals to a given treatment condition would be unethical.

- Numbers are used to represent different amounts of quantitative variables and different classifications of categorical variables.

- Nonexperimental studies may be classified along two dimensions: one based on the purpose of the study and the other on the time frame of the data collection.

- Evidence of a relationship is not convincing evidence of causality.

- Alternative explanations for results in nonexperimental research should be explored and ruled out.

OVERVIEW OF NONEXPERIMENTAL RESEARCH

QUANTITATIVE RESEARCH is empirical, using numeric and quantifiable data. Conclusions are based on experimentation and on objective and systematic observations. Quantitative research may be divided into two general categories: experimental and nonexperimental. The essential elements of experimental research, which was discussed in detail in the previous chapter, are presented here first as a contrast to nonexperimental research. A primary goal for experimental research is to provide strong evidence for cause-and-effect relationships. This is done by demonstrating that manipulations of at least one variable, called the treatment or independent variable (IV), produce different outcomes in another variable, called the dependent variable (DV). An experimental study involves at least one IV that is manipulated or controlled by the researcher, random assignment to different treatment conditions, and the measurement of some DV after treatments are applied. Any resulting differences in the DV across the treatment groups can then be attributed to the differences in the treatment conditions that were applied.

In contrast to experimental research, nonexperimental research involves variables that are not manipulated by the researcher and instead are studied as they exist. One reason for using nonexperimental research is that many variables of interest in social science cannot be manipulated because they are attribute variables, such as gender, socioeconomic status, learning style, or any other personal characteristic or trait. For example, a researcher cannot randomly place individuals into different groups based on gender or learning style because these are naturally existing attributes.

Another reason to use nonexperimental research is that, in some cases, it would be unethical to randomly assign individuals to different treatment conditions. A classic example of this is that one could not study the effects of smoking by randomly assigning individuals to either a smoking or a nonsmoking group for a given number of years. The only ethical way to investigate the potential effects of smoking would be to identify a group of smokers and a group of nonsmokers and compare them for differences in their current state of health. The researcher, however, would also need to take other variables into account, such as how long people had smoked, their gender, age, and general health level. To do so would be important because the researcher cannot take for granted that the groups are comparable in aspects other than smoking behavior. This is in contrast to experimental groups, which, due to the process of random assignment, start out equal in all respects except for the treatment condition in which they are placed. In nonexperimental research, groups based on different traits or on self-selection, such as being or not being a smoker, may differ for any number of reasons other than the variable under investigation. Therefore, in nonexperimental studies, one cannot be as certain as in experimental studies that outcome differences are due to the independent variable under investigation. The researcher needs to consider possible alternative explanations, to jointly analyze several variables, and to present conclusions without making definitive causal statements.

In this chapter, you will learn how to characterize nonexperimental studies that do not rely on either manipulation of variables or random assignment of subjects to groups. Different types of nonexperimental studies will be explained, and you will learn how to characterize them using a two-dimensional classification system. By the end of the chapter, you will understand the basic elements of nonexperimental studies, as well as the rationale for their use. Nonexperimental research examples, including published studies, will be incorporated into the discussion to facilitate understanding. At the end of the chapter, text and Web resources are provided to help you locate supplemental materials and additional information.

VARIABLES AND THEIR MEASUREMENT

To facilitate reading the remainder of the chapter, a brief review of variables and some of their different aspects is presented. A **variable** is any characteristic or attribute that can differ across people or things; it can take on different values. Some variables are inherent traits, such as gender or height. Others may vary due to experimenter manipulation, such as treatment groups of drug versus placebo, or due to self-selection, such as attending a two- or a four-year college. In quantitative research, variables are measured in some way and those numerical values are then used in statistical analyses. The nature of variables is important because, to some extent, it dictates the way research questions are asked and which analysis is used.

One basic distinction is that variables can be either categorical or quantitative. **Categorical variables** are those that differ across two or more distinct categories. The researcher assigns arbitrary numbers to the categories, but the numbers have no interpretable numerical meaning. For example, for categories of the variable "employment status," we could assign the value "1" to employed full-time, "2" to employed part-time, and "3" to not employed. Additional examples of categorical variables that are individual traits are gender, ethnicity, and learning style; some that are self-selected are marital status, political party affiliation, and field of study.

Quantitative variables can be measured across a scale, their numeric values have meaning, and they can be subjected to arithmetic operations. The following are all examples of quantitative variables: age, height, weight, grade point average (GPA), job satisfaction, and motivation. There is an important distinction between the first three and the last three variables in this list. For such variables as age, height, and weight, zero is a meaningful value that indicates the absence of the characteristic being measured, as in something that is brand new or has no weight. The numbers have interpretable meaning. We know what five years or five feet means because there is no arbitrariness about these values or how to interpret them.

In contrast, zero is an arbitrary value for variables such as GPA, satisfaction, or motivation. A zero motivation score does not mean one has no motivation, but merely that one attained the lowest possible score for the particular instrument being used. GPA in most schools in the United States is given on a continuum from 0.0 to 4.0 but, for example, at the Massachusetts Institute of Technology (MIT), it goes from 0.0 to 5.0 (see GPA calculation and unit conversion on MIT Web page at http://web.mit.edu/registrar/gpacalc.html). The International Baccalaureate grades range from 1 to 7, based on a rubric developed from the standardized curriculum.

For another example, consider measurements for temperature. The freezing point of water is represented as zero on a Celsius thermometer, but as 32 on a Fahrenheit thermometer. In neither case does a zero represent the absence of temperature. In each case, we understand what the numbers mean because specific interpretations have been assigned to them.

Interpretation of different grading schemes or thermometers is possible because of commonly understood unit descriptors. This is not so for such variables as job satisfaction or motivation, where scores are arbitrary and depend on the measurement instrument being used and how it has been designed. Typically, such scores are the sum or the average of responses to a set of items. The items may be statements, constructed so that all are related to the variable to be measured, and responses are often, but not always, on a Likert scale from 1 (strongly agree) to 5 (strongly disagree). The terms **scale** and **index** are often used to describe such sets of related items that, together, produce a score about some characteristic or phenomenon. For example, the Multidimensional Job Satisfaction Scale (Shouksmith, Pajo, & Jepsen, 1990) contains eleven different subscales, each a multi-item scale measure of a different dimension of job satisfaction. Another instrument, the Job Satisfaction Survey (Spector, 1985), consists of nine four-item subscales to assess employee attitudes about the job. As you can see from this example, different researchers developed different measures of the same construct, job satisfaction.

Exact interpretation of a scale score's value, or measure, for variables such as motivation or satisfaction is not important. What is important is to know that the higher the score, the more one has of the characteristic being measured and vice versa. One could, for example, examine whether males or females had higher levels of job satisfaction or if people with higher levels of job satisfaction also tended to have higher levels of motivation. To be confident of results, it is also important to know that the measures being used are reliable and have been validated.

Reliability relates to the consistency or dependability of a measure. Basically, if it is reliable, you can be confident that all the items that make up the measure are consistent with each other and that, if you were to use the measure again with the same individuals, they would be rated similarly to the first time. **Validity** relates to whether it is measuring what we intend it to measure, and represents the overarching quality of the measure. The purpose of using the measure is an important consideration in evaluating validity because it could be valid for one use but not for another. These concepts are complex and beyond the scope of this chapter (see Trochim, 2005, for a very understandable description of validity and reliability of measures). As a consumer of research, you should at least be aware of them and look for how research authors deal with these concepts. Do they describe their measures in detail and provide some indication of reliability and validity?

Defining Variables

Although some variables are inherently categorical or quantitative, others may be defined in either way. Imagine, for example, that you are interested in measuring the education level of a group of individuals. You could do this categorically, by defining education as "highest degree earned" and using five values representing none, high school, college, masters, or doctorate as different levels of education. Or, you could do this quantitatively by defining education as "number of years of schooling," where the resulting values would be meaningfully interpreted. This distinction is important if one is interested in studying the relationship between educational level and salary, a quantitative variable, because it relates to how the data might be analyzed and how research questions would be phrased. Using the categorical definition, you could compare the median salary value across the five categories of "highest degree earned." The **median** represents the midpoint when all the salaries are listed from lowest to highest. One could then determine if there were any appreciable differences in salary across the five groups and whether more education (represented by having a higher degree) corresponded to higher salary.

Using the quantitative definition, you could graph the two variables in a **scatterplot** or compute a **correlation coefficient** (a measure of strength and direction of relationship for two variables) for the number of years of schooling and salary. The first would provide a visual representation of their relationship and the second a numerical one. Figure 4.1 shows how resulting data might be depicted in the two cases described. The table shows the number of people in each group and their median salary. The scatterplot shows all the data points. The correlation for this data set is 0.66. Correlation

---

FIGURE 4.1. *Two Representations of the Relationship Between Salary and Education Level*

Highest Degree	N	Median Salary
Doctorate	30	68,438
Master's	20	65,938
Bachelor	181	33,150
High School	190	24,975
None	53	24,000
Total	474	28,875

Education is measured as a categorical variable (highest degree). The size of each group (N) and the median salary are given in the table.

Education is measured as a quantitative variable (number of years in school). Each point in the scatter plot represents years in school and salary for a single individual.

values range from -1 to $+1$, with zero indicating no relationship and 1 indicating either a negative or a positive perfect relationship depending on the sign. We could say these data showed a moderate positive relationship. Fewer years of schooling tend to correspond to lower salaries and more schooling to higher salaries.

Phrasing Questions

In the first case demonstrated in Figure 4.1, you would be comparing groups with different levels of education on some measure (salary), and in the second case, you would be relating two sets of numeric scores (years and salary). The research questions of interest in the two cases would be: (1) how do groups, based on highest degree earned, differ from each other with respect to salary? and (2) how does number of years of schooling relate to salary? Phrased generically, the key questions in the two situations are: How do groups differ from each other on some measure? How are the variables related to each other? The distinction between these two cases depends only on the fact that education was conceptualized as either categorical or quantitative and not on the nature of the relationship involved.

REFLECTION QUESTIONS

By now, you should be able to:

1. Describe the difference between experimental and nonexperimental studies

2. Give an example of an independent and a dependent variable within the context of a research question

3. Give an example of a categorical and a measured, quantitative variable

CLASSIFYING NONEXPERIMENTAL RESEARCH

In the literature on experimental studies, there is agreement on the distinction between true and quasi-experiments. Although both involve treatment manipulation, **true experiments** use random assignment of subjects to groups *and* random assignment of groups to treatments. **Quasi-experiments** use preexisting intact groups (see Chapter Three for details).

For nonexperimental designs, there appears to be no consistent agreement on typology. In 1991, Elazar Pedhazur and Liora Schmelkin stated that "there is no consensus regarding the term used to refer to designs" which were presented in their chapter on nonexperimental designs (p. 305). Two commonly used terms for nonexperimental studies are "correlational research" and "survey research." However, the term *correlation* relates more to an analysis strategy than to a research design, and the term *survey* describes a method of gathering data that can be used in different types of research.

Ten years later, Burke Johnson (2001) came to the same conclusion. Based on a review of twenty-three leading methods textbooks in education and related fields (thirteen explicitly from education and the rest from anthropology, psychology, political science, and sociology), he found little consistency in how nonexperimental studies were classified. He discovered over two dozen different labels being used, sometimes with slight variations in the wording. The most frequently used labels in these texts were survey (twelve times), correlational (ten times), descriptive (eight times), and causal-comparative (five times). The result of my informal review of six additional research methods texts was consistent with Johnson's findings.

In an attempt to remedy this confusion, Johnson (2001) proposed a categorization scheme consisting of two basic dimensions, each with three categories. The first dimension represents a characterization of the basic goal or main purpose for conducting the nonexperimental quantitative study. The second dimension allows the research to be classified according to the time frame in which data were collected. These two dimensions will be presented here and discussed separately in the next two sections. In your reading of published articles or research methods textbooks, you will probably encounter other terms for nonexperimental research. You may want to read Johnson (2001) to familiarize yourself with these terms and with the problems that arise because of their use.

Classification Based on Purpose (Dimension 1)

The categories of the first dimension for classifying nonexperimental studies, which are based on the main purpose of the study, are:

1. **Descriptive** nonexperimental research, in which the primary focus for the research is to describe some phenomenon or to document its characteristics. Such studies are needed in order to document the *status quo* or do a needs assessment in a given area of interest.

2. **Predictive** nonexperimental research, in which the primary focus for the research is to predict some variable of interest (typically called the **criterion**) using information from other variables (called **predictors**). The development of the proper set of predictors for a given variable is often the focus of such studies.

3. **Explanatory** nonexperimental research, in which the primary focus for the research is to explain how some phenomenon works or why it operates. The objective is often to test a theory about the phenomenon. Hypotheses derived from a given theoretical orientation are tested in attempts to validate the theory.

The three categories could be seen as answers to the question: Was the main purpose of the research to describe a phenomenon, to study how to predict some future event, or to understand how something operates or what drives it?

To help explain these three categories, consider the use of exit interviews. Such interviews are often conducted by organizations with employees who leave or by school systems with departing teachers and graduating seniors. An exit interview study can be **descriptive** if the purpose is to collect data in order to get a comprehensive picture of reasons for employees leaving their organization or school. These descriptions might be used to determine if people leave for reasons related to the organization or for personal reasons. On the other hand, the study would be **predictive** if exit data were collected and then related to hiring data for the same individuals for the purpose of using the results to screen potential employees and hiring people who might be less likely to leave. Finally, the study would be **explanatory** if the data were analyzed with the purpose of testing hypotheses about how personal characteristics might be related to employee or student feelings about their organization or school.

A good example of a published **descriptive** study is the "39th Annual Phi Delta Kappa/Gallup Poll of the Public's Attitudes toward the Public Schools" (Rose & Gallup, 2007). Begun as an effort to inform educators, the annual survey now provides information that has policy implications. Although the accumulated database can be used to track changes in attitudes about pre-K–12 schooling over a long period of time, the design for each yearly survey is purely descriptive in terms of its purpose. Results are a descriptive representation of how the general public feels about different aspects of public schools.

A study by Leslie Halpern and Thomas Dodson (2006) to develop a set of indicators that could identify women likely to report injuries related to intimate partner violence is an example of a **predictive** study. They tried to develop markers that could be used in hospital settings to make predictions about likelihood of intimate partner violence. They identified two variables as potential predictors: injury location and responses to a standard screening questionnaire. They included these, along with demographic variables, in developing a prediction model.

An **explanatory** study was done to examine the relationships among the variables of attachment, work satisfaction, marital satisfaction, parental satisfaction, and life satisfaction (Perrone, Webb, & Jackson, 2007). This research was informed by attachment theory, which describes "parental attachment as a stable connection that provides a feeling of safety and security for the child" (p. 238). The researchers used five published instruments and present a very good description of reliability and validity for each one.

Classification Based on Time (Dimension 2)

The categories of the second dimension for classifying nonexperimental research, which refer to time, are:

1. **Cross-sectional** research, in which data are collected at one point in time, often in order to make comparisons across different types of respondents or participants.

2. **Prospective** or **longitudinal** research, in which data are collected on multiple occasions starting with the present and going into the future for comparisons across time. Data are sometimes collected on different groups over time in order to determine subsequent differences on some other variable.

3. **Retrospective** research, in which the researcher looks back in time using existing or available data to explain or explore an existing occurrence. This backwards examination may be an attempt to find potential explanations for current group differences.

These categories could be seen as answers to the question: Were the data collected at a single time point, across some time span into the future, or were already existing data explored? You could think of them as representing the past (retrospective), present (cross-sectional), and future (prospective) with respect to timing of data collection. As an example, suppose you were interested in assessing differences in college students' attitudes toward potential careers. In a **cross-sectional study**, you might take a random sample of first-year college students (freshmen) and fourth-year college students (seniors) and compare their attitudes. Your purpose might be to show that more mature students (seniors) view career options differently from less mature students (freshmen).

Now consider assessing career attitudes in a **prospective study**. There are actually three options: trend, cohort, or panel study. To distinguish among these three approaches, think of a four-year prospective study starting in 2008 with college freshmen. The population of interest is all college freshmen in the United States. In 2008, a **random sample** of college freshman is taken for all three approaches. Table 4.1 describes the samples in the subsequent three years for each approach. In the trend study, the same *general population* (college freshmen) is tracked. In the cohort study, the same *specific population* (college freshmen in 2008) is tracked. In the panel study, the *same individuals* are tracked. One of the advantages of a panel study is that you can look for changes and not simply report on trends. A disadvantage is that you have to start with a fairly large sample due to attrition over time, particularly for a lengthy study.

An example of a **retrospective** study could be an examination of the educational background and experience of very successful teachers and less successful teachers. The idea is to look backward in time and examine what differences existed that might provide an explanation for the present differences in success. To the extent that such a study needed to depend on people's memories of relevant background information, it would be less accurate than if prior data were available for examination.

For a published example, consider one question addressed by Michael Heise (2004), which was whether key actors in a criminal court case view case complexity in the same way. The results of his **cross-sectional** comparison of three key actor groups (juries, attorneys, and judges) suggest that they do possess slightly different views on whether crimes are complex.

Examples of both prospective and retrospective research are based on the *Nurses' Health Study*, a large-scale longitudinal study started in 1976 with a mailed survey of 121,700 female registered nurses between thirty and fifty-five years of age who lived in eleven states. Descriptive information about risk factors for major chronic diseases and related issues was gathered every two years. Although most of the

TABLE 4.1. Description of Samples After Initial 2008 Sampling of College Freshmen

	2009	2010	2011
Trend	New sample—college freshmen	New sample—college freshmen	New sample—college freshmen
Cohort	New sample—college sophomores	New sample—college juniors	New sample—college seniors
Panel	Same sample from 2008, who are now sophomores	Same sample from 2008, who are now juniors	Same sample from 2008, who are now seniors

information gathered was identical, new questions were added periodically. The *Nurses' Health Study* Web page (www.channing.harvard.edu/nhs) contains a complete list of publications based on these data.

One such study was conducted by Francine Laden et al. (2000). They examined the responses from the 87,497 women who answered newly included questions about lifetime use of electric blankets and heated waterbeds. Using data from the larger study, Laden and her colleagues focused their attention on the relationship between electric blanket use and breast cancer from both a prospective and retrospective view. This was done because electric blanket use is a source of electric and magnetic fields (EMFs) exposure, and EMF exposure had been hypothesized to increase the risk of breast cancer. The relevant year is 1992, when information about use of electric blankets and waterbeds was first documented. For the **prospective** part of their study, they considered women who had not been diagnosed with cancer as of 1992 and analyzed the occurrence of breast cancer from 1992 to 1996 for groups according to electric blanket or waterbed usage. For the **retrospective** part, they used records from 1976 to 1992, considering only women who were cancer free in 1976. In the prospective part of the study "exposure to electric blankets and waterbed use was assessed prior to the occurrence of breast cancer," while in the retrospective analysis "exposure was ascertained after diagnosis" (Laden et al., 2000, p. 42).

Retrospective studies may be based on past records, as in the previous example, or on retrospective questions, that is, on questions about past behaviors or experiences. Merely using already existing data, however, does not make it retrospective. The key distinction is the study's purpose. Are you looking backwards to discover some potential cause or explanation for a current situation, or are you using data from one point in time to predict data from a later time? Notice that Laden and her colleagues (2000) used preexisting data for both retrospective and prospective studies. For the prospective part, women who had not been diagnosed with cancer in 1992 were divided into groups based on whether they did or did not use electric blankets, and the groups were then compared with respect to breast cancer incidents by 1996. For the retrospective part, they divided the women into two groups based on whether they had or had not been diagnosed with cancer as of 1992 and then compared them in terms of reported prior use of electric blankets.

Combining Classification Dimensions

When used together, Johnson's two dimensions (2001) combine to form a 3×3 design for a total of nine distinct categories that may be used to describe nonexperimental research. Examples of all nine may be found in the *National Education Longitudinal Study of 1988* (NELS:88), which was a large-scale data collection effort National Center for Education Statistics, 1988. A nationally representative sample of eighth graders were first surveyed in 1988, with subsequent follow-up surveys every two years until 1994, and then once again in 2000. The National Center for Education Statistics Web page (http://nces.ed.gov/surveys/nels88) describes this study, and also provides an annotated bibliography of research done using the various data sets. Depending on which data were selected for each study and the study purpose, different NELS:88 studies might be classified using all nine of the purpose by time frame classifications. To help clarify this cross-classification scheme, Table 4.2 gives the titles of articles representing each type, which are then described.

Type 1—Descriptive retrospective. Using retrospective chart review, Anne Marie Higley and Karen Morin (2004) described the behavior of infants whose mothers had a drug history. Their findings supported the use of an assessment tool to guide parents in providing a supportive care environment to help infants recover.

Type 2—Descriptive cross-sectional. This study was discussed earlier as an example of a cross-sectional study. It is descriptive because the goal was to document the extent to which juries, attorneys, and judges held similar or different views about a case. The results have implications for legal reform efforts.

Type 3—Descriptive prospective. This was an investigation of the stability of test anxiety measures over time and testing formats, with data collected at three time points in an academic semester, therefore making it prospective. The purpose for the description was to determine if test anxiety was a stable condition or if it is necessary to

TABLE 4.2. Articles Classified According to Both Research Objective and Time of Dimensions

	Retrospective	Cross-Sectional	Prospective
Descriptive	*Type 1*	*Type 2*	*Type 3*
	Behavioral responses of substance-exposed newborns: A retrospective study (Higley & Morin, 2004)	Criminal case complexity: An empirical perspective (Heise, 2004)	The stability of undergraduate students' cognitive test anxiety levels (Cassady, 2001)
Predictive	*Type 4*	*Type 5*	*Type 6*
	Electric blanket use and breast cancer in the Nurses' Health Study (Laden et al., 2000)	A predictive model to identify women with injuries related to intimate partner violence (Halpern & Dodson, 2006)	Electric blanket use and breast cancer in the Nurses' Health Study (Laden et al., 2000)
Explanatory	*Type 7*	*Type 8*	*Type 9*
	A further look at youth intellectual giftedness and its correlates: Values, interests, performance, and behavior (Roznowski, Reith, & Hong, 2000)	Relationships between parental attachment, work and family roles, and life satisfaction (Perrone, Webb, & Jackson, 2007)	Thirty-year stability and predictive validity of vocational interests (Rottinghaus, Coon, Gaffey, & Zytowski, 2007)

include a test anxiety measure with every test in a longitudinal study. Results indicated that it is not necessary to measure anxiety with every test; it is only necessary to measure anxiety in one test-taking situation.

Type 4—Predictive retrospective and **Type 6—Predictive prospective**. The two parts of this study were described earlier as examples of retrospective and prospective studies. Both parts were predictive in nature, using a backward and a forward perspective to determine the extent to which electric blanket and waterbed use could be used to predict breast cancer. Although results did not exclude small risks, neither analysis supported an association between breast cancer risk and use of electric blankets and waterbeds.

Type 5—Predictive cross-sectional. In this study, discussed as an example of a predictive study, a one-time data collection was used. The authors' aim was to develop and validate a predictive model. They subdivided their sample, using one group to develop their model and the second group to validate, or test it. Their work produced a predictive and validated model of three components: risk of self-report of intimate partner violence–related injury, age, and race. The researchers then hypothesized that these three variables could be used to develop a protocol to assist in the early diagnosis of intimate partner violence in an emergency department and outpatient clinical setting.

Type 7—Explanatory retrospective. This study was explanatory because a goal was to further previous work on giftedness and knowledge and understanding of several related variables. The data came from the High School and Beyond database, a longitudinal study with baseline information on 14,825 students who were high school sophomores in 1980. The data for this study included the base year and the third follow-up survey, four years later, after graduation. The data set "allowed for more comparisons than could reasonably be included in a single study. Variables were chosen that would either serve to replicate previous findings or expand psychological and behavioral profiles of gifted male and female students into more detail" (Roznowski, Reith, & Hong, 2000, p. 96). A retrospective conclusion was that educational attainment differences of gifted males and females had their origins in the early high school years.

Type 8—Explanatory cross-sectional. Already discussed as an example of an explanatory study, this study was based on data from the fifteenth annual survey of a longitudinal study that started in 1988 with 1,724 participants. About 1,200 participants were lost in the first three years. Only 108 participants were left for this study, which shows the dramatic attrition that can happen in a longitudinal study. Although the data were from a longitudinal study, these authors only used the fifteenth year's data, thereby making it cross-sectional.

Type 9—Explanatory prospective. The authors suggested that "Assessing the predictive validity of an interest inventory is essentially answering the question, 'Do early interest scores match one's future occupation?'" (Rottinghaus et al., 2007, p. 7). To answer this question, they did a thirty-year follow-up of 107 former high school juniors and seniors whose interests were assessed in 1975. The first author had collected the initial data. Their results extend research on vocational interests, indicating that interests were fairly stable even after such a long time span.

REFLECTION QUESTIONS

1. How do descriptive, predictive, and explanatory studies differ?

2. How do retrospective, cross-sectional, and prospective studies differ?

3. Find several recent articles in your field of study where a nonexperimental design was used. Classify their main purpose as being descriptive, predictive, or explanatory and classify the time dimension as retrospective, cross-sectional, or prospective.

CAUSAL EXPLANATIONS AND NONEXPERIMENTAL STUDIES

Under Johnson's classification system (2001), many nonexperimental studies are either descriptive or predictive. For those, the notion of causation is not relevant. However, a goal for many explanatory nonexperimental research studies is to explore potentially causal relationships. A causal relationship is one in which a given action is likely to produce a particular result.

The terms *independent* and *dependent* refer to the different roles variables play in experimental studies. If a causal relationship exists, then the outcome (the measured DV) depends on, or is a direct result of, the nature of the assigned independent treatment condition. Strictly speaking, these terms are not applicable in nonexperimental research, although they are often used. The more appropriate terms in nonexperimental studies are **criterion** and **predictor** variables, criterion being the presumed outcome of one or more predictor variables. When the intent is to use nonexperimental research to study potential cause-and-effect relationships where experimentation is not possible, the concept of IV and DV may still be of interest, but conclusions about causation that can be made from nonexperimental studies are weaker than those that can be made from true experimental studies. Additionally, great care needs to be taken to assure that nothing essential has been overlooked.

As explained earlier, the distinction is often made between nonexperimental studies that involve both categorical and quantitative variables and those that involve only quantitative variables. Considering only two variables for the sake of simplicity, an example of the first type of study is a comparison of gender differences in mathematics achievement in high school. Gender, with male and female as the two categories, is considered the independent variable and some mathematics achievement score is the measured dependent variable. Examples where both variables are quantitative might be an examination of the relationship between test scores and time spent studying, or between scores on some measure of motivation and scores on an achievement test. Examples like these, of very simple cases involving only two variables, are neither very interesting nor very informative. Additional variables could be included in order to examine more complex relationships.

No matter which type of design or which type of variable is used, evidence of a relationship would not be convincing evidence of causality. Recall the example described earlier about investigating the relationship between education level and salary and the two ways that education level could be measured. Regardless of whether education level was construed as categorical (highest degree earned) or as quantitative (number of years of schooling), it should not be concluded that one's educational level *caused* or produced a different level of salary. If dramatic differences across the five groups with different degrees were found such that those with higher education had higher median salaries, all that can be concluded is that there was a *relationship* between educational level and salary. This same conclusion would be possible if results indicated a strong positive correlation between years of schooling and salary: that people with fewer years of school tended to have low salaries and people with more years of school tended to have high salaries (see Figure 4.1 for graphical representation of a positive relationship). The scatterplot for a negative relationship would go from the upper left corner to the lower right corner, indicating that low scores on one variable tended to go with high scores on the other variable.

The differences in the wording of the research questions in the previous two cases reflect the nature of the variables used (categorical or quantitative). They would require different analysis strategies, either to test if the median values did differ more than you might expect by chance, or to determine the strength and direction of the relationship. Differences in wording or analysis do not, however, reflect any difference in the nature of the relationship between the variables. Explanatory nonexperimental research articles often have conclusions phrased in causal language. Therefore, the next section is a review of the essential elements needed to establish cause-and-effect relationships and a discussion of their applicability to nonexperimental studies.

Requirements for Causality

There are three conditions necessary in order to be able to argue that some variable X (the presumed independent) causes another variable Y (the presumed dependent).

1. The two variables X and Y must be related. If they are not related, it is impossible for one to cause the other. For nonexperimental research, that means that it must be demonstrated that differences in X are associated with differences in Y.

2. Changes in X must happen before observed changes in Y. This is always the case when X is a manipulated treatment variable in an experiment. But establishing that a cause happened before an effect needs to be documented in some way or logically explained in nonexperimental studies. This is impossible to do when the data are cross-sectional and collected simultaneously.

3. There is no possible alternative explanation for the relationship between X and Y. That is, there is no plausible third variable that might explain the observed relationship between X and Y, possibly having caused both of them.

In nonexperimental studies, the first requirement can be established easily with correlational analyses. The second could also be established if longitudinal data are used so that predictor variables are measured before the criterion. The third requirement is more difficult to demonstrate. To do so requires a thorough knowledge of the literature and the underlying theory or theories governing the topic being investigated, logical arguments, plus testing and ruling out of alternative possibilities.

The fact that two variables are related does not inform us of which one influences the other. There are at least three reasons why two variables could be related, and it is not possible to know from the correlation which one is the correct reality. Three potential explanations are: (1) that X causes or influences Y, (2) that Y causes or influences X, or (3) that Z, a third variable, causes both X and Y. Consider the following headline: "Migraines plague the poor more than the rich." It could be argued that the stresses of living in poverty and other poverty-related conditions could trigger migraine headaches. It could also be argued that migraines cause one to miss work and eventually lose employment, thereby inducing poverty for a subset of individuals prone to migraines. Which is the correct interpretation? It is impossible to tell.

Although there is no formal way to prove causation in nonexperimental research, it may be possible to suggest it. This is done through careful consideration, by referring to the three conditions for cause, by presenting logical arguments, and by testing likely alternatives in order to make a case for the *likely* conclusion of a causal relationship. One must be careful, however, not to phrase conclusions as proof of causation.

Ruling Out Alternative Hypotheses

To demonstrate the process for ruling out alternative hypotheses, we will use a medical example. Consider the process a doctor goes through in diagnosing a new patient's illness. First, the doctor considers the symptoms. The list of symptoms is used to select potential problems with similar symptoms and to rule out problems with different symptoms. Tests are ordered to confirm the most likely diagnosis and remedies are tried. If the test results are negative or the remedies do not work, then the original diagnosis is discarded, and other possible diagnoses are considered and tested. How does this process relate to research? The first step is matching observations (the reported symptoms) to theory (known symptoms for an illness). The second step is to test a hunch or tentative hypothesis (initial diagnosis) and rule out alternative hypotheses (other potential diagnoses). The process continues until a reasonable conclusion is reached. The analogy breaks down because, ideally, the correct diagnosis is made and the patient is cured, although results are never as conclusive in nonexperimental studies.

Given a theory that is driving the research, how does one rule out potential alternative hypotheses? One way is to consider all likely **confounding** or **lurking variables**. In an experimental study, two variables are confounded when their effects on a dependent variable cannot be distinguished. The following example, although purely correlational, should clarify the concept of confounding or lurking variables.

One would expect that grades and standardized test scores, such as SAT scores, would be related more to each other than they would to socioeconomic status (SES). In many studies, however, SES and SAT appear to have a much stronger relationship than do grades and SAT. Rebecca Zwick and Jennifer Green (2007) explored reasons for such results with data from a random sample of 98,391 students from 7,330 high schools. They performed two different analyses. In the first analysis, they found the correlation for grades and SAT for the entire sample and, in the second analysis, they did so for each school individually and then averaged the school-level results to get one overall measure of relationship. The second analysis produced a much stronger relationship between grades and SAT scores than did the first analysis. This is because the first analysis ignored the fact that there are school-level differences in SES as well as other variables.

Figure 4.2 should help you visualize this discussion. In part A, the two smaller ovals represent a scatter plot of scores for two schools, where both grades and SAT scores tend to be higher in School 2 than in School 1. The lines bisecting these two ovals provide a linear representation of the relationship between the variables within each school and are called **regression lines**. Both ovals are rather narrow in width, being fairly close to their regression lines, and thereby give a visual representation of a relatively strong positive relationship between grades and SAT *within* each school. The larger oval represents the relationship between grades and SAT scores as it would appear across or *between* schools, that is, if school membership were ignored in the analysis. It is much more spread out around its regression line (the dotted line), erroneously indicating a much weaker relationship between grades and SAT. The two smaller ovals correspond to Zwick and Green's second analysis (2007) and the larger oval to their first analysis. Ignoring the differences between the schools confounds the relationship between grades and SAT being investigated.

Part B of Figure 4.2 shows a worst-case scenario of ignoring a lurking variable. Suppose the relationship between two variables, X and Y, is negative for each of two groups. This is shown by the two smaller ovals, where lower scores on X tend to go with higher scores on Y and vice versa within each group. Ignoring groups,

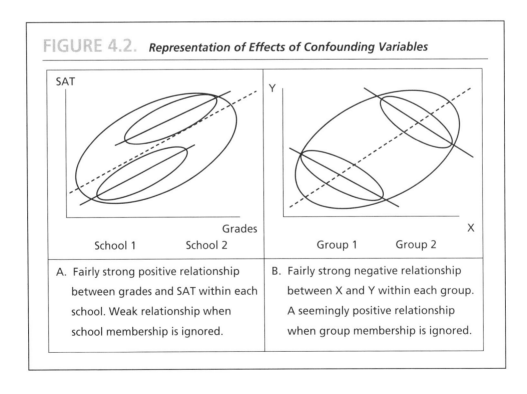

FIGURE 4.2. *Representation of Effects of Confounding Variables*

A. Fairly strong positive relationship between grades and SAT within each school. Weak relationship when school membership is ignored.

B. Fairly strong negative relationship between X and Y within each group. A seemingly positive relationship when group membership is ignored.

however, would produce a positive relationship, which would be a completely wrong conclusion.

REFLECTION QUESTIONS

By now, you should be able to

1. List and explain three essential requirements to argue cause.

2. Explain why even a strong correlation does not imply causation.

3. Describe why ruling out alternative hypotheses is important.

4. Find one or two nonexperimental studies in your field of study where hypotheses were tested or where a theory was explored. What extraneous variables or potential alternative hypotheses were discussed? Can you think of others that were not discussed? How might inclusion of those variables have changed results?

ANALYSIS AND INTERPRETATION IN NONEXPERIMENTAL STUDIES

Data analyses in nonexperimental studies depend on both the goal for the study and the nature of the variables in the data set. Almost any analysis may be possible and a useful presentation is not reasonable here. There are ample books and sources for details about statistical methods and their use. A few examples are given at the end of the chapter; also see the discussion on understanding quantitative data in Chapter Six.

You need to be aware of the basic distinction between descriptive and inferential statistics. **Descriptive statistics** involve summarizing and describing quantitative information in meaningful ways. For example, a mean, or arithmetic average, is a statistic used to describe a central value for a set of numbers. **Inferential statistics** are used to make conclusions beyond the data collected and to test hypotheses. Statistical tests are used to make conclusions about populations based on results from random samples or to determine the probability that results are not due to random chance.

Interpretation of results in nonexperimental studies should be consistent with the nature of the work, which is based on nonmanipulated variables. Therefore, conclusions about cause and effect are not appropriate in *any* nonexperimental study. As you read empirical articles, you should be attuned to how conclusions are discussed and be wary of causal language. Robinson, Levin, Thomas, Pituch, and Vaughn (2007) reviewed 274 empirical articles in five teaching-and-learning research journals in 1994 and 2004. They recorded causal and noncausal language use in abstracts and discussion sections. Their two main conclusions were: (1) experimental articles in teaching-and-learning declined in the ten-year span, and (2) on average, the use of causal conclusions made in nonexperimental and qualitative studies increased. They conclude by saying that "as journal readers, we have an obligation to search an article for information about how the data were collected so we are not unduly influenced by unwarranted conclusions" (Robinson et al., 2007, p. 412). Ideally, after studying this chapter you will be able to search through articles for information about how the study was conducted and use that to consider conclusions.

SUMMARY

The goal for this chapter was to present adequate information about nonexperimental designs so that a practitioner could read the literature and have a basic understanding of methods used. Nonexperimental research is described in many ways and covers any quantitative study that does not have manipulated variables or random assignment. A topic of research interest can be modified to serve alternative purposes, and data can be collected over different time frames. The two-dimensional classification system presented here should help you categorize articles. Reading any of the articles listed in Table 4.2 that are of interest to you could be useful in understanding why it was classified according to the two dimensions given. A good place to start, with a relatively straightforward example, would be the Cassady (2001) article, which is an example of Type 3, a descriptive prospective study. A good exercise would be to find other nonexperimental studies and classify them according to the two dimensions of purpose and time of data collection.

A key to understanding published research is to identify the goal of the research, evaluate what was done in relation to that goal, and consider aspects and variables that may have been overlooked. Most important, consider the language used in published works and be skeptical if overzealous researchers present their nonexperimental results in causal terms. Regardless of what type of research is presented, be a wary consumer.

KEY TERMS

attribute variables
categorical variables
confounding or lurking variables
correlation coefficient
criterion
cross-sectional research
dependent variable
descriptive nonexperimental research
descriptive statistics
experimental research
explanatory nonexperimental research
independent variable
index
inferential statistics
median
nonexperimental research

predictive nonexperimental research
predictors
prospective or longitudinal research
quantitative variables
quasi-experiments
random assignment
random sample
regression lines
reliability
retrospective research
scale
scatterplot
true experiments
validity
variable

Note: My thanks to Professor Bill Frakes, from the Computer Science Department at Virginia Tech, and to students, including many from my Research Methods class in Fall 2007, for reviewing a prior draft of this chapter. Their insightful comments and suggestions helped improve this version. I take responsibility for any elements of confusion that may remain.

FURTHER READINGS AND RESOURCES

Suggested Readings

Allison, P. D. (1999). *Multiple regression: A primer.* Thousand Oaks, CA: Pine Forge Press.

This basic text, discussing an analysis technique often used in nonexperimental studies, is written in an understandable manner, using examples from social science research literature to develop the concepts.

Johnson, R. B., & Christensen, L. See lecture in Chapter Eleven: Nonexperimental quantitative research, based on *Educational Research: Quantitative, Qualitative, and Mixed Applications.* Retrieved March 13, 2008, from www.southalabama.edu/coe/bset/johnson/2lectures.htm.

Discusses steps in nonexperimental research, ways to control extraneous variables in nonexperimental research, and Johnson's classification scheme for nonexperimental research, and provides a graphic description of controlling for a third variable.

Locke, L. F., Silverman, S. J., & Waneen, W. S. (2004). *Reading and understanding research* (2nd ed.). Thousand Oaks: Sage.

Although this book deals with research in general, it is an easily understandable resource with good examples to help you read and understand published research articles. Aimed at consumers of research, the approach is nontechnical and user-friendly.

Lowry, R. (1999–2008). *Concepts and applications of inferential statistics.* Retrieved October 10, 2007, from http://faculty.vassar.edu/lowry/webtext.html.

Chapter Three of this free, full-length statistics textbook provides an introduction to linear correlation and regression using examples and diagrams. This is useful for understanding the basic analyses used with nonexperimental data.

Meltzoff, J. (1997). *Critical thinking about research: Psychology and related fields.* Washington, DC: American Psychological Association.

This text should help develop critical thinking skills via research by critiquing exercises of different types of research studies. It combines fundamental content with practice articles.

Trochim, W. M. *The research methods knowledge base* (2nd ed.). Retrieved October 20, 2006, from www.socialresearchmethods.net/kb.

Of particular use is the "Language of Research" part of the "Foundation" section, where types of relationships are clearly described, using simple examples and graphs.

CHAPTER

A PRIMER OF SURVEY METHODS

MARK BERENDS AND GENEVIEVE ZOTTOLA

KEY IDEAS

- Survey questions yield results that require an understanding of the difference between "concepts" and "constructs," as well as an understanding of how constructs create a framework for survey questions.

- A key part of survey research means being able to distinguish between good survey questions and those that are poorly worded, as well as being able to measure the quality of a question by the degree to which it supports the construct.

- Identifying independent and dependent variables, and being able to provide examples of each, are valuable skills for those who are interpreting survey results.

- The four tests for reliability are key to understanding survey research.

- The various types of probability and nonprobability sampling are important for those involved in survey research to know.

- Pretesting, pilot testing, and cognitive interviews are key stages of survey research.

- For those involved in the reading and application of survey results, it is helpful to know the five phases of data reduction.

- Each type of survey has key advantages and disadvantages important for practitioners to understand.
- Those involved in survey research should be able to articulate key ethical issues prevalent in the field.

WHAT IS SURVEY RESEARCH?

WE ARE currently living in the Information Age, an era that is characterized and propelled by information on preferences, needs, and behavior. With a dramatic increase in use over the past fifty years, administering surveys to samples of individuals, groups, or organizations is one of the most important basic research methods of the social sciences—serving important purposes in both the public and private sectors. Data from such surveys allow for monitoring important trends in society, testing our theoretical understanding of social processes, providing information to firms through market research, guiding politicians through polling of public opinion on key political issues and strategies, and providing key indicators of what is going on in our society.

The aim of this chapter, which has been adapted from *Survey Research Methods in Educational Research* (Berends, in Green, Camilli, & Elmore, 2006), is to provide an introduction to some key issues and concepts of survey research methods to pique the interest of those new to the field. Volumes of books and articles have been written on the subject, but this chapter is intended to provide an overview of the issues that practitioners will need to consider as they investigate social life through survey research methods.

Surveys You Know

There are times when researchers are interested in the broad population, and there are times when it is beneficial to obtain information on more limited populations of interest. For example, the United States government conducts the decennial census of the population, as required by the U.S. Constitution and conducted by the U.S. Bureau of the Census. Such information is used to determine how many seats each state will have in the U.S. House of Representatives as well as to provide key information to state and local policy makers and organizations. This information also indicates important demographic trends, such as the racial-ethnic composition and income distribution of the U.S. population. The census of the population is called a census because information is gathered from everyone in the U.S. population. In other words, when collecting data from all the people in a particular population, researchers refer to this as a census, not a survey.

Yet one need not wait every ten years to get such information when information on societal trends is gathered monthly as well. Initiated by the U.S. government, the *Current Population Survey* (CPS; see www.stats.bls.gov/cps/home.htm) is conducted by the Bureau of the Census for the Bureau of Labor Statistics. The CPS is a monthly survey of a sample of roughly fifty thousand households that provide survey data to understand demographic indicators of the U.S. labor force. Carefully selecting those fifty thousand households allows the federal government to make estimates of the entire U.S. population in regard to employment, unemployment, earnings, and hours of work for individuals sixteen years and older. Other information includes demographic characteristics such as age, race-ethnicity, gender, marital status, and educational attainment. Additional questions in the CPS periodically ask about school enrollment, work experience, health, and employee benefits.

Another example of periodic surveys in education includes the annual Phi Delta Kappa/Gallup Poll of public attitudes toward the public schools in the United States. For years, Gallup and Phi Delta Kappa have reported key attitudes about public schools based on a random sample of about one thousand adults, eighteen years and older. The findings from this survey provide estimates for the U.S. population as a whole. For example, information from this poll includes the consistent finding that since 1985 between 20 and 26 percent of U.S. adults give a grade of A or B to the nation's public schools. Grades increase if adults consider the schools in their community. That is, since 1985, between 40 and 50 percent of adults give a grade of A or B to the schools in their community. Such annual surveys provide some key indicators about continuing attitudes of the U.S. population toward schools but also provide opportunities to poll about timely educational issues, such as the public's attitudes toward school choice, test-based accountability, and teacher salaries (Rose & Gallup, 2007).

In education, there is a host of surveys conducted by the U.S. Department of Education. These surveys range from following a cohort or group of students over time, including young children in the Early Childhood Longitudinal Study or high school students in the Education Longitudinal Study (see Further Readings and Resources at end of chapter). In addition to monitoring several different cohorts of students, the U.S. Department of Education also conducts other surveys on repeated cross sections of students and teachers over time. That is, rather than following the same group over time as in the cohort studies, the repeated cross-sectional studies involve taking different national samples of schools, teachers, and students over time. As national samples, cross-sectional samples can be compared over time to monitor trends in the United States. However, one cannot assess individual change (of the student, teacher, or school) over time in these cross-sectional national samples. Examples of studies that monitor trends by examining different national samples include the Schools and Staffing Survey and the National Assessment of Educational Progress (see Further Readings and Resources at end of chapter).

THE RESEARCH PROCESS

It is natural for the majority of the population to use everyday patterns of thought when trying to make sense of the world around them. Generally speaking, we formulate nonscientific questions in an attempt to get answers to the way our world works from the perspective in which we live. Through our limited experiences we selectively give our attention to that which we choose, thereby forming our own generalizations and beliefs. This nonscientific mode of thought inevitably produces biased, subjective questions and answers regarding the world we want to know more about (Nardi, 2006).

Scientific thinking, however, uses empirical observations, systematic processes, and procedures that can be easily repeated. Thinking scientifically to first form research questions enables researchers to then be objective as they conduct each stage of the survey research process. High-quality, unbiased data are the result of a study that is rooted in scientific thought.

Choosing a Topic

The first part of the research process involves choosing a topic or theoretical issue. The research must stimulate interest around general topics for the purpose of finding specific ideas from which the research questions will develop. Reading published research and using other resources such as Internet search engines and library databases are ways to generate ideas. High-quality research begins with a theoretical issue, question, or topic. Therefore it is important to keep in mind that a theory involves a set of statements that are logically linked to explain some social phenomenon in the world around us.

Focusing the Research: Concepts and Constructs

Once a topic or theoretical issue is selected, such as *the impact of charter schools on parent satisfaction*, a set of questions containing constructs and concepts related to the topic are developed. Concepts are very similar to constructs, but there is a slight distinction made in that a "concept is an abstraction formed by generalizations from similar phenomena or similar attributes. *A construct is a concept that is systematically defined to be used in scientific theory*" (Hox, 1997, pg. 49, emphasis added). In other words, a **concept** is a specific idea that encompasses particular attributes such as "gender," an idea that represents masculinity and femininity, whereas **constructs** are more dynamic because they are ideas that are harder to define objectively. For example, "satisfaction" and "sense of belonging" are constructs because they are defined in different ways by different people. Concepts and constructs, terms that are often used interchangeably, must be defined in a way that is relevant to the study. When reading survey results, concepts and constructs help one to derive meaning from the results and conclusions articulated by the researcher.

There is a great deal of work in untangling social theories to articulate clear relations among constructs. **Conceptualization** refers to the theoretical work in defining constructs and their interrelationships. Having a clear definition for each concept as it relates to the research topic is key to the process of conceptualization.

Hypotheses, Variables, and Operationalization

Hypotheses are statements derived from previous research and theory that can be tested with empirical data, and show a relationship between two or more constructs. A hypothesis might state that voter apathy is greater when the conditions presented specifically during a time of war characterize the sociopolitical climate. Or a study might hypothesize that the prevalence of adolescent pregnancy is directly related to the quality and comprehensiveness of the public schools' sex education curriculum.

Beyond developing constructs and hypotheses, constructs must be translated into measurable form. A construct contains a depth of meaning represented by the variation that exists within it; through these **variables** the construct derives its whole meaning. For example, the construct "parent satisfaction" might contain the following variables:

- Overall quality of school
- Likeliness to recommend school
- Teacher expectations
- Likeliness of returning to school next year
- Quality of homework assignments
- Degree of challenge
- School standards
- Teacher care
- School safety
- Opportunities for parent involvement
- Grades received
- Facilities
- Class size
- School size
- Extracurricular activities
- Student and teacher sense of pride

Through the process of operationalization, the indicators of the construct are specified, those that can be measured, and thus assign values to the variables. For researchers and practitioners alike, this process of operationalization is key to ascertaining in a more detailed way what is being measured through the research. Knowing what variables were examined enables the reader of research to determine whether or not the study is relevant for his purposes.

Operationalization is an intricate process, particularly when we are thinking about how each variable will be measured. Most concepts have multiple categories or values that represent the variability occurring within the concept. Variables used to indicate parent satisfaction, such as those mentioned above, range in intensity. For example, the variable "overall satisfaction with school" can be measured in degrees of intensity from "very satisfied" to "very dissatisfied." Some variables, however, do not include such a range. For example, the construct "family background" contains the variable "mother's labor force participation" which may be measured as "yes" or "no" in terms of the mother working for pay outside of the home.

Independent Versus Dependent Variables

Research is conducted to find out why a particular variable varies. The outcome or effect that the researcher is trying to understand is called the **dependent variable**. The degree to which the outcome (dependent variable) varies depends on certain causes or predictors (**independent variables**) (Nardi, 2006). A hypothesis such as *Public service employee job satisfaction depends on the degree to which the employee feels empowered* could be modified to read *Public service employees who feel empowered are more satisfied than those who feel disempowered.* The level of satisfaction will be dependent on the degree of empowerment (set forth by specific, measurable variables to measure empowerment). However, there is nothing about a variable that makes it fundamentally dependent or independent; the hypothesis characterizes variables as independent or dependent. Therefore, it is crucial for a practitioner interested in utilizing the results presented by researchers to be able to discern between these two types of variables, so as to determine how the research relates to the topic of interest.

REFLECTION QUESTIONS

1. What topics in your discipline might be examined using survey research?

2. Create two research hypotheses and identify the independent and dependent variables for each.

WRITING GOOD SURVEY QUESTIONS

Questions and the answers they provoke are key to the process of measuring outcomes. The answers are only meaningful to the extent that they help the researcher understand more about the question that is being asked. Also, questions that facilitate measurement do so in a way that when applied they produce valid results, results that are meaningful for both researchers and practitioners. **Validity** implies accuracy, meaning that the respondent's answers correctly indicate what the question set out to measure. This depends largely on the way the questions are worded.

According to Fowler (2002), there are four causes of reduced accuracy:

1. Respondents do not understand the question

2. Respondents do not know the answer

3. Respondents cannot recall the answer, although they knew it at one point

4. Respondents would rather not share the answer, although they know it

To increase validity, questions should be worded simply, clearly, and in a direct manner so as not to confuse the respondent.

There are many ways to increase validity when writing survey questions (Chambliss & Schutt, 2003). It is important to avoid **negative phrases**, especially double negatives. **Double-barreled questions** can also be confusing on surveys, making responses less than accurate. If the respondent is being asked two questions at once with only one response option provided, this is confusing and the resulting answer will be meaningless. It is effective in this case to split the question up into two separate questions. (See Exhibit 5.1 for examples.)

EXHIBIT 5.1. **Negative and Double-Barreled Question Examples**

Negative phrase: Do you feel that this workplace shouldn't provide better child-care services for employees?

Double negative: Don't you agree that there are not many services available to make this workplace "family-friendly?"

Double-barreled: The child-care services and the business functions at this workplace are . . .

Bias increases when words are used that suggest that the respondent should answer in a certain way. Minimizing bias is important to increasing validity as well. This can be accomplished by choosing words and phrases that are rather neutral. Avoiding bias is as important as allowing for disagreement. Respondents should feel comfortable providing a "no" answer without feeling as if they have chosen a politically or socially incorrect answer. (See Exhibit 5.2 for examples.)

EXHIBIT 5.2. **Revising Questions to Minimize Bias**

Poorly worded, with bias: Aren't charter schools, which are founded upon cohesive ideas and a strong mission, better than traditional public schools?

Better wording, minimized bias: In your opinion, how would you describe the presence of the mission of the charter school in which you currently have your child enrolled as compared to the presence of the mission in the traditional public school he or she previously attended?

Does not allow for disagreement: Parents should make an effort to get involved at their child's school; it is not always the school's responsibility to chase after parents to get them involved.

Also, surveys should be designed with careful consideration given to the respondent's ability to answer the questions being asked. Using **skip patterns** (see Exhibit 5.3) to direct respondents to the next applicable question ensures greater validity.

Chambliss and Schutt (2003) emphasize that good survey questions are mutually exclusive, exhaustive, and allow for indecision. There are respondents who, even if they do not know the answer, will choose one anyway unless they are given a "don't know" response option. Those who are not leaning toward one answer more than another need to be given the opportunity to remain neutral by choosing a response option marked "neutral."

To ensure accuracy, response categories should be both exhaustive and mutually exclusive. This means that all conceivable answers are offered (**exhaustive**), and response options do not overlap (**mutually exclusive**). (See Exhibit 5.4 for example.)

EXHIBIT 5.3. **Examples of Question Skip Patterns**

4. Which type of school does your child now attend? (check the school that applies)

 a. Traditional public school (non-charter) _____

   ■ Did you look for information about Indianapolis charter schools?
   Yes (go to Q. #5) _____ No (go to Q. #7)

 b. Charter school _____

   ■ Did you look for information about Indianapolis Public Schools?
   _____ Yes (go to Q. #5) _____ No (go to Q. #7)

EXHIBIT 5.4. **Example of Overlapping Question Responses**
Question Fails to Provide Responses That Are Mutually Exclusive

Choose the appropriate age category to describe yourself:

 a. 25–35 b. 35–45 . . .

 Note: an exception to the rule of mutual exclusivity is the response option: "check all that apply"

To establish **reliability**, it is necessary to examine the way that two respondents taking the same survey approach the questions on the survey (Fowler, 2002). The less likely all respondents are to interpret and answer the questions in the same way (that is, go through a similar thought process), the less reliability the survey instrument has. A survey that has a high level of validity will in many cases be more reliable than it would be if its validity was low. However, a highly valid measure is highly reliable as well.

There are several ways to test reliability (Chambliss & Schutt, 2003). If a test taker produces a different score on a test each time the test is taken with all other circumstances remaining constant, the measure is unreliable. This check for reliability is called **test-retest**. Also, the reliability of a measure can be tested by examining how the questions on the survey internally "work together." The extent to which the questions derive meaning from the relationship they have with each other determines the measure's **internal consistency**. Next, if the order of the questions is changed or the phrasing of the questions is slightly modified, and the survey outcomes are similar, **alternate-forms reliability** has been established. Along the same lines, the **split-halves reliability** approach splits the group of survey respondents in half and administers the slightly different forms of the questions to the two halves. If the results are similar in this case, split-halves reliability has been established. Finally, if multiple observers are using the same instrument to report on the same situation or occurrence, their responses should be similar (Chambliss & Schutt, 2003). This indicator is called **inter-observer reliability**.

REFLECTION QUESTIONS

1. Identify the problem with each of the following survey items and then rewrite each item, improving upon its wording to increase its validity.

    a. Don't you feel that this school doesn't provide enough extracurricular activities for its students?

    b. Isn't it about time teachers in this school began caring more about student engagement?

    c. Indicate your age by choosing the appropriate category.

    ___ 30–35 ___ 35–40 ___ 40–45 ___ 45+

2. How would you know if the published results of survey research are likely to be valid?

Piloting and Cognitive Interviews

One way of testing survey questions to see how accurately respondents will interpret them is to discuss the questionnaire with experts in the field. As experts, they are knowledgeable about how questions should be phrased to ensure accuracy, which layout and response format is most effective for the specific purpose at hand, and how best to order questions.

Also during a **pilot** (also called field testing), the survey is administered to a group of respondents (ranging from ten to one hundred) who resemble the individuals in the actual sample. Sometimes on the pretest version of the survey, researchers will offer additional space beside each question for respondents to make comments about their thought process or points about which they were less than clear. This process of piloting indicates about how long the survey takes to complete.

Although pilot testing is a valuable method to determine survey length and general problems with select items, it is helpful to know more about how exactly the respondent's cognitive process is working to interpret the survey questions. Specifically, effective survey questions are interpreted by the respondent so as to uphold the validity of the question and the construct that it measures.

Cognitive interviews explore reasons why respondents answer the way that they do, identify the degree to which survey items measure the key constructs, find gaps where additional questions might be needed, and pinpoint misleading items that might deviate from measuring the target construct.

During the cognitive interview process, respondents are asked to explain the question using their own words and to describe the process they used to choose their answer. The goal of the interview process is to answer four key questions (Fowler, 2002):

1. Are the key questions clearly understood?

2. Do respondents have access to the information needed to effectively answer the question?

3. Do the response options provide the answers the respondents want to choose so that they can be accurate?

4. Are the response options accurately measuring what the questions set out to measure?

Revisions to the survey and changes in the survey format are made using the data from the cognitive interviews.

Interviews are audio- or videotaped and they are intended to encourage respondents to share their thought process as they answer each question. The respondents point to specific aspects of the survey questions that evoke genuine thoughts and feelings that match the experience the survey instrument is measuring. Also, through the interview the respondent indicates which items are unclear, in what ways they are unclear and, if relevant response options have been omitted, the interview is a good time for respondents to share this too. Follow-up interpretative questions not on the survey itself are sometimes used by the interviewer to gain insight into how well the questions are designed. These "think alouds" provide important data for researchers as they aim to understand how the respondent thought about the question before answering it.

SAMPLING, RESPONSE RATES, AND NONRESPONSE

Survey research aims to describe relevant characteristics of individuals, groups, or organizations by collecting information from a **sample**, a group of representative individuals from a population, through their responses to standardized questions. Although it is sometimes possible to survey an entire **population**, a group of individuals or other entities to which the findings are being generalized, most of the time a smaller representative group is used. Researchers gather information on the characteristics of the population, and these combine to form the **population parameters**. An example of a population parameter would be "the educational attainment of teachers in the nation or state."

Social researchers most often have the goal of creating a sample that best represents the characteristics of the general population in which they are interested. The purpose is to generate values from the sample that can be statistically analyzed to produce meaningful conclusions about the population. Likewise, readers of research derive great meaning from research that is based on representative samples.

This process is one that involves the sample frame, sample size, and the method of selection. First, the **sampling frame** is a general term used to identify the selected group. The degree to which this group has the same characteristics as the general population of interest (from which the group was chosen) determines its representative quality.

There are three ways the sampling frame is classified:

1. Sampling from a complete list of individuals in the population.

2. Sampling from a group that attends or participates in something (such as a meeting).

3. Sampling in multiple stages is used when a full list of the individuals in the population is not available. Individuals are selected beginning with larger clusters (groups) and at each stage the clusters get smaller (Nardi, 2006).

Overall, a sampling frame should include all distinct characteristics of the entire population and it should be created in such a way that the probability of selection for each individual included in the sample can be determined. It is imperative that the limitations of the study presented by the sampling frame be disclosed.

Sample size is only relevant for random samples that are scientific by nature. Nonrandom samples produce results that are based only on the group chosen, regardless of size. It is important to pinpoint subgroups of the population of interest. Although there is not an exact rule on how large a sample should be, looking at the subgroups to determine the smallest size group that would still yield meaningful results can help to determine an appropriate **sample size**. A general rule for determining a good sample size is "the bigger the sample, the better the data."

Probability or Random Sampling

The objective of a representative sample is to produce results that are generalizable; that is, to permit the researcher to make inferences about the sample that are valid in the broader population.

In order to create a representative sample, the group chosen for the sample should be made up of individuals who have similar characteristics to those in the larger population. If the researcher is interested in dropout rates in choice versus traditional public schools, for instance, the sample of individuals chosen from the traditional and choice schools in a particular area should be similar on most levels to the greater population of traditional and choice school students.

If indeed the distribution of demographics between the sample and the population from which it is drawn is very similar, then the researcher can be comfortable that any inferences made about the sample are equally valid in the population.

Simple, Stratified, and Systemic Samples

To generate a **simple random sample**, a list of all possible members of the population and all members in the sampling frame must appear on a numbered list. Then, members are chosen by random numbers (tables of such random numbers are generated by computers and are readily available), or names are chosen out of a box as in a lottery. Also, each member is selected independently of another and is therefore not affected by any other selection, nor can any name be selected more than once. Telephone surveys use a random sample technique called random digit dialing (RDD), in which machines generate phone numbers within various area codes and then dial the numbers. The drawback to this method of random sampling is that bias is introduced when those who use only a cell phone as their main phone line are not given the opportunity to be included in the sample.

If selected randomly from the population, comparison groups are sometimes not the right size for measurement purposes. **Stratified sampling** is a method of sampling that can be used to alter the size of the comparison groups in this case. For example, if the population contains more females than males, but the researcher's goal is to have an even number of each gender, the stratified random sampling allows for an over- or undersampling of a subgroup. Likewise, if the goal is to replicate the exact subgroup distributions present in the population, samples can be stratified on certain characteristics to obtain a sample that is an exact match from which the group was selected.

Systematic random sampling is a method used to make obtaining stratified samples more efficient. There are three key points to remember when generating a systematic random sample (Fowler, 2002):

1. When drawing samples from a list, first determine the exact number of entries on the list and the number of elements from the list that are to be selected.

2. A start-point is designated by choosing a random number that falls within the sampling interval. This random start creates chance selection.

3. By using a random start-point (any random number such as forty-five), the researcher then chooses every forty-fifth person from that start-point.

Most often a systematic random sample creates a sample similar to that which a simple random sample would create. However, if the population itself is ordered in some distinct way, this method would not be random and therefore it would not be representative either.

Nonprobability Sampling

True random sampling (probability sampling) is necessary to produce generalizable data. However, there is not always enough time or money to allow for such elaborate processes. In this case, nonprobability sampling is used. The following is a brief description of the four **nonprobability** sampling methods.

Convenience (or **accidental**) **sampling** is nonscientific in that the results gathered from such a sample are not reliable. If, while walking down the street, you are stopped to answer some questions about your cable service, this is an accidental sample. The people selected are only those who are on that particular street at that certain time of day in that particular city. If it were midmorning on a weekday on Fifth Avenue in New York City, the people strolling around with their shopping bags are probably very affluent and do not likely have typical jobs because they are not working on a weekday morning. Not every person from every diverse group has the opportunity to participate in this particular accidental survey. Readers of research should be aware if convenience sampling has been used, as it produces unreliable data.

Another example of a convenience or accidental sample is demonstrated in the case of volunteer samples. For example, those who respond to an ad for an online survey that, upon completion, enters them into a drawing for a prize of a fifty-dollar gift card to Target are not the same as all other people who did not have a chance to participate in this survey. Others might not have access to the Internet, and still others might not feel a need for a fifty-dollar gift card because they are not in need of any financial assistance.

Purposeful sampling is directed at a particular purpose the researcher might have to examine certain qualities in a group of people. For example, if prior research reveals that members of the YMCA are typically people who donate at least once a year to a charity, this group, based on this characteristic they possess, might be surveyed.

By singling out YMCA members for the study, not everyone has the opportunity to participate and therefore the sample is nonrandom.

Quota sampling builds on accidental sampling, adding the goal of creating a sample that represents comparison groups equally. Demographic characteristics such as gender, age, and race-ethnicity are categories for which a researcher might set a quota. If the quota is ten people under twelve years of age, ten people over twenty-one, and ten people over fifty, and these desired numbers are chosen—as in the case of the Fifth Avenue survey, as people walk down the street—this generates a quota sample.

Snowball sampling is used to target a certain group that might be difficult to sample with convenience or purposeful sampling. For example, if the goal is to survey men and women who have had plastic surgery, not all (or even many) would disclose such information if you stopped them on the street to ask them. The best way to get this kind of nonrandom sample is to gather a few respondents you might know as acquaintances and ask them to pass the survey along to others they know who have had the same kind of procedures. The sample snowballs from there.

Response Rates and Nonresponse

For a quality sample, data should be collected from as many individuals in the sampling frame as possible. When the percentage of respondents from which data are collected is low, this contributes to survey error and therefore threatens the validity of the survey. The **response rate** is the term used to identify the number of individuals who have provided data, proportional to the total number of individuals in the sampling frame. This number is presented as a percentage. Response rates of more than 70 percent are ideal, but response rates of 20 to 33 percent are more common, unfortunately. The U.S. Department of Education has required in its research contracts response rates of 80 percent or higher.

Data collection methods and procedures play a large role in determining response rates. Procedures should be created to ensure that all respondents who give consent to participate are afforded every possible opportunity to do so. Following up more than once with respondents who haven't provided data is an effective method of increasing response rates.

Nonresponse in survey research can lead to bias because those who fail to provide data may be different from those who do respond. Depending on the type of survey being conducted, bias is introduced in different ways. For the purposes of this text, it is necessary only to mention a few.

Nonresponse in mail surveys directly affects the research purpose and outcome because those who do not provide data are generally less interested in the overall topic of the survey. The low response rate shows that a certain large group of individuals from the sample frame were not particularly concerned with the topic that the survey intended to measure. Fowler (2002) uses the example of a health care mail survey. Respondents who do not return the mail survey are given a follow-up phone interview. Studies have shown that in the case of such health surveys the group of people who were given the follow-up phone interview were younger, healthier, and a greater number of them were male, as compared to the group that responded during the first data collection effort. Nonresponse in mail surveys has also indicated that the nonresponse groups are on average less educated and are of a lower income bracket than those who provide data.

Telephone survey nonresponse creates bias in a different way. If the surveys are conducted during normal business hours (9 AM to 5 PM), the people who are able to be contacted are distinctive in that they are generally either home taking care of young children, unemployed, or retired. This makes the group of respondents who provide data different in terms of their income level, interests, education, or age.

Is the Framework Intact?

After the pretesting phase, it is important to revisit the theoretical framework of the survey. It is advantageous to reexamine the survey after the pretesting data has indicated whether or not there is a need for changes to the survey. More often than not, modifications will take place during this phase; therefore, after such changes are applied, it is crucial that researchers check that all key constructs are intact and correctly measured.

REFLECTION QUESTIONS

1. Give an example of a research study that would work well with each of the following types of sampling: purposive sampling and snowball sampling.
2. Explain the significance of response rates and nonresponse.

DATA REDUCTION

After surveys are administered and data are collected, data must be put into a computer format. This process is called **data reduction** and it consists of five phases (Fowler, 2002). First, the data must be organized within a computer file. Next, a code is designed to translate respondents' answers into a quantifiable format that can be understood by a computer. Third, the code is implemented so that the responses are categorized. Fourth, the data are entered into the computer. And in the last phase, the data are cleaned, a process that ensures that all data fields are complete, correct, and consistent.

Although this text will not address the intricacies of data analysis, it is valuable for our purposes to highlight a few key elements essential to formatting the data file, coding, and cleaning the data. Before data analysis can begin, the researcher must decide on which software to use. Statistical Analysis Software (SAS), Stata, and Statistical Package for the Social Sciences (SPSS) are commonly used programs in social research. These and others vary in terms of their format and how they treat missing data. After choosing a program, it is important to be aware of how the program reads blank fields. Some programs do not recognize the blank as a nonresponse or necessarily read the blank field as a zero.

Within the coding phase there are critical elements to keep in mind. Survey answers are, through the establishment of code, given numeric value and at the same time missing data are coded. Codes should differentiate between incomplete information, information that was not relevant to the respondent, and "don't know" responses attributable to inadequate access to information or the respondent's inability to recall the information. It is best to keep codes the same for answers that have the same meaning in terms of research purposes. Furthermore, a code should organize responses that, from an analysis perspective, are related to each other and in effect support the same construct, into the same category.

After coding, data must be cleaned. This phase involves checking for consistency throughout the entered data. Even if checks on the data are installed within the program itself, it is best to look for missing data, extra information, or any other inconsistencies that may have occurred in the process.

TYPES OF SURVEYS

As a popular form of quantitative research, survey research involves writing questions for surveys and interviews, measuring responses, and analyzing data. Common methods for collecting survey data include face-to-face interviews, telephone surveys, mail surveys, and Web-based surveys. An extensive review of all the issues related to each approach is beyond the scope of this chapter, but there are many texts available on the subject (Babbie, 2001; Fowler, 1993; Groves et al., 2004; Mangione, 1995; Tourangeau, Rips, & Rasinski, 2000). Practitioners who read research should be aware of the issues presented by each survey method, because such issues affect the limitations of the study results and conclusions.

Face-to-Face Interviews

Face-to-face interviews are an effective method for gathering high-quality information. The interviewer has the opportunity to clarify confusing questions and encourage the respondent to elaborate to clarify answers. Face-to-face interviews are advantageous because complete control is with the interviewer; this ensures that the respondent is indeed the person for whom the interview is intended. For example, to obtain quality data when conducting surveys of school administrators about school strategies, it is important to interview the principal, not one of the key administrative staff. Face-to-face interviews enable the researcher to have more control over who is actually answering the questions, which is not the case with mail surveys.

At the same time, there are reasons for the face-to-face interviewer to exercise caution. The person who conducts the interview plays an important part in securing cooperation to increase response rates. However, interviewers need to be careful about the way that they motivate respondents so that they do not encourage respondents to provide socially "desirable" or "expected" answers. This creates the potential for bias. Readers of research should remain aware of this potential for bias, as it affects the validity of the results of the study. Groves et al. (2004) suggest that to avoid such problems researchers can create questions that do not require interviewers to change their behavior for different respondents.

The following are ways in which bias can be avoided: (1) interact with respondents in a task-oriented, professional manner; (2) read questions exactly as worded; (3) explain the survey procedures to the respondent; (4) probe in a neutral manner to avoid increasing the likelihood of one answer over another; and (5) record answers without making interpretations or inferences about what respondents did not say.

The high costs of transportation, personnel, and time to conduct the interviews make this approach less common for large sample studies that are geographically dispersed. One can imagine the costs involved of face-to-face interviews of a nationwide random sample of teachers aimed at answering questions about compensation and working conditions. Even within one state, the costs of this type of interview may be too great. Thus, face-to-face interviews are often geographically clustered, which can add to measurement error. Cost is a key issue to consider in face-to-face interviews.

Telephone Surveys

There are several advantages to using telephone surveys. Telephone surveys are significantly less expensive than face-to-face interviews, but maintain some of their advantages. Rather than traveling to a respondent's place of residence or work, a phone call is a much less expensive approach in terms of time and money. As in face-to-face interviews, the purpose of the survey, why it is important, and what information is requested can be explained during the phone interview. Although not as personal as a face-to-face interview, it is much more so than a mail survey, even with a carefully crafted cover letter. Also, during a telephone interview, the interviewer can gather additional information about questions that are unclear, making sure that the respondent clearly interprets questions so as to preserve their intent; respondents can also provide additional comments on particular survey items. Finally, if there is a central administration of several individuals conducting phone interviews, procedural changes can be made uniformly across interviewers to maintain consistency of survey administration to secure high-quality information.

However, like any research approach, telephone interviews are not without their weaknesses. One weakness is that not everyone has a phone. Although about 95 percent of the U.S. population reports having a telephone, there are some subpopulations that are underrepresented in their phone use (for example, the poor); therefore, depending on one's desired sample and research question, understanding who is likely to have and use a phone is important during the sampling phase. Second, with the growth of cell phone use, many people use their cell phone as both a mobile and a home phone because of the cost-effectiveness of having just one phone bill. Hence, this part of the population cannot be contacted for the survey because cell phone numbers are unpublished. As a final consideration, with the proliferation of market research and solicitations, many are suspect of phone calls requesting information. The screening of phone calls with answering machines is all too common. Some ways to bypass this problem include sending a letter in advance describing the project, its significance, information requested, and range of dates when a phone call will occur, or providing the respondent with an 800 number to call during selected times, thus allowing the respondent to select a time convenient for him or her.

Mail Surveys

The biggest advantage of mail surveys is that they are relatively cheap. When a researcher needs to administer surveys to a large sample that is geographically dispersed, mail surveys are a reasonably cost-effective option. Traveling all over the country conducting face-to-face interviews may not be feasible and telephone interviews tend to be more expensive than questionnaires sent in the mail; therefore, mail surveys may be the best option within budget constraints.

However, the disadvantage of this approach is that many study participants will often not mail back their surveys. Mail survey response rates may be disappointingly low. For some surveys, only half the respondents mail back the questionnaires.

The problem with low response rates (below 70 percent) is that survey nonresponse can severely bias the results; the quality of the information can be called into question. There may be important biases in the information received because those who fail to return the surveys may be different in systematic ways from those who did. It is difficult to know for sure that those who responded to the surveys are just like those who did not; problems arise by saying that the survey information represents the larger sample drawn. For example, if the survey is administered to a random sample of teachers within a particular state to ask about working conditions, and most of the teachers in large urban areas fail to respond, then researchers cannot know for sure about the inferences they make about teachers' working conditions in the state. The results may be biased favorably because the survey data are based mainly on teachers from rural and suburban areas vis-à-vis urban teachers. Rural and suburban teachers may report more favorable work conditions when compared with urban teachers.

Overall, mail surveys can work well if they are short, easily understood, and accompanied by clear directions and some sort of incentive (for example, a coupon or gift certificate). It should be as easy as possible for respondents to answer the questions and mail the survey back to the researcher. A clear, easy-to-read cover letter introducing the study, the survey, and the importance of the person's responses is an important element. Also, surveys should always include an envelope with a return address and postage. There are other ways to help increase response rates for mail surveys that have been suggested by others and are worth consideration (see Babbie, 2001; Dillman, 1978; Salant & Dillman, 1994; Yammarino, Skinner, & Childers, 1991).

Internet and Web-Based Surveys

An approach for gathering survey data that is growing in popularity is self-administration of surveys with computers (Nesbary, 2000). One only need to think about the unwanted "pop-ups" at the computer terminal that sometimes include an online survey for some marketing firm. Despite the fact that this type of survey is annoying to most, Internet-based surveys can be used to gather data efficiently. Questionnaires can be sent to desired respondents by e-mail, or respondents can click on a link to answer the survey.

Typically, there are three types of Internet-based surveys (Simsek & Veiga, 2001). First, an e-mail message with the survey embedded in the e-mail text can be sent to respondents. The respondent simply returns the e-mail with the answers. Second, an e-mail can be sent with an attachment that the respondent must open, answer, and then send back as an attachment. Third, researchers can use a URL-embedded message in the text of the e-mail, so the respondent simply clicks on the hypertext link, which then evokes the Web browser to present the respondent with the Web-based survey.

There are several advantages of Internet-based surveys. First, the marginal costs of conducting Internet surveys can be much lower than the costs of traditional surveys, especially face-to-face interviews, but also mail surveys (Mehta & Sivadas, 1995). Although there are the primary costs of assembling and obtaining sampling frames, creating and buying software to support the databases, and accessing the Internet, there are no costs associated with paper, printing, mailing, and transferring the data from paper to electronic form. Second, Web-based surveys can be designed in ways that are more aesthetically appealing to respondents—providing motivation for them to complete the questionnaire. The programs used to construct such surveys are also set up to allow for automated coding of the data. This eliminates a step in the process of having individuals key in the data from questionnaires—often a source of error. In fact, some programs can print out up-to-date descriptive statistics to assist in monitoring the survey administration. Although Web-based surveys have a certain elegance and efficiency, there is a significant limitation: Not everyone has access to computers or the Internet or the motivation or capacity to handle Web-based surveys. Depending on the desired sample, it is important to be mindful of the fact that even in this modern age of computers there are still differences in computer use by age, race-ethnicity, income, and education. Depending on a preferred sample to address these questions, such differences may result in bias in the survey results obtained.

ETHICAL ISSUES IN SURVEY RESEARCH

Because respondents voluntarily participate and therefore always have the ability to opt out of the research, there are fewer ethical considerations in survey research than in experimental or field research. The procedures and methodology are disclosed, making respondents aware of their exact role in the study.

The key concern in survey research is confidentiality. If revealed to the public, the data collected during survey research often contain information that would be detrimental to the respondents in some way. Giving respondents the confidence that their answers will not be made public protects the respondents and insures validity. Respondents are more likely to provide honest, accurate answers if they trust that the data will not be disclosed.

Ways to Ensure Confidentiality and Increase Anonymity

It is best that only researchers who need to deal directly with the data have contact with it. This reduces the chance of data "leaking out" and potentially sacrificing confidentiality. Data that are linked to respondents should use numbers rather than names on the data itself. The numbers and the corresponding names should appear on a separate list kept apart from the data in a secure location.

Mailings and phone calls are used to increase response rates during the follow-up phase, which requires identities to be linked to numbered surveys. This phase should be performed only by the most trustworthy members of the project team. For electronic survey confidentiality, encryption technology should be used to secure Web information. True anonymity would mean the absence of identifiers linking respondents with their responses. This is not feasible in most cases, because without identifiers, follow-up techniques cannot be employed. Also, without name links, which allow the research team to repeat the procedures with the same people at various points in time, follow-up techniques become impossible to employ.

Ethical research is conducted in such a way that the survey process ensures that no individual suffers any negative consequences. Furthermore, research subjects should benefit through their participation in the research process. When researchers launch a new project that requires federal funding, they must report to their institutional review board (IRB). The IRB is responsible for approving research that involves human subjects. The IRB reviews the research proposal before the project begins. This review is aimed at protecting three parties: subjects, researchers, and the research institution. Most specifically, the IRB is focused on protecting the well-being of the subjects. (For more information on ethics and IRB review, see Chapter One.)

According to the Department of Health and Human Services (1995, in Fowler, 2002), educational tests are subject to IRB review when (1) subjects are identifiable, and (2) when the release of data gathered from the human subjects could incriminate, make subjects civilly liable, hurt them financially, or affect their employability or reputation.

Informed Consent

Key to ethical research is the process of informing respondents and gaining consent for their participation in the study. Respondents should be provided with all the necessary information in simple terms before asking for their agreement to participate, including the name of the organization conducting the study, the research person with whom the respondent will have contact, the source of funds for the project, a brief description of the questions the research is setting out to study, the level of confidentiality of the research, their freedom to opt out of the study, and their freedom to skip any question they do not want to answer.

Throughout the process of obtaining informed consent, it is emphasized that researchers foster a strong rapport, high level of trust, and mutual respect as they interact with the respondent. This ensures that the respondent is provided a comfortable environment while making a decision about whether or not to participate in the research (Sieber, 1992).

The following are additional ways to protect respondents:

1. Confidentiality agreements should be signed by all who have contact with the data.

2. Names and addresses that link respondents to the surveys should be kept to a minimum and should be kept apart from the survey results. These links should also be severed after the process is over.

3. Only those who are directly involved in the data collection itself should have access to the data.

4. When respondents present results gathered from small populations or categories they should be aware of the risk of identifying individuals in such small groups.

5. After survey data are collected and entered into computer-readable format, researchers should destroy original documents.

Ethics Beyond Data Collection

There are ethical considerations beyond the data collection phase. In reporting the data, researchers are faced with the challenge of how to interpret results without speculation, bias, or selectivity. It is the researcher's duty to have a well-rounded understanding of the topic and of the research already published on the topic. The researcher should understand the context into which his new findings will emerge. Nardi (2006) presents important questions to be considered before findings are reported:

1. What happens if your findings have major repercussions on public policy and people's lives?

2. What are the ethical issues involved in reporting some of your findings and not others (especially those that may conflict with the main beliefs held by the agency sponsoring the research)?

3. How can your research be ethically presented when selection bias occurred (as with a Web page or a log-in survey)?

Being mindful of these questions can help to keep research ethical. Best practice is that all limitations of the research are clearly and openly laid out.

 REFLECTION QUESTIONS

1. Although readers of research and practitioners do not perform the actual steps that comprise the data reduction process, they should be aware of how this process occurs. What are some of the challenges researchers are faced with throughout this process of data reduction?

2. The type of survey researchers choose to use is key to understanding the results and conclusions. What are some of the limitations and advantages presented by each type of survey instrument?

3. Confidentiality is the main ethical consideration in survey research. Name four ways respondents are protected.

SUMMARY

Through survey research, we can establish a clearer and more objective picture of how and why individuals behave the way they do. Interestingly, survey research not only provides researchers with information at the point of data collection and analysis, and through the process of survey design and development, but readers of research are enlightened by this process as well, leading them to a greater understanding of the results and conclusions set forth by researchers. From start to finish, survey research is a process that unfolds the many layers of questions that continuously emerge around us.

KEY TERMS

alternate forms reliability
bias
cognitive interviews
concept
confidentiality
constructs
conceptualization
convenience sampling
data reduction
dependent variable
double-barreled questions
exhaustive
independent variables
informed consent/protecting respondents
institutional review board (IRB)
internal consistency
inter-observer reliability
mutually exclusive
negative phrases
nonprobability sampling
nonresponse

operationalization
pilot
population
population parameters
purposeful sampling
questions that allow for disagreement
quota sampling
reliability
reliability tests
response rate
sample
sampling frame
sample size
simple random sample
skip patterns
snowball sampling
split-halves reliability
stratified sample
systemic random sample
validity
variables

FURTHER READINGS AND RESOURCES

Suggested Survey Article

Newmann, F. M., Smith, B. A., Allensworth, E., & Bryk, A. S. (2001). Instructional program coherence: What it is and why it should guide school improvement policy. *Educational Evaluation and Policy Analysis*, *23*, 297–321.

Suggested Reading

Babbie, E. R. (2004). *The practice of social research* (10th ed.). Belmont, CA: Wadsworth.

The strengths of this textbook lie in the coverage of social science theory and research and the pragmatics of experimental, survey, and field research. All through the book, Babbie utilizes up-to-date, real-life examples instead of overwhelming the beginner with irrelevant studies on unfamiliar topics.

Web Sites

U.S. Department of Education: Surveys of Longitudinal Cohorts— Early Childhood Longitudinal Study

http://nces.ed.gov/ecls

The *Early Childhood Longitudinal Study, Kindergarten Class of 1998–1999 (ECLS-K)* is a longitudinal study that followed a nationally representative sample of approximately twenty-two thousand children from kindergarten through fifth grade. The ECLS-K began collecting data from kindergarten students, their teachers, and schools in the fall of 1998. Data were collected periodically until the spring of 2004, when the students were in the spring of fifth grade. Although ECLS-K is designed primarily as a longitudinal survey of students, teachers and school administrators were sampled in each wave. This makes it possible to use the data to examine changes in schools over time. In the first year, for example, sample students were in kindergarten, so the sampled teachers were largely kindergarten teachers. In subsequent years, first-, third-, and fifth-grade teachers have formed the primary sample. This has great advantages in a study of student achievement.

The *Early Childhood Longitudinal Study, Birth Cohort (ECLS-B)* is an additional longitudinal study, providing detailed information on child development, health, early care, and education. The study followed a nationally representative sample of approximately 13,500 children born in 2001 from nine months of age through the first grade. This longitudinal study gathers information on children's cognitive, social, emotional, and physical development from multiple sources—from the children, their parents, their child care providers, their teachers, and their school administrators. In this longitudinal cohort, the same children were followed up from birth through first grade with data collected when the children were nine, twenty-four, and forty-eight months old, in kindergarten, and in first grade.

U.S. Department of Education: Surveys of Longitudinal Cohorts—Education Longitudinal Study

http://nces.ed.gov/surveys/els2002

Fielded for the first time in 2002 when students were high school sophomores, Educational Longitudinal Study (ELS) is a longitudinal study that will follow a nationally representative cohort of high school students over time. By surveying the same young people over time, researchers and policy makers can monitor changes taking place during the life course and compare these trends to early cohorts of students for which the U.S. Department of Education has gathered data. In the first year of data collection (2002 is called the base year), ELS measured students' tested achievement and surveyed students about their attitudes and experiences. These same students were tested and surveyed again, when they were seniors in the 2004 follow-up. Study participants will be followed for a number of years to examine whether adult outcomes (for example, higher education and labor force participation) can be understood in terms of their earlier aspirations, achievement, and high school experiences. ELS gathers information from a variety of sources, not only students. For instance, ELS also contains survey information from students' parents, their teachers, and their school administrators. The teacher surveys provide information about the student and about the student's experiences in that teacher's class. By gathering survey information from multiple sources, researchers will have a more comprehensive set of data about students' lives in their home, schools, and communities.

U.S. Department of Education: Surveys of Repeated Cross Sections—The Schools and Staffing Survey (SASS) and the Teacher Follow-up Survey (TFS)

http://nces.ed.gov/surveys/sass

SASS is a survey-based design that gathers data from a nationally representative sample of teachers. Rather than a cohort design (following the same group of teachers over time), SASS is designed as a repeated cross-sectional survey. This means that periodically (for example, in 1990–1991, 1993–1994, 1999–2000, 2003–2004) the U.S. Department of Education gathers data on a cross section of the nation's teachers to gather nationally representative information. Although the teachers may differ across waves (for example, different teachers in 1993–1994 versus 1999–2000), each wave is representative of teachers in the nation's schools. SASS surveys of teachers, school administrators, district administrators, and the teacher follow-up survey (TFS) gather information on teacher demand and shortage, teacher and administrator characteristics and attitudes, school programs, school climate, teacher compensation, district hiring practices, and characteristics of the student population. Surveys are sent to respondents in public, private, and Bureau of Indian Affairs tribal schools. Many of the same survey questions have been used in each cross-sectional wave of the survey, allowing researchers to investigate trends over time.

The aim of the TFS is to examine how many teachers remained at the same school, moved to another school, or left the profession in the year following the SASS administration. For example, in 2000–2001 the TFS was administered to a sample of teachers who completed the SASS in the previous year. Surveys are administered to (a) a set of teachers who left teaching since the previous SASS and (b) those who are still currently teaching. Topics in the survey range from asking teachers who left teaching about their current jobs and their decisions to leave teaching, as well as strategies for retaining them in the profession by asking teachers who remained in teaching about their teaching assignments, aspects of their profession, time spent on various job tasks, and professional development opportunities and experiences.

U.S. Department of Education: Surveys of Repeated Cross Sections—National Assessment of Education Progress (NAEP)

http://nces.ed.gov/nationsreportcard

NAEP is often referred to as "the Nation's Report Card." The NAEP is the only nationally representative assessment of the nation's students in various subject areas, including reading, mathematics, science, writing, U.S. history, civics, geography, and the arts. In different years, different subjects are tested. Additional surveys of students, teachers, and administrators provide important data to link to the student achievement scores to understand students' instructional and school experiences. Many do not know that there are several different components to the national assessment, including the national NAEP, the state NAEP, and the long-term trend NAEP. The national NAEP provides information for the nation as a whole. A national sample of public and private schools is drawn, with students randomly selected within those schools to test achievement in grades 4, 8, and 12. The tests in these national data continue to change over time as technology, educational goals, and cultural concerns change over time.

Since 1990, the state NAEP has provided achievement and survey results for state representative samples of schools. Results from these state NAEP surveys can be used to make statements representative of each state. In 2002, combined samples of schools were drawn for both the state and national NAEP to reduce the burden on schools. To monitor trends in student achievement over time, one needs to ask the same thing over time. For such purposes, the NAEP long-term trend assessment is designed to provide information on changes in achievement of students aged nine, thirteen, and seventeen years old. Since the early 1970s, nationally representative samples are administered mathematics and reading tests, asking the same set of questions each time. Such procedures allow researchers to assess changes in achievement over time.

CHAPTER

QUANTITATIVE DATA ANALYSIS

MARYLYNN T. QUARTAROLI

KEY IDEAS

- Descriptive statistics provide important information about quantitative data.

- Patterns in quantitative data can be represented graphically and numerically.

- The type of data collected is a critical factor in determining which statistical tests are appropriate.

- Descriptive statistics reveal patterns in the distribution of quantitative data, plus measures of central tendency, variability, relative position, and relationship.

- Inferential statistics are used to determine whether the findings in a research study are due to chance alone.

- Critical to inferential statistics is the determination of statistical significance and effect size.

AS YOU will see throughout this text, researchers use many strategies to collect data in at least two distinctly different forms: numbers and words. **Quantitative data** are those scores, counts, values, or ratings that are recorded in, or can be transformed into, numbers; **qualitative data** are the words or images that are obtained from interviews, observations, written documents, photographs, artifacts, or recordings.

As a practitioner, you may never have to analyze data yourself for publication. But as a reader of research studies, if you want to determine whether you should incorporate the findings into your professional practice, it is important for you to determine not only the quality of the research design, but also how the data collected have been analyzed and represented in the published articles. Many readers are particularly intimidated by the statistics used to analyze quantitative data. In this chapter, I will explain some of the basic strategies that are used to interpret and represent the quantitative data collected by social scientists. I will also indicate what questions readers need to ask as they review published research reports.

WHAT DO THOSE NUMBERS MEAN?

Now you may already be saying to yourself: "I'm not good at math," "Don't confuse me with all those numbers," "I can't make sense of all those tables and graphs," or "Statistic is just a synonym for sadistic." But wait, do not despair—the field of statistics is not really a foreign land with an incomprehensible language, as you might think.

Although it is true that there are many highly sophisticated statistical techniques used to analyze numerical data, a familiarity with the basic foundations of quantitative data analysis will go a long way toward facilitating your comprehension and evaluation of published research articles. Be forewarned: By reading this chapter you may not be able to analyze, or even interpret, all the numerical data presented by researchers. Further study, either by taking one or more statistics courses, or by working your way through some of the cited and recommended texts at the end of the chapter, is required to develop a more thorough understanding of quantitative data analysis, enabling you to more critically evaluate the researchers' use of statistical procedures and their interpretation of the results.

With that said, let us begin to examine what all those numbers, tables, and graphs in published research articles might be telling us.

Meanings of Numbers

A number is a number is a number . . . right? Not exactly. Although we have all had experience with the arithmetic meanings of numbers and counting since kindergarten, depending upon the context within which these are used, numbers can represent different types of data.

On a typical day, you might pick up the morning newspaper and find the results of opinion polls on the front page, indicating what citizens believe about the government's economic or foreign policies. You check out the weather forecast to find the predicted high and low temperatures for the day. You turn to the sports pages to find out how your favorite basketball team is doing in the standings. Finally, you look at the movie reviews to help you select which movie you want to see that night. As you drive to school, you check your watch and your wallet to see if you have the time and cash to stop at the local coffee shop to get a latte to help you stay awake in class. Your teacher returns a graded test that you took last week. You spend some time on the computer completing the end-of-term evaluations of your courses before you go home. You have been generating or analyzing different types of quantitative data all day long. With some examples and explanations provided in the next sections, you will be able to understand how researchers also analyze and interpret similar types of quantitative data.

SUMMARIZING DATA: DESCRIPTIVE STATISTICS

The use of **descriptive statistics** is the first step in analyzing quantitative data. As the name implies, these are strategies for representing and summarizing collected data to provide a basic description of that data, including any patterns or trends. In some studies, such as survey research (discussed in Chapter Five), these may be the only procedures used to summarize the data. Most studies analyze quantitative data using descriptive statistics. Therefore it is very important to understand what these statistics represent. What are these procedures likely to be?

Frequency Distributions

Let's suppose that I am interested in finding out if there are any gender enrollment patterns in classes that have thirty-five students in the political science department. I find that there are only six classes that have an enrollment of thirty-five this semester. I count the number of female and male students in each of those classes. How will I show my findings to others?

There are a number of different techniques for representing how often each condition, score, or event occurs; these are called **frequency distributions**. One way is to create a table of all **values**, the numerical representation of quantities, such as Table 6.1, to present the findings, listing each class and the number of females and males in each.

From this table, readers can see that in the American and World Politics courses, the gender distribution tends to be about the same. The Environmental Politics course seems to attract more females than males, whereas the pattern is reversed in the State Politics course. Local and Native American Politics courses appear to be highly preferred by males and females, respectively.

However, if the data set was very large, representing many, many classrooms (as would be likely if I examined all 150 classes across campus that had an enrollment of thirty-five total students, for example), the resulting table would be very long indeed. It would take several pages just to list all the classes and the student counts. To make it easier to look for patterns, simpler ways to represent the data are necessary. One solution to this challenge would be to group the data into ranges representing different numbers

TABLE 6.1. **Frequency Table of Number of Males and Females in Political Science Classes with Thirty-Five Students**

Class	# Females	# Males
American Politics	17	18
Environmental Politics	22	13
Local Politics	5	30
World Politics	19	16
Native American Politics	33	2
State Politics	11	24
Totals	107	103

of female students in the classes. Because the total enrollment is thirty-five students, I might decide to create five categories (in this example, simply because thirty-five is divisible by five). This would result in the following groups: classes with very few female students (less than 7), classes with fewer females than males (7–13), classes with approximately the same number of females and males (14–20), classes with mostly females (21–27), and classes with almost all female students (more than 28). A grouped frequency table similar to Table 6.2 presents these results.

From this table, readers can see that most classes of thirty-five students have equal numbers of females and males (79 classes with 14–20 females), with fewer classes having mostly female students (22 classes with 21–27 females, and only 5 with 28 or more females), as compared to those with mostly male students (35 classes with 7–13 females, and only 9 with 0–6 females).

For some people, reading tables is not initially very clear, especially if the data are much more extensive or complicated than these examples. A picture or graphical representation might be helpful to use; one choice is a **histogram** (a bar graph of a frequency distribution), as in Figure 6.1.

TABLE 6.2. **Grouped Frequency Table of Female Students in Classes with Thirty-Five Students**

Number of Female Students	Number of Classes
0–6	9
7–13	35
14–20	79
21–27	22
28 or more	5

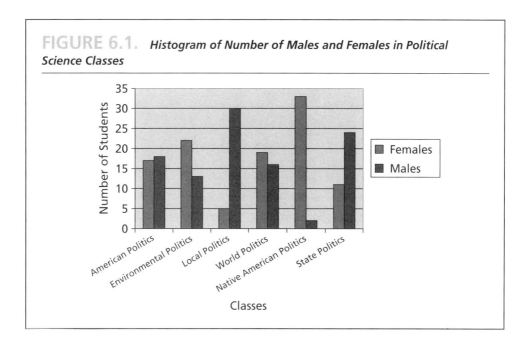

FIGURE 6.1. *Histogram of Number of Males and Females in Political Science Classes*

Another choice for representing the same data is a **frequency polygon** (a graph of a frequency distribution with the data points joined by straight lines), as shown in Figure 6.2.

Because the lines in this frequency polygon crisscross several times, some readers might find this confusing to interpret and therefore prefer the histogram. Both reveal the same patterns in the data as in the original table—which classes have approximately equal numbers of males and females and which are greatly preferred by one gender.

One thing that is apparent in this example is that the Native American Politics class has an unusually large number of females, compared to the other classes in the set of data. In this study, this class is an **outlier**, a count which does not fit into the general pattern of values collected; in this case it is extremely large. Another outlier might be when a value is extremely small, as it is in the number of females in the Local Politics class. This is an important piece of information to notice that is clearly evident in the graphic displays; it will radically affect the mathematical calculations on this data, as you will see in a later section of the chapter.

Distribution Patterns

Let's graphically reexamine the data on the number of females in 150 classes with enrollments of thirty-five students, and grouped in Table 6.2. Using a histogram (see Figure 6.3), the reader can clearly see a pattern: most classes have 14–20 female students. The number of classes with progressively more or fewer females tapers off in both directions from this high point, with very few classes representing the extreme cases of almost all or almost no female students.

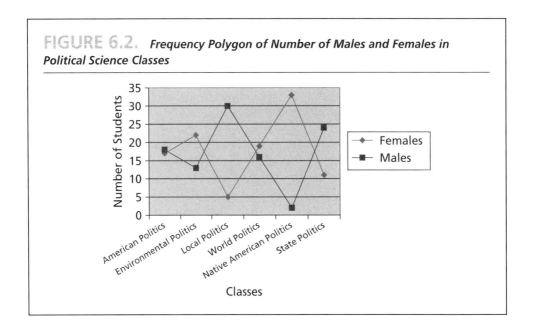

FIGURE 6.2. *Frequency Polygon of Number of Males and Females in Political Science Classes*

This type of distribution pattern commonly occurs when larger numbers of values are collected. In published research, this general pattern may be displayed not as a histogram; rather, the histogram is converted into a frequency polygon, by connecting the data points using straight lines, as shown in Figure 6.4.

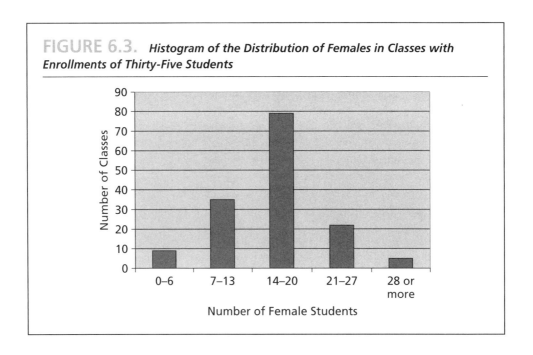

FIGURE 6.3. *Histogram of the Distribution of Females in Classes with Enrollments of Thirty-Five Students*

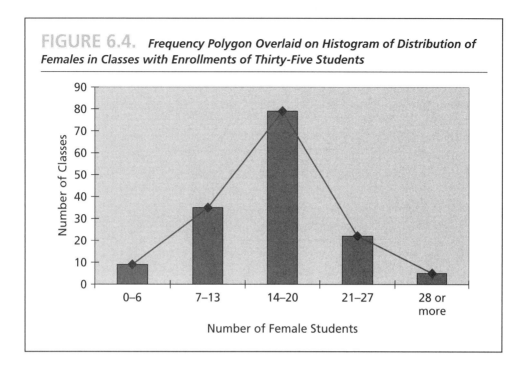

FIGURE 6.4. *Frequency Polygon Overlaid on Histogram of Distribution of Females in Classes with Enrollments of Thirty-Five Students*

The straight lines in the frequency polygon are then smoothed into a curve and the histogram bars are removed, as shown for this data in Figure 6.5.

As you can see, this distribution pattern approximates the shape of a bell, with the most common values clustered in the center of the distribution, tapering off smoothly toward the minimum and maximum possible values. With larger sets of data, this shape becomes even more symmetrical, with each side of the curve as a mirror image of the other. I collected data from a group of only 150 classes; but what would happen if I examined a collection of data, a **data set**, with many more cases? For example, 550,000 students take the General Test of the Graduate Record Examinations every year. Graphing the scores of all these students should produce a very smooth pattern indeed, with the highest point on the curve, representing the most frequent scores (or **mode**), in the middle of the distribution, and with substantially fewer students scoring much higher or lower than the predominant group. The result would be a perfect bell-shaped curve.

Statisticians refer to a perfectly symmetrical, bell-shaped curve as a **normal curve** (see left curve in Figure 6.6); as explained in the next sections, a normal curve has important characteristics, and any changes from a normal distribution affect the statistical choices that researchers have available for quantitative data analysis.

But sometimes, plotting the data does *not* result in a normal curve. If I had counted the number of females in classes in an engineering program, rather than all across the campus, most classes would probably have few female students. Or, if I counted the number of females in classes in a women's studies program, I would probably find that most classes had high numbers of female students. Curves of these data sets would be lopsided, rather than bell shaped. I would describe these distributions as

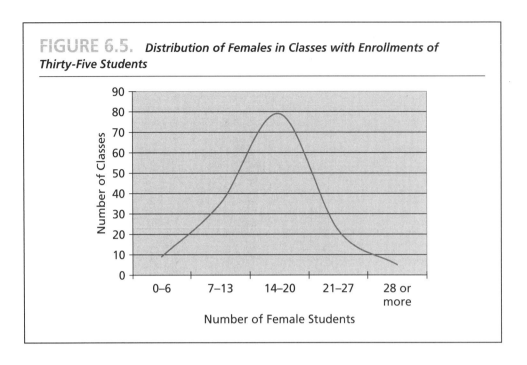

FIGURE 6.5.   *Distribution of Females in Classes with Enrollments of Thirty-Five Students*

asymmetrical distributions and refer to the curves as skewed. For the engineering classes, the curve would look similar to the one in the middle of Figure 6.6 and be described as positively skewed, with a longer leg or "tail" sloping toward the left side of this graph, because few classes would have high numbers of females and many classes would have low numbers of females. For the women's studies classes, the curve would look like the one on the far right in Figure 6.6, because there are not as many classes with low numbers of females. This data is negatively skewed; in this case, the longer leg or "tail" extends more toward the side of the graph with few female students. Therefore, the idea of skewed distributions or skewness refers to distributions

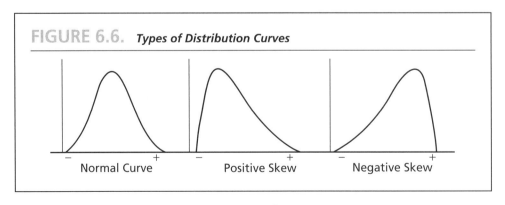

FIGURE 6.6.   *Types of Distribution Curves*

Source: Gene V Glass, personal communication, December 11, 2007.

in which more of the data fall toward one side or the other of the graph, rather than being normally distributed.

Not all distributions of data result in curves with only one peak, or mode, where the most common value occurs. For example, student evaluations of courses often show about the same numbers of students who like the professor and those who do not, with very few students feeling neutral. When graphed (see Figure 6.7), these data result in a curve with two peaks and a "valley" in between; this is known as a **bimodal distribution**, in which there are two values that are most common, representing two modes.

Why is determining the shape of the data distribution pattern important for both researchers and readers of research to know? It is because the procedures of many **statistical tests** (different mathematical calculations used to analyze and interpret the numerical data), which will be explained in subsequent sections of the chapter, assume that the distribution is normal. This means that when graphed, the data look very much like the normal, bell-shaped curve. If it is skewed or bimodal, other statistical choices must be made to adequately interpret the data.

Types of Numerical Data

Before beginning to understand the statistical tests commonly used to analyze and interpret quantitative data, you need to recognize that there are different types of numerical data. In the opening section of this chapter describing a typical day in your life as a student, I mentioned many different numbers that you regularly encounter. The

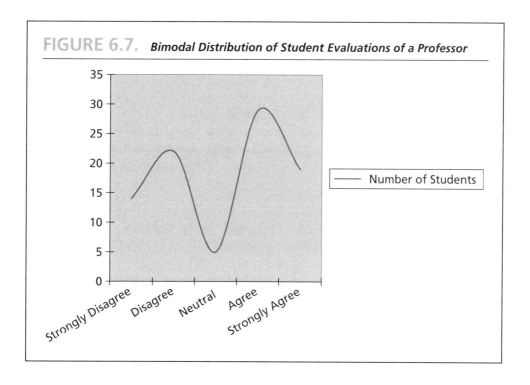

FIGURE 6.7. *Bimodal Distribution of Student Evaluations of a Professor*

selection of statistical tests depends upon which type of numerical data is collected. As a reader of research, you should be able to identify the type of data collected, because this is one key factor in determining if the statistics used in the report are appropriate.

As in the previous examples of the gender of students in classes, some things can be counted as belonging in one and only one category. A person is either male or female. There was no option for some intermediate label. Similarly, another category or label might name a person's marital status: single, divorced, married, or widowed. This scale of measurement generates **nominal data,** essentially counting the membership in distinct, named categories; it may also be called **categorical data.**

Returning to the examples of collecting and interpreting quantitative data that you might be doing on a typical day, on the sports page, you look for your favorite basketball team's current position in the National Basketball Association (NBA) list of standings. Your team is a member of only one conference in the league—either the Eastern Conference or the Western Conference. This is another example of nominal data. To see how well your team is doing, you would be able to find your team and its statistics listed only in the appropriate conference.

You looked at the movie reviews in the newspaper, which often use one or more stars (or "thumbs-up" symbols) to indicate how good the reviewer believes these movies to be. The morning newspaper also reported the results of opinion polls on citizens' beliefs about the current government's economic and foreign policies. When you filled out the end-of-the class evaluation form, you were also participating in an opinion poll about your class. You were asked to indicate your level of agreement with several statements or prompts, such as "My instructor is interested in helping me be successful in this class," "My instructor is very knowledgeable about this subject," or "I would take another class from this instructor." Many polls and evaluation forms ask the respondents to indicate their level of agreement with these types of statements or prompts using a scale of "strongly agree, agree, neutral, disagree, or strongly disagree." All of these ratings or indications of rank represent **ordinal** data. Your newspaper will also report many other kinds of ordinal data, such as who finished first, second, or third in the county spelling bee or in the high school graduating class.

What makes ordinal data unique is that the levels of performance for the rankings are not necessarily equally spaced. As an example, you may read the reviews of a single movie by several different critics; one may assign four stars, another may give it three stars, and one may only give the movie one star. You can see that the criteria for assigning number of stars are probably not the same for all three reviewers. Similarly, on course evaluations, the difference between "strongly agree" and "agree" is not likely to be the same amount for all students. Therefore, interpreting what rankings actually mean requires a reader to be cautious, recognizing that differences between levels of measurement may not be equal.

As a student, you are very familiar with another type of data. In the typical day example, you received results back on a test that you took in class. You can add this score to your total points earned in the course so far this semester. You can also average the scores you made on all the tests. These calculations will give you an idea about how you are doing in the class. If you compared a score of 80 with a score of 85, this difference of 5 points should represent the same difference in levels of performance as the difference between a score of 65 and a score of 70. However, a score of 0 really doesn't indicate a complete lack of knowledge, nor does a score of 100 indicate a complete mastery of the content. Neither does a score of 100 mean that you know twice as much as another student who scored 50 on the test.

Your newspaper reported yesterday's high and low temperatures, the projected high and low temperatures for today, and the average daily temperature. Like test scores, for temperatures each degree also represents an equally sized increment of difference. But if it is winter, you can see that for the Fahrenheit and Celsius scales, a temperature of 0 does not mean there is no heat. In fact, the newspaper may report a temperature below zero. Both properties (equally spaced intervals between values and no absolute zero) are characteristics of **interval** data.

But what about stopping to buy that latte at the coffee shop? What types of quantitative data are time and money? The difference between each interval is the same; the difference between 5 and 6 is the same as between 11 and 12. Each minute represents the same amount of time. You can figure out what your average income is and the difference between the cost of the coffee and how much cash you have in your pocket. You can also calculate the average time it takes you to drive to class and the difference between the time it is now and when class starts. So, like interval data, time and money represent equal intervals of value; but unlike interval data, there is a possibility of absolute zero. You could have no time and no money.

For time and money, you can also correctly say that 12 is twice as much money as 6 and 15 minutes is one-fourth of an hour. If your favorite basketball team has played 49 games and won 31 of these so far, you can calculate that the team's winning percentage is 63.3 percent by dividing 31 by 49. In my study of class gender patterns, I can use the same strategy to calculate the percentage of females in each political science class, and in all the political science classes combined. These calculations are all indicating ratio relationships in the numbers; therefore, this type of data is known as **ratio** data. Height and weight are also commonly reported ratio data. If a child weighs 55 pounds and his mother weighs 110 pounds, the child's weight is 50 percent of the mother's. If the child is 4 feet tall and his father is 6 feet tall, the father's height is 1.5 times the child's height.

These four types of measurement scales (nominal, ordinal, interval, and ratio) are summarized in Table 6.3.

It is important for you to identify the kinds of data used in research in order to determine whether researchers selected the appropriate statistical tests to analyze and interpret their findings. In the variety of simple statistical procedures described below, pay attention to which kinds of data are most appropriately analyzed using these calculations.

Measures of Central Tendency

As illustrated earlier in the chapter, the frequency distributions of females in political science classes and across the university revealed several different patterns in the data;

TABLE 6.3. **Scales of Measurement with Descriptions and Examples**

Scale or Type of Data	Description	Examples
Nominal	Categories or labels	Gender, sport team division membership, marital status
Ordinal	Rankings	Race results (1st, 2nd, 3rd . . .), rank in graduating class, preferences or opinions
Interval	Equally spaced values; no absolute zero	Test scores, Fahrenheit and Celsius temperature scales
Ratio	Equally spaced values; absolute zero is possible	Time, money, frequency counts (wins/losses; females/males), age, weight, height

in some classes there were many more females than males, and in other classes the opposite was true. But to summarize these gender patterns, I will need to find a way to represent a *typical* classroom. One method is to mathematically determine the central tendency, or average, number of females and males in classes. Although there are three measures of central tendency that are commonly used (mean, median, and mode), you are most likely to encounter the mean as representative of the average, or typical, value.

Mean   Look back at the frequency counts of students in political science classrooms in Table 6.1. In six classrooms, each with 35 students, I counted 107 females and 103 males, for a total of 210 students. Dividing the number of female students (107) by the number of classrooms (6) yields an average of 17.8 females in the *typical* classroom; making a similar calculation shows that there are typically 17.2 males per classroom. These two values represent the **mean** number, an arithmetic average, of males and females in the data set.

In reality, it is not possible to have fractions of a person, either male or female; but from the means, you would expect that most classrooms would have approximately 18 females and 17 males (rounding the decimals to the nearest whole numbers). You know from the frequency counts that this is not exactly true. If you look at how many females are actually in each classroom (5, 11, 17, 19, 22, and 33), you'll notice that there are actually no classrooms with 18 females; one did have 17 and one did have 19. Similarly, there were 2, 13, 16, 18, 24, and 30 males in the six classrooms; no classroom had 17, but one did have 16 and one had 18. Even though in some classes there were many more or less females and males, overall the typical class has *on average* 18 females and 17 males.

The mean is undoubtedly the most common descriptive statistic reported in the research literature. The symbol used to represent the mean is an X with a bar above it, $\overline{X}$, or a capital M in some publications. Means are often reported for opinion polls and surveys (ordinal data), a group of test scores (interval data), and average ages or incomes (ratio data).

Median   Earlier in the chapter, I hypothesized that the gender distribution in class-rooms of a women's studies program would likely be skewed, with most classes having large numbers of female students. Table 6.4 is a sample data set for the seven classes with thirty-five enrolled students in this program.

Making the calculation as explained in the previous section, the mean number of females in these seven classes is about 25 (actually 24.6). The number of females in these classes arranged in order from highest to lowest results in this sequence: 33, 30, 29, 28, 27, 17, and 8. You can see that five of the seven classes have more than 25 females, none have 25, and two have much fewer than 25 female students. It appears that the mean does not really represent what is typical in the classrooms. The midpoint in this series, another way to visualize the center of a distribution, is 28 females. This is a closer representation of what is the typical situation in the women's studies classrooms than the mean.

This measure of central tendency is called the **median** (symbol is *Mdn*). This is the value that represents the exact midpoint in the data, when the values are arranged from highest to lowest. Half of the scores or values will be higher than the median and 50 percent of the scores or values will be lower than the median. To remember what a statistical median is, some students find it helpful to remember the location of the median of a road—in the middle. As illustrated in the above example, the median is a better measure than the mean to indicate the central tendency, or typical condition, if a data set is skewed. Authors might report median values on ordinal, interval, or ratio data sets.

What happens when two data sets have the same means? Looking at Table 6.5 for the test scores for two classes, you will see that the mean test score in each class is 73.41.

TABLE 6.4. **Frequency Table of Students in Women's Studies Classes with Thirty-Five Students**

Class	# Females	# Males
Introduction to Gender Studies	28	10
Sociology of Gender	27	8
Domestic Violence and Criminal Justice	8	27
Women, Health, and Healing	30	5
Race, Gender, and the Media	17	18
Gender and Indigenous Representation	29	6
History of Feminist Movements	33	2
Totals	*172*	*76*

TABLE 6.5. **Test Scores in Two Classrooms**

Class X	Class Y
97	93
96	92
89	86
88	85
86	84
85	84
85	83
83	82
82	82
82	80
79	75
79	75
78	74
78	74
77	74
77	73
76	73
76	72
75	72
75	72
74	71
74	70
66	67
65	67
65	66
64	65
64	65
63	64
58	63

(Table 6.5, continued)

56	60	
31	55	
26	51	
73.41	**73.41**	**Mean**

The 32 test scores in each class are arranged from the highest to the lowest. Because there is an even number of scores in these classes, there is no single score that is right in the exact middle of the distribution. The 16th and 17th scores in each list are closest to the midpoint. In Class X these scores are 77 and 76; in Class Y these are both 73. To find the median, you should find the arithmetic average of these two scores. Therefore, the median for Class X is 76.5 (halfway between 76 and 77); the median for Class Y is 73. The median and mean for Class Y are very close to the same value (73 and 73.41), but this is not the case for Class X. Depending upon how the scores in data sets are distributed, the means and medians may or may not be close to the same.

The more different the means and medians, the less likely that the data are distributed in a normal curve. Thus, even without a graph, a reader of research can interpret whether a distribution is normal if both the mean and median are reported by the authors. The farther apart these values are, the more skewed, or asymmetrical, the distribution is, making it more difficult to interpret what the "typical" condition is using the mean alone.

Mode   As mentioned in the section about the shapes of distributions, the **mode** is the value or score in a data set that occurs most frequently. Many students find it helpful to use the alliteration "mode is most" to remember how to find this statistic. In the political science classroom gender data set (see Table 6.1), there is no specific number of females that occurs in more than one classroom. Therefore, there is no mode. In some data sets, there may be more than one mode. In Table 6.5, there are many pairs of test scores for Classroom X, but no score occurs more than twice in the list. Classroom Y has two modes: there are three scores of 74 and three scores of 72. These conditions are not uncommon in data sets—there may be no mode, two modes, or many modes. In general, the mode simply summarizes the frequency of a single value or score; therefore, it is somewhat imprecise and is not often found in the research literature, except to describe shapes of distributions when these are bimodal (having two common values) or multimodal (having more than two common values).

Measures of Variability

Frequency distributions and different measures of central tendency, or averages, are two descriptive statistics measures that represent data sets. However, these do not provide a complete picture of the distributions. Another important consideration is how much **variability** there is in the data sets—that is, how spread out or clustered together the values are.

Reconsider the test scores from Classroom X and Classroom Y (see Table 6.5). The top scores are different, as are the lowest scores for these classes. But how much do the test scores really vary between these two classes?

Range   By far the simplest way to measure variability is to calculate the **range**; this is the difference between the highest and lowest scores in this data set. For Class X, the high score (97) minus the lowest score (26) is 71; for Class Y, the high score of 93 minus the low score of 51 is 42. The variability in test scores in Class X is apparently quite large, with a range of 71; Class Y's scores are much less variable, with a range of only 42. Unfortunately, the value for this measure can change a great deal if only one score (either endpoint—the highest or the lowest score) changes. Because the range also ignores the values of the scores between the endpoints, this statistic is not commonly used and there is no common symbol. Most often, you will find researchers reporting the variability in a data set using the standard deviation, explained in the next section.

Standard Deviation   In the discussion of ordinal data, I suggested that you generate this kind of data all the time when you rate your instructors on a course evaluation form. Let's say that the form is using a 5-point scale (5 = strongly agree, 4 = agree, 3 = neutral, 2 = disagree, and 1 = strongly disagree) and the mean for "My instructor is interested in helping me be successful in this class" is 3.2, with a standard deviation of 1.0. How should your instructor interpret this information? Does he assume that he is doing all right in this area because his rating is slightly on the "agree" side of the scale? To interpret this result, he needs to know what the standard deviation of 1.0 means.

The **standard deviation** is the average distance between each of the values in a distribution and the mean of that distribution. Now what does that mean? Think of it this way. We are trying to show the amount of variability in a data set. We know that the arithmetical average, the mean, is one measure of the central tendency of the data. Then, we need to consider the average amount by which the rest of the scores vary, or deviate, from this mean. The larger the value of the standard deviation, the more variability is present in the data set. The instructor looking over his evaluation reports should be careful to note that the standard deviation value of 1.0 represents a large proportion of a 5-point scale. He should expect that the *typical* student rated him between 2.2 (mean of 3.2−standard deviation 1.0) and 4.2 (mean of 3.2 + standard deviation 1.0). Therefore, he should be aware that some students disagree that he is interested in their success, some are neutral, and others agree. For those of you who need to see how a standard deviation is calculated, I refer you to the statistical texts listed at the end of the chapter.

It is enough to say that researchers report both the means and standard deviations of interval (such as test scores) and ratio (such as frequency counts) data as numbers, typically including decimals. The larger the value of the standard deviation, the more widely the values in the data set deviate from the mean. Two symbols may be used in research reports to represent standard deviations, *SD* or σ (the lowercase Greek letter sigma), so you should keep your eye out for either one.

For the test scores in Table 6.5 the means are the same (73.41) but the standard deviations are quite different (15.46 for Class X and 9.93 for Class Y). What does this tell you? It says that even though the class averages are identical, the distributions of the scores are much more varied for Class X as compared to Class Y, as predicted from the range calculations. But the SD is a statistic that does not change dramatically with the value of a single endpoint. And because it is calculated using all of the data points (in this case, all the test scores), it is much preferred by researchers as representative of the entire group of data, rather than just the highest and lowest scores. But what does a standard deviation look like, and why is a normal distribution of the data assumed to be the case when calculating this statistic?

Relationship Between Normal Curve and Standard Deviation   Let's stop for a moment to reconsider the normal curve discussed earlier. If the values in a data set are distributed normally, the mean, median, and mode are all located at the very center of the bulge and the legs, or "tails," of the graph are evenly sloping away from the mean in each direction. "There is a special relationship between the mean and the standard deviation with regard to the area contained under the curve" (Pagano, 2001, p. 83), as illustrated in Figure 6.8. In this diagram, the central tendency measure (for simplicity's sake, called the mean) is designated by the value μ (lowercase Greek letter mu) and the number of standard deviations away from the mean is shown as $\pm 1\sigma, 2\sigma, 3\sigma$, and beyond.

You will notice that 68.2 percent of the area under the curve is within one standard deviation on each side of the mean (34.1 percent on each side of the mean, the darkest shaded areas). For the instructor looking at his evaluation ratings, this means that about 68 percent of the students rated him between 2.2 and 4.2 on his interest in helping students be successful in class.

If this relationship between the mean and the standard deviation is applied to the Class X and Class Y test scores (assuming that the distributions are normal) in Table 6.5,

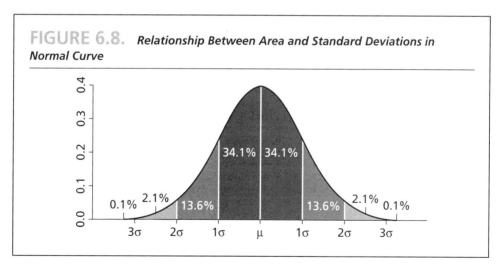

FIGURE 6.8.   *Relationship Between Area and Standard Deviations in Normal Curve*

Source: Creative Commons Attribution 2.5, licensee for Wikipedia; modified by P. Strandmark, April 7, 2007.

68 percent of the students would score within one standard deviation of the mean. For Class X, you should expect that 68 percent of the students will score between 57.95 (M 73.41 − SD 15.46) and 88.87 (M 73.41 + SD 15.46). For Class Y, you should expect about 68 percent of the students to score between 63.48 and 83.34. You could project further that 95.4 percent of the students would score within two standard deviations (includes 34.1 percent + 13.6 percent = 47.7 percent on each side of the mean) and 99.6 percent (adds an additional 2.1 percent to each side) within three standard deviations. Even farther away from the mean, the legs of the graph would never quite reach the horizontal axis, but would apply to much, much smaller percentages of students.

But what does this relationship between normal distributions, means, and standard deviations show? I'll explain in the next section.

Measures of Relative Position

If you were told that your IQ was 132, would you be happy? The number really does not mean anything by itself (although it sounds wonderful when you are used to receiving test scores in class with a maximum value of 100); you must have a reference against which to compare the score. For that, you would need to know something about relative positions of scores, and that is what the normal curve, the mean, and standard deviations are used to show. There are several measures that are commonly reported for test results in the research literature; among these are percentile ranks and standard scores. The underlying assumptions are that the distribution of values or scores is normal and that the measurement scale is either interval or ratio.

Percentile Rank   Imagine that you are a parent; you receive the following results from the annual achievement test that your third-grade child took this year in school. Among the many numbers that are included on the report form, you notice the following confusing values:

Percentile:	84
z score:	+1.0
T score:	60
Stanine:	7
Grade Equivalent Score:	9.6

How are you to interpret this? These numbers look to be very inconsistent. Is your child doing well? Should you be concerned and schedule a meeting with the teacher? It is amazing how many different numbers there are to represent your child's performance on a single test.

The first value recorded is a percentile of 84. Does this one mean that your child got 84 percent of the questions correct? This is what you might think from the number and from your past experience with taking tests in classes. But unlike a percent, which represents the proportion of correct answers on a test, a **percentile rank** indicates the percentage of test scores that fall below a particular score. For example, a percentile rank of 97 means that this score is higher than 97 percent of all the scores earned on this test; it does *not* mean that the test taker answered 97 percent of the questions on the test correctly.

Examine Figure 6.9 carefully; the longest vertical line represents the mean of the distribution. If you look at the standard deviations scale on the figure, you will see that the SD for the mean is zero. There are shorter lines to the right and left of the mean, representing $\pm$ 1, 2, 3, and 4 SD (labeled σ) away from the mean. The percentile rank values are shown below the scales for the standard deviations and cumulative percentages. Remember—the middle point (median) in a set of scores has 50 percent of the scores higher than the mean and 50 percent lower than this value, which also corresponds to the 50th percentile. One standard deviation above this value (+ 34 percent) is approximately the 84th percentile (adding 34 to 50); one standard deviation below the mean (34 percent) is roughly the 16th percentile (subtracting 34 from 50). You can see on the graph that your child's 84th percentile aligns with SD + 1.0, as you would predict from this calculation.

Standard Scores   First of all, you should know that the achievement tests typically given in school are **standardized**; this means that the tests are given to many groups of students across the country under identical conditions, and the **raw scores** (how many questions each student got right in each section of the test) are plotted on a graph. To

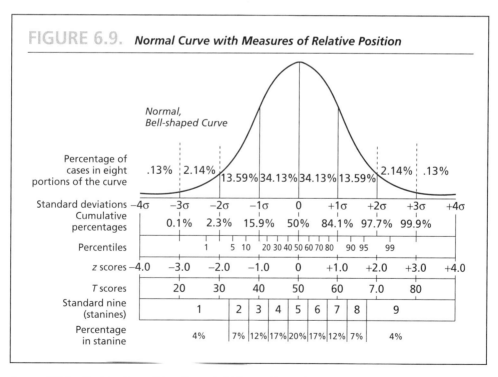

FIGURE 6.9.   *Normal Curve with Measures of Relative Position*

Source: Wikipedia, http://en.wikipedia.org/wiki/Image:PRtoNCE.JPG, 2007.

make comparing the results between different sections of the test and between different groups of students easier, the raw scores are then converted to standard scores.

A **standard score** represents how far a raw score is from the center of the distribution. These can be written several different ways: z scores, T scores, stanines, and normal curve equivalents. If you look at the values of the z **scores**, for example, you will see that these are equivalent to the values of the standard deviations from the mean, except that these are not marked with σ. If you look back at the test results in the example above, you will notice that your child's z score is 1.0. How would you interpret this test score?

Find the T **scores** on the graph in Figure 6.9; you can see that these are direct mathematical conversions of the z scores, so that the mean is 50, rather than 0, and each standard deviation is $\pm$ 10 units, not $\pm$ 1.0, 2.0, 3.0, or 4.0. For your child with a z score of +1.0, the T score is 60, which is 10 points above the mean.

Stanine scores are another type of conversion of z scores. In this case, the normal distribution is divided into nine equal parts (the "standard nine" thus "stanine"), each of which is equal to one-half, or .5, of a standard deviation. How might you interpret your child's stanine score of 7?

Grade Equivalent Score   The final number on your third grader's achievement test report form is 9.6 for a grade equivalent. This is perhaps the most often misinterpreted score on the report. A **grade equivalent score** represents a student's knowledge and ability expressed in terms of grade level in school; for example, a value of 7.5 would mean seventh grade, fifth month. So, you might think that your third grader's 9.6 grade equivalent score means that you should immediately transfer your child to the ninth grade. Nothing could be farther from the truth! This score is correctly interpreted to mean that the score your child earned is likely to be the same score earned by a student in the ninth grade, sixth month taking the same test your child did. It is *not* saying that your child can do ninth-grade, sixth-month level work. In fact, the test your child took had mostly third-grade-level work on it. What a grade equivalent score of 9.6 does tell you is that your third grader is working well above the average third-grade student, which you also know from the other reported standard scores.

Your IQ Score   Now, back to the question at the beginning of this section of the chapter about measures of relative position: Would you be happy to find out that your IQ score is 132? You should now suspect that you need to know the mean score and the standard deviation for this test in order to interpret your performance. If the Wechsler IQ test was the one you took, the mean for this distribution is 100 and the standard deviation is 15. What stanine score and percentile rank would this represent?

Measures of Relationship

So far, I have been discussing statistics that researchers use to describe the characteristics or traits of categories, groups, or individuals. A final component in examining a data set is to determine if there are any relationships between these factors or variables.

A **variable** is anything on which humans can vary. Said another way, it is "a concept that can assume any one of a range of values, for example, intelligence, height, test score, and the like" (Gay, Mills, & Airasian, 2006, p. 11). Other variables you might think of are age, income level, gender, ethnicity, attitudes, motivation, and many other characteristics. The chapters on experimental, nonexperimental, and survey research (Chapters Three, Four, and Five) provide more complete explanations of the different types of variables.

Correlation   As a basketball fan, you might be thinking about where your team ranks in the standings and wonder if the team would perform better and improve in the rankings if the owners of the team spent more money on player salaries. This is a question that is looking for a possible relationship between team performance and salary expenditures; in other words, you would like to see if there is a predictable pattern, or **correlation**, in the relationship between player salaries and the team's position in the National Basketball Association standings.

A researcher could help you by collecting the average salaries and rankings for each team and calculating a **correlation coefficient**, a numerical value indicating both the degree and direction of a relationship. There are a number of different statistical calculations that can be used to express a correlation; among the most commonly used are the Spearman rho and the Pearson *r*. Exactly what these are or how they are calculated is not critical at this point; you can find out how to do it in any of the textbooks listed at the end of this chapter.

What you *do* need to know is whether the correlation is positive or negative. Consider possible relationships between team performance and player salaries. If the researcher finds out that the more money the team owner spends on player salaries, the better the team does in the rankings, this is a positive correlation. However, if the findings indicate that increased player salaries result in a poorer showing in the standings, this is a negative correlation.

Correlation coefficients can range in value from +1.00 to −1.00. The closer the value is to 1.00, the stronger the relationship whether it is positive or negative; a value of 0 indicates that there is no relationship at all. Values of 0.80 or higher indicate strong relationships; moderately high correlations have values of 0.60 to 0.80, with values less than 0.60 indicative of a less than clear relationship. In a study of the NBA salaries and team wins, Berri, Schmidt, and Brook (2006) found a correlation coefficient of .39. How would you interpret the correlation?

In reading research that examines the relationship between factors or variables, you should keep one axiom in mind: Correlation is *not* causation. Even if the sports salary researcher reported a correlation coefficient of .75, this doesn't necessarily mean that the high player salaries *caused* the team to perform better; it only means that there appears to be a moderately high positive relationship between the two variables: salaries and successful performance.

To emphasize that caution is necessary when interpreting correlation results, Pagano (2001) described a newspaper article he read that reported a positive correlation between obesity and female crime. Does that mean that if a woman gains forty pounds, she will become a criminal? Conversely, does it mean women criminals are doomed to be obese? Of course not. The researchers (and the reader) should consider what other factors might be contributing to a positive correlation.

Another way to examine which variables might relate to particular outcomes is to use regression analysis, as described in the chapter on nonexperimental research (Chapter Four). Regression calculations allow researchers to use data sets to predict the value of one variable when the value of another variable is known. You have had experience doing a similar task when you were asked to interpret a line graph; given a value on the horizontal axis, you project the corresponding value on the vertical axis. For a more complete discussion of regression analysis, refer to one of the suggested texts at the end of this chapter.

More sophisticated statistical techniques examine multiple factors simultaneously for multiple correlations and multiple regressions; you may find these in your reading. Just remember to ask yourself what the researchers are trying to do: show the direction and strength of the relationship (correlation), as in the basketball salaries and team performance, or use one variable to predict values for another variable (regression)?

Descriptive Statistics Are Important

Let me end this section of the chapter by stressing the importance of descriptive statistics in research studies. In many cases, analyses of quantitative data stop here. As you can see from the above explanations, we can get a lot of information from the data sets just by using descriptive statistics. Researchers decide to take the next step into inferential statistics if their intention is to examine whether or not the results of the research are due strictly to chance, as you will see in the next section.

 REFLECTION QUESTIONS

1. How are the values for these three measures of central tendency (mean, median, and mode) the same? How are they different?

2. What would happen to the values of the mean and the median of the income of students in your class if Bill Gates suddenly decided to enroll?

3. Why is knowing the standard deviation important when interpreting the findings in a research study with quantitative data? Think of an analogy you can use to explain the concept of standard deviation to your partner.

4. In your professional practice, what factors or variables might be useful to examine for possible relationships?

GENERALIZING RESULTS: INFERENTIAL STATISTICS

If correlation does not indicate causality, as discussed in the preceding section, then what type of statistics might be used to suggest that one or more variables *do* cause changes in other variables? As a reader of research, you should consider the purposes of the different research methodologies explored in the chapters in this text; not all research attempts to determine or "prove" causal relationships. But some methodologies, such as experimental or nonexperimental research, *do* intend to establish cause-and-effect relationships.

Pretend that you are the head of the Community Outreach Unit in an urban police department. You are interested in finding out if the new version of Drug Abuse Resistance Education (D.A.R.E.) program is effective in reducing both violent and drug offenses by middle school students. It will take a lot of personnel time and money to retrain the D.A.R.E. officers in your unit to use the new instructional techniques and equipment, and you want to be assured that it is worth the effort before you suggest it to your superiors and the local school district. You find information about the new program online and in several published research studies. What do you look for in these reports to help you make your decision?

The question to be answered is this: "Are any differences between the outcome variables (number of middle school drug and violent offenses) due to the intervention (the new D.A.R.E. program) under study, or could the differences simply be due to chance?" This is the question that inferential statistics can answer.

Tests of Significance

All inferential statistical procedures test the **null hypothesis**, which is a statement or prediction that there will be *no* true differences between groups or factors and that any differences found are due strictly to chance. In the D.A.R.E. example, the null hypothesis would state that there are no differences in the number of drug and violent offenses committed by middle school students who receive the new D.A.R.E. training, as compared to middle school students who receive no D.A.R.E. training or who receive an older version of it. In some research reports, the authors might write their hypotheses in an alternative format, stating the effect that they *expect* to find; for a research study about the new D.A.R.E. program, such an alternative hypothesis may say, "Middle school students who participate in the new D.A.R.E. program are less likely to commit drug and violent offenses when compared to students who had no training or who were trained using the older D.A.R.E. curriculum."

For you to consider adopting the new D.A.R.E. program, of course, you would want to see research that rejects the null hypothesis and concludes two things: (1) differences between groups are due to the specific factors or interventions in the new program, and (2) the differences found within the sample are generalizable to (apply to) an entire population, including the youth in your jurisdiction. In making your decision about implementing the new program, you want to be assured that there *are* differences not due to chance between the different groups of middle school students that participated in the research studies. You also want to feel confident that the new program is likely to work in your locality with the middle school student population that you will serve, as it did for the students in the community where the research was conducted.

To draw these conclusions requires that the researchers examining the new D.A.R.E. program apply a **test of significance** to the study data to determine if the findings are substantially different from chance. But first, the researchers must specify what level of probability is acceptable for rejecting the null hypothesis. Is it good enough to be

90 percent sure that the null hypothesis is incorrect, or is it important to be 95 percent or even 99 percent sure? In most social science research, the generally accepted level of probability is 95 percent. This is usually identified by the reverse statement: The probability level (**p value**) that any differences found in a study are due solely to chance is less than 0.05, or 5 times out of 100.

When reporting findings, researchers should identify the p value in the narrative of the "Findings" section and in any data tables: Be sure to look for this as you read the studies. Significance is usually marked by one or more asterisks (*) in statistical data tables. In many studies, p values of both 0.05 and 0.01 are indicated. Statistical computer programs also calculate the exact level of significance; in some studies you may notice that the p value is 0.000, implying no likelihood that any differences are due to chance. Just remember, this is a mathematical calculation and may not be accurate in all cases in a population. Probability values greater than 0.05 ($p > 0.05$) are considered not significant, and researchers should explain these results, especially if they expected to find significant differences.

Selection of the Statistical Tests

Before the computer age, researchers had to make all their statistical calculations by hand. As you can imagine, this process could take a long time and require careful attention to each step of the mathematical process. Nowadays, there are many statistical tools available in modern computer software programs (such as SAS, SPSS, and SIMSTAT, listed in the resources at the end of this chapter) that can be easily applied to numerical data. How do the researchers decide which statistical test(s) to apply? There are several criteria that influence this decision.

- Purpose or goal of statistical analysis
- Type of data or scale (nominal, ordinal, interval, and ratio)
- Number and type of variables (**independent variables** are the hypothesized "causes" of change; **dependent variables** are the "effects" or "outcomes"). In this example, D.A.R.E. is the independent variable, and lower offenses the dependent variable or desired outcome.
- Underlying assumptions of each statistical test (such as a normal distribution of data and a sufficiently large sample of participants, usually greater than thirty)

Of course, some researchers have their favorite statistical tests and they design studies in which it is appropriate to use these tests.

Table 6.6 shows a small sample of commonly used statistical tests. Notice that the first criterion is the type of quantitative data collected. The next criterion is the number and types of variables, and the hypothesized relationships between them.

The speed of calculations done by computer has allowed for the development of even more complicated and powerful statistical tests that can be applied to quantitative data, such as analysis of covariance (ANCOVA), factor analysis, multiple regression analysis, and structural equation modeling (SEM). The researchers will identify which are used in the "Methodology" section. What you should be looking for when you read the reports is whether the results are statistically significant, as indicated by asterisks and p values.

TABLE 6.6. **Commonly Used Inferential Statistical Tests**

Goal	Type of Data	Number and Type of Variables	Statistical Test Choice
To test the difference between two group means (for example, number of offenses committed by students before and after participating in D.A.R.E., or between number of offenses committed by students who did or did not participate in D.A.R.E.)	Interval	1 independent; 1 dependent	t test
To test the difference between the means of two or more groups (for example, number of offenses committed by students before and after participating in the new D.A.R.E., the old D.A.R.E., or not at all)	Interval	1 or more independent; 1 dependent	Analysis of variance (ANOVA)
To test whether the observed frequencies (the frequency counts or percentages from nominal data) show a true difference from the frequencies expected if all categories were equal	Nominal	2 or more frequency counts or percentages	Chi-square
To test the difference between two group means of rankings	Ordinal	1 independent, 1 dependent	Wilcoxon matched-pairs signed ranks test
To test whether the relationship between the two variables is greater than would be expected due to chance	Interval	2 variables that are both measured	Pearson product-moment correlation (Pearson r)

Source: Adapted from Lodico, Spaulding, & Voegtle, 2006, p. 257.

Using Inferential Statistics for Decision Making

After the statistical tests have been completed, the researchers must use the results to make a decision—should the null hypothesis be rejected? As discussed above, they selected a p value (usually $p < .05$), which they will use to make this decision. For the D.A.R.E. program, if the studies you read show statistically significant differences between groups of middle school students who have been trained using the new program when compared to those trained under the old program, you might decide to go to the expense of adopting the new one. But there is another piece of information you would need to have in order to make a decision before adopting the new program.

Besides knowing that the results of the new program are statistically better than expected from chance, you would also need to know how important this difference is. One way that researchers express this is by reporting an **effect size**. (Another explanation of effect size can be found in Chapter Seven on meta-analysis or in the recommended resources for this chapter.) Although there are several different statistical tests that can be used to measure effect sizes, the most common one is Cohen's d. By convention, the effect size values are interpreted as follows:

- Small effect sizes: $d = .2$ to $.5$
- Medium effect sizes: $d = .5$ to $.8$
- Large effect sizes: $d = .8$ or higher

Be sure to look for a discussion of effect sizes in the "Findings" and "Discussion" sections of published research reports.

The authors of the studies you have been reading about the new D.A.R.E. program report statistically significant results, $p < .01$, with effect sizes of $.6$. From this information what will you decide about whether or not you should spend the time and money to implement the new D.A.R.E. program in your local middle schools?

EVALUATING REPORTS WITH QUANTITATIVE DATA

As a reader of research studies that have included the analysis of quantitative data, you will want to look carefully at how the researchers collected, analyzed, and interpreted the data. From the discussions above, you should be able to identify the types of data collected, understand the descriptive statistics that are reported, begin to determine whether the statistical tests selected are appropriate, and verify that the interpretations made by the researchers are consistent with the statistical results included in the report. The following questions provide a checklist of what you should look for as you read and evaluate the reports:

- What types of data are used in the research?
- What are the demographics of the study participants? How typical or representative are they of the population important to you?
- How large is the data set? How many participants are in the study?
- Have the appropriate descriptive statistics been thoroughly reported and explained?
- Do the statistical tests selected match the types of data collected?
- What is the shape of the data distribution? Is it a normal curve?
- Do the statistical tests used meet the underlying assumptions, such as a normal distribution and an adequate sample size (usually more than thirty)?

- Do the researchers explain any anomalies in the findings (for example, a skewed distribution or no significant differences between groups)?
- How do the researchers interpret the results from different types of data?

Reexamine the suggested article from one of the preceding chapters on the different kinds of research: experimental (Chapter Three), nonexperimental (Chapter Four), or survey (Chapter Five). Carefully examine the "Methodology" and "Findings" or "Results" sections of the report to answer these questions.

REFLECTION QUESTIONS

1. How is the concept of statistical significance different from the popular use of the word "significant" to mean important?

2. Why must a reader of research be able to identify the types of data collected during a study?

3. Why is it important to consider the effect size in addition to whether or not a finding is statistically significant as you read published research reports?

SUMMARY

Although the statistics used to analyze quantitative data can intimidate many readers of research, the information in this chapter provides a starting point for overcoming such fears. Descriptive statistics provide an important basis for interpreting the numerical data collected during research. The use of descriptive statistics reveals patterns in the distribution of the data, plus measures of central tendency, variability, relative position, and relationship. Authors of the reports may represent the patterns in quantitative data graphically, numerically, or both. Inferential statistics are used to determine whether the findings in a research project are due to chance alone, or if the factors or treatments under study result in statistically significant and important differences. The type of data collected, the variables, and the relationships between them are critical factors in determining which statistical tests are appropriate. To make the best decision about whether to incorporate research findings into your professional practice, you should carefully examine the methodology, findings, and conclusion sections of published articles for appropriate and consistent data analyses and interpretations.

KEY TERMS

asymmetrical distributions
bimodal distributions
categorical data
correlation
correlation coefficient
data set

dependent variables
descriptive statistics
effect size
frequency distributions
frequency polygon
grade equivalent score

histogram
independent variables
inferential statistics
interval data
mean
median
mode
negatively skewed
nominal data
normal curve
null hypothesis
ordinal data
outlier
p value
percentile rank
positively skewed
qualitative data

quantitative data
range
ratio data
raw scores
skewed distribution
skewness
standardized
standard deviation
standard score
stanines
statistical test
T scores
test of significance
values
variability
variable
z score

FURTHER READINGS AND RESOURCES

Suggested Readings

The following are classic texts used in statistics classes. These are listed in progressively more complex order.

Howell, D. C. (2007). *Fundamental statistics for the behavioral sciences.* Belmont, CA: Wadsworth.

Pagano, R. R. (2006). *Understanding statistics in the behavioral sciences* (8th ed.). Belmont, CA: Wadsworth.

Tabachnick, B. G., & Fidell, L. S. (2005). *Using multivariate statistics* (5th ed.). Boston: Allyn and Bacon.

Data Analysis Computer Programs

There are many programs available, either as shareware or proprietary. Commonly used ones, with links to the Web sites, are provided here.

SAS: www.sas.com

SIMSTAT: www.provalisresearch.com/index.html

SPSS: www.spss.com

Web Sites
AllPsych Online: The Virtual Psychology Classroom

http://allpsych.com/researchmethods/index.html

This online resource is a ten-chapter research methods textbook for both undergraduate and graduate students in psychology, education, and the social sciences. It has separate chapters on descriptive and inferential statistics, plus a chapter on how to be a critical reader of research.

The Research Room: Online Guide to Social Science Research

www.uh.edu/~srama/index.htm

This is a University of Houston reference source for information and resources on social science research, both qualitative and quantitative.

CHAPTER

UNDERSTANDING
META-ANALYSES

GENE V GLASS

KEY IDEAS

- Meta-analysis is a technique to summarize the results from a large number of research studies on the same topic or issue.

- The statistical techniques used in meta-analysis calculate and compare hundreds of effect sizes.

- Cross-tabulations of effect sizes can reveal important distinctions within the research data.

- Meta-analysis is helpful in the practical evaluation of treatments, interventions, or instructional methods.

DECADES AGO, prior to the explosion of research on education in the 1960s, summarizing the research on a topic was relatively simple. There might be five relevant studies to consider, and a **narrative review** was possible. "Jones (1945) found superior reading achievement at grade three for students initially taught by the Whole Language method; however, Lopez (1938) found no such differences for a group of 125 students whose home language was Spanish." However, as early as the 1970s, the number of empirical research studies on many topics of interest to educators and policy makers was multiplying wildly. By the late 1970s, a hundred studies of the relationship between school class size and achievement confronted anyone wishing to review that literature. The narrative review no longer sufficed. The typical narrative review of the 1970s—as would have been reported in the *Review of Educational Research*, for example—became a long list of "positive" and "negative" findings followed by a call for additional research. Systematic methods of coding, organizing, and displaying information were needed; traditional statistical analysis methods in the form of meta-analysis proved to be sufficient to the task. Although meta-analysis was originally developed for summarizing research in education and psychology (Glass, 1976), today it is applied much more frequently in medicine.

WHAT IS META-ANALYSIS?

Meta-analysis is a collection of statistical analysis techniques used to summarize a body of empirical research studies on a particular topic; for example, Is Whole Language a better method of initial reading instruction than Phonics? Or, Do students who are retained in a grade for an additional year benefit subsequently more than those who are not? Its findings are expressed in **quantitative** terms; for example, "Aggregating the findings of eighty-five experiments on the effects of Ritalin on classroom behavior, we find that there are on average 22 percent fewer discipline problems reported in a year's time for the children placed on Ritalin than in a comparable group on a placebo or receiving no treatment at all for attention-deficit disorder."

Meta-Analysis Illustrated

An illustration of a simple meta-analysis will clarify how these techniques are applied in performing a meta-analysis. Suppose that we are interested in what the existing research studies say about the effectiveness of Whole Language versus Phonics as methods of initial reading instruction. From the very first step a controversial decision must be made in conducting a **literature search**: Which studies and how many studies should be included? This is in part a question about how one should go about searching for the relevant literature, and in part about what type of studies should be included. On the latter question, experts can disagree. Some maintain that only the "best" studies should be included (Slavin, 1986); others advise including every relevant study, whether it is "good," "bad," or "indifferent" (Glass, 1978). As to how relevant studies should be located, the life of the meta-analyst has never been better. The Internet has greatly facilitated the collecting of research; Google Scholar (http://scholar.google.com), and the online ERIC collection (www.eric.ed.gov) are invaluable resources for locating studies. The old-fashioned technique of **branching bibliographies** is still an important means of collecting research for a meta-analysis: find a very recent study on the topic, inspect the list of references cited in that study, go to those studies and do likewise; in this way, one will quickly compile a list of most of the relevant research. The only glitch might occur if newer studies exist than the "recent study" one began with; but "search forward" resources are available in which one can start with an older study and find all later studies that reference it (see the ISI Web of Knowledge, http://scientific.thomson.com/isi).

Assume that our meta-analyst studying Whole Language (WL) versus Phonics (PH) has collected most of the relevant literature and is prepared to take the next steps. Suppose that two hundred experimental studies comparing the two methods of teaching reading have been located. Two of these many studies are "Jones (1945)" and "Lopez (1938)." In order to keep straight all of the information contained in these many studies, the meta-analyst has devised a database structure for **coding** the studies. Coding involves defining key features of the studies (for example, when the study was published, the ages of the children, the length of the instruction, and the like) and describing these features by means of numerical, alphabetical, or word codes. The two studies by Jones and Lopez are coded in Table 7.1.

TABLE 7.1. **Study Coding for WL Versus PH Meta-Analysis**

Study Characteristic	Jones	Lopez
Date of publication	1945	1938
Source	Journal article	Dissertation
Grade level at testing	3	2
Teachers' experience	1–2 years	6 or more years
Students' home language	English	Spanish
Number of students	N-WL = 70; N-PH = 68	N-WL = 38; N-PH = 36
Achievement test results	Mean-WL = 4.4; SD = 1.1	Mean-WL = 3.1; SD = 0.9
	Mean-PH = 3.8; SD = 1.0	Mean-PH = 3.0; SD = 1.1
Type of test	California Achievement Test	Iowa Test of Basic Skills
Attitude test results	Mean-WL = 76; SD = 12.6	Mean-WL = 9.4; SD = 3.2
	Mean-PH = 65; SD = 11.9	Mean-PH = 9.2; SD = 3.4
Type of attitude scale	Moore Reading Interest Scale	Hopkins Reading Inventory
Effect size for achievement	ES = 0.57	ES = 0.10
Effect size for attitude	ES = 0.90	ES = 0.06

In reality, many more characteristics of studies would be coded than the few illustrated in Table 7.1.

1. Why was meta-analysis developed?
2. What are the initial steps in conducting a meta-analysis?
3. How can the preferences and biases of the researcher influence a meta-analysis?
4. What topic or issue is important to you that might be explored using a meta-analysis?

For **comparative experimental studies** like these, the focus of attention is on the **outcome measures**, such as the achievement or attitude results. Jones administered the California Achievement Test and found a six-month grade equivalent (GE) superiority for the WL group when compared to the PH group's test results. Lopez administered the Iowa Test of Basic Skills and found a one-month GE superiority for the WL students initially taught to read by the WL method. There are dozens of ways to measure reading achievement of elementary grade students. If the meta-analyst is required to keep all of the findings separate depending on which test was administered, the general trends in the two hundred studies will be lost in the confusion of dozens of individual results. In truth, the standardized tests of reading achievement differ only in insignificant particulars; they test vocabulary and comprehension, and that's about it. The meta-analyst calculates for each study a general measure of the relative superiority of WL versus PH known as the **effect size** (ES). The effect size is like a **standard score** in that it expresses the comparison of WL and PH on a scale that is independent of the **mean** and **standard deviation** (SD) of the original scales used to measure outcomes. For example, suppose that on the Scholastic Aptitude Test (SAT) verbal test women score on average 550 and men score 500. The SAT has a standard deviation of 100 points; therefore, women exceed men by one-half standard deviation, or, the ES comparing women and men is 0.50, favoring women. Now suppose that on the American College Test (ACT) Reading test, women score 21.5 on average and men score 19.0. The ACT Reading test has a standard deviation of 5 points, so the ES comparing women and men on the ACT Reading test is also 0.50. We have compared women and men on verbal tests even though those tests use quite different measurement scales.

In the current example of WL and PH, the Jones study gives an ES as follows:

$$ES = (Mean\text{-}WL - Mean\text{-}PH) \div [(SD\text{-}WL + SD\text{-}PH)/2]$$

$$ES = (4.4 - 3.8) \div [(1.1 + 1.0) \div 2] = .6 \div 1.05 = 0.57$$

The two standard deviations are averaged to estimate the standard deviation of a group of students taught by either method. The effect size is interpreted as follows: the mean of the WL group is approximately six-tenths of a standard deviation higher on reading achievement than the mean of the PH group. The significance of the ES becomes clearer when it is displayed graphically, as in Figure 7.1..

Figure 7.1 depicts the results of the Jones study on a scale of reading achievement that can be compared from one study to the next. The two curves in Figure 7.1 are separated at the mean by 0.57 standard deviations. One important implication of

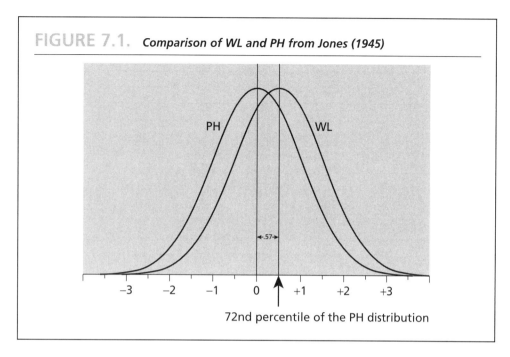

FIGURE 7.1. *Comparison of WL and PH from Jones (1945)*

this effect size is that, assuming normal distributions of reading achievement scores, the average student taught by the WL method scores above the 72nd **percentile** of the distribution of scores of students taught by the PH method. So a student at the center of the reading achievement distribution benefits by 22 percentile ranks (50th versus 72nd) when taught initial reading by the WL method.

For the students whose home language was Spanish in the Lopez study, the ES comparing WL and PH is

$$ES = (3.1 - 3.0) \div [(0.9 + 1.1) \div 2] = .1 \div 1.0 = 0.10$$

When two normal distributions of scores differ at the mean by .10 standard deviations, the average student (at the 50th percentile) in the higher distribution exceeds 54 percent of the students in the lower distribution, an advantage of only 4 percentile ranks.

A typical meta-analysis might involve the calculation of hundreds of effect sizes. Obviously, such a huge collection of data cannot be comprehended without the aid of further statistical analysis. This is where meta-analysis makes its entrance as the **analysis of analyses**. We suppose that "Jones (1945)" and "Lopez (1938)" are just two of two hundred comparative experiments on WL and PH. When the ES measures from all two hundred studies are calculated and averaged, the meta-analysis has begun. Suppose that across all two hundred studies the average ES is equal to 0.45 favoring WL over PH. This finding can be depicted as in Figure 7.2.

Surely among these two hundred effect size measures there is variability that can illuminate the choice between WL and PH. Whole Language teaching might be superior for one type of student, but Phonics could be superior for another type. Or, perhaps, inexperienced beginning teachers have more luck with Phonics instruction than with

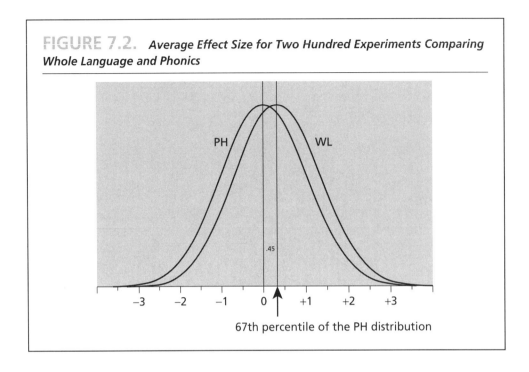

FIGURE 7.2. *Average Effect Size for Two Hundred Experiments Comparing Whole Language and Phonics*

Whole Language. The meta-analyst will investigate these questions by categorizing the data according to the coding conventions of the database and then reporting the average ES for various **cross-tabulations**, as in Table 7.2.

Here, the cross-tabulation of the effect sizes paid big dividends. WL was seen to be somewhat insignificantly inferior to PH for inexperienced teachers (in the first or second year of teaching), and insignificantly superior to PH for moderately experienced teachers, but extraordinarily superior to PH for teachers with six or more years experience. In fact, an ES of 2.0 implies that the average student taught by WL exceeds in reading achievement more than 97 percent of the students taught by PH. (Of course, this illustration is hypothetical and exaggerated to make the point clearer.) At the same time, the subdividing of the database by "teacher experience" revealed the value of greater specificity in the questions being asked and the inadvisability of lumping together data arising from dissimilar circumstances that ought not to be ignored. The meta-analyst

TABLE 7.2. **Average Effect Size Comparing WL and PH for Various Levels of Teacher Experience**

Teacher Experience	Number of Studies	Average ES
First or second year teaching	30	−0.15
3–5 years teaching	120	0.15
6 or more years teaching	50	2.05

never knows in advance which distinctions will prove to be important or whether the corpus of studies being analyzed will permit making the important distinctions.

Achievement is just one of the outcomes that would be measured in an experiment comparing WL and PH. Attitude, or how much the children enjoy and seek out reading on their own, would likely also be evaluated in many studies. Jones, for example, administered the Moore Reading Interest Scale to the 138 students in her study. The Moore Scale consists of twenty items, for example, "I like to go to the library," each of which the student rates on a 5-point scale from 1 (Disagree) to 5 (Agree). A maximum score of 100 is possible, though rarely obtained. The summary statistics for the two groups, WL and PH, in the Jones study appear in Table 7.1. An effect size can be calculated for these data in the same manner that it was calculated for the California Achievement Test data:

$$ES = (\text{Mean-WL} - \text{Mean-PH}) \div [(\text{SD-WL} + \text{SD-PH}) \div 2]$$

$$ES = (76 - 65) \div [(12.6 + 11.9) \div 2] = 11 \div 12.25 = 0.90$$

The Lopez study also measured children's interest in reading at the end of the experimental period. The Hopkins Reading Inventory is an interest inventory consisting of a list of fifteen activities: "I ask my parent to take me to the library," "I want to get a book for my birthday," and the like. A child's score is the number of activities he or she reports engaging in. Scores can range from 0 to 15. The summary statistics for the Lopez study appear in Table 7.1. The effect size on the Hopkins Inventory for the seventy-four students in the Lopez study is as follows:

$$ES = (\text{Mean-WL} - \text{Mean-PH}) \div [(\text{SD-WL} + \text{SD-PH}) \div 2]$$

$$ES = (9.4 - 9.2) \div [(3.2 + 3.4) \div 2] = .2 \div 3.3 = 0.06$$

The superiority of WL over PH on children's attitudes toward reading is very evident in the Jones study (ES = 0.90), but far less so in the Lopez study. In fact, one could conclude that there is no real difference in reading interest at all in the Lopez study. The meta-analyst will begin to search for explanations. As the WL method was much less effective relative to PH for the children whose home language was Spanish, is this the reason why no important difference in attitude toward reading was also seen in the Lopez study?

At this point, the critic of meta-analysis might say that things have gone too far. Lumping together results (ESs) from the California Achievement Test (CAT) and the Iowa Test of Basic Skills (ITBS) might be acceptable, but comparing the results on two different reading attitude inventories is comparing apples and oranges. But the two achievement tests were also "different." In fact, CAT and the ITBS have separate forms that pose slightly different questions ("old . . . young; same or opposite?" or "weak . . . strong; same or opposite?"). Any meta-analysis involves the comparison of "different studies." Only "different studies" can be compared, for if two studies were "the same," there would be no point in comparing them; they would show the same results. (The "apples and oranges" criticism is addressed in more detail below.)

Comparative experimental studies lend themselves to description of their results with the effect size measure. Other kinds of studies are appropriately described by different measures. For example, studies of the relationship between parents' level of education and their children's academic achievement might be best described by a **correlation coefficient** (see, for example, White, 1982). A body of studies might show an average correlation coefficient between mother's level of education and child's level of 0.35, but an average correlation of .20 between father's level and child's level.

REFLECTION QUESTIONS

1. What kinds of data or measures can be examined in a meta-analysis? How does this limit the use of meta-analysis?

2. What is an effect size? Describe an example, without using a mathematical calculation, to explain or illustrate what is meant by effect size.

3. Why is calculating the average effect size not the final step in meta-analysis?

EVALUATING META-ANALYSES

You might never perform a meta-analysis yourself, but the chances are good that in your role as a professional practitioner or even as an individual who faces important choices about your health or the education of your children, your relatives, or a friend, you will encounter a published meta-analysis. You will then want to know if you should believe what it says. The following list of questions, with some suggestions about what to look for in their answers, should help you in evaluating the claims emanating from a particular meta-analysis.

How Good Was the "Literature Search" That Drew Together the Collection of Studies to Be Analyzed? There are several characteristics of how the studies to be analyzed were collected that will bear on the strength of the results. Did the literature search catch the most recent work? Any well-performed meta-analysis will provide the reader with a list of the studies included in the analysis. It's an easy matter to check the dates of the studies to make sure that current work has been included. On the other end of the date spectrum, one ought to ask whether arbitrary decisions by the meta-analyst about when to cut off the search, such as "nothing before 1970 will be included," might have excluded important work.

Did the meta-analysis miss important studies merely because the analyst was lazy or underfunded? For example, for certain topics, the dissertation literature is rich and significant, but often analysts ignore it, either because it is thought to be of "low quality" or because it is too costly to access.

Did the meta-analyst exclude important work on arbitrary grounds that may have biased the results? Meta-analysts tend to be statistics experts or methodologists. As such, they often have strong opinions about what research is "good" and what research is "bad," even when those opinions are entirely **a priori** in the sense that the "good" and the "bad" studies show essentially the same thing. Any meta-analyst must draw boundaries around the literature and exclude some work for practical reasons. Drawing these boundaries is a matter of judgment. Beware when the meta-analyst reports that only the "best evidence" was included in the analysis. Too often, that "best evidence" is the work of the analyst, the analyst's students, or like-minded friends (Slavin, 1986).

Does the Meta-Analysis Compare Apples and Oranges?   The single most frequent criticism of meta-analysis is that it compares "apples and oranges." It is also the single most wrongheaded criticism. Nothing will prepare the reader for understanding meta-analyses more than to get one's thoughts straight on what it means to compare apples and oranges.

Of course meta-analysis mixes apples and oranges; in the study of fruit nothing else is sensible; comparing apples and oranges is the only endeavor worthy of serious inquiry; comparing apples to apples is trivial.

The unthinking critic will claim that it only makes sense to integrate any two studies if they are studies of "the same thing." But these critics who argue that no two studies should be compared unless they were studies of the "same thing" blithely compare persons (such as experimental "subjects") within their studies all the time. This is inconsistent. It is self-contradictory to assert that "No two things can be compared unless they are the same." If they are the same, there is no reason to compare them; indeed, if "they" are the same, then there are not two things, there is only one thing and comparison is not an issue. One study is an apple, and a second study is an orange. I compare fruits when I'm hungry and have to decide between an apple and an orange.

Any two studies differ in an infinite number of ways, even when they are on the same topic. Study 1 compares students' achievement in class sizes of thirty-five and twenty; the subject taught is beginning algebra. Study 2 compares class sizes of twenty and fifteen; the subject taught is beginning geometry. Can their results be compared? Yes, of course, for some purposes. They can even be compared with Study 3 that evaluates achievement in class sizes of forty and twenty in American history. If all three studies show superior achievement for the smaller class size, we learn something. For the reader who is interested only in individualization of mathematics instruction, Study 3 might be the orange that will have to be separated from the apples, Studies 1 and 2. Different readers will have different opinions about how much the studies in a meta-analysis can differ before the findings cease to be relevant.

If a critic wishes to dismiss a particular meta-analysis from anyone's consideration because it *compares apples and oranges*, it might be well to ask whether the critic simply doesn't like the findings of the analysis.

Does the Meta-Analysis Ignore Important Differences Among Studies?   This question gets at the other side of the coin of the apples and oranges problem. Similar to the wrongheaded opinion that any two studies that are different can't be integrated, ignoring important differences in the integration of multiple studies is ill advised. Suppose that a meta-analysis is performed on a hundred experimental studies comparing distance learning with traditional large-group lecture instruction for college-age undergraduates. And suppose further that these one hundred studies yielded an average ES of .10—not impressive, perhaps, but not zero. In fact, the finding might be regarded as so unimpressive that readers of the meta-analysis decide that the added cost and trouble of mounting a distance education program just isn't worth it. This conclusion might have been different if the meta-analyst had reported the average effect sizes separately for different types of subject taught, as in Table 7.3, for example.

A meta-analysis that failed to take into account the important distinction of what subject is being taught via distance learning would surely leave its readers with a misleading, if not false, conclusion. Mathematics teaching by means of distance instruction works quite well; in fact, the average student studying math by distance teaching outperforms 74 percent of the students studying math in traditional large-group college instruction. But distance education doesn't do so well in teaching composition, perhaps because the interaction between the instructor and the writer is curtailed, or in chemistry and biology classes, perhaps because there is just no adequate online substitute for laboratory work.

A good meta-analysis will make every attempt to examine and compare the results of the studies after they have been grouped according to important distinctions that may bear on the strength of the results. Often, the original studies being integrated in a meta-analysis do not do a good job of reporting the particular circumstances under which the study was performed; for example, distance learning was compared with large-group instruction, but the author of the study failed to record what subject was taught. There's not much that the meta-analyst can do about this situation, but that does not necessarily mean that the study should be ignored or discarded.

Another Example

Consider an example that may help illuminate these matters. Perhaps the most controversial conclusion from the psychotherapy meta-analysis that my colleagues and I published in 1980 was that there was no evidence favoring behavioral psychotherapies over nonbehavioral psychotherapies. This finding was vilified by the behavioral therapy camp and praised by the Rogerians and Freudians. Some years later, I returned to the database and dug a little deeper. What I found appears in Figure 7.3. When the nine experiments extant in 1979 in which behavioral and nonbehavioral psychotherapies are compared in the same experiment between randomized groups, and the effects of treatment are plotted as a function of follow-up time, the two curves in Figure 7.3 result. The findings are quite extraordinary and suggestive. Behavioral therapies produce large short-term effects which decay in strength over the first year of follow-up;

TABLE 7.3. **Average Effect Size Comparing Distance Learning (DL) and Large-Group (LG) Instruction for Various Subjects Taught**

Type of Subject Taught	Average ES = [(Mean-DL − Mean-LG) ÷ SD]
Mathematics	0.65
Composition	0.04
Chemistry	0.08
Biology	−0.18

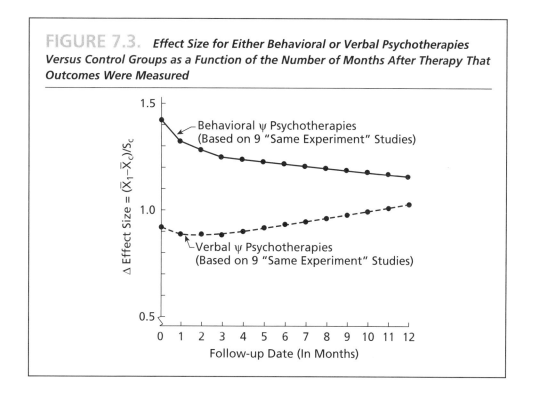

FIGURE 7.3. *Effect Size for Either Behavioral or Verbal Psychotherapies Versus Control Groups as a Function of the Number of Months After Therapy That Outcomes Were Measured*

nonbehavioral therapies produce initially smaller effects which increase over time. The two curves appear to be converging on the same long-term effect. I leave it to the reader to imagine why. One answer, I suspect, is not arcane and is quite plausible.

Figure 7.3, I believe, is a truer reflection of reality and how research, even meta-analysis, can lead us to more sophisticated understandings. Indeed, the world encompasses all manner of interesting differences and distinctions, and in general, gross averages do not do it justice. However, denying the importance of an average effect size that one does not like for personal reasons simply because the data are not broken down by one's favorite distinction is not playing the game fairly. Not every distinction makes a real difference, as for example, when a graphologist (handwriting expert) claims that a pile of negative findings really hides great successes for graphologists trained by vegetarians.

Are the Findings of the Meta-Analysis Generalizable?   Surely a fact that doesn't generalize is of no use to anyone. But it does not follow that the methods of **inferential statistics** (significance test, hypothesis tests, confidence intervals) are the best means of reaching a general conclusion. The appropriate role for inferential statistics in meta-analysis is not merely unclear; it has been seen in quite disparate ways by different methodologists since meta-analysis first appeared.

Inferences to populations of persons seem quite unnecessary, because even a meta-analysis of modest size will involve a few hundred persons (nested within studies) and lead to nearly automatic **rejection of null hypotheses**. Moreover, the chances are remote that the persons or subjects within studies were drawn from defined populations with anything even remotely resembling **probabilistic techniques**. Hence, probabilistic calculations advanced as if subjects had been randomly selected would be dubious.

At the level of "studies," the question of the appropriateness of inferential statistics can be posed again, and the answer again seems to be negative. There are two instances in which common inferential methods are clearly appropriate, not just in meta-analysis but in any research: (1) when a well-defined population has been randomly sampled, and (2) when subjects have been randomly assigned to conditions in a controlled experiment. The latter case is of little interest to meta-analysts who never assign units to treatments. Moreover, the typical meta-analysis virtually never meets the condition of probabilistic sampling of a population—though in the case of Smith, Glass, and Miller (1980), the available population of psychoactive drug treatment experiments was so large that a random sample of experiments was in fact drawn for the meta-analysis. Inferential statistics has little role to play in meta-analysis.

It is common to acknowledge, in meta-analysis and elsewhere, that many data sets fail to meet probabilistic sampling conditions, and then argue that one ought to treat the data in hand "as if" it were a random sample of some "hypothetical population." One must be wary here of the slide from "**hypothesis about a population**" into "**a hypothetical population**." They are quite different things, the former being standard and unobjectionable, the latter being a figment that we hardly know how to handle.

The notion of a hypothetical population appears to be circular. If the sample is fixed and the population is allowed to be hypothetical, then surely the data analyst will imagine a population that resembles the sample of data. If I show you a handful of red and green M&Ms, you will naturally assume that I have just drawn my hand out of a bowl of mostly red and green M&Ms, not red and green and brown and yellow ones. Hence, all of these "hypothetical populations" will be merely reflections of the samples in hand and there will be no need for inferential statistics. Or, put another way, if the population of inference is not defined by considerations separate from the characterization of the sample, then the population is merely a large version of the sample. With what confidence is one able to generalize the character of this sample to a population that looks like a big version of the sample? Well, with a great deal of confidence, obviously. But then, the population is nothing but the sample writ large, and we really know nothing more than what the sample tells us, in spite of the fact that we have attached misleadingly precise probability numbers to the result.

Hedges and Olkin (1985) have developed inferential techniques that ignore the pro forma testing (because of large N) of null hypotheses and focus on the estimation of regression functions that estimate effects at different levels of study. They worry about both sources of statistical instability: that arising from persons within studies and that which arises from variation between studies. The techniques they present are based on traditional assumptions of random sampling and independence. It is, of course, unclear to me precisely how the validity of their methods is compromised by failure to achieve probabilistic sampling of persons and studies.

Does the Meta-Analysis Test a Theory?   This answer may surprise you. Meta-analysis has nothing to do with theories. In spite of its superficial similarity to things that look very scientific, such as statistical formulas, meta-analyses are not tests of theories. Rather, meta-analysis is useful in the practical evaluation of techniques and methods. Do students learn more in small classes than in large? Do students who are made to repeat an elementary grade do better or worse throughout their subsequent years in school? Technological evaluations are mostly, though not exclusively, matters of cost-effectiveness estimation. Meta-analysis can be helpful in assessing the effectiveness side of the equation. When joined with cost analysis, meta-analysis can make its best contribution to practical affairs. (See Levin, Glass, & Meister, 1987, listed in references as an example.)

REFLECTION QUESTIONS

1.   What are the strengths and weaknesses of meta-analysis as a research strategy?
2.   How can you tell if you should believe what you read in a meta-analysis?

SUMMARY

Prior to about 1975, the most common mode of reviewing a collection of studies on a topic was the narrative review. That method tended to break down as the literature grew to dozens and in some cases hundreds of studies. Methods of describing ("coding") and statistically analyzing the results of multiple empirical studies were developed and now are classified under the name "meta-analysis." A typical meta-analysis might result in a conclusion such as, "Twenty studies comparing guided discovery versus the lecture method of teaching addition of fractions show that on average the typical student learning by the guided discovery method outperforms 70 percent of the students learning by the lecture method." The validity of a meta-analysis rests on such considerations as the thoroughness of the literature search, the care exercised in coding studies, and proper methods of statistical analysis. Generalizing the findings of a meta-analysis is a topic on which even the experts disagree.

KEY TERMS

analysis of analyses
a priori
branching bibliographies
coding
comparative experimental studies
correlation coefficient
cross-tabulation
effect size
generalizable

hypothesis about a population
hypothetical population
inferential statistics
literature search
mean
meta-analysis
narrative review
outcome measures
percentile

probabilistic techniques
quantitative
rejection of null hypotheses

standard deviation
standard score

FURTHER READINGS AND RESOURCES

Suggested Readings

Waxman, H. C., Lin, M-F., & Michko, G. M. (2003). A meta-analysis of the effectiveness of teaching and learning with technology on student outcomes. Naperville, IL: Learning Point Associates. Retrieved November 2, 2007, from www.ncrel.org/tech/effects2.

A meta-analysis of teaching and learning aided by educational technologies authored by Hersh Waxman and his colleagues is an excellent illustration of the technique and its practical interpretation.

Glass, G. V (1976). Primary, secondary, and meta-analysis of research. *Educational Researcher*, 5, 3–8.

Glass, G. V (1978). Integrating findings: The meta-analysis of research. *Review of Research in Education*, 5, 351–379.

Glass, G. V, McGaw, B., & Smith, M. L. (1981). *Meta-analysis in social research*. Beverly Hills, CA: Sage Publications.

Glass, G. V, Cahen, L. S., Filby, N. N., & Smith, M. L. (1982). *School class size: Research and policy*. Beverly Hills, CA: Sage Publications.

This series of papers and books from the earliest stages of the development of meta-analysis gives the reader an introduction to the method and illustrates its application to education and the behavioral sciences.

Hedges, L. V., & Olkin, I. (1985). *Statistical methods for meta-analysis*. New York: Academic Press.

The quantitative methods involved in meta-analysis received their definitive treatment in 1985 by Larry Hedges and Ingram Olkin.

Cooper, H. M., & Hedges, L. V. (Eds.). (1994). *The handbook of research synthesis*. New York: Russell Sage Foundation.

Every aspect of meta-analysis, from the literature search through coding, analysis, and reporting, is covered in detail by the various contributors to *The Handbook of Research Synthesis*.

Hunt, M. (1997). *How science takes stock: The story of meta-analysis*. New York: Russell Sage Foundation.

The science writer Morton Hunt was commissioned by the Russell Sage Foundation to write a history of meta-analysis. His book makes interesting reading for a general audience.

Web Sites

Several Web sites contain literature on meta-analysis, examples, and even freeware (no-cost software) for performing meta-analyses.

http://en.wikipedia.org/wiki/Meta-analysis

The Wikipedia entry on meta-analysis is concise, informative, and constantly updated with relevant links and new information.

http://edres.org/meta

The most comprehensive and informative Web site on meta-analysis was created and is maintained by Lawrence M. Rudner. His site contains links to other Web sites and offers freeware for conducting meta-analyses (http://edres.org/meta/metastat.htm).

www.archive.org

Note: These Web sites were accessed in the summer of 2007. If in the future the addresses reported above are obsolete, you can still access the material as it looked then by means of the World Wide Web archive known as the "Wayback Machine."

CHAPTER

8

EVALUATING HISTORICAL RESEARCH

LAURIE MOSES HINES

KEY IDEAS

- The purpose of historical research is to provide more than a simple accounting of what happened in the past; it interprets and explains the past to illuminate the present.

- Historians use their historical imaginations to pose answers to important and intriguing questions, to fill a gap in our understanding of the past, to reconsider how existing historical data are interpreted, and to examine current policies.

- Historical researchers analyze and interpret information gathered from both primary and secondary sources to present their arguments.

- Historians base their analyses and conclusions on their own perspectives, which are influenced by their particular foci, their philosophical beliefs, and their topics of interest.

MOST PEOPLE encounter history frequently. They may listen to their parents or grandparents tell stories of their youth. They may look at old letters, photographs, or newspaper clippings about important events in a person's life. They may find a box of old toys or clothing in their attic or garage. These are all pieces of history, like pieces of a jigsaw puzzle. Individually, they may be interesting, but they do not tell us a story or complete a picture of the past. Some people seek out more complete stories or histories of an earlier period. They may watch the History Channel, visit ancient Pueblo ruins or a museum, or read a history book. These things tell a story of the past, oftentimes using old newspapers or documents, accounts given by people who witnessed events, or even historical artifacts such as old tools, toys, or even buildings to uncover earlier times. If these stories are examples of good historical research, however, they tell us more than a story about ancient times or a chronicle of events. Historical research provides historical analysis—an interpretation about the past based on consideration of relevant pieces of history and intended to explain an earlier time and come to some conclusions about what the story means for the present. So, although we may all encounter history, historical research is a way to make sense of the past by following certain methods of analysis.

How, then, does one distinguish between a good story about the past and historical research? There are some basic elements to historical research.

BASICS OF HISTORICAL RESEARCH

Historical research, unlike stories about the past, intends to explain an earlier time on its own terms. It goes beyond the telling of a story or the compilation of facts, to explain a previous period or event as a way to understand humanity and possibly to illuminate current issues or dilemmas. Based on analysis of information, historical research advances an interpretation of an earlier time.

Although people today can never truly leave their own era and go back in time, historians use their **historical imagination** to understand the subject in its own right and on its own terms. Historians consider Herodotus, an ancient Greek who lived during the fifth century B.C.E.[1] the father of history because he took the perspective of other people—the people who lived during that time and experienced a historical event—when writing about the past. Herodotus did not apply his own cultural or historical sensibilities to an earlier time or people. Likewise, historians try to emulate this by not judging or evaluating earlier people, events, or concepts using today's standards. Although we cannot shed all of our current principles and beliefs, using today's values to evaluate the past is called **presentism**, and historians consider this a violation of basic standards of historical research. Rather, historians use their historical imagination to recreate another time in its entirety—the events, the cultural, social, or moral beliefs and values, the intellectual ideas, and the economic and political climate—because they can never actually be there.

Historians aim to understand the past by considering the **context**, or the circumstances, of a particular time. The context gives meaning to events in the past. There are various kinds of contexts that historians consider: economic, cultural, social, intellectual, and political. The context allows historians to assess a historical event or person on its own terms because the context exposes the norms, values, and ideas of that time. Context helps answer such questions as: What were the economic circumstances of families in Kansas during the 1930s? How did European society view children in the seventeenth century? Without knowing this context, information or historical facts carry little meaning. For example, one cannot comprehend the Civil War without understanding the political issue of states' rights, the economics of the slave system, and social attitudes about slavery in general.

Historical research requires identifying who or what are the **historical actors** that played a critical role in shaping the time and topic under investigation. More than likely, these are people, but sometimes historical actors are organizations (including governments), demographic groups (such as working-class women), or ideas (such as republicanism). In understanding the influence that these historical actors have, historians take great caution in ascribing a motive. Likewise, understanding how or why things happen or change or why they stay the same (**continuity**) is an important aspect of historical research; yet historians take similar vigilance in implying **causation**, the idea that something caused certain circumstances, events, or changes. Historians tend to describe the events or changes and only attribute cause or motive on the part of historical actors if there is clear and compelling evidence. It is one thing to make the historical leap of using one's historical imagination to understand the past; it is quite another to use imagination to point a finger at the cause of change or motivation for an action. Good historical research will consider all relevant sources of information, weigh the facts, and show any evidence of causation or motive, if indeed it is evident.

Analysis and interpretation are the heart of historical research. This is what distinguishes it from a compilation of facts or the telling of stories. As implied above, analysis is the consideration of information within its multiple contexts, the weighing of facts, and the careful attribution of any causation and motive. In making this analysis, historians interpret the evidence. They then must present their interpretation by organizing the evidence into a coherent and logical argument.

Of course, these basic elements or methods of historical research are more complex than stated. The concepts of historical imagination, context, historical actors, continuity and causation, and analysis and interpretation are more like minimal standards of thinking that all historians follow in their research than methods of research. One could follow these minimal standards and still produce historical research that is not too good. How, then, does one tell the difference between good and bad historical research? How should one evaluate historical research? In understanding the methods that historians use to do research, one learns how to evaluate historical research.

1. What is the purpose of historical research?
2. In what way is doing historical research different from telling a story? In what way is it the same?

HOW ARE QUESTIONS POSED, OR "SO WHAT?"

One way of evaluating historical research is to ask whether the question posed by the historian is a good one—that is, one worth asking because the answer may tell us something important and worth knowing. In essence, we can ask of any piece of historical research, "So what? What is its significance? Will this tell us anything of importance, help us understand humanity, or help illuminate a problem in today's society?" Therefore, as one way to evaluate historical research, we want to understand how historians come upon the questions they ask of the research evidence. Historians find their topics of study in a number of ways.

Intriguing and Important Questions

Historians, just like anyone, become intrigued by some idea or topic about the past. Not all questions, however, are worth asking. Fundamentally, historians try to address relevant questions that can be answered. As historian Jules R. Benjamin notes in *A Student's Guide to History* (2007), historians do not want to waste time pursuing questions with no answers, such as "What is the purpose of the universe?" Nor do they wish to ask questions that are insignificant, such as "Who wore the first pair of pants with a zipper?" (Benjamin, 2007, p. 4). The former question belongs in the realm of philosophy, not history; the latter in a game of trivia. Good historical research would not address these questions.

Good questions are often "good" because they deal with relevant or perennial issues, such as children's health and upbringing, people's religious beliefs, and church or state authority. Others explore aspects of humanity or social relations: Why did Puritans engage in witch-hunting? How and why did various people participate in the American civil rights movement? Still other questions look at issues about change and continuity, such as when and why did governments begin to provide for the poor? Comparisons also trigger historical investigation, such as when historians question the differences and similarities among the experiences of Jewish, Italian, and Irish immigrants.

As a reader of historical research, you must evaluate the study to see how or, indeed, if the specific topic addresses a larger issue about humanity or its problems. Is it addressing an intriguing, important, or relevant topic, beyond the unanswerable or trivial? It could be an interesting or even entertaining story, but truly good historical research also addresses these important and larger questions. Sometimes historical research that is important to one group of people, such as studies on historical conceptions of family, which may be important to those in nontraditional family units, may seem unimportant to another group of people. However, you must strive to see how the topic of study addresses questions of importance, even if it is not important to you personally. Typically, the more important the questions that are addressed, the more significant the historical research—assuming, of course, that other criteria of good historical scholarship are met.

Filling a Gap

Often, historians will identify a gap or hole in existing historical scholarship and seek to fill it. This requires that historians be very familiar with the current historical scholarship to recognize an untold part of a story or to see how certain ideas or concepts may vary in different contexts. As a new reader of historical research, you may not be entirely familiar with existing historical scholarship and therefore would not necessarily see how any one piece of research would fill a gap. The historian may or may not lay this out for readers in the preface or introduction of the study. If he or she does, it is a bonus for you as a reader. Even if the historian does not specifically write that the research fills an opening in the scholarship, he or she usually will discuss what is known about a topic or time period. In this case, the reader would turn to the footnotes (as most historians use footnotes or endnotes) to see the references to existing scholarship. Again, familiarity with existing scholarship helps in determining if the study is considering all prior research in identifying any gap.

A prime example of historical research that fills a gap in the research is the work of Linda Perkins, who studies the history of African American teachers. Consistently, Perkins takes the history of teachers, whether in teacher education, hiring, or pay policies, and shows how it often does not include African American teachers. To Perkins, for the history of teachers to be complete—to fill the gap in the research—one must include the experiences of African American teachers, and this is what she does with her research. Perkins's scholarship both finds an untold story (that of African American teachers) and shows how concepts applied to white teachers change when historians consider the experiences of African American teachers.

Interpretive Differences

Occasionally, historians do not look to fill a gap in existing scholarship but to reconsider how existing historical data are interpreted. In these cases, historians will use historical information that other historians have used and sometimes consider additional data or sources that they think change the conclusions. The questions posed in these instances probably are significant, or else there would not be such debate among historians. Examples of these types of questions are the studies on the creation of the public school system in Massachusetts by Michael B. Katz (1968) and by Carl F. Kaestle and Maris A. Vinovskis (1980). With these studies, the historians are making arguments that they have a new (and better) way of interpreting historical evidence. Similarly, a historian can use different concepts and evidence in probing a topic and therefore provide an interpretation that has a unique perspective. For instance, Jared Diamond, an evolutionary biologist, has applied concepts from that field to understand the much larger topic of the emergence and extension of human societies in his *Guns, Germs, and Steel* (1999). We will discuss more about interpretive differences later.

When reading a study advancing an interpretive difference, the reader of historical research must see himself as a judge or juror and consider whether and how this latest explanation addresses previously accepted scholarship on the topic. Are weaknesses in prior research exposed in a convincing manner? Does the new analysis conflict with or extend prior scholarship? What fresh understanding does it bring to the topic? Innovative interpretation may advance historical knowledge and usher in a reconsideration of existing scholarship. This, indeed, would be one marker of good historical research.

Exploring Current Policy

Some historians address current governmental or social policy and practice by researching a particular issue in the past. This kind of historical research may help to inform how the policies and practices came to be and are enacted, or to critique current policy by exposing aspects of similar policies not considered in current debates. Historians sometimes look into the past to draw comparisons with today's policy and practice. Such historical studies typically are significant because they have direct relevance to policy issues. They help policy makers and practitioners consider present policies and practices in light of what we know about the past, as well as assist in addressing existing problems.

With this kind of historical study, the researcher should overtly make the connection between earlier and current times, rather than forcing you, the reader, to intuit such connections. You should ask whether the study directly addresses today's issues or makes the link between past and present. Does it recommend changes in policy or practice or perhaps state why such suggestions are not made or are inappropriate? If, indeed, the historian's intention is to have the research speak to policy, then he or she should articulate the relationship between the history and contemporary issues. As a reader, you may find this stated in an introduction, a conclusion, or a specific section of the writing devoted to applying the research to current policy or issues.

Good examples of this type of historical research are David Tyack and Larry Cuban's *Tinkering Toward Utopia: A Century of Public School Reform* (1995) and Diane Ravitch and Maris Vinovskis's *Learning from the Past: What History Teaches Us About School Reform* (1995), both of which deal with past efforts at school reform. Other policy-focused histories include Fraser and Gerstle's *The Rise and Fall of the New Deal Order* (1990) on U.S. government policy from Franklin D. Roosevelt until Ronald Reagan; the study on the ethics of medical policies and practices in relation to African Americans titled *Medical Apartheid* (Washington, 2007); and the exploration of how World War I veterans shaped government social policy in the United States, *Doughboys, the Great War, and the Remaking of America* (Keene, 2003).

Once you as a reader determine if the question posed is a good one, you must then determine whether the research itself—the means or methods used to address the question—is good.

REFLECTION QUESTIONS

1. What is a topic of interest to you that might lend itself to historical research?
2. Pose two or three different questions about this topic that require different historical approaches.

WHAT DATA ARE USED, OR "HOW DO YOU KNOW?"

Unlike other kinds of research in which the investigator may create data to analyze by distributing a survey, giving a psychological, physical, or subject-specific test to a group of people, or even creating an experiment to observe, historians find existing—and often old—data that they use to know about the past. There are two sources of evidence on which historians base their analyses and interpretations: **primary sources** and **secondary sources**. These are the materials from which historians know something about an earlier time and which they use to make conclusions. If you asked a historian, "How do you know this?" she would point to her sources. Before we discuss these two sources of data in detail, let us consider general things about sources as a way to evaluate historical research.

As a reader of historical scholarship, you can ask many questions about the sources used that will help in determining the quality of the research. One must realize that to find references to the sources used by a historian, you will have to refer to the footnote or endnote number (usually within or at the end of a paragraph in the text) and check the corresponding note at the end of the document. Unlike other social scientific research, historical scholarship does not have a specific section of the text devoted to a literature review. Previous scholarship is embedded throughout a historical piece, and references to those works arc found in the footnotes. Historians are actually notorious for reading the references (the footnotes or endnotes) of a piece of scholarship as much as they read the actual text!

First, you can ask if the sources used are appropriate to the topic under analysis. For instance, a study of U.S. federal government policy on immigration and employment during World War II should rely on federal documents, not local or state documents, unless those latter documents shed light on federal policy in terms of its creation, enactment, or influence. Similarly, an exploration of the effects of federal immigration and employment policies on Hispanics in Los Angeles should utilize local documents, perhaps from city government, businesses, organizations, or local newspapers, as well as any evidence from the people being studied, such as diaries, letters, or even interviews. As a reader, you must ask if the sources used by a historian provide the necessary data on which to build an analysis.

Second, you can check to see if the sources used are original. If historians want to study psychiatric care in Austria during the generation before Sigmund Freud practiced, they should study documents from Austria and preferably in the original language. Relying on translations of documents removes the historian one step from the original source. There is also the possibility that the translator did not adhere to the original meaning. Additionally, if a document has been edited or shortened, this further deteriorates the integrity of the historical research because someone other than the researcher has determined what is important to read. Check the references to see if the documents used are in the original language and in their original form.

Third, the reader must ask if the historian is interpreting and analyzing the sources appropriately, or, as historians would say, within the proper context. Historians must strive, as noted above, to understand the documents in light of their time. They must consider the source's purpose when it was created. Was it to express feelings, persuade others, explain a phenomenon, provide social, moral, or legal guidance or regulation, or do something else? Historians must also learn about the person or organization that wrote or produced the source, because this sheds light on the context and may indicate any biases of the source's creator. In our previous example of federal immigration policies, it would be helpful to know if a source's author was a business owner, a Hispanic worker, or a white native of Los Angeles, as all may have had different perspectives on migrant labor. Knowing about the background, beliefs, social status, and biases of an author of a primary source helps to provide context or meaning to that source. Historians use these pieces of evidence in interpreting sources.

The historian does not just use this evidence to understand the documents and make an analysis; the historian also must include this information and evidence in the narrative or text of the research article or book. This is how the historian supports the analysis and conclusions made—by showing or telling all the information that was considered. This same process is also how the historian brings to life the past and re-creates the context of life in an earlier time—by discussing the details surrounding the evidence. Think about how you would describe life in your community or city today. The more detail and description you provide, the better understanding someone would have of what it is like to live there, what people do, the values they have, and the things that animate life in your city. Historians do the same thing, except they do it for people and places in an earlier time by using the records or documents of that era. And historians show their evidence in footnotes or endnotes to illustrate how they have come to their conclusions.

Unless you are willing to do the background legwork to locate and read the sources that the historian has used—most people are not and many sources may not even be accessible to you—then you must rely upon the professionalism of the historian in interpreting the documents and weighing the evidence in making analyses and conclusions. As a reader, you can assess the quality of research by asking if the context is evident and if the analysis and interpretation make sense in light of the context. Additionally, readers rely on the judgment of other historians in their assessment of the historical interpretation and analysis. Is the article or book published in a reputable journal or at a reputable publishing house? Has this research been referred to by other sources? These things help to attest to the quality of the historical research.

Historical research is based on interpretation and analysis of both primary sources and secondary sources. Let us now turn to understanding these sources as a way to consider the quality of historical research.

Primary Sources

Primary sources are data that were created during the time under investigation. These were created by people who actually witnessed or experienced an event. Primary sources can be any number of documents or artifacts—newspaper articles, personal journals, photographs, toys, interviews—and historians use a variety of these sources to interpret and analyze the past.

Sometimes, primary sources provide conflicting accounts or experiences of the past. This is known as **counterevidence**. Knowing about the sources' authors or producers and their purposes assists the historian in weighing the evidence. Historians must also cross-check their documents with other sources and with existing knowledge and information to resolve any factual errors and expose any biases in creating an accurate interpretation of the past.

Often, the interpretation made by the historian depends on what primary sources are used. Recall our example of the study of federal immigration policies during World War II. Using only federal documents would provide one kind of interpretation; using local sources or archival documents, especially from people affected by the policy, could lead to a different interpretation. Historians argue that new interpretations about a certain topic or time are necessary either when new primary sources have become available or when the historian considers different primary sources than those found in earlier research. The sources will shape the interpretation. Thus, it is important for the reader of historical scholarship to understand the variety of primary source documents available for use.

Public Records   Some primary sources are **public records** or **public documents** that typically have been published and therefore are accessible to anyone, especially in the Internet age. Unless classified, government documents and information are examples of public documents, and with the Internet you can simply click to get historical census data, for example. Public documents are not just government-produced documents, however; they include any published or reproduced source that was made available to the public. Examples of public documents include newspapers, magazines, books, published debates, and pamphlets. Local, state, or federal government documents, such as laws, reports, legislative records (such as the U.S. Congressional Record or even the minutes of a local city council or school board meeting), census data, tax records, deeds, school enrollment figures, and birth, marriage, and death certificates are also public records. Sometimes private organizations such as labor unions or professional associations publish documents for general consumption. All these sources are available to a researcher with enough ingenuity to find them, either through a library or even through the Internet. Digitization projects currently aim to make older material accessible online. For instance, you can find online the text of published sermons from the seventeenth century and back issues of newspapers from the 1950s.

Archival Documents   Other primary sources were not created to be widely distributed or available to the general pubic but were private or **archival documents**, such as letters, diaries, personal photographs, or even the documents of a private corporation or organization. These documents were created for personal or internal use, and there may be only one copy of them. (Some private documents have been published, as in the case of the letters and diaries of historical people. The correspondence between John and Abigail Adams is a prime example.) These private documents usually are accessible only through archives, specialized libraries that hold and preserve historical documents. To use these documents, the researcher must actually go to the archive, sometimes even requesting permission in advance to use a source. Depending on the source's condition and age, strict rules may apply for its usage, such as handling certain materials with special gloves or not making photocopies of materials.

Artifacts Non-written items that historians analyze are **artifacts**. Any object produced during an earlier time can be an artifact. This includes such items as toys, tools, clothing, furniture, and buildings, to name a few. Artifacts can even be images and recordings, photographs, paintings and sculptures, music, movies, television productions, and advertisements. Historians can find additional information about artifacts produced for public enjoyment, such as artwork and entertainment media, including movies or novels from a previous time period, and this helps the historian understand the impact or importance of the item. For instance, historians can scour critics' reviews, book reviews, and publication records that provide the numbers of editions a book went through, the numbers of copies printed and sold, or the revenue earned by a movie or record to determine the influence that the artifact had on popular culture and society. When reading histories that use artifacts, check to see if the historian both interprets the artifacts (says what they mean) and gauges their influence on the broader culture. A historian can provide an illuminating description of an item, but if that item was culturally insignificant, then we learn little about the past. You can read in the text whether the author has given a rationale for the importance of the artifacts being analyzed.

Two different examples illustrate the use of artifacts. The older *Child Life in Colonial Days*, first published in 1899 by Alice Morse Earle, reconstructs the life of children in the colonial period by describing in exceptional detail numerous artifacts—from clothes, shoes, and wigs to toys, pens, examples of penmanship, and portraits, among other things. Thomas Doherty, in his *Teenagers and Teenpics: The Juvenilization of American Movies in the 1950s* (1988) uncovers both the business side and social perception of movies made for teens in the 1950s by looking at various movies, their reception by teenage audiences and adults as measured by box-office receipts and social commentary, and the decisions of major motion picture corporations in producing and advertising movies to a new teen market. Both pieces of research use artifacts—one using tangible artifacts, the other using media artifacts—as a way to understand the past.

Oral Interviews Within the last few decades, historians have begun to utilize interviews with people who have direct knowledge of a historical topic or event. Oral history interviews do create a new primary source, or at least elicit information that otherwise would not be part of public record. (Technically, the information exists, just not in a form that is accessible to a researcher until he or she asks questions of a direct observer of a previous time.) Just like written documentation, oral interviews can sometimes conflict with other sources of information. With oral interviews, this is doubly problematic because individuals may not remember things as they were or they may be influenced by their subsequent experiences, including the researcher's questions. Additionally, there may be a great length of time between the original event and the time when the person is giving the recollections, and this can affect the person's ability to remember the past as he or she experienced it. As a reader of historical scholarship, it is important to recognize these limitations and determine whether the researcher has accounted for any potentially faulty information through the confirmation of data by other witnesses or documented sources. Although oral interviews do help historians understand the experiences of people, researchers also must be careful not to overgeneralize this experience to all people. You should examine the historical scholarship you are reading to determine what group of people the interviewees represent as well as whether and how their experiences reflect that of, or relate to, the larger society.

Quantitative Information   Quantitative data are numbers, facts, or figures that help historians show the significance of an issue under investigation, illustrate changes, make comparisons, and generally interpret the past. However, they provide their own set of interpretive issues. In our society, numbers in and of themselves give an aura of scientific exactness, but readers of historical analysis must be savvy when evaluating them. Here it is wise not to be wowed by numbers simply because they are numbers. Some figures themselves are problematic. Take, for instance, colonial literacy rates and the statistics associated with them. How does the researcher define literacy? As those people who can sign their names to legal documents or as people who read? For example, E. Jennifer Monaghan, in her 1989 study of colonial literacy in America, has shown that learning to read was separate from learning to write, so literacy figures that consider only the writing of one's name would not include those people, mostly women, who learned how to read but not how to write. When using quantitative data, the historian must ensure that the statistics actually measure the concept or category being studied. What, then, were the researcher's methods in determining this statistic? The number, as we see, may not actually say what it implies. It may be more complex than that, and in evaluating historical research that utilizes quantitative data, the reader must ask what indeed the statistics are illustrating. Are the numbers and even the categories of the things being tallied reliable? Do they actually measure what the historian claims that they measure?

Historians sometimes compile statistical data from existing census records, survey statistics, or other quantifiable information. Historians will sometimes "create" quantitative data by counting, for instance, church membership records in a city, then organizing them according to ethnic, residential, or other categories. How do they do this? They cross-check the information with books that provide common ethnic origins of surnames or with city documents recording residences. Statistical data may help to show the relationship between, say, income, ethnicity, and church membership. Historians will use sophisticated methods of computer analysis to determine how significant the relationships are among these categories.

Historians also use statistical information to track or illustrate changes over time or to make comparisons among groups or even across time. The numbers or figures often can be quite illustrative. To assist readers in seeing such comparisons or changes, historians will often place statistical information into charts, graphs, or other forms of visual representation. Table 8.1 is adapted from Joel Perlmann's *Ethnic Differences: Schooling and Social Structure Among the Irish, Italians, Jews and Blacks in an American City, 1880–1935* (1988). It shows the percentage of young people enrolled in high school by race and nativity (whether or not a person was born in the United States).

Not only does the table allow you to see the increase in school enrollment of the various ethnic groups across time, but it also allows you to compare the percentages of

TABLE 8.1. **High School Enrollment Patterns in Percent, 1880–1925**

Father's Ethnic Group	1880	1900	1915	1925
Native white, native parent	27.4	36.2	52.5	57.8
Native white, foreign parent	15.9	15.2	45.3	—
Foreign-born white	3.5	11.5	29.4	46.1
Black	3.7	12.3	22.4	30.7

Source: Adapted from Perlmann, 1988, p. 186.

students of the various ethnic groups enrolled in school at different times. For instance, the children of immigrants (in the foreign-born white category) and black children had nearly equal high school enrollment rates in 1880 and in 1900; yet their rates of enrollment diverge beginning in 1915 and show clear differences by 1925, with black youths enrolling in high school at a lower proportion. We could, as did Perlmann, ask what economic, cultural, or social circumstances accounted for these differences.

When reading historical research that incorporates quantitative data, therefore, it is important to ask if the measurements are consistent over time and reliable and if the statistical information presented helps to illustrate change or comparisons, or even if it provides instructive information that aids in describing or analyzing an earlier period of time.

Secondary Sources

Secondary sources are any interpretations or histories about the past. Historians learn about earlier times not only through primary sources but through what other historians have written. Secondary sources provide historians with existing knowledge about an earlier period. This assists the historian in understanding the past and even in finding those unanswered questions or interpretative differences that may be the starting points for his own research. Secondary sources also are good places to begin identifying primary sources.

As mentioned before, history articles or books do not have a literature review section. However, historians must consult all relevant and related secondary materials in doing their research. References to the secondary literature are embedded into the body of the text and referenced in the footnotes or endnotes. As a new reader of historical scholarship, you may not know if an author has considered all previous work, but when you begin to read on a topic or time period, you will learn this. Once you begin to gain proficiency in this literature, you will be able to read the footnotes or references and identify when historians are considering all important secondary sources or when they have missed or ignored any.

When historians consider both primary and secondary sources, they must then weigh the evidence about the topic or issues under investigation and come to an analysis or interpretation about that time period. As noted, different sources may very likely yield different conclusions or interpretations, but sources are not the only things that shape an interpretation.

1. What are the differences between primary and secondary sources?
2. For the historical research questions that you posed in the last section, what sources might provide appropriate data for your analysis and interpretation?

WHAT IS THE INTERPRETATION, OR "WHY DO YOU THINK THAT?"

Many different things shape an interpretation of the past. Historians base their analyses and conclusions on their own perspective or **interpretive lens**, which they use in seeing earlier times. The interpretive lens used in analyzing the past can be seen in the foci of a study, categories of analysis employed, and the historian's general perspective on history.

When evaluating historical research for the interpretation it makes, you can pose some general questions about interpreting the evidence or source materials. Most histories should advance an organized and cogent argument or thesis about the time or issue under consideration based on good interpretation of evidence. Thus, you can ask a few questions: Is the argument logically made? Can this conclusion or interpretation be drawn from the sources used? Would the conclusion have been different if other sources were used? Additionally, historians must acknowledge **counterevidence**, or sources and evidence that do not support the conclusion being advanced. How did the study address counterevidence? Did the historian provide compelling evidence to show why his or her analysis was correct, given counterevidence?

Historians also should speak to **counterarguments** and alternative interpretations that either have been previously advanced in other secondary research or that can be made given the evidence. The historian must argue why his or her interpretation is different and perhaps more accurate or compelling than other interpretations and arguments. As a reader, you can check if the characterizations of other interpretations are oversimplifications or if they misrepresent that research. Ethical historical scholarship will do neither.

Foci of Historical Studies

Historians can look at topics and events from a number of different ways. Recall again our example of immigration policy during World War II, and let us use this to understand the variety of foci historians can take. We can look at the effect of federal immigration policy on Los Angeles, using some federal sources and local sources, such as local newspapers or diaries and interviews of people in Los Angeles. This would be a local scope of study. Or we could examine the effect of this same immigration policy on the American Southwest, using state and maybe some local sources throughout that region. This would be a regional scope of historical study. Another alternative is studying the effect of these policies nationally. We would have to look at documents at the federal level as well as sources throughout most, if not all, of the states, including national-level publications, such as newspapers with a national circulation. We can extend our study even further if we begin to consider the effects this United States policy had on other nations, such as Canada and Mexico. Thus, the scope of historical research can be local, regional, national, or even international. Remember, however, that the sources used must reflect and be from the same scope of exploration. One could not use only newspapers local to Los Angeles and claim to be doing an international history. The scope of a study determines how wide a net historians cast in finding sources and influences the interpretation made.

Related to the scope of study is how historians view or "see" a topic. Do they look at it from the top down, which, in the case of our immigration policy example, would lead the historian to focus on the bigger picture about policy, rather than a smaller picture about people, their work, and their lives? Focusing on people, especially common people as opposed to famous or historical people such as presidents or labor union leaders, is considered a bottom-up focus. Simply pursuing a local scope of study would not, by default, lead to a bottom-up interpretation, because one could examine the wartime aircraft industry in Los Angeles and its growth and economic influence on the city, and still say very little about the lives of people who worked in those factories. Bottom-up histories look at common people, and historians who pursue such studies often believe in the importance of those common people in shaping history. How the historian sees the topic—bottom up or top down—influences who or what is studied. Those doing bottom-up research often explore people and use sources that get at them, such as diaries, letters, and oral interviews. They also immerse themselves in the local culture of those people, from sources getting at their neighborhood or city politics to the organizations, groups, clubs, churches, or other bodies that influenced common people. Those doing top-down research may focus on government policy, institutions and how they operate, and influential people—those movers and shakers of a particular time or place. Beyond determining the sources used, how historians see their topics influences what they think is important about the past and who they believe are the historical actors that effect change. Are the historical actors the policies and actions of the state, or are they common people and their actions and responses? Does the historian see institutions, such as organizations, as influencing the course of events or do they see a give and take between people and policies? When reading historical research, you should determine how the author sees the topic and how that is part of his or her interpretation.

Historical research also varies according to the length of time under study. Some historians focus on a very limited time period, for instance, immigrant labor from 1940 to 1945. Others take a much longer approach, such as the laboring classes from the dawn of industrialization in the eighteenth century to today. What the former provides typically in extreme detail, the other usually treats in much broader form, providing interpretations about continuities and sweeping changes over time.

These different aspects of foci of historical studies—the scope, the view, and the time frame—are part and parcel of the kind of interpretation of the past the historian makes. They shape a historian's interpretation and are shaped by how the historian sees the world and history.

Perspective on History

Do you think that people who do not understand history are doomed to repeat it? Do you believe that history shows how much progress humanity has made over the centuries? Both of these are examples of **philosophies of history**, and they shape how people see the past. Studying the field of history and how historians interpreted the past is called **historiography**. One can look at approximately the last one hundred years, when history became a professional field of study, to see different trends in historical interpretation. You can ask of the historical research you read what philosophy of history the author has and where he or she fits in the historiography. These questions will help you understand the interpretative lens of the historian.

Philosophies of History   One's philosophy of history explains the basic relationships between events and their causes, and among the past, the present, and the future. Believing that history repeats itself or that society is doomed to repeat history if it does not learn from the past embodies the **cyclical** philosophy of history. The **providential** philosophy sees history as "determined by God, and . . . represent[ing] struggles between forces of good and evil . . . but the eventual victory of good is foreseen" (Benjamin, 2007, p. 6). Thinking that history shows continuous progress or improvement in society based on humankind's efforts and abilities is a **progressive** philosophy. With all these philosophies, the historian is seen as an objective interpreter who simply is uncovering the past. Although most historians strive for objectivity and to honestly portray an earlier time in its own light by shedding their personal and cultural biases and values, some have begun to question the ability of historians to leave their present times behind in interpreting and understanding the past. This philosophy, called **postmodernism**, believes that the present taints and corrupts historians' views of the past and that historians do not uncover the past as much as create it. The underlying philosophy of history that a historian has influences how he or she interprets evidence.

As a reader of historical research, you should question if the history suggests patterns that are repeated in history (the cyclical view) or if it implies that things are improving (the progressive view). Does the history cast the events as "good versus bad," even if there is not the presumption that God has preordained the conflict but rather that humanity's goodness or moral righteousness will prevail? Not only does this help to clarify the historian's philosophy, but it aids you in analyzing and evaluating the historical research because you can possibly predict the moral or lesson of the story.

Historiography   There are trends in how historians view history and interpret the past. Many historians consider the years between 1900 and 1950 as a time when scholarship pursued a **Whiggish interpretation** of history, especially in social science fields such as education, where history was not the main mission but in which scholars explored historical topics, such as the emergence of tax-supported public education, the juvenile justice system, or librarianship. Whig histories oftentimes focused on the development of institutions and prominent people, events, and ideas by using official public documents and taking them at face value, rather than questioning their purpose and biases. It often celebrated progress. In the 1950s, many historians began to question Whig histories' methods and sources and their interpretations and conclusions. These historians believed that considerations about and sources from common people should be included in history. These historians wanted to revise history, and thus produced **revisionist** interpretations by examining new sources, asking new questions, and using such concepts as socioeconomic class in analyzing the past. This development of using new categories of analysis has dominated historical scholarship since the 1950s.

Categories of Analysis

Historians come to the conclusions they do based on their analysis of evidence. There are three major categories of analysis and interpretation: class, race-ethnicity, and gender. When considering class, historians must ask how social or economic differences shaped the past. For analyses based on race or ethnicity, historians look at the influence of racial or ethnic groups. Considerations of women's experiences or of the conceptions of masculinity and femininity are part of gender analysis. These kinds of analyses are not just about considering the experiences of people within these categories but the recognition of how these concepts structured events, social relations, policies, and ideas in the past. Historian Ruth Mazo Karras, in *Boys to Men* (2003), explores what it meant to be a man in medieval Europe, and thus begins to uncover social conventions about gender in medieval society. Research on the Atlantic slave trade and slavery in North America not only describes the experiences of millions of forcibly transplanted Africans and their descendants, but also explains how their labor contributed to and was a critical component of the economic growth of Britain and the United States between 1680 and 1860 (Williams, 1944).

Within the last few decades, concepts and theories from literary theory and the social sciences have further enriched historical scholarship. For instance, researchers have begun to "relate sociological theory and methodology to historical research," in scholarship now called **historical sociology** (McCullough & Richardson, 2000, pp. 52–53). Historians have employed Marxist theory, feminist theory (see Chapter Twelve), and reader response theory, to name only a few, in historical analysis. Although borrowing concepts and theories from various disciplines may help historians to explain and interpret the past, historians may face difficulties in applying sociological or other social scientific and literary terms and concepts to an earlier time because the context may be different.

What you must recognize is that historical scholarship has continuously expanded the areas of research and the ways in which the past can be analyzed. Additionally, historians often see the world through a specific interpretive lens, thus shaping how they view all historical events, actors, and contexts. It is for this reason that two historians can come to different interpretations of the same evidence: Each is informed by a way of looking at the world, finding meaning in it, and coming to some understanding of it.

TYPES OF HISTORICAL RESEARCH

Historians can use their craft—the analysis of primary and secondary sources, the weighing of evidence and counterevidence, and the interpretation of data—in writing a variety of types of history (summarized in Table 8.2). **Social history** plumbs the

TABLE 8.2. **Topics Addressed in Different Types of Historical Research**

Types of Research	Topics Addressed
Biography	The life of one person
Cultural history	Cultural phenomena and their influence in society
Intellectual history	Ideas, the people who advance them, and their influence
Oral history	Any topic can be explored, but the sources used are interviews with people who experienced a past time or event
Political or diplomatic history	Politics and diplomacy, usually at a regional, national, or international level, with a focus on political figures
Quantitative history	Any topic can be explored, but statistics are used to understand the past
Social history	The experiences of common people

experiences of common people, as when historians try to reconstruct life on frontier settlements in 1850 or in cities in 1890. Related to social history is cultural history, which examines any range of cultural phenomena, from sports and entertainment to popular culture and cultural divergences. Histories of country music, gay and lesbian culture in the 1920s, or the temperance movement are examples of cultural history. Political or diplomatic history focuses on politics or diplomacy, usually at a regional level or higher. Political and diplomatic history often center on public figures (such as presidents and diplomats) and the agencies or bodies in which they operate. Intellectual history explores ideas, their formation, and their influence in society. The development of the idea of feminism in the 1920s or the notion of republicanism in early America are examples of topics for intellectual history. Biographies are histories focused on the life of one person, either because the person was historically significant, such as Abraham Lincoln, or because the person represents or speaks to the experiences of a larger group of people or community, as with the history of an eighteenth-century midwife written by Laura Thatcher Ulrich (1991). Some kinds of histories are grounded in the use of specific sources, as with quantitative history that utilizes statistics or oral history based on interviews.

These diverse types of histories often use different kinds of sources because they are focusing on various phenomena. Social history and biography are prone to incorporate personal materials such as diaries and correspondence, in addition to materials local to the area studied. A history of female factory workers or even a specific worker in Lowell, Massachusetts, would explore all aspects of life in Lowell, from church life and schools to local politics. Intellectual history would examine documents in which ideas are put forth, such as scientific or political treaties, manuscripts, or journals, as well as the personal documents of the people who advanced those ideas. Cultural history explores cultural items, from movies and music to novels and other paraphernalia. Of course, any historian can use any source; he or she simply may use that source in different ways.

There also are topical areas of history, such as history of education, history of labor, military and diplomatic history, and history of science and technology. Then there are histories about geographic regions and demographic groups, such as world history, European history, African American history, women's history, or Chinese history. Some histories specifically engage in historical comparisons, called comparative history. Even within these types of histories there are lengthy lists of topics. History of education, for instance, includes history of higher education, history of public education, history of the curriculum, and history of teachers, among others.

There are specific academic journals and associations devoted to all these different types of history, and many more not mentioned here. Some of the major organizations are the Organization of American Historians (www.oah.org), the American Historical Association (www.historians.org), and the World History Association (www.thewha.org). In particular, the American Historical Association has a link on its Web site to all the scholarly societies that are affiliated with it (see www.historians.org/affiliates). Additionally, there are historical societies in many cities and states across the United States that not only display exhibits on history but archive and store documents and artifacts. Museum and historical sites also house historical materials and have a specific educational mission to explain and interpret history to visitors. Many historical associations and societies sponsor journals (some available online) and Web sites for information and even access to primary and secondary sources. There are even online discussion forums for a variety of historical topics; visit www.h-net.org to subscribe, see the various topic areas (such as H-world for world history), and join the discussion.

LEARNING MORE

There are many different specialized resources to help you learn more about historical research. Some resources help in understanding topics and others assist in locating sources. Still others help you in doing historical research of your own and in following conventions of writing style and bibliographic entry. Even more specialized sources provide introduction to the historiography of a specific subtopic or genre within historical scholarship and point to directions for future research. Because of the wide variety of topics within the social sciences and because historical research often explores a similarly diverse array of subjects, we cannot survey this territory here, but a few are mentioned in "Further Readings and Resources" at the end of the chapter.

Jules R. Benjamin's *A Student's Guide to History* (2007) not only provides practical advice on how to analyze sources and research and write a historical paper, but also offers a lengthy list of resources on a variety of historical topics, including history organizations, bibliographies arranged by topic, reference guides, online resources, and digital reference sources and online discussion lists in history, to name a few. A more concise guide to the historian's craft is *A Pocket Guide to Writing in History* (2004) by Mary Lynn Rampolla. Both of these resources can help you do historical research.

For a critical discussion of the treatment of historical research within the social sciences, see Gary McCulloch and William Richardson's *Historical Research in Educational Settings* (2000). This does focus only on the subtopic of history of education, but the authors approach it from a theoretical perspective that can help you consider historical research within the tradition of the social sciences. McCulloch and Richardson think that historical research has not been adequately addressed in scholarship on social science research because of history's association with the humanities. They do believe, however, that historical research has been influenced by critical theory, and they address historiography to show changes in historical scholarship over the last fifty years.

However, the best way to become familiar with historical research is to begin reading the scholarship. With these basics on how to evaluate historical research, you will start to distinguish "good" studies from those of lesser quality, find models of good research, and enter into the larger discussion about the past. Either of the exemplary works listed in the "Further Readings" at the end of this chapter would be a great place to start.

 ## REFLECTION QUESTIONS

1. How do you view history? Has this changed after reading this chapter? If so, what influenced your new perceptions? If not, what information corroborates your previously held perspective?

2. What types of historical research would be useful for you to seek out to expand your understanding of your discipline and to improve your professional practice?

SUMMARY

Historians attempt to recreate the past by examining primary source documents, uncovering the ideas, beliefs, and values that shaped an earlier time, and drawing conclusions from their work. Historians may address all kinds of topics, using all different sorts of documents and sources, and they certainly are influenced by their own philosophies of history and their own interpretive lens. Even when historians come to conflicting conclusions about the past, they all try to discover the complexities and details of that earlier time in a way that brings the past to life for readers.

KEY TERMS

archival documents
artifacts
categories of analysis
causation
continuity
context
counterargument
counterevidence
cyclical philosophy
historical actors
historical imagination
historical sociology

historiography
interpretive lens
philosophies of history
postmodernism
presentism
primary sources
progressive philosophy
providential philosophy
public records or documents
revisionist interpretation
secondary sources
Whiggish interpretation

FURTHER READINGS AND RESOURCES

Exemplary Works of Historical Research

Kim, J. K. (2004). The political economy of the Mexican Farm Labor Program, 1942–1964. *Aztláan: A Journal of Chicano Studies*, *29*, 13–53.

This article is the winner of the 2007 EBSCOHOST: American History and Life Award, awarded through the Organization of American Historians.

McClellan, J., & Dorn, H. (2006). *Science and technology in world history: An introduction*. Baltimore, MD: The Johns Hopkins University Press.

This book is the winner of the 2000 World History Association Book Prize.

Suggested Readings

Benjamin, J. R. (2007). *A student's guide to history*. Boston: Bedford/St. Martin's.

Jules R. Benjamin's book not only provides practical advice on how to analyze sources and research and write a historical paper, but also offers a lengthy list of resources on a variety of historical topics.

Clark, V. A. (2008). *A guide to your history course: What every student needs to know*. Upper Saddle River, NJ: Pearson Education.

A wonderful book that describes how to study history textbooks, how to write papers, how to avoid plagiarism, and how history as a discipline works.

Rampolla, M. L. (2004). *A pocket guide to writing in history* (4th ed.) Boston: Bedford/St. Martin's.

This is a more concise guide to the historian's craft than Benjamin's book. Both of these resources can help you do historical research.

McCulloch, G., & Richardson, W. (2000). *Historical research in educational settings*. Berkshire, England, and Philadelphia: Open University Press.

The book provides a critical discussion of the treatment of historical research within the social sciences. This does focus only on the subtopic of history of education, but the authors approach it from a theoretical perspective that can help you consider historical research within the tradition of the social sciences. McCulloch and Richardson address what they see as the limitations of treatments of historical research, as well as historiography and the influence of critical theory.

Web Sites and Associations

As described in the chapter, there are many historical associations and Web sites; some of the more prominent ones are the following:

Organization of American Historians (www.oah.org)

American Historical Association (www.historians.org) in particular, there is a link on this Web site to all the scholarly societies that are affiliated with it (see www.historians.org/affiliates)

World History Association (www.thewha.org)

Online discussion forums on a variety of historical topics; visit www.h-net.org to subscribe, see the various topic areas (such as H-world for world history), and join the discussion

ENDNOTE

1. B.C.E. is "Before the Common Era." Historians have begun to use the terms "before the common era" and "common era" (C.E.) instead of "B.C." ("before Christ") and A.D. ("anno Domini," or translated from the Latin to mean "in the year of the Lord"). The new terms reflect a more inclusive terminology than the previous ones, which were based on the Christian marker of Jesus's birth for the dating system.

CHAPTER

CASE STUDY RESEARCH

STEPHEN D. LAPAN AND SHADOW W. J. ARMFIELD

KEY IDEAS

- Case studies seek rich descriptions about people, events, topics, or programs by researching them in their natural environment.

- In contrast to the broad surface data collected through survey research, case studies produce details about local phenomena.

- Case studies may be conducted to explain aspects of a program to stakeholders or as devices for building or testing theories.

- The term "case" refers to the portions or aspects of a given phenomenon that will be studied.

- Case studies can be completed over varying time periods as single cases or as multiple cases or sites.

- Steps followed in case study research include case selection, study question formulation, collecting data, and reporting the findings in a meaningful way.

- Most case studies share the characteristics of describing the context, using mixed methods, cross-checking findings, applying purposeful sampling techniques, and summarizing findings.

- Readers can make naturalistic generalizations, learning from case study reports by comparing them to their own practices.

■ Case study reports are more trustworthy when the case is clearly defined, evidence of validity is present, voices within the case are well represented, alternative views are incorporated, and researcher interpretations are supported by concrete examples.

CASE STUDY is a form of research that endeavors to produce rich descriptions about singular contemporary events or topics (not historical ones), such as the thorough study of a recent teachers' strike or a close examination of a new hiring policy at an insurance company. The study of people falls under this category of investigation, which is called **narrative research**, and is concerned with the contemporary retelling of how people interacted with significant past events (re-storying), as in the study of individuals who were retained in school (Powell, 2005). Although there are several possible objectives for case study research, this chapter will focus exclusively on the inspection of educational and social programs.

In program case studies, the researcher first identifies the case to be investigated as some aspect of the program, sharpens the focus of the study by formulating questions about the case, spends significant time on-site collecting observational and other complex descriptions, attempts to answer study questions posed during planning, and sets out to discover other relevant information related to the case. Rather than focusing on large samples used in experiments and other traditional frameworks, the case study's target is a particular setting and the inspection of real-life contexts where data are collected about daily activities, routines, and participant interactions with the case.

Case study research is characterized by a microscopic approach where intensive examination of the "particular" is emphasized; this is what some call "peeling the onion" to carefully view each layer of identified case-related program activity. Typical of this research is what many label **naturalistic inquiry**, where the case researcher makes every attempt to leave the program undisturbed during observation. Unlike many forms of research, case study does not try to affect results or manipulate variables. The primary goal of case study research is to present an authentic portrayal of typical program functions using observation, participant dialogue, and other firsthand accounts to illuminate and reflect actual everyday program activities.

Scriven (1991) describes case study as the polar opposite of survey research (see Chapter Five). Survey studies cast a wide net to gather broad, useful, surface-level information, such as regional incidences of flu cases or national high school dropout rates. Conversely, case studies drill deeply below the surface into single instances, much more locally, to gain a thorough understanding about the complexities of a program. Using this research approach, one might examine the case of flu treatment at a local emergency care facility or the case of one high school's attempt to prevent dropouts.

Traditionally, the term "case study" referred to a patient's clinical workup or diagnostic exploration in medicine, psychiatry, or psychology for the purposes of guiding treatment strategies. Case studies are also used in other fields as instructional devices in which students in professional training produce solutions to problems posed in actual or fictionalized case stories. Law students, for example, would be given a court case report to analyze; business trainees would discuss a case of stock market fraud.

For several decades now, however, case studies have been thought of in a remarkably different way, not as clinical or training devices, but rather as social scientific research used to discover the complicated interactions between people, settings, and programs. These multilayered case studies focus on the "how" and "why" questions about educational and social programs.

In the well-regarded study *Boys in White* (Becker, Greer, Hughes, & Strauss, 1961), for example, the purpose was not to study or describe medical students for clinical purposes, but rather "to discover what medical school did to medical students other than giving them a technical education" (p. 17). This study met the general criteria of social scientific case study research by observing the rich detail of one class of medical students in one medical school at the University of Kansas as they experienced their daily routines, schedules, and interactions with medical training.

REFLECTION QUESTION

1. What do you think are important distinctions between clinical case work and case study research?

PURPOSES OF PROGRAM CASE STUDIES

Many writers have classified the purposes that case studies could serve. Yin (2003), for example, suggests that they can be used to explore, describe, explain, and compare. Simons (1977), on the other hand, suggests their role can be to discover and communicate innovative ideas and programs. Perhaps the most parsimonious characterization of case study uses has been offered by Stake (1995), who outlines two purposes. The first is the investigation of a case for the sole purpose of understanding the case itself. This is what Stake (2005) identifies as **intrinsic**, case studies that seek answers to questions about the case alone, designed within the framework of the program of interest only. Intrinsic case reports offer stakeholders and other readers sharpened views and new insights about program operations. Stake (2005) cautions, "the researcher at least temporarily subordinates other curiosities so that the stories of those 'living the case' will be teased out" (p. 445).

A distinctly different purpose for case study research is that of **theorizing**, where the investigator considers the case as a device or set of findings to be applied beyond the case being studied. Stake (1995) calls this the **instrumental** role of case study research. **Theory building** is one instrumental function that first gained prominence with the pioneering work of Glaser and Strauss (1967), who demonstrated the power of understanding a phenomenon by studying it in action. They developed the concept of **grounded theory**—building theory from the ground up by thoroughly examining example after example of concrete instances of an idea or case, followed by the construction of an explanation for all of these concrete events. For example, researchers might conduct theory-building case studies of elementary students who set about solving a range of problems while the researcher carefully records their problem-solving behavior. Using these observations, the researcher begins to construct a theory of problem-solving ability among young children.

In addition to the theory-building role, researchers may employ instrumental case studies to test existing theories (**theory testing**) to determine whether these theories can be confirmed when applied to real-life contexts. When applied to real-life contexts, these theories can be confirmed. Case study investigators might follow through with the theory constructed about the problem-solving abilities of children in several new settings with different populations. These case studies may support a theory or uncover inconsistencies as the theories are tested. In both building and testing theories, researchers are likely to include multiple cases in their designs, thus enabling them to make stronger arguments for findings.

REFLECTION QUESTIONS

1. What does the term "grounded theory" mean to you?
2. What is a theory you know about and how might you test it?

PROGRAM CASE STUDY DESIGNS

Case study researchers may use either intrinsic or instrumental reasons as they set about designing their studies. These case study formats are distinguished by the time committed to completing the research and the number of cases included.

One-Shot or Snapshot Design

The first of these, the **one-shot** or **snapshot** case study, is a design used when the research involves one case to be studied at a single point in time. The typical time frame for the one-shot study ranges from six weeks to six months. Such studies are timely in that they offer **stakeholders** (those affected by the program) and other interested readers early evidence of program functions. By meeting the goal of case illumination, study results offer insights for the participants but they can also offer findings for program improvement. This improvement role opens the opportunity for case studies to be used as **program evaluations** (see Chapter Ten), where the researcher provides conclusions and suggestions for program changes, not just summary interpretations. This evaluative role may or may not be the goal of the one-shot case study and should be negotiated between the researcher and the stakeholders during the planning stages.

Longitudinal Design

Longitudinal case study designs, another type of case research, are conducted over longer periods of time, usually six months to a year or more, and are more thorough in representing typical patterns of activity. The researcher has the opportunity to recheck program functions, collect data from the same participants on more occasions, and play the role of a **participant observer**, where the researcher is thought of as more of a program member than as a visiting observer. These longitudinal case studies may be intentionally designed as **ethnographic research** (see Chapter Eleven) if the aim of the investigator includes the cultural interpretation of program and participant practices. Care is taken in ethnographic case study designs to understand and even anticipate the nature of group roles and belief systems as they evolve. Therefore, the case study researcher must be a trained ethnographer. It is notable that longitudinal case study evaluations are also common, especially when large-scale programs require extended study.

Comparison Design

Another case study format often employed is the **comparison design**, in which different cases are studied at a given site or at more than one location. The unique purpose served in this approach is not only to generate individual case patterns, but also to note commonalities and differences found when comparing the cases. These cross-case comparison studies may share the characteristics of the snapshot or the longitudinal approach and the intrinsic purposes of producing illuminative results for stakeholders at each site. They are often used instrumentally (for theorizing) as well.

IDENTIFYING THE CASE

One key to understanding any case study is the ability to recognize and identify the **case** of the case study. The **case** represents the focus of the study, what some call the *main character*, although it is not a character at all, but rather the segments or aspects of a program that receive the attention of the researcher. Case studies might identify cases as program adoptions, new innovations, or attempts to resolve social ills. The actual research might be the case study of the implementation of new computer software, the application of new management techniques, or an innovative employee-recruiting program.

   As you are reading case study reports, it is of primary importance to keep the case or main focus of a study at the forefront. Reminding oneself of the focus or case at hand helps to organize all the information presented in the report. The reader should always ask: "What does this have to do with the case?" and "How does this information improve my understanding of the case being studied?" In their report, case study researchers are responsible for making the case clearly identifiable to the reader. The five case study titles and descriptions listed in Exhibit 9.1 are examples of how cases are identified.

 REFLECTION QUESTION

1. In your own words, how would you define the term "case" in case study research?

EXHIBIT 9.1.   **Examples of Case Study Titles and Descriptions**

Lapan & Hays (2004). *Collaborating for Change.*

   Case study of the preparation of teams of classroom teachers to develop and implement programs of gifted education for underrepresented populations

Mabry & Ettinger (1999). *Supporting Community-Oriented Educational Change: Case and Analysis.*
   Case study of a program to implement community-oriented social studies curriculum

Markus (1983). *Power, Politics and MIS Implementation.*
   Case of resistance to the adoption of Management Information Systems (MIS)

McFadden (1999). *College Students' Use of the Internet.*
   Case of student pornographic use of computers in one university laboratory

Myers (1994). *A Disaster for Everyone to See: An Interpretive Analysis of a Failed IS Project.*

   Case of the attempted but failed implementation of a centralized payroll Information System (IS) in the New Zealand Education Department

---

PLANNING AND CONDUCTING CASE STUDIES

Understanding the anatomy of case study research is best revealed by reading examples of case reports. Here, we offer an excerpt of a school program case study investigating the Technology Integrated Learning Environment (TILE) program for middle school students (Armfield, 2007). As with most case studies, the following are the common elements of the TILE study:

1. *Case selection:* The case study is framed by setting boundaries of place and time. The TILE program was located at the Sentinel Middle School and studied during the spring of 2007. Specifically, this is an intrinsic, one-shot case study describing the adoption of the TILE program.

2. *Study question formulation:* In this step, Armfield refined his case by selecting which aspects of the TILE program would be the focus of observation. This is where he adjusts the knob on the microscope to bring into even finer focus what parts of TILE will be studied. Although several questions were posed, this excerpt highlights two: How do students, teachers, and others influence instructional planning? What patterns of lower- and higher-level thinking are emphasized during instruction? These questions were chosen in part because they reflect the middle school philosophy espoused by the program adopters.

3. *Collecting data:* This is an essential problem-solving stage of the design, as the researcher determines how best to answer the study questions posed. For the questions included in the excerpt, Armfield decided to learn about instructional planning and student thinking by observing class instruction, collecting interview

and questionnaire data from students and teachers, and inspecting lesson plans related to the two research questions.

4. *Synthesizing results:* The role of the researcher in this final phase of case study work is synthesizing data, which provides answers to the study questions. Reporting this synthesis is enhanced by direct quotations and other firsthand accounts of the program as observed by the investigator. Often too, the researcher will uncover other findings not sought in the questions but considered useful in explaining how the program functions. Where possible, Armfield reported firsthand accounts using quotations or observation to explain his results. He expressed his findings as direct answers to each research question. Case researchers may decide to present their findings in many other formats, such as stories, plays, or even as video documentaries.

 REFLECTION QUESTIONS

1. If you were doing a case study of this course, what particular "case" within the course would you choose to study?

2. What questions might you pose about the case you have identified?

Case Study Example: The Sentinel Middle School TILE Program

The excerpts of the TILE case study that follows (Armfield, 2007) represent a useful example of an intrinsic, one-shot investigation. It is *intrinsic* in that the research design focused on and was framed by the TILE program only; it was a *one-shot* study where all data were collected during a single two-month time period. Using observations, interviews, questionnaires, and inspection of lesson plans, the researcher attempted to uncover answers related to his study questions. In this abbreviated excerpt, two of the questions identified by the case study investigator relate to influences on instructional planning and student thinking encouraged during lessons. All person and location names used in this case study are pseudonyms to disguise and protect participants' identities.

The Case. The new program being implemented is called the Technology Integrated Learning Environment (TILE). The purpose of this case study was to observe and describe this program as these teachers and students at Sentinel Middle School (SMS) implemented it beginning in 2006.

In the fall of 2003, two middle school teachers and approximately 55 seventh-grade students began a new program called the Technology Integrated Learning Environment (TILE) at SMS. In addition to this being a case of the adoption of this program, the teachers were expected to follow the middle school's philosophy of exploration and nurturing student thinking, as well as promoting student achievement, which would be assessed on a statewide test.

Short History. In its first year, the TILE program consisted of two seventh-grade teachers and 55 students. In the three years up to the time of the research, the TILE program had grown to twelve teachers and 330 students. Six of the teachers worked with 165 of the students at the seventh-grade level; the other six teachers worked with the remaining students at the eighth-grade level. Each grade level had three academic teams. Each team consisted of two teachers and approximately 55 students. The teachers on each team taught the school's four core academic disciplines: English, mathematics, social studies (geography or American history), and general science.

Community Setting. The community is a regional center with a population of approximately sixty thousand that lies at the intersection of two interstate highways. Although the city was developed around the logging and railroad industries, the three largest employers now are a state university, a regional health center, and a private industry specializing in the development of medical products. Vital to the community's survival is a large tourism industry. This industry is supported by temperate weather and a number of internationally recognized natural landscapes in the vicinity. Nearly 40 percent of the residents twenty-five years of age or older have bachelor or graduate degrees. Seventy-two percent of the community population is age forty-four or younger. The percentages of population by ethnic background are:

Asian or Pacific Islander	1.8%
African American	6.1%
Native American	10.0%
Hispanic	16.1%
European American	77.9%

School Setting. Sentinal Middle School (SMS) is one of two public middle schools in this community. The school was built at the end of the 1960s and designed for community activities. The building plan included four classroom pods with few walls. Over the years the philosophy of the school has changed and walls have been erected between some of the classrooms. In the early 1990s, SMS made a transition from junior high school to middle school. All students are placed on teams and work with two to four core teachers. SMS serves a population of approximately 750 students in the seventh and eighth grade, ages eleven to thirteen. Fifty-two percent are eligible for the free and reduced lunch program. The percentages of student population by ethnic background are:

Asian or Pacific Islander	1.4%
African American	3.1%
Hispanic	18.8%
Native American	19.9%
European American	56.8%

According to school records, the socioeconomic backgrounds of students in the TILE program reflected those of the entire school population.

At the time of this study, the school was split into two unique schools within the school, with approximately 44 percent of the students participating in the TILE program and the rest attending the school in its original design. The students and teachers on the TILE teams had access to three new computer labs, creating a 4-to-1 student-to-computer ratio. The remainder of the school population shared one lab of five-year-old computers, creating a 14-to-1 ratio.

The Players. The sample of the study was one team in the TILE program. This consisted of 57 seventh-grade students, two teachers, and one student teacher. All members of the team were observed and most participated in a questionnaire. Teachers and students were interviewed during the study period. At the conclusion of the observations, ten students were selected to be interviewed. These students were both male and female, of African American, Native American, Hispanic, and European American descent, and had multiple levels of academic ability. The students were chosen based on their abilities to share multiple perspectives on the TILE program. The students who shared their experiences in the TILE program were Aaron, Alisa, Belinda, Bethany, Frida, Heather, Kevin, Laurie, Michael, and Turner. The teachers were Mr. Kelvin, who taught English and science, Mr. Lincoln, who taught geography and math, and Ms. Roberts, a student teacher in English. Each teacher is European American. Mr. Lincoln, the school principal, and two professors from the university were behind the initial development of the TILE program.

The Story. The purpose of this research was to describe the activities, roles, and behaviors of students and teachers in a learning environment designed to meet the needs of these stakeholders with varied and possibly conflicting philosophies of education. Data collection included multiple methods and sources, such as interviews with both students and teachers. The researcher's observations contained descriptive data developed through both qualitative and quantitative methods, and he collected teacher lesson plans and other documents describing classroom activities.

Case Study Question 1: Influence on Instructional Planning

The weekly learning objectives are listed on the whiteboards in the back of each of the classrooms in the TILE program. The objectives are located in a grid with five columns and two to four rows. The columns represent the days of the week and the rows represent the classes held in that room. To understand the source of those learning objectives, the students and teachers had to be questioned and lesson plans had to be reviewed. When asked in interviews about who plans learning objectives, the students and teachers gave the following statements about student involvement:

Belinda: Mr. Lincoln decides most of the time and Mr. Kelvin decides most of the time, but then he'll, both of them will let us put our opinion of what we want to do. Sometimes they'll let us put our opinion in.

Frida: The teachers, and every now and then, Mr. Lincoln and Mr. Kelvin give us a little free time to figure out what we want to do, kinda like a miniature study hall.

Mr. Kelvin: Me, not so much, the kids more than anything.

Mr. Lincoln: We also allow the students to make decisions at times, you know to where they begin to take more responsibility for some of their learning, more than maybe some other classes would.

Although both students and teachers indicated student involvement in the development of learning objectives, more often reference was made to the teacher as engineer of learning objectives.

Alisa:	Mr. Kelvin, Mr. Lincoln, and Ms. Roberts [Mr. Kelvin's student teacher].
Bethany:	Usually the teacher, which would be either Mr. Lincoln or Mr. Kelvin. But if they're on the same subject, like the rockets, they'll decide it among themselves and tell the class.
Mr. Lincoln:	These, I'm basically doing on my own. Mr. Kelvin is doing his own projects right now, but we are going to be getting back on a common math project here before long, so basically me.
Mr. Kelvin:	Ms. Roberts and I work together.

Finally, both teacher and students referred to outside entities as the developers of learning objectives.

| *Michael:* | I think it's pretty much the teachers have a pre-planned schedule or the whole school district has a year curriculum that they plan on having the teachers teach throughout the year. |
| *Mr. Lincoln:* | In math, the math activities are geared in part to making sure that they do understand the basics; standards. |

The teachers' lesson plans also provided evidence of how the TILE program develops its learning objectives. Each of these plans placed "meeting state standards represented on the statewide test" near the beginning.

Summary for Question 1: Influence on Instructional Planning The conspicuous placement of learning objectives in each of the TILE classrooms demonstrates their importance, but did not indicate how they were derived. Both the teachers and the students were aware of student involvement in instructional planning, suggesting that students were "sometimes" allowed to share opinions about planning. In interviews, both students and teachers indicated that teachers were "usually" and "basically" the developers of learning objectives. Finally, one student and one teacher pointed out that district and state policies determined goals for instruction. These latter influences were evident in the teachers' lesson plans.

Case Study Question 2: Student Thinking in Classroom Discussions

Conversations among the teachers and the students in the TILE classrooms were observed throughout the duration of the case study. A total of 594 minutes, or nearly ten hours, of classroom activity were observed. These data were collected during nearly fifty 48-minute classes. Each of the teacher's classrooms was observed for three consecutive days during January and three more days in February. The observations were divided into three five-minute intervals at the beginning, middle, and end of each class period. The findings indicated that teacher talk was responsible for 328 minutes, or about five and one-half hours (55.2 percent), of the total time. Student talk accounted for 216 minutes (36.4 percent) of the time observed. Fifty minutes (8.4 percent) was observed as all talk–no talk activities—those in which students were engaged silently, and those during which students were all talking at once. These data, summarized in Table 9.1, reflect all observations, although each class deviated from this to some extent.

TABLE 9.1. **Minutes and Percentages of Time in Classroom Talk and Behavior**

	Teacher	Student	All Talk–No Talk
Time in Minutes (%)	328 (55.2%)	216 (36.4%)	50 (8.4%)

These data show that the teachers are largely responsible for communication in the classrooms. Some of this time was spent giving directions and answering questions. The remaining time was spent on teacher questions. The levels of thinking addressed by teacher questioning became a clear theme in data gathered by the researcher.

During observations on January 18, 2006, Mr. Lincoln had the following discussion with his students:

Mr. Lincoln: What is the name of a second object that makes the shape of a third object?

Student: I know, net.

Mr. Lincoln: Can someone tell me one thing about this object?

Student: It has a square in the middle.

Mr. Lincoln: What is the general name of an object with four sides?

Student: Quadrilateral.

Mr. Lincoln: Quad? What does quad mean?

Mr. Lincoln: What else has quad in it?

Student: Quadriceps.

Mr. Lincoln: How about quadruped? What does that mean? Quad means four.

One week later, Mr. Kelvin was observed talking with his students who were about to present something to their classmates. He asked, "What questions will you ask your classmates? What do you think their response will be?" He tells them that they need to think about this so that they will have the right questions for the presentation.

The observations above demonstrate how questioning and answering are conducted in the TILE classrooms. Throughout the classroom data collection period the researcher observed many conversations between teachers and students. The conversations at times were teachers asking and students answering questions. Knowing the types of questions asked can further help define teaching and learning through an understanding of what it is the teachers want the students to get from the questioning.

The first type of question addressed is that which is based on **memory.** Questions in this realm aim for answers that can be based on the recall or recognition of facts. The answers are generally narrow in scope and have one correct answer. In the observation above, Mr. Lincoln asks the students, "What does quad mean?" This is an example of a memory question. Of the 769 questions asked during the observation period, 698 fell into this category. That is, 90.8 percent of all questions observed required memory.

The second type of question most often asked were those classified as **application and analysis.** Although these questions require memorized information, they also require more than the first type of question. The memorized information is not considered the end result but rather serves as the catalyst for finding an answer. The respondent analyzes the memorized information or integrates it into a new situation. In the observation above, Mr. Kelvin asks the students, "What questions will you ask your classmates? What do you think their response will be?" This is an example of an application and analysis question, one that requires the students to use what they know in a new situation. Fifty-two questions, or 6.8 percent of all questions observed, fell into this category.

Whereas application and analysis questions ask the respondent to begin to integrate memorized content, **creative thinking** questions ask respondents to project or predict different outcomes based on their understandings of the information given. An example of creative thinking questioning was observed during the examination of geometric shapes. Mr. Lincoln asked his students to consider how time would have affected Egyptian pyramids had they been made into other three-dimensional shapes. Throughout all of the question-and-answer periods, 18 of 769 (2.3 percent) of the questions fell into the creative thinking category.

The last type of student thinking observed involved questions classified as **evaluative**. Evaluative questions call for the respondent to offer suggestions of judgment, value, or choice. An example of this type of question was observed in a discussion of drought. Mr. Kelvin asked his students to compare and contrast drought conditions in desert locales with those in mountain locales. One percent (.1) of the 769 questions that were observed fell into this category. A summary of the question levels found is presented in Table 9.2.

Summary of Findings for Question 2: Student Thinking in the Classroom   The amount of time spent in conversations between the teachers and the students demonstrates the importance of communication in the TILE classrooms. Transcriptions of teachers' questions were included here to demonstrate the types of verbal interchanges that occurred in the TILE classrooms. The data revealed here indicate that there are specific levels of thought emphasized in these classrooms, with the overwhelming majority of questions found to be at the memory level (90.8 percent). These questions required students to express memorized information. The remaining 71 questions recorded (9.2 percent) encouraged students to move beyond memory by requiring that they apply previous knowledge to new problems, predict how ideas would work in new settings, and evaluate their observations or answers.

REFLECTION QUESTIONS

1. Do any of the ideas in this case sound familiar; that is, can you identify with this case?

2. What, if anything, did you learn from this case?

TABLE 9.2. **Type of Questions Asked in the TILE Program**

	Memory	Analysis and Application	Creative	Evaluative
Raw (%)	698 (90.8%)	52 (6.8%)	18 (2.3%)	1 (0.1%)

COMMON CASE STUDY CHARACTERISTICS

The TILE investigation contains elements characteristic of most case studies. These include:

- **Contextualization** of the case, where details are given to the reader about the history of the program, explanations of community and school, and identification of the cast of players in the case. This provides the surrounding characteristics in which the case is studied.

- **Mixed methods data collection**, where both qualitative words and quantitative numbers are used to document the case. Interviews, questionnaires, lesson plan analysis, and observations of questions and classroom talk are represented in words and numbers in the TILE study.

- **Triangulation** of data collection methods and data sources, where at least two types of observations are used (such as questionnaires and interviews), and at least two sources are used (for example, students and teachers). This triangulation offers more complex, overlapping descriptions of the case and makes the report more trustworthy as well.

- **Purposeful (purposive) sampling**, where data sources such as people and documents are sought because that is where the answers to the study questions are likely to be found. There is a purpose for selecting students, for example, because they know what class is like when teachers step out of the room. Traditional studies often use representative sampling to reflect populations of people; case studies seek information-rich sources, just as a detective would in locating witnesses.

- **Summaries** are used by the case researcher to review and synthesize observations, offering interpretations that do not reflect conclusions, judgments, or recommendations.

LEARNING FROM CASE STUDIES

Readers of case studies find them enlightening to the extent that the reports capture the complexities of the case and parallel the readers' own definitions of accepted practices and contexts. The reports should be presented as authentic reproductions of daily activities and events without evidence of researcher views, unless an evaluation purpose of the design was negotiated beforehand. This allows the reader to reflect on the case material, drawing conclusions independent of the investigator.

Unlike reports of most traditional research findings, case studies offer narrative portraits that should communicate the complexities of the case in terms familiar to participants and other practitioners knowledgeable about the focus of the case. Stake and Trumbull (1982) suggest that case studies offer opportunities for learning and change when the findings authentically represent the daily events of most practitioners. They call this **naturalistic generalization**, where reader-practitioners can identify with the experiences reported and even gain new insights to guide new practice. "The naturalistic researcher observes and records what readers are not placed to observe for themselves, but who, when reading the descriptive account, can experience vicariously the various perplexities" (Stake & Trumbull, 1982, p. 5).

The usefulness of any case study relies not only on the thoroughness and accuracy of its reports, but also on what the reader finds applicable. This idea of learning from case studies depends in turn, at least to some degree, on the extent of a practitioner's trust in the overall quality of the investigation.

TRUSTING CASE STUDY REPORTS

Extensive discussions regarding **validity** (trustworthiness of study results) as it applies to case study work can be found in the chapter on program evaluation (Chapter Ten). For example, the reader may want to review in greater detail ideas in those chapters related to **triangulation**, cross-checking findings using various methods and sources, as well as the concept of **member checking**, reviewing preliminary findings with participants to determine consistency with their experiences in the program. In addition, readers of case studies can apply the questions below as a way of testing the quality of any report produced from case study research. There should be few, if any, negative answers to the issues raised here.

- Is the case clearly defined, including its boundaries of place and time?
- Are study results linked to the identified case?
- Is the intrinsic or instrumental purpose of the case study clearly communicated?
- Are study results used intrinsically or instrumentally as indicated?
- What design (one-shot, longitudinal, comparison) was used in the case study and is the report consistent with that format?
- Was sufficient time spent in collecting data about the case?
- Is there supporting evidence, including firsthand reports, for all findings?
- Are the findings a complete and representative reproduction of the case?
- Were most participants included as data sources?
- Were participants consulted (member checking) about the authenticity of the findings?
- Was triangulation (multiple sources and methods) used to insure consistency of findings?
- Were pseudonyms used to encourage stakeholder honesty?
- Is the report presented in a form that communicates to its intended audiences?
- Were differing views of events in the case acknowledged and reported?
- Is there always a clear distinction between the descriptions of the case and the researcher's interpretations?

REFLECTION QUESTIONS

1. What, in your opinion, should you be most skeptical about when reading a case study report?

2. Do you think case study investigations are "real" research studies? Why or why not?

SUMMARY

Historically, case studies were thought of as clinical reports about individuals, but in the last forty years they have been used to develop thick descriptions of events, topics, and programs. Case study results can be used to inform stakeholders about program functions or to build or test theories.

Case study research may be conducted on single or multiple cases over varying lengths of time. All case studies contain the identification of the case to be examined, formulation of questions to sharpen the focus, and the collecting and reporting of case findings using various formats for different audiences. Readers of these studies often learn from them when they recognize similarities with their own practices and determine that the studies offer authentic findings.

KEY TERMS

application and analysis
case
case study
comparison design
contextualization
creative thinking
ethnographic research
evaluative
grounded theory
intrinsic case
instrumental case
longitudinal design
member checking
memory

narrative research
naturalistic generalization
naturalistic inquiry
one-shot or snapshot design
participant observer
program evaluations
purposeful (purposive) sampling
stakeholders
theorizing
theory building
theory testing
triangulation
validity

FURTHER READINGS AND RESOURCES

Suggested Case Study Articles

Jenkins, K. (2008). Practically professionals? Grassroots women as local experts—a Peruvian case study. *Political Geography*, *27*, 139–159.

This case study is developed from a feminist perspective.

Smith, T. W., & Strahan, D. (2004). Toward a prototype of expertise in teaching: A descriptive case study. *Journal of Teacher Education*, *55*, 357–371.

This case study of expertise in teaching is based on data from three expert teachers gathered through interviews, observations, and questionnaires. The results are to be used to inform practitioners and to improve practice.

Suggested Readings

Jacelon, C. S., & O'Dell, K. K. (2005). Uses of qualitative research, or so what good is it? *Urologic Nursing*, *25*, 471–473.

This a good example of the practical application of case study reports as authors examine standards for judging qualitative research and then describe how to use the results in new settings.

Jack, S. M. (2006). Utility of qualitative research findings in evidence-based public health practice. *Public Health Nursing*, *23*, 277–283.

   This source offers readers helpful ways to read and use qualitative reports such as case studies as ideas for change and improvement in their own professional practice.

Myers, M. D. (1994). A disaster for everyone to see: An interpretive analysis of a failed IS project. *Accounting, Management, and Information Technologies*, *4*, 185–201.

   This is a case study in a large organization demonstrating the failed implementation of a technology-related innovation. This case presents a story of intentions and pitfalls encountered when changes are attempted on a broad scale.

Simons, H. (1971). Innovations and the case-study of schools. *Cambridge Journal of Education*, *3*, 118–124.

   Good example of the use of case studies to document innovations as the author recounts the process during the curriculum innovations at several schools. The purpose was to make the experience of innovation accessible to the public.

Stake, R. E., & Easly, J. (1978). *Case studies in science education*. Urbana-Champaign, IL: Center for Instructional Research and Curriculum Evaluation.

   A firsthand account of the adoption of a K–12 science curriculum in U.S. schools. It offers a good example of case study reports presented as vignettes, scenarios, and reports of experiences to illustrate the adoption process.

Organizations and Web Sites

American Educational Research Association—Special Interest Group on Qualitative Research (SIG #82)

   www.aera.net/Default.aspx?menu_id = 208&id = 772

   Provides opportunities for discussion related to the philosophy, purposes, and methodological issues surrounding the use of qualitative research in social and educational contexts.

National Science Foundation Workshop on Qualitative Research in the Social Sciences

   www.nsf.gov/pubs/2004/nsf04219/start.htm

   Special conference on the importance of qualitative studies including guidelines and presented papers.

Center for Instructional Research and Curriculum Evaluation

   www.ed.uiuc.edu/circe/Publications/CIRCE_Publications.html

   This site offers several papers on case study and qualitative research.

CHAPTER

PROGRAM EVALUATION

STEPHEN D. LAPAN AND CAROL M. HADEN

KEY IDEAS

- Evaluation involves the systematic determination of worth or merit.

- Evaluation reasoning includes the selection of criteria and standards, measuring if standards are met, and synthesizing the results.

- Qualitative and quantitative data can be used in examining antecedents, transactions, and outcomes in personnel, policy, materials, and program evaluation studies.

- Purposes of program evaluations may be for accountability, improvement, or enlightenment.

- Trusting program evaluation study results includes the effective use of member checking and various forms of triangulation.

WHAT IS EVALUATION?

UNDERSTANDING PROGRAM evaluation begins with the idea of ranking, assessing, judging, or in some other way determining worth or merit. The logic that professional evaluators use can be found in the familiar publication *Consumer Reports* (Consumers Union, 2007), the magazine that offers guidance to consumers about the value and quality of products and services. They may report their evaluations of high-definition televisions (HDTVs), digital cameras, and automobiles. They even offer advice on how to negotiate with building contractors.

In reporting their evaluation findings on HDTVs, for instance, *Consumer Reports* would choose elements (called criteria) on which the TVs will be judged. They might identify the following as criteria: repair records, picture and sound quality, cost, and ease of use of the remote control. The television evaluations are then carried out by measuring these criteria, comparing each TV's performance to that of the others—the Panasonic television has a sharper picture, but the Samsung has a better repair record. Each television is evaluated to see how well it performs on each of the criteria.

Consumer Reports then offers final rankings and ratings for all brands examined by combining the varying evidence. Some TV sets may score high on picture and sound but low on remote use. It is the final work of the evaluator to synthesize all of this data and make clear recommendations so that readers can decide which purchases to make.

The Logic of Evaluation

Thinking about how *Consumer Reports* uses **criteria**, **standards**, **measures**, and **synthesis** to contribute to our understanding of how most evaluation studies are organized, evaluation reasoning or logic can be represented in these four steps:

1. **Criteria:** Selecting characteristics or elements to study (TV sound, picture, and so on)

2. **Standards:** Identifying how these criteria will be judged; using benchmarks to determine growth, improvement, or minimum expectation, not just standards set by state or federal requirements (comparing TVs to one another in terms of picture quality)

3. **Measures:** Explaining how information or data will be collected to evaluate the criteria (judges rate picture quality, examine past repair records)

4. **Synthesis:** Combining findings and drawing conclusions based on measuring the criteria against standards (final rankings, ratings, recommendations for which TVs to buy—for example, Panasonic has better picture, Samsung has better repair record, but Sharp is better overall when all criteria are explored)

The evaluation of programs in the public and private sectors follows a similar logic when evaluation studies are implemented. In a high school mathematics program, for example, an evaluation study could include as criteria the review of the teaching materials, the observation of teaching, and evidence of student learning. The standards used in such an evaluation may be comparing the goals set out in the materials with the actual instruction, comparing the materials with state standards or graduation tests, and measuring student achievement on grades and exams. Measuring performance on each of these criteria would produce data that could then be synthesized to summarize how well the mathematics program was meeting its goals and serving the students.

Using the *Consumer Reports* model is useful to a point, but real-world evaluation studies are more complicated than studying television sets. For one thing, all of the participants in evaluation studies may not agree on which criteria should be used. There are different constituencies who represent interests and perspectives that often conflict. Parents may not know or even care about the curriculum goals; teachers may not agree with all of the content on the state test. It is the professional evaluator's responsibility to work out differences in criteria so that the final results can be used by all who have a stake in the quality of the program being evaluated. The primary audiences for most evaluation studies are these constituencies (**stakeholders**). In the math program, students would be one primary audience or set of stakeholders, for example.

 REFLECTION QUESTION

1. If you were evaluating this course, what would be a few appropriate criteria and associated standards you might use?

Qualitative Versus Quantitative Data

In the *Consumer Reports* and high school math examples, several kinds of information or data are compiled to arrive at conclusions about the best televisions and the quality of math education. These data can be words developed using visual observation or interviews (**qualitative data)** or they might be ratings or test results (**quantitative data)**. For years there were heated debates in program evaluation over which kind of data would best serve evaluation studies. Qualitative supporters made the case that words from participants and descriptions from observations offered the most complete picture of program quality and operation. Quantitative proponents argued that such reports were too subjective and that test scores and systematic counting offered the most accurate measure of program performance. Lapan (2004) summarizes the current state of this argument in program evaluation: "This debate has been resolved by both sides recognizing the place of both quantitative and qualitative data and that the best studies would incorporate both kinds" (p. 239). The choice of the kinds of data collected should be dictated by the questions being asked according to stakeholder needs and program purposes. Such choices commonly involve the use of both qualitative and quantitative data.

Forms of Evaluation

Although this chapter will focus primarily on **program evaluation** (for example, the nursing program at a local hospital, a firefighter training school), evaluation studies occur in other forms, including the evaluation of personnel, policies, and materials. In each instance, the determination of worth or value is the goal, as noted earlier, by selecting criteria, identifying standards, measuring performance, and reporting results (synthesis). **Personnel evaluation** involves gathering information (data) about the performance of individuals and what they produce, such as the evaluation of college professors by judging their teaching and scholarly publications. Factory workers, doctors, janitors, psychologists, and CEOs are among the many personnel who could be the focus of this form of evaluation. In each case, the criteria and standards for evaluation would vary.

Policy evaluation, on the other hand, focuses on the careful examination of the nature and effect of rules, regulations, procedures, and even unwritten policies intended to set boundaries and expectations in formal and informal settings. International, national, and various state and local entities might be the focus of policy evaluation. Venues could include hospitals, government agencies, professional offices, schools, private industry, and condominium associations. Policy issues for evaluation might be many, including hiring and firing criteria, guidelines for salary adjustments, and standards for promotion. The evaluation of such policies would be conducted to draw conclusions about their clarity, fairness, equity, and overall effects.

Probably the closest to the *Consumer Reports* model, **materials evaluation** focuses on any set of materials used for teaching, training, learning, reporting, communicating, or even entertaining. Evaluation or the determination of worth may involve assessing the material's goal achievement, appropriateness of purposes, and how the content compares to outside standards, when available, such as state or federal requirements. A college dental hygiene curriculum might be evaluated, for example, by comparing it to the content on a national examination or how it compares to acceptable standards in private practice. The evaluator might inspect documents or other written sources as well as observe the implementation of the materials when presented.

The subject of this chapter, program evaluation, represents a more comprehensive perspective on evaluation with a potential focus on all aspects of programs in education, government, social service, and business settings. To understand this approach to determining worth, we look at the nature of programs themselves.

 ## REFLECTION QUESTIONS

1. Consider a parent, sibling, or friend who is employed. What criteria might be used to conduct a personnel evaluation in his or her workplace?

2. What criteria might be used to evaluate the policies or materials found at this same workplace?

Definition of a Program

Evaluators focus on a wide range of activities that are usually referred to as programs. The idea of a **program** can be defined as any effort that includes a set of expectations or goals, guidelines or procedures, regular activities or routines, and other characteristics that form any enterprise that aims to create a desired result. These program elements may be explicit or implicit, written or unwritten. There are professional training programs in such fields as medicine, law, teaching, and counseling as well as in other activities that seek well-defined ends, such as military recruitment efforts. Additionally, there are all sorts of programmatic efforts at the international and national levels, such as those sponsored by the World Health Organization and the National Science Foundation, as well as those found in other public and private settings. They all have purposes, desired proceedings, and expected results. Thus, they all can be and often should be evaluated to determine their effectiveness, and whether they operate in the manner intended, produce desired results, and do not create unknown problems in the process.

The role of program evaluation is to assist program participants, managers, outside funding agencies, and other interest groups in the collection of pertinent information, and by offering findings that may help stakeholders understand how their programs work.

One useful way to view programs is by organizing them into three convenient segments (Stake, 1967):

- **Program antecedents:** Those plans and activities that occur in preparation for implementation, when the program is being conceived, discussed, and in other ways prepared before it begins

- **Program transactions:** The functions and operations of the program once it is implemented, as defined by routine and nonroutine activities established to achieve its purposes and goals

- **Program outcomes:** The expected or actual short- and long-term effects of the program efforts that justify the program purposes, usually indicated by participant performance or program goal achievement

Program antecedents in an elementary reading program would include elements such as selection of reading texts and identification of students. In a counseling center, antecedents could include choosing psychological tests and developing group-therapy guidelines. When evaluating program transactions, elements might be lesson plans and support-group activities, and program outcomes could include measures of student reading performance and client mental health. Depending on the purposes of the evaluation study, these and other program elements might be the target of program evaluations in which stakeholders and the evaluator design a study to determine the quality of the reading or counseling program efforts.

Purposes of Program Evaluation

In general, program evaluation studies are conducted for one or more of three reasons:

1. Assess **accountability** by studying whether a program meets the expectations of taxpayers, funding agencies, or other outsiders

2. **Improve** the program by collecting data that will offer answers to program participants about effectiveness

3. **Enlighten** audiences about how certain programs work so that other program developers or academics may learn from these results

Accountability evaluations are usually required or requested by outside agencies or interest groups, including international, national, state, and local funding agencies, school boards, or community organizations. These individuals and agencies may identify evaluation as one requirement for receiving funding, for example. In most cases, the goal is to determine if resources and tax dollars are being used in the ways intended. These outsiders are often more interested in "bottom line" or "final results" information such as whether recruiting numbers are increasing at the police academy, infection rates are falling among patients, or students are scoring well on tests. They also want to know if money is spent as directed and if there is an efficient use of funding (**cost-effectiveness**). This accountability role of evaluation studies has been labeled by Scriven (1991) as **summative**, indicating that the results are a summary or final judgment of the program's worth.

Program improvement evaluations are more often the interest of insiders, especially program managers, administrators, and participants who want evidence of program strengths and shortcomings so that successful efforts can be supported and weaknesses can be remedied.

In program improvement evaluation, the managers and participants are just as interested in the effectiveness of the day-to-day routines, the quality of materials or curricula, and the value of other ongoing program operations as they are in results or bottom line performance data or test scores. It often contributes more to overall improvement when program functions can be studied so that positive aspects can be highlighted and problems can be corrected. This form of evaluation is characterized as **formative** evaluation (Scriven, 1991), where the purpose is to use findings to make midcourse corrections rather than a final assessment of quality. "The distinction between formative and summative evaluation has been well summed up by Bob Stake: 'When the cook tastes the soup, that's formative; when the guests taste the soup, that's summative'" (Scriven, 1991, p. 169).

Enlightenment evaluations usually exist as an adjunct to accountability and improvement studies. However, when conducted for the purpose of enlightenment alone, such evaluations are ordinarily carried out by academics whose main interests are to learn about program history, implementation, functions, and results. They like to find out what distinguishes good and bad practices and how such programs compare with ideals they hold or those presented in the literature. The findings of these studies are shared with colleagues, presented in courses or at conferences, and published in professional journals. These enlightenment evaluations may also serve either formative or summative purposes.

REFLECTION QUESTION

1. Thinking again of evaluating this course, would you use a formative or a summative evaluation orientation? Why?

Program Evaluation History

In the early decades of the twentieth century, program evaluation existed as a sideline activity engaged in mostly by academics who served as consultants to schools and other agencies in need of evaluation findings. When called upon, these evaluators would find out the primary purposes of the program in question and locate a standardized test that would parallel those objectives. Test scores would then be used to calculate the program's worth and these results reported to the sponsors. This testing or "outcomes only" approach to program evaluation is generally associated with the work of Tyler (Smith & Tyler, 1942) and persisted as the dominant evaluation model until the 1960s. Tyler, Lapan, Moore, Rivers, and Skibo (1978) did argue in later years for additional evaluation evidence to complement test scores.

Today, professional evaluation has become a prominent field with at least a half dozen of its own journals as well as evaluation organizations in more than twenty countries around the world. The American Evaluation Association alone has approximately twenty-five hundred members. This burgeoning growth of program evaluation finds its beginnings in the Great Society programs of the 1960s in the United States. Most agree that it was Senator Robert F. Kennedy's demand for program accountability in Title I of the Elementary and Secondary Education Act of 1965 (ESEA) that signaled the need for evaluations throughout government-funded programs. Kennedy sought evidence that the Title I ESEA programs were delivered as designed and that the expenditures were distributed as intended. This expanded definition for program evaluation implied more and different kinds of evidence than test scores offer and eventually spread to additional government-supported efforts in education and other human services. Now virtually every federal and state agency includes program evaluation as part of funding requirements, even if testing remains a part of the overall evaluation framework.

HOW IS EVALUATION DONE?

Program evaluations vary with the purpose and specific focus of the studies, but typically begin by holding discussions with program developers, managers, leaders, participants, and others who have an interest in the evaluation results. The evaluator would learn from these stakeholders why the evaluation is to be conducted and for whom. It is essential to determine if accountability or program improvement is more important to these audiences. Most evaluations serve more than one of these purposes and are likely to enlighten audiences about such programs as well, but it is necessary that primary purposes be made explicit during the planning stages to ensure that the study design is consistent with these aims.

The evaluator develops a preliminary description of the program based on information from the aforementioned meetings and from any available written documents that contain goals, purposes, intentions, expectations, desired outcomes, and any other explanations about the program antecedents, transactions, and anticipated outcomes. This description should include any background, objectives, resources and materials, participant preparation, guides, schedules, routines, and tests or other performance measures. A draft of this description is then shared with the stakeholders (for example, the sponsors, managers, and participants) to correct any misunderstandings or capture evolutionary program changes not recorded in documents. Programs are dynamic and ongoing, making them hard to pin down in writing, and any program description developed by the evaluator should represent as contemporary a rendition as possible.

The exchange between evaluator and stakeholders brings to the surface differing views and beliefs about program goals, expectations, and operations, allowing the evaluator either to obtain consensus or to incorporate these differences. Funding agencies and other outsiders may have differing expectations that must be taken into account as well. The evaluator is likely to generate a few drafts of the program description before all appropriate stakeholders can reach agreement on its content.

REFLECTION QUESTIONS

1. Who would be the main stakeholders for your evaluation of this course?
2. In what ways might these stakeholders differ in their expectations for the course?

Evaluation Agreement

During the early planning of the study, it is useful to offer the stakeholders a written plan stating the purposes of the study, the questions, standards, sources, and methods to be used, along with the data to be collected and a time line of all study events. At this point an evaluation agreement should be signed by the evaluator and sponsors of the study. This written agreement can be part of the evaluation plan and makes a matter of record the costs, deadlines, responsibilities, and potential audiences for the final report. Among the specific questions answered in the signed agreement are:

- Who will oversee the study?
- Who will collect the data?
- Who will write the final report?
- In what forms will the final report be presented?
- How will preliminary findings be made available?
- What provisions are made for alternative findings (**minority report**)?
- Who will have access to the evaluation findings?
- What are the costs associated with the study?
- What time lines and deadlines are expected?

This evaluation agreement can anticipate later potential misunderstandings about the study process and findings. In particular, program evaluation sponsors all too often change their minds about who might have access to final results, as these findings are not always flattering. Office managers may not want their supervisors or clients to find out about certain problems or school administrators may prefer that parents remain in the dark about weaknesses of a school program.

Criteria and Standard Selection

By writing and revising the program description, the evaluator has come to know the program antecedents, intended transactions, and expected outcomes. The evaluator must now engage in complicated decision making, working with the stakeholders to decide which program elements will guide the evaluation study. This process is complicated by the several deserving voices involved in the program that are likely to claim that their program concerns are the most important. Sponsors may want to know about program costs, participants might request information about daily operations, and funding agencies are likely to require test scores or other performance results. The evaluator has a perspective about criteria selection as well, given past experience and knowledge about similar programs.

The evaluator will usually begin by listing all concerns and criteria identified by the stakeholders. The next step is to pare down the original set by combining similar criteria and deleting low-priority elements, thus determining which items best reflect the purpose of the evaluation—that is, accountability (summative) versus improvement (formative). This stage of revision is guided by two essential questions posed by the evaluator:

1. For whom is this evaluation being conducted?

2. What do these audiences need to know?

In this genuine problem-solving task, the evaluator can use the list of criteria and translate those into evaluation questions that will guide the study. These questions are the lifeblood of evaluation studies where findings can be judged by the extent that each was reasonably answered. An example will clarify this criteria- and question-development process. Suppose that the director of a job placement agency requests an improvement evaluation of her program. The director, agency employees (consultants), and the evaluator agree to focus on two program criteria:

1. The accurate identification of client background and job skills by consultants

2. The successful matching of each client with suitable employment

These criteria can then be used to generate evaluation questions and the standards against which the questions would be measured—remember our *Consumer Reports* framework criteria, standards, measurement, synthesis. The first criterion above, accurate identification, might be translated into the evaluation question: What process do agency consultants use to learn about client background and skills? The standards for this evaluation question would be (1) that the process has been explained thoroughly, and (2) the extent to which client background and skills were accurately identified by the consultants. The evaluator might listen to taped sessions when consultants are first working with clients, interview the consultants about this process, and have clients complete a short questionnaire as measurements.

An evaluation question linked to the second criterion above could be: What is the rate of accuracy in placing clients in jobs that match their background and skills? The evaluator could ask the client about this match, inspect the job agency placement records, and perhaps interview personnel directors at job placement sites. The standard here would be the extent of the match between client background and skills in their job placement.

The evaluator may develop as few as one or two or as many as six or more evaluation questions with suitable parallel standards provided for each. Much depends on the complexity of the program, and time and budget constraints.

1. If you were planning an evaluation of this job placement agency, what other criteria and questions might you develop? What different questions would you pose if it were a summative evaluation?

Measuring Through Data Collection

Evaluation study planning depends on the careful selection, adaptation, or development of **data collection tools**, sometimes called **instruments**, which include questionnaires (also called surveys), interview guides or **protocols**, observation protocols, and pencil-and-paper devices such as attitude scales and performance tests. The professional evaluator has knowledge of how and when to use these instruments when they are available, but often may need to develop new ones because most studies must answer questions unique to the special setting and program under review. To find ready-made instruments, the evaluator would depend on the *Mental Measurements Yearbook* (Spies & Plake, 2005) for performance and attitude measures and on other sources, such as Simon and Boyer's *Mirrors for Behavior III* (1973), which offers dozens of classroom observation protocols.

Because new instruments are nearly always needed, the evaluator should spend adequate time trying out each new measure (called **field testing**) with individuals, groups, or in situations similar to those that will be used in the study. One would not, for example, try out a questionnaire with a forty-two-year-old, if seventeen-year-olds will be completing it for the evaluation. The field tester needs to know how seventeen-year-olds will react to the questions. Field-testing also provides useful practice for those newer to evaluation work, allowing them to practice giving directions, following procedures, and in the case of interviews, getting taped feedback about the interview effectiveness.

Interview Protocol Always considered one of the best data collection methods, face-to-face and telephone interviews provide in-depth information that cannot be obtained in any other way. Program participants, managers, and others close to the program have special perspectives about the experience that no one else could have. This is called **tacit knowledge** or **knowing-in-action**, as contrasted with in-head or book knowledge, based on experiences that only participants, clients, and other insiders possess. "This practical or experiential knowledge is . . . not some mysterious intuition but a genuine form of understanding" (Stake & Schwandt, 2006, p. 409). Although sometimes labeled as "just their opinion," the evaluator is collecting two important kinds of data: the participants' *recounting of events*, reporting what transpired from an insider's view, and their *opinion of the events*, their reaction to the experience. Both kinds are useful.

Developing interview protocols and conducting the actual interviews are complex tasks. It is therefore important that trained professionals collect this kind of data. Amateurs do not know how to build these protocols and make common errors during interviews, even when they follow the questions they are given. They might agree with interviewees, for example, causing the respondent to give answers shaded by the interviewer's opinion. And many new to interviewing will not know when to follow up to obtain more complete answers.

Visual Observations Making physical connection with the program through observation always contributes to understanding in evaluation studies where data can be obtained about daily routines and real reactions to events, thus producing a visual record of concrete examples. There are hundreds of observation guides or inventories available such as the Simon and Boyer (1973) source noted earlier, but as with other evaluation tools, the investigator ordinarily must adapt old instruments to new settings, or more often construct new protocols to fit the particular program. Like interviews, observations are subject to researcher bias. When evaluators interview or observe, they must take extra precautions to keep their personal beliefs and interpretations from being part of the findings. This is reason enough to use at least two data collectors when observing; each one can watch the same video independently and then both can compare observations for agreement. Even when observation checklists and ratings are highly concrete and easily observed, disagreement is possible. These agreement checks are a necessity.

Tests and Scales Obtaining performance and attitude measures can offer useful additional evidence in evaluation studies. Although there is no substitute for program observations and participant interviews, performance and attitude data can offer answers to special questions in the evaluation plan. For example, if observations reveal that program participants have ready access to relevant materials, it is sensible to test for knowledge contained in these materials. Also, obtaining a pencil-and-paper measure of participant attitudes can be combined with interview findings to make a stronger case. In the job agency example, managers, consultants, and clients could be asked to rate their experiences related to job placement, perhaps on a scale of 1 (not very effective) to 5 (very effective). These data could be used to complement other reports.

Testing is a very popular proxy for understanding programs, as the early history of program evaluation would suggest, but tests only have limited value, because several essential elements of the program cannot be revealed by measuring participant knowledge or skills. Although tests can reveal what was learned in a training experience, such scores may also reflect the test taker's ability or study habits rather than overall program quality. In addition, most currently available commercial tests or attitude measures are not aligned with specific programs. Thus, even when used, they should be adjusted to fit the individual program's content and goals.

Questionnaires and Document Inspection These data collection techniques are most often used as background information to support other findings from interviews and observations. Questionnaires might be sent to those not at a program site or those who have left the program for some reason. These insights would be different and add depth to an overall evaluation study. Also, questionnaires allow the evaluator to obtain large amounts of information more quickly than the labor-intensive interview and observation approaches useful for more in-depth inspection. Consumers of evaluation studies should know that low return rates are a common problem in questionnaire reporting. The reader should be able to determine the real number of returned questionnaires and what portion that rate is of the total sent (see the discussion of "Response Rates" in Chapter Five).

Documents are most often used to learn about program purposes, history, original expectations, and earlier institutional or company commitments. When balanced against current program operations, these data offer some insight about the extent of program support and overall changes in goals. Perhaps documents reveal that only 70 percent of the dollars originally promised were actually spent on the program. Subsequent program weaknesses could be linked in part to this lowered financial support.

 ## REFLECTION QUESTION

1. If you had to select one way of collecting data for this course, which method would you choose and why?

Sampling   Probability sampling, or what some call **random sampling**, is the act of obtaining a smaller group more convenient to study, but a group that accurately represents the larger population from which it was sampled. This is done by randomly selecting a large enough number of participants, instructors, managers, administrators, parents, community members or other appropriate stakeholders to ensure that the sample is representative of each whole group. This is usually the "gold standard" in research, especially when representativeness of people is the key. In evaluation studies, however, representativeness of information is more important. Thus, the data sources must be those who know certain information or who have experienced the program in some way. Evaluators want answers about the program, how it functions, its history, and its purposes. There are certain individuals considered the most information-rich sources for these questions. The evaluator must locate these people to find out what they know. This is known as **purposeful sampling** (also called purposive), the deliberate selection of sources who can best answer each kind of question the evaluator needs to ask. Some of these questions would include:

- How did the program get started and why?
- Who sought the grant funding for the program and who contributed to the writing of the grant itself?
- What were the original plans for starting and implementing the program?
- What reasons were most prominent in wanting to initiate such a program?
- What expectations were thought of at the time of the grant writing?
- What changes in these goals have occurred over recent years?

The evaluator does not want answers to such questions from a representative sample of managers or participants. That would only reveal who seems to know something about the program history and early operation and who does not. Instead, the evaluator seeks **key informants** (see Chapter Eleven)—those who were there or who would best know these answers. Most sampling in evaluation studies is done in this manner. The professional evaluator must always ask: Who would know this? Which data sources are most likely to give me these answers? Who would be best suited to answer these questions? This is why good evaluation plans identify known key informants but leave room for locating others during the data collection stages.

In special cases, of course, random sampling is an appropriate choice. In school program settings, for instance, the evaluation study plan may include pre-post testing of a sample that is representative of all students in the program to determine if the students learned relevant material. Although making up a small portion of the overall evaluation plan, this would offer important data for the evaluator. In many cases, by the way, sampling is not even necessary. Participants may number fewer than one hundred or so, and therefore all could be given the pre- and posttests.

Synthesizing and Reporting Study Results

When practitioners hear about evaluation findings, they are most likely to get them in the form of a concise set of statements answering such basic questions as: Were the materials used as planned? Could the participants demonstrate knowledge of the material? This set of statements or concise paragraphs is usually called an **executive summary**. In this summary the reader can examine the shortest version of what the evaluation study found. For some, this is all they want to know. Others may also want the next section, which usually contains recommendations for changes or the identification of program elements that should be supported or receive greater emphasis. Two examples of such recommendations could be:

- Because students were found to be much more actively engaged in learning and problem solving during science lab work, much less emphasis should be given to classroom lecture and discussion.

- Supervisor training produced the best results; even more resources and time should be used for this part of the program.

Following these first areas of summary and recommendation, the reader can find specific details that reveal more about the program implementation, operation, and effects, where examples of various program elements are explained in detail. Examples of daily routines, participant insights, and program manager decisions are often outlined in these pages, giving the reader the specific information that produced the preceding summaries and recommendations.

Findings might be offered in writing, or visually in multimedia formats, or as outlines for informal discussions with stakeholders. Different formats and words may be required for different audiences. It is the evaluator's responsibility to ascertain each audience's expectations, levels of understanding, and common language so that communication is clear and ample opportunity is offered for questions and rival explanations. Final evaluation reports should incorporate these concerns and alternative views (minority report) about the program and its quality.

Program evaluators wrestle with the complex issue of whether their findings will be understood, heeded, or ultimately applied to future program efforts. In some cases, communication, orientation, seminar, and training plans are included in the evaluation study design where the evaluator's intent is to increase the likelihood that evaluation results can be internalized and applied by the program participants and managers. This decreases the possibility that, like so many studies, the evaluation report quickly finds a home in the back of a file drawer or is lost somewhere in an administrator's computer.

 REFLECTION QUESTION

1. Why might some audiences want to read just the executive summary of a study, while others decide to read the entire evaluation report?

Trusting Program Evaluation Findings

In most research studies an essential part of the effort is to demonstrate how much readers can trust the results of the research. This is usually called **validity** or **study validity**, although in evaluation it is sometimes called *trustworthiness* or *credibility*. Program evaluation validity is especially important when a majority of the information collected is qualitative data (words) rather than numbers, percentages, or statistics (quantitative data). Audiences are usually more accustomed to seeing reports expressed as quantitative results and may need some convincing if most of the data is qualitative. Two common approaches for validating qualitative evaluation results are member checking and triangulation.

Member Checking   One way for a consumer or practitioner to test the believability of an evaluation study is **member checking**, a technique that involves pulling together preliminary summaries of study findings throughout the evaluation process. If, for example, the evaluator has finished collecting data from students in a high school English program (but may still be collecting data from teachers and administrators), this student data can be reduced to a few accessible pages, perhaps in outline form, shared with the students, and used as opening starting points for a discussion about the program and their experiences in it. The primary goal for the evaluator is to ask: "Does this information fit with your understanding of the English program? Is this similar to your experience in English classes?" The idea of member checking, then, is to test findings with those who have experience in the program. "Is there anything in this report you might question or say, 'Gee, that doesn't happen!'?"

Member checking is done with as many stakeholders or groups associated with the program as possible to allow early results to be tested against the lived experience of those inside the program. Checking must be done only after information has been obtained from each respective group, thus avoiding any contamination of earlier data. If not done in this sequence, information shared in member checking sessions is very likely to show up as data later in the study. An additional advantage of member checking is that the sharing itself establishes a direct and personal connection with program members, making the evaluator and even the final report more trustworthy. They know that they were involved and their opinions were considered. In fact, if enough disagreement or questions are raised during member checking, the evaluator may need to collect more data to get a better idea of what transpires, or at least to report the alternative views offered by each group.

In a final important note on member checking, it is *not* to be used for editing or fact checking; that is, the evaluator does not provide verbatim transcripts of interviews or exact reproductions of observations and ask: "Is this what you said?" or "Do I have your words just right here?" Fact checking has a different purpose and should occur in the same time frame as when data are being collected to increase each respondent's best memory of events.

Triangulation   Consumers of any evaluation report will want to inspect the study to make sure various kinds of triangulation were employed. This validation approach refers to the use of more than one data source (such as managers and participants) and more than one method of collecting information (such as interviews and question-naires). When evaluators use **source** and **method triangulation**, they are building on the strengths of each source and method while correcting for their shortcomings. If participants and managers, for example, report similar observations in both interviews and questionnaires, these findings are much more believable than if reported by one group or obtained from only one instrument.

Good evaluation reports explain the credibility of each finding, offering explana-tions such as: "All the data point to the conclusion that the police academy training is both rigorous and challenging, but disagreement was found from one source to another about whether cheating was possible." Or, "Although questionnaire results indicated that cheating was a problem, this was not reported in interviews." These various levels of certainty make the reader aware of not only the program's complexity, but also of how thoroughly and authentically the evaluator has reflected events and actions. If everything is rosy or if most program elements are reported in a negative way, readers begin to wonder about the evaluator's thoroughness or trustworthiness.

An additional form of triangulation, usually called **researcher triangulation**, is used when evaluators have close ties to the evaluated program. The evaluator may have social contacts with the program director or may have assisted in the program's development. This closeness causes at least the potential for increased **bias** (beliefs and expectations based on prior knowledge and experience about the program). Most would agree that some kind of counterbalance or monitoring of this potential bias should be done. Using researcher triangulation, an outside professional evaluator or other researcher who has no program ties is given the data collected from the evaluation study, but is not allowed to see any summaries, conclusions, or findings produced by the "inside" evaluator. This outside researcher then draws conclusions from the data itself. These conclusions are then compared to those of the inside evaluator to check for discrepancies. Important disagreements must be addressed by questioning the inside evaluator's conclusions or by collecting additional information about the program to confirm one conclusion over the other. At the very least, alternative interpretations by the outside evaluator are incorporated into the final report.

REFLECTION QUESTION

1.   In evaluating this course, how might you use source and method triangulation?

Ethics in Evaluation Studies

With the growth of the evaluation field, more attention has been paid to the need to conduct evaluation studies that reflect ethical practice. The American Evaluation

Association (2003) has developed *Guiding Principles for Evaluators*, which includes many ethical considerations that need attention in all phases of any evaluation study. For example, during the planning phase of an evaluation, the evaluator should make all aspects of the study transparent to program planners, managers, and participants to avoid even the appearance of a "hidden agenda" in the study. During the data collection phase, the evaluator must seek informed consent from participants, explaining the purpose of the study and any potential risk that could result from participating (see Chapter One).

To be ethical, an evaluation must include the perspectives of all relevant stakeholders, not just those who hold the most power in the program under review. The evaluator has the added responsibility of gaining an understanding of the cultural and social contexts in which the program operates, such as local history, population characteristics, and community standards.

Finally, during the reporting phase of the evaluation study, the evaluator must avoid the usual pitfall of portraying the program in the way that the sponsors or others in power would want to see it. The evaluator is obligated to represent all findings without regard to the interests of those in charge or sponsoring the study.

REFLECTION QUESTION

1. In what ways might an evaluator of this course be unethical?

JUDGING PROGRAM EVALUATION STUDIES

There are aspects of evaluation plans and studies that require attention if the studies are to be of high quality. Evaluation studies might be conducted by amateurs, can be poorly designed, are sometimes improperly implemented, and in some cases are reported in unacceptable ways. Although not exhaustive, the following elements of quality should assist the consumer-practitioner in judging evaluation studies. As an interested consumer of evaluations, you will want to find out about these evaluation elements by asking the evaluator and by reading the evaluation plan and final report.

Evaluator Qualifications

In too many cases, persons are thrust into the role of evaluator whether or not they are prepared for the experience. Professional evaluators have formal training in most aspects of research studies, have course work in measurement and statistics, and have specialized preparation in evaluation design and methods. These professionals also have conducted several evaluations so that their practical experience qualifies them to work through the routines and respond flexibly to surprises.

Professional evaluators also know the importance of making transparent any potential conflicts of interest, such as having a prior relationship with the sponsors or perhaps being involved in some earlier stage of the program's development. Seasoned evaluators know how to minimize the negative effects of such conflicts.

Two questions the consumer might ask are:

1. To what extent does the evaluator demonstrate appropriate training and experience?

2. Have any potential conflicts of interest or special relationships been communicated and addressed?

Evaluation Planning

Qualified evaluators recognize the importance of building understanding with all of the stakeholders in the program by obtaining their ideas regarding program purposes and operations. Developing and revising a program description through discussions with these groups is a vital precondition to planning an effective evaluation study. The evaluator reads all documents and listens to participants, managers, and other audiences to construct and revise a program description and to obtain essential contributions about how the evaluation should be planned.

Two questions the consumer might ask are:

1. To what extent were appropriate stakeholders involved in evaluation planning?

2. Was a preliminary program description developed, shared, and revised to reach consensus?

Evaluation Design

Although evaluation designs vary for each program being evaluated, some characteristics remain constant. As noted at the beginning of this chapter, evaluations are characterized by four elements:

- Identifying criteria
- Setting standards
- Measuring performance
- Synthesizing and reporting results

Professional evaluators understand the need to make transparent to stakeholders what criteria and standards have been selected and how they will be measured. Synthesis comes later in reporting. Further, these elements should be explicit in the evaluation plan, usually as part of the questions, methods, and data sources presented.

Two questions the consumer might ask are:

1. Are the criteria, standards, and their measurement made clear in the study plan?

2. Are the evaluation questions, methods, and sources consistent with the criteria and program purposes?

Evaluation Process

As complicated as evaluation studies may be, certain aspects should be monitored to ensure quality. Among these are confirming that information is collected fairly and objectively, and that these data are verified in several ways including both member checking and triangulation. Fairness is increased when information about typical program operation is obtained from those who would have the best knowledge about the program, including participants. Data confirmation is achieved by getting reactions about early findings from stakeholders during the study (member checking). The information gathered in these member checking sessions should then be used to revise findings, which may include collecting additional data for verification, or at least be included in the final report. Also, cross-checking information should be done using more than one method and more than one source. In some cases, researcher triangulation should be used as well.

Four questions the consumer might ask are:

1. Are the data collected typical and representative of the program operation?
2. Is the information collected from those who would know most about the program, its purposes, and daily activities?
3. Is member checking used systematically as part of the evaluation study?
4. How is triangulation used to improve the believability of the study?

Data Richness

Evaluation studies begin with a preliminary program description, but offer greater detail and revisions of that description as the study itself unfolds. Richness of description is essential in capturing how the program was implemented (antecedents), how it functions (transactions), and what effects it has (outcomes). Too much dependence on quick summaries and numbers can reduce the full disclosure of how the program looks when reconstructed and explained. There is never enough time or resources to fully explain every aspect of a program from inception to final effect, but wherever in-depth description is not produced by the evaluator, he or she must offer good reasons for this decision, and the stakeholders must approve.

Two questions the consumer might ask are:

1. Is there clear evidence of thorough and in-depth description of the program history and operation?
2. Are there full explanations of program effects observed in both daily results and overall outcomes?

Study Validity

For practitioners and other consumers of evaluation studies to believe in the results of these investigations, several approaches need to be an integral part of the study and reporting. The three most important areas needing attention are cross-checking data by using additional sources and methods (triangulation), checking preliminary findings with stakeholders (member checking), and accounting for any potential evaluator bias or conflict of interest. If evaluators make it clear how these validation approaches have been addressed in their plans and in their final report, audiences will be able to judge the extent to which they can trust in these findings.

Four questions consumers might ask are:

1. Was the triangulation of data sources evident and as thorough as it could have been?

2. Was the triangulation of methods sufficient to convince the reader that the findings were cross-checked?

3. Was member checking systematically done with appropriate groups, and were the results of these sessions used appropriately?

4. Was potential evaluator bias or conflict of interest addressed and accounted for in the plan and in the final report?

Study Report

The evaluation study report itself may be made available in different forms for different audiences, but must be accessible and understandable. In some instances, managers or administrators may not want clients or parents to know about program weaknesses. In addition, this final study should reflect careful attention to reasonable alternative descriptions and interpretations, especially those reported during member checking discussions. If there is no mention of disagreements or minority views of findings, consumer suspicion should be aroused.

Three questions consumers might ask are:

1. Was the final report available to any audience who might be interested or affected by the program and its operation?

2. Were the findings reported in a form accessible and understandable for all audiences?

3. Were alternative interpretations or minority renditions included in the study?

Study Use

It is all too common to find the end of evaluation work defined by the submission of final reports sent to the outside funding agency or filed with the local sponsors, without effecting actual program changes. Some of the many reasons for this lack of follow-through may be found in the report itself. It is the professional evaluator who must make recommendations that stakeholders can understand and use in their situation given their resources. Some evaluators make this follow-through a part of their evaluation plans, but most do not.

Two questions consumers might ask are:

1. Can the evaluation findings be readily translated into decisions about program changes and improvements?

2. Are the recommendations from the study realistic given the resources available to the program?

SUMMARY

Evaluation differs from other forms of research in its intent. Rather than generating "knowledge for knowledge's sake," the findings of an evaluation study are intended to inform decision making about programs, products, materials, or personnel. Program evaluation studies can achieve the purposes of improvement, accountability, or enlightenment.

Evaluators are responsible for conducting evaluations that provide meaningful, authentic information without compromising ethical considerations. For an evaluation study to be credible, it must be relevant to the needs of stakeholders and should involve collecting appropriate data from key participants about program operations.

KEY TERMS

accountability evaluations
antecedents
bias
cost-effectiveness
criteria
data collection tools
data richness
document inspection
enlightenment evaluations
evaluation agreement
evaluation design
evaluation ethics
evaluation process
evaluation questions
evaluator qualifications
executive summary
field testing
formative
instruments
interview protocol
key informants
logic of evaluation
materials evaluation
measures
member checking
method triangulation

minority report
outcomes
personnel evaluation
policy evaluation
program
program evaluation
program improvement
protocols
purposeful sampling
qualitative data
quantitative data
questionnaires
random sampling
researcher triangulation
source triangulation
stakeholders
standards
study validity
summative
synthesis
tacit knowledge (knowing-in-action)
tests and scales
transactions
validity
visual observations

FURTHER READINGS AND RESOURCES

Suggested Evaluation Article

Lewis, N. S., & Jeanpierre, B. (2006). An evaluation of a master's degree in K–8 mathematics and science: Classroom practice. *School Science and Mathematics*, *106*, 231–240.

Suggested Readings

Davidson, E. J. (2005). *Evaluation methodology basics.* Thousand Oaks, CA: Sage.

A book that not only serves as a comprehensive, accessible introduction to the practice of evaluation but also offers useful guidance for planning and conducting an evaluation study.

House, E. R. (2007). *Regression to the mean: A novel of evaluation politics.* Charlotte, NC: Information Age.

This one-of-a-kind resource is a novel written about how evaluations are planned and conducted, and the political struggles that often emerge when competing interest groups debate the findings. This is the single most accessible source for understanding the structure and nuance of program evaluation.

Patton, M. Q. (1987). *How to use qualitative methods in evaluation.* Newbury Park, CA: Sage.

This very accessible introduction to the world of evaluation clarifies what readers of evaluation reports should understand. Although intended for those learning how to conduct evaluations, this small paperback offers clear ideas for the practitioner about planning, sampling, collecting data, and making sense of qualitative results.

Sanders, J. R., & Sullins, C. D. (2006). *Evaluating school programs: An educator's guide* (3rd ed.). Newbury Park, CA: Sage.

This practitioner-friendly guide to planning evaluations in school settings uses language and examples that allow readers from most social science fields to gain an understanding of evaluation studies and the reasoning used to plan and conduct these investigations.

Associations

American Evaluation Association (AEA). AEA is an international professional association of evaluators in many fields, including education. AEA has approximately five thousand members in all fifty states in the United States and has members from over sixty foreign countries. Web site: www.eval.org.

American Educational Research Association (AERA). AERA is a professional organization of over twenty-five thousand members with interests in educational research. AERA's Division H: School Evaluation and Program Development has over fifteen hundred members who are interested in "applied research and evaluation studies and/or assessment and accountability activities in pre-K–12 settings." Web site: www.aera.net.

Journals

American Journal of Evaluation (AJE) Published by the American Evaluation Association, AJE contains articles related to evaluation methods, theory, practice, and findings.

New Directions for Evaluation This quarterly publication of the American Evaluation Association contains articles for practitioners related to evaluation practice and professional and societal issues relevant to the field.

Educational Evaluation and Policy Analysis This journal of the American Educational Research Association publishes articles related to the formulation, implementation, and evaluation of educational policy.

Testing Web Site

To find out which tests and attitude measures are available, what their purposes are, and their overall quality, go to: www.unl.edu/buros.

See also *The Sixteenth Mental Measurements Yearbook* by Spies and Plake (2005), listed in the references.

CHAPTER

ETHNOGRAPHY RESEARCH

FRANCES JULIA RIEMER

KEY IDEAS

- Ethnography is a systematic study of a particular cultural group or phenomenon, based upon extensive fieldwork in one or more selected locales.

- Ethnography research focuses on cultural interpretation for the purposes of description or extension of social theory.

- The ethnographer is the data collection instrument.

- Ethnographers use multiple data sources and methods of data collection to increase the validity and trustworthiness of the findings.

- Ethical ethnographers are careful to reduce any risks to themselves and the other participants before, during, and after the research process.

- Ethnography brings complex, personal, and thoughtful insights and meaning to the inner workings of social settings.

GROPING IN THE DARK

WHEN I began my first ethnographic research project, I was not an ethnographer. I was a teacher and a student, living in the city, pondering questions about education and social mobility, poverty and work. I had enrolled in a doctoral program and taken classes in research methods, but I became an ethnographer by doing the things that ethnographers do. I learned how to ask questions by asking, and how to watch, listen, and document the moments of everyday practice by watching, listening, and recording. My experience was what ethnographic evaluator David Fetterman (1989) described when he wrote, "Ethnography is what ethnographers actually do in the field. Textbooks . . . together with lectures—can initiate the newcomer to the field and refresh the experienced ethnographer, but actual fieldwork experience has no substitute" (p. 26). During this entire ethnographic research effort, however, I felt as though I was groping in the dark, making decisions with the discomforting tentativeness of most first-time ethnographers. Uncertainty was my own repetitive refrain. Over and over I asked myself such questions as, "Is this an appropriate site to do research? Should I be spending more time there instead of here? Should I be observing more, or observing less? How can I make myself more visible? How can I make myself invisible?" Months passed before I came to understand that uncertainty was a fundamental part of the ethnographic method. Much more time passed before I began to feel even slightly comfortable fumbling with the unfamiliar.

In addition to my own somewhat bewildering experience, I have heard students speculate about ethnographic research after reading a classic ethnography conducted in an exotic locale or a more recent ethnography conducted in a classroom or neighborhood somewhere. But all too often, they are enticed by the lure of ethnography without understanding or appreciating its strengths, constraints, and demands. In this chapter, I address these gaps in awareness by drawing on my own journey through unfamiliar ethnographic territory, as well as on the work of classic and contemporary ethnographers. Writing this chapter for the reader of ethnography who hopes to gain a general familiarity with the theoretical assumptions, methodological procedures, and standards of quality involved in ethnographic research, I discuss ethnography as a research methodology and examine ethnographers' assumptions about knowledge, characterizations of culture, considerations of methodology, and the toolbox of methods.

WHAT IS ETHNOGRAPHY RESEARCH?

So what exactly is ethnography and what does an ethnographer do? **Ethnography**, embedded in an anthropological tradition, is essentially the study of a particular cultural group or phenomenon. **Fieldwork** is a fundamental part of that study, and for anthropologists, ethnographic fieldwork involves documenting people's beliefs and practices from the people's own perspectives. Margaret Mead (1928) went to the Pacific for nine months to document the ways adolescence is negotiated by Samoan islanders. Clifford Geertz (1965) studied religious practices in Bali, and Sherry Ortner (1978) traveled to Tibet to study the relationships among cultural symbols in the organization of a society. For educational anthropologists, the field may be a classroom, a school, a literacy group, or any other place where learning or teaching takes place. To conduct his first ethnography, Harry Wolcott (1967/2003) spent a year in a Kwakiutl Blackfish village in British Columbia. He taught in the village's one-room school while documenting the ways children learned their culture's values both in and outside the classroom. Alan Peshkin (1986) lived in a midwestern United States community and studied the social dynamics of Bethany Baptist Academy, the town's fundamentalist Christian school. Dorothy Holland and Margaret Eisenhart (1990) spent time at two colleges, examining what they came to call a pervasive "culture of romance" on the campuses.

Other ethnographers conduct research in hospitals and family dining rooms, in geriatric centers and on the shop floor, in jungles and recreational parks, wherever the activity in which they are interested takes place. For me, the field was the workplace. In an attempt to understand how men and women marked by the status of welfare recipient entered, were received by, and participated in the social organization of work, I spent two years watching new workers assemble science kits in a nonprofit business, care for elderly residents in a long-term care facility, fill prescriptions in an inner-city hospital pharmacy, and build spiral staircases at a woodshop in the suburbs (Riemer, 2001).

But whether the culture under study is a village, classroom, or shop floor, the ethnographer's aim is **cultural interpretation**. "Cultural interpretation involves the ability to describe what the researcher has heard and seen within the framework of the social group's view of reality" (Fetterman, 1989, p. 28). In order to craft descriptions of culture, cultural events, and cultural practices, an ethnographer studies real people doing what they do to meet the everyday demands with which they are confronted. In other words, ethnographers collect data in natural settings. Basic to the fieldwork approach is the belief that what individuals believe, understand, and act upon cannot be detached from their context. Fieldwork provides the opportunity to take into account individuals' beliefs and actions, or what anthropologists call their everyday practices, within the context in which they are enacted.

The ethnographer, then, must be a keen surveyor and interpreter of culture from the "**emic**,"[1] or the insider's view of reality. Yet because seeing is always filtered through our own ideas, capturing the insider's perspective is neither straightforward nor easy. We bring our cultural selves with us wherever we go, and even with the best of intentions, an ethnographer can never see life completely through another person's eyes. In a similar fashion, the ethnographer is never able to completely write him- or herself out of the ethnography. As the anthropologist Vincent Crapanzano (1977) asserts, "however objective they may seem, there is an autobiographical dimension to all ethnographies" (p. 72).

To further complicate matters, an "**etic**,"[2] or the outsider's perspective, is also fundamental to ethnographic research. Returning to the writing of David Fetterman (1989), "an etic perspective is the external, social scientific perspective on reality" (p. 32). The ethnographer's task, then, is not only to include insiders' meanings, but to translate them into concepts comprehensible to individuals outside the society. This balance between insider and outsider perspectives places special demands on the researcher. The ethnographer must remain open and nonjudgmental about the actions and beliefs of the social group under study, while making these understandings and practices intelligible to outsiders.

 ## REFLECTION QUESTIONS

1. What is cultural interpretation?
2. What do the terms "etic" and "emic" mean?
3. Why are both etic and emic perspectives fundamental to ethnographic research?
4. Why and where do ethnographers engage in fieldwork?

Ethnography Is Descriptive

How, then, is ethnographic research conducted? Ethnography begins with what the anthropologist Bronislaw Malinowski described as a **foreshadowed problem**, that is, with a problem or topic of interest. Foreshadowed problems are generated from all sorts of places: established theories, a personal need to explain a particular phenomenon, an unanticipated outcome or set of outcomes, or even a chance encounter. Although ethnographers are encouraged to identify problems that focus their research, they must also remain open to the unexpected. As Malinowski wrote (1922, p. 9), "Preconceived ideas are pernicious in any scientific work, but foreshadowed problems are the main endowment of a scientific thinker."

But because they reflect the study's conceptual and theoretical grounding, foreshadowed problems can feel vague and abstract. **Research questions** are based on foreshadowed problems, but are written to guide the ethnographer through the research process (LeCompte, Preissle, & Tesch, 1993). For example, an ethnographer interested in gender might ask, "How is masculinity constructed among a group of Spanish males living in the same town?" An educational ethnographer, on the other hand, might ask, "What are the attitudes of a particular group of children towards schoolwork?" Anthropological studies can also help identify the kinds of questions ethnographers ask.

In collecting data for their classic text *The Navaho*, Clyde Kluckhorn and Dorothea Leighton (1947) wanted to know what "aspects of Navaho culture [*sic*] . . . bear most immediately upon the government's capacity to help The People strike a working balance between human needs and fluctuating resources" (p. xix). Margaret Mead (1928) went to Samoa to answer questions about "coming of age in Samoa." She wanted to learn whether "the disturbances which vex our adolescents [were] due to the nature of adolescence itself or to the civilization? Under different conditions does adolescence present a different picture?" (p. 11). *Boys in White* (Becker, Greer, Hughes, & Strauss,

1992) was driven by the question of what medical school does "to medical students other than giving them a technical education" (p. 17). As Howard Becker and colleagues explained, "Our original focus, then, was on the medical school as an organization in which the student acquired some basic perspectives on his later activity as a doctor" (p. 18). What's important to note here is that each of these examples sets out to describe a particular set of circumstances, rather than fashion a cause-and-effect explanation of their foreshadowed problem. According to Margaret LeCompte, Judith Preissle, and Renata Tesch (1993), "Ethnography always is descriptive; it also involves the study of an interplay among empirical variables as they occur naturally, rather than as they may be manipulated or arranged in advance by an investigator. The naturalistic setting both facilitates on-the-spot and holistic analysis of causes and processes and precludes precise control of so-called extraneous factors" (p. 39).

Ethnographic Methods

What do ethnographers do during their time in the field? They gather information by watching and talking with people, and by reading available reports and records. **Observation** is a main tool in an ethnographer's toolbox, and ethnographers spend a good deal of their time in the field observing, either as nonparticipant or participant observers. **Participant observers** take part in whatever is going on in the site in order to better understand the insider, or emic, experience. The Polish anthropologist Bronislaw Malinowski (1922), for example, the first and perhaps the most famous participant observer, spent three years in a small village with the Trobriand Islanders, watching and talking with men as they constructed canoes, tilled their horticultural plots, and traded kula shells with neighboring islanders. In an effort to better understand the role of social structure in creating conformity in institutional environments, sociologist Erving Goffman (1961) worked in a mental hospital providing care for and talking with patients. William F. Whyte, who titled his autobiography *Participant Observer* (1994), studied the life of urban young men in Cornerville, an Italian neighborhood in Boston (1981). He spent three years with the neighborhood's gangs on street corners, in the local bowling alley, and in rent strike demonstrations. In my own research (Riemer, 2001) on welfare-to-work transitions, I worked alongside new workers packing science kits for area schools and piling boxes on skids. In a nursing home, I helped the nursing assistants. I was studying by wheeling elderly residents to and from lunch, making their beds, and listening to their stories. But I could not legally fill prescriptions at a pharmacy, nor did I have the woodworking skills to assist in building stairs in a custom wood shop. In those sites I was a **nonparticipant observer**, trying to watch unobtrusively while technicians filled prescriptions and woodworkers shaped wood into custom-built spiral staircases.

Participant and nonparticipant observations are at two ends of a continuum, and most ethnographers engage in a mix of the two, depending upon the context and circumstances. But regardless of level of participation, "the most important element of fieldwork," as ethnographer David Fetterman (1989) wrote, "is being there—to observe, to ask seemingly stupid yet insightful questions, and to write down what is seen and heard" (p. 19).

Life histories and other kinds of in-depth interviews are also part of an ethnographer's fieldwork. "Ethnographers use interviews to help classify and organize an individual's perception of reality" (Fetterman, 1989, p. 50). However, **ethnographic interviews** are less formal and less interviewer-driven than traditional interview formats. As anthropologist Michael Agar (1980) wrote, in an informal interview "everything is negotiable. The informants can criticize a question, correct it, point out that it is sensitive, or answer in any way they want to" (p. 90). In fact, the best ethnographic interview is more like a conversation than a traditional interview. The ethnographer probes, reacts, questions, responds, expresses surprise, and discloses. "The field researcher, then, regards the interview as a lengthy conversation. The way the researcher probes for detail, for clarity or explanation, and his gestures which signal normal surprise and even disbelief, provide him with the means for shaping an interview in this way" (Schatzman & Strauss, 1973, p. 72). This informality doesn't mean ethnographers don't prepare for interviews. Ethnographers plan questions and develop interview protocols to ensure that the interview flows and questions aren't forgotten. The interview itself, however, does not necessarily follow a preset format or linear line of questioning (Ellen, 1984). It is guided instead by the talk itself, by what gets said, and what is left unsaid.

In addition to observation and interviews, ethnographers also collect and examine **site documents** for information related to their research questions. The term *document* refers here not only to public and private texts,[3] but to photographs, videos, and film as well. In his classic study of a school principal, Harry Wolcott (1978) examined the contents of the school's *Teacher Handbook*, documented the type and frequency of materials distributed by the school's office staff, perused the school's bulletin boards, and reviewed letters and memos written by the principal. In his study of school and community in small-town America, Alan Peshkin (1978) had access to diaries in which students responded to teacher prompts such as "Today I was thinking about . . ." (p. 151). According to Peshkin, the diaries became an important data source on students' conversations, private thoughts, and feelings about after-school jobs and future possibilities. In my current research, an examination of literacy practices in Botswana, I look at both public and private text, and pay special attention to the printed material that men and women encounter on a daily basis. I visited libraries and shops where I counted numbers and kinds of books. I scanned daily and weekly newspapers, attended church services to observe how text is used in Christian rituals, conducted a house-to-house survey on text ownership, and interviewed participants of the government's literacy program on their literacy needs. In Gaborone, Botswana's capital, I listened to men and women talk about the text they encountered in their work as security guards, domestic help, and laborers in wholesale outlets. "After I got a job I got the idea of coming here [to a literacy class], because there's too much documentation," a security guard in Gaborone explained. A warehouse worker offered, "Signing the [pay]check, I could only put a cross. There's still some difficulty. I can scribble my name on paper." Men and women in rural villages, however, talked about enrolling in literacy classes so they could read letters from family members working in the mines or as domestics in South Africa, decipher prices of items in shops, and sign for government farming subsidies and identity documents. Because these texts, whether personal, public, or housed in a library's archives, are reflections of shared practice, societal norms, and public relationships, they are potentially rich sources of data.

Data Collection

Ethnography is notoriously eclectic in its employment of multiple methods of data collection, and ethnographers will typically observe, conduct interviews, and scrutinize relevant archives and artifacts during a single research effort. In ethnographic research, data collection is tailored to meet the information needs of each study; the ethnographer determines the information required to address the study's research questions, and designs a mix of techniques to elicit that information. In his study of Harlem drug dealers, for example, Philippe Bourgois (1995, p. 13) "spent hundreds of nights on the street and in crackhouses observing dealers and addicts . . . regularly tape recorded their conversations and life histories, . . . visited their families, attending parties and intimate reunions, interviewed and in many cases befriended, the spouses, lovers, siblings, mothers, grandmothers, and when possible, the fathers and stepfathers of the crack dealers, [and] spent time in the larger community interviewing local politicians and attending institutional meetings" (p. 13). Dorothy Holland and Margaret Eisenhart (1990) followed twenty-three young women through their first three semesters at two colleges, designed and administered a survey to a random sample of young women at both colleges, and conducted follow-up interviews by phone two and four years later with the twenty-three focus women.

This diversity of research methods also allows the ethnographer to **triangulate**, or cross-check, the accuracy of collected data and analytic statements. "Just as a surveyor locates points on a map by triangulating on several sites, so an ethnographer pinpoints the accuracy of conclusions drawn by triangulating with several sources of data" (LeCompte et al., 1993, p. 48). Merely watching an event, or simply talking with individuals at the scene, does not provide checks for either researcher or participant bias. Analyzing data from multiple sources collected by diverse methods and supported by a range of theories allows the ethnographer to make comparisons, verify emergent assertions, and convey a sense of trustworthiness to the reader.

Given the range of activities inherent in collecting data, ethnographic fieldwork is time-intensive. In order to gain the perspective of a community's members, an ethnographer lives in the community for an extended period of time. I spent three years, for instance, in Botswana during my most recent investigations of literacy. In fact, ever since the Polish anthropologist Bronislaw Malinowski was sequestered while collecting data in the Trobrand Islands during World War I, one year, or a **full cycle of activities**, has been considered the minimum duration for fieldwork. Although ethnography is time- and labor-intensive, most ethnographers actually have difficulty leaving the field. In deciding when sufficient data has been collected, ethnographers are guided by what David Fetterman calls the **law of diminishing returns**. "The law of diminishing returns can determine that it is time for the ethnographer to leave the field. When the same specific pattern of behavior emerges over and over again, the fieldworker should move on to a new topic for observation and detailed exploration. Similarly, when the general picture reaffirms itself over and over again, it is probably time to wrap things up and return home" (Fetterman, 1997, p. 20).

Risks of Ethnography Research

As this section suggests, a common outcome of fieldwork is the development of close relationships between the ethnographer and individuals in the field. Living and working with people over long periods of time can foster intimate bonds that come with the obligations of friendship. Ethnographers can develop particularly close ties with their **key informants**, those individuals who take on the role of sponsor and gatekeeper, introducing the ethnographer to other members of the community, and sharing their own insider information about the setting. Key informants are those special individuals who like to talk, who know the setting, and who understand the ethnographer's mission.

In his ethnography *Street Corner Society*, William F. Whyte (1981) writes about one of the most famous relationships between ethnographer and key informant, that between himself and his friend Doc. Introduced to each other by a social worker at a local settlement house, Doc became Whyte's guide, advisor, and mentor. Upon their first meeting, Doc offered, "Well any nights you want to see anything, I'll take you around. I can take you to the joints—gambling joints—I can take you to the street corners. Just remember that you're my friend. That's all they need to know. I know these places, and, if I tell them that you're my friend, nobody will bother you. You just tell me what you want to see, and we'll arrange it." As Whyte explained, Doc's role quickly evolved from informant to collaborator. "My relationship with Doc changed rapidly in this early Cornerville period. At first he was simply a key informant—and also my sponsor. As we spent more time together, I ceased to treat him as a passive informant. I discussed with him quite frankly what I was trying to do, what problems were puzzling me, and so on. Much of our time was spent in this discussion of ideas and observations, so that Doc became, in a very real sense, a collaborator in the research" (p. 28).[4]

Informants can also place themselves at risk by disclosing information about their private lives. In my research on welfare-to-work transitions, I was particularly concerned about the risk new employees might incur in talking with me about their work. Most of these men and women occupied low-wage, low-status jobs, and they often reminded me of their precariousness in the workplace. In order to avoid any risk of their losing their jobs, I maintained their anonymity and recorded our conversations in my own shorthand rather than audiotaping. I also transcribed my notes into text format and returned them to the men and women for their review, modification, and feedback. I honored any objections they voiced about the transcripts and removed any passages they found distressing. My situation, however, was nowhere as serious as that of the anthropologist Edward Bruner, who was collecting data in a village in Sumatra when civil war ignited in the region. Bruner (2004) writes, "Villagers in Sumatra, for example, welcomed my wife and me, and adopted us into their kinship system, but no one could have predicted that a civil war between pro- and anti-American forces would subsequently develop in the region. It created a situation where our very presence in their village, as Americans, placed them in grave physical danger. The greatest risk to them was us just being there, irrespective of informed consent or research protocols" (p. 2).

Unlike researchers who only know their respondents through surveys, telephone conversations, or as numbers in statistical runs, ethnographers enter **interdependent relationships** with their informants. As Edward Bruner asserts (2004), "When you live for long periods intertwined with others, immersed in their lifeways, it is hard to separate yourself from them. Research is no longer something out there, separate from self, apart from life" (p. 1). Given these personal relationships, ethnographers have a distinctive obligation to the people they are studying. They abide by a **code of ethics** developed and advanced by the American Anthropological Association (1998) and honored by institutional review boards. These guidelines include gaining **informed consent** from anyone who participates in the research; individuals must not only agree to participate, but must fully understand the purposes of the research and the implications of their participation. In addition, the ethnographer must assure the **confidentiality** of all research participants, and guarantee that they will be neither harmed nor exploited by their participation. The need to protect research participants is so critical that all ethnographers, even students conducting ethnographic research for a class, must abide by this code of conduct.

 REFLECTION QUESTIONS

1. What is an example of a "foreshadowed problem" that interests you?

2. What do ethnographers do in the field?

3. How does participant observation differ from nonparticipant observation?

4. How do ethnographic interviews differ from other interviews?

5. What are the risks to participants and researchers during ethnographic work?

6. How might information gained from archives complement that obtained by observation and interviews?

7. What is the importance of a key informant?

Ethnographic Data Analysis

Ethnography is local by nature; that is, the ethnographer collects data necessary to describe and interpret local practices. The focus may be site-specific, as in a classroom, a school, a village, or a training program, or multisited (Marcus, 1998), as in a dynastic fortune, a legal network, the emerging middle class, or as in my current research, literacy practices across geographic distances and ethnic groups. But whether single- or multisited, the research remains local, and in all cases, has a particular focus. In fact, ethnographers avoid terms like "typical" or "representative" when describing their findings, and are justly cautious about sweeping statements that go beyond what their data can support. Rather than generalizing from a particular case, ethnographers position themselves as producers and disseminators of information, and leave the reader to apply the research findings as appropriate.[5]

Because ethnographic research is local, its focus is deep, rather than broad. This capacity to delve deeply into a particular site or issue allows for another fundamental aspect of ethnographic research, what anthropologist Clifford Geertz (1973) called "**thick description**" (p. 6). By "thick," Geertz was referring to description that includes all possible meanings of an event, including meanings conferred by members of the culture itself. He illustrated the concept of "thick description" with the example of "the wink of any eye." Geertz contrasts the actions of three boys, each blinking his right eye. One boy is winking, one boy's eye is twitching, and the third is parodying a wink. According to Geertz, ethnography differentiates a wink from a twitch from a parody of a wink by its capacity "to capture the thick description of cultural categories." An ethnographer's job is "to capture" the thick description of an event, experience, or scene—that is, to write a description that is layered, rich, and contextual.

But an ethnography is not simply descriptive; it also situates insider beliefs and practices within a larger theoretical context. In this linking of the local to the theoretical, "the aim . . . is the enlargement of the universe of human discourse" (Geertz, 1973, p. 14). In other words, says Geertz, an ethnographer's task is to generate **theory**. But what is theory? According to educational anthropologists Margaret LeCompte, Judith Preissle, and Renata Tesch (1993), "theories are statements about how things are connected. Their purpose is to explain why things happen as they do" (p. 118). For example, in his book *God's Choice*, Alan Peshkin (1986) argues that the Christian fundamentalist school he studied embodied a contradiction inherent in a pluralist society. The school, wrote Peshkin, benefits from the country's "tradition of religious liberty, which is a cornerstone of American pluralism" (p. 293). At the same time, the school itself does not support pluralism; its fundamental theology promotes inflexibility rather than tolerance and absolute belief over debate and compromise. He encapsulated his theory in the following: "The existence of fundamentalist Christian schools creates a paradox of pluralism in the United States. Paradoxes of pluralism testify to our ideological health" (p. 298). Peshkin deals in **mid-level theorizing**, which speaks to "general areas of human experience, makes statements which apply to this kind of experience in a variety of settings, and often utilizes an explicit empirical data base as its foundation" (LeCompte et al., 1993, p. 134).

Bronislaw Malinowski, on the other hand, dealt in the **Big T theory**. During his fieldwork among the Trobriand Islanders, Malinowski developed a theory of social interaction that he named "functionalism" (1922). Particularly interested in the islanders' kula ring exchange, a systematic exchange of prized kula shells across islands, Malinowski argued that the kula shells were not nearly as valuable to the islanders as the kula partnerships that developed through the exchange. The development of these partnerships ensured peaceful contact and communication across the islands. At the same time, they reinforced status distinctions, as traditional chiefs controlled the most valuable shell resources and organized the island-to-island expeditions. Drawing on the kula exchange, Malinowski argued that each aspect of the culture played a role in fulfilling the biological and psychological needs of the society's members. In other words, social institutions and social relations had particular functions that together formed a stable, enduring system.

These theories, Malinowski's functionalism and Peshkin's paradox of pluralism, for instance, originated out of data collected in the field and began to form when the ethnographers were in the field. Unlike researchers who set out to prove or disprove a predetermined hypothesis, the ethnographer begins with data, looks for patterns and regularities, formulates tentative hypotheses for further investigation, and finally develops some general conclusions or theories. The analytic process moves from the bottom up, from specific observations to broader generalizations and theories. This movement from data to theory has been dubbed **grounded theory** (Glaser & Strauss, 1967, p. 1) and has been defined as "the discovery of theory from data." In ethnographic research, then, generating theory begins in the field; field notes are collected, written (or typed) up, and immediately become the ethnographer's focus of analysis.

Writing Up Field Notes

The timely write-up of field notes is essential, but for ethnographers, it is neither a quick nor a pleasant task. As anthropologist Annette Lareau explained,

> I made one very serious mistake in the field; I fell behind in writing up my field notes. Writing up field notes immediately is one of the sacred obligations of field work. Yet workers I have known well all confessed that they fell behind in their field notes at one time or another. Researchers are human—we get sick; we have an extra glass of wine; we get into fights with our spouses; we have papers to grade, due the next day; or we simply don't feel like writing up field notes immediately after an interview or a participant-observation session. On top of that, at least for me, writing field notes is both boring and painful: boring, because it repeats a lot of what you just did and it takes a long time to write a detailed description of a fifteen-minute encounter/observation; painful, because it forces you to confront unpleasant things, including lack of acceptance, foolish mistakes in the field, ambiguity about the intellectual question, missed opportunities in the field, and gaping holes in the data. (Lareau, 2000, p. 216)

Writing up field notes as soon as possible after collecting data is indeed "essential," but in truth my sentiments mirror those of Lareau. I also find the write-up of field notes to be a time-consuming and tedious process. But like it or not, avoidance is impossible. New researchers talk about the promise of voice translation machines, but for now, sitting at a computer expanding field notes from elaborated "scratch notes" to richly detailed narratives continues to be a fundamental part of field work.

This process is one in which I engaged during my examination of individuals' welfare-to-work transitions. Over my two years in the field, I came to know 162 employees in four companies, 52 training and workplace supervisors, 12 trainees, and 18 administrators at the city and state levels. My discussions with these men and women, my observations, and the other data collection strategies produced piles of field notes that I transcribed, **coded** according to categories that emerged as I examined the data, and sorted by these codes to detect **emerging themes**. I constituted and reconstituted the categories to accommodate new sources of data and divergent experiences and meanings. The process was like making a jigsaw puzzle without a predetermined frame, adding pieces to create an image, and rearranging pieces to accommodate the additions. I spent an entire winter reading everything I could find about poverty and welfare, human capital, stratification and reproduction, the construction of identity, and structure, agency, and resistance, in order to know how to talk about the images that began to form. My process was consistent with ethnographer David Fetterman's description of analysis (1997): "Ethnographers look for patterns of thought and behavior. Patterns are a form of ethnographic reliability. . . . The ethnographer begins with a mass of undifferentiated ideas and behavior, and then collects pieces of information, comparing, contrasting, and sorting gross categories and minutiae until a discernible thought or behavior becomes identifiable. Next the ethnographer must listen and observe, and then compare his or her observations with this poorly defined model" (p. 96). For ethnographers, then, developing theory involves an analysis process that is open-ended and exploratory, and at times, daunting and unsettling.

REFLECTION QUESTIONS

1. Identify a phenomenon that can be characterized with thick description. What are the multiple explanations that might be developed?
2. How do ethnographers analyze the data they've collected?
3. How does "grounded theory" differ from hypothesis-driven research?
4. Why are ethnographers loath to generalize from their findings?

Writing Up Ethnography Research

Ethnography has always been conducted in natural settings, but over time the focus of ethnographic research has shifted and expanded. Ethnographic research was originally a form of **salvage anthropology**; its aim was to record the exotica of rapidly vanishing societies. These first-generation ethnographies were compilations of societies' cultural components, and included information on kinship, social control, economic and property relations, religion and ritual. The goal of the research was twofold: to document the ways of life in rapidly vanishing societies, and to discover cultural patterns that were similar across societies. Over time, specialized subfields developed, and ethnographers began to restrict their focus. Examining specific institutions in order "to get at the whole through one of its parts" (Clifford, 1988, p. 31), researchers focused specifically on archaeology, art, childhood and socialization, development and change, ecology, production and exchange systems, ethnic identities, family and kinship, gender and difference, systems of health and healing, biological inheritance, power and social control, religion and belief systems, or visual representations (Coleman & Simpson, 1998).

These early ethnographers wrote in a style they termed **ethnographic realism**, which was characterized in part by the use of the ethnographic present. Writing in present tense was seen as more authentic; it put the reader in a role of observer viewing an ongoing event. Note the difference, for example, in "The boy played with the dog," and "The boy plays with his dog." In the first example, the boy, whether real or not, has finished playing with the dog and has perhaps moved on to other activities. The scene is finished, and the reader cannot return to observe the action. In the second case, however, the action is not complete; the boy may be playing with his dog all day today. If we went to the location, we might very well see the boy as he plays with his dog. The effect is more immediate. It brings the reader into the action; it places the reader in the scene.

But in addition to writing in the ethnographic present, other narrative techniques were employed, at times deliberately and at others simply procedurally to give the reader a sense, as anthropologist James Clifford (1983) wrote, that "you are there, because

I was there" (p. 118). In order to establish "**experiential authority**" (Clifford, 1988, p. 35), for instance, the teller was positioned as an anonymous, omnipresent narrator; after all, who could question the authenticity of an account if the narrator was so godlike in his telling? Other conventions believed to authenticate the ethnographer's account included a comprehensive description of the culture under study, profiles of composite rather than actual individuals, and oversimplification in place of the complexity and variability of real life. As George Marcus and Dick Cushman (1982) wrote, "what gives the ethnographer authority and the text a pervasive sense of concrete reality is the writer's claim to represent a world as only one who has known it first-hand can" (p. 29).

However, in the 1960s and 1970s, a shift from ritual to **everyday practice** altered both ethnography's focus and writing style. As defined by anthropologist Sherry Ortner (1984), everyday practice is "the little routines people enact, again and again, in working, eating, sleeping, and relaxing, as well as the little scenarios of etiquette they play out again and again in social interaction" (p. 154). In privileging practice over ritual, the focus of ethnographic research has expanded to include not only "the sublime and the beautiful," to quote Ralph Waldo Emerson (1837), but also the mundane and the secular. This stance on culture begins, argues Michel de Certeau (2002), the author of the groundbreaking *The Practice of Everyday Life*, "when the ordinary man *becomes* the narrator, when it is he who defines the (common) place of discourse and the (anonymous) space of its development" (p. 5).

Problems of Representation

At the same time, critiques of ethnography as ahistorical and apolitical began to surface, and the assumed authority of both the ethnographer and ethnographic realism were accused of being imperialist and patronizing (Asad, 1973; Clifford, 1988; Marcus & Fischer, 1999; Said, 1979). In response to these alarms, ethnographers began to address what George Marcus and Michael Fischer (1999, p. 34) called the "**crisis of representation**"—that is, they scrutinized how "others" are represented in ethnographic texts. Described as "methodological self-consciousness and a concern for reflexivity" (van Maanen, 1995, p. 8), the soul searching that ensued resulted in a range of experimental texts, including critical ethnographies, auto-ethnographies, and other versions of what George Marcus (1998) named "messy texts." In order to make the behind-the-scenes of the ethnography more apparent, some ethnographers, Paul Rabinow (1977) and Jean-Paul Dumont (1978) being the most noted, wrote personal accounts of the trials and tribulations of their fieldwork experiences. In an attempt to lend credibility to the ethnographer's interpretation, others, including Paul Willis (1977), June Nash (1979), and Doug Foley (1990), wrote about the culture they studied, whether it be marginal youth, a Bolivian mining town, or a small southwestern U.S. town, within a historic, economic, and political context (even though the described context was most often outside the awareness of group members themselves).

Other ethnographers crafted their stories using the **multiple voices** of their informants rather than with the researcher's single voice. In an effort to create space for the voices of both the researcher and the researched, for example, Patti Lather and Chris Smithies (1997) wove voices of women affected with HIV/AIDS into their narrative

Troubling the Angels. In a similar approach, Ruth Behar framed the personal account of Esperanza Hernandez, an indigenous Mexican street peddler, with her own feminist interpretation of ethnicity and Latina identity. "Se lleva una historia muy grande, compadre (I carry a heavy history)," explained Esperanza in Behar's *Translated Woman: Crossing the Border with Esperanza's Story* (2003, p. xi).

Another response to this crisis of representation has been the emergence of texts that are loosely named **auto-ethnographies**. The term auto-ethnography actually contains two distinct strands, "the study of one's own people or group" and "autobiographical accounts presented as ethnographies of the self" (Wolcott, 1999, p. 173). The essays in Deborah Reed-Danahay's edited text, *Auto/Ethnography: Rewriting the Self and the Social* (1997), for instance, all examine issues of voice, representation, and power, but take a range of forms, from witness narratives, autobiography, and biographies to self-reflexive accounts and life histories. Alternatively, in his *Poker Faces: The Life and Work of Professional Card Players*, David Hayano (1982) documents the culture and social organization of "the cardroom and its players" from his own vantage point as poker player. He asserts that participant observation was essential to his research, because "an insider's view of the work of professional poker players could only be accomplished by prolonged immersion and, most important, *by being a player*" (p. 155). As Deborah Reed-Danahay writes (1997), "We are in the midst of a renewed interest in personal narrative, in life history, and in autobiography among anthropologists" (p. 1).

These changes in ethnographic writing did not evolve on their own; they were shaped by the changes that accompanied the breakup of European colonial empires. As distinctions blurred between civilized and savage, modern and traditional, and first and third worlds, and the subjects of ethnographic research became readers of ethnographic research, ethnography's responsibility in creating exoticized images of non-Western peoples both became apparent and was made problematic. The alternative forms of ethnographic writing described previously were part of larger attempts to shift relationships between the researcher and the researched, powerful and powerless, voiced and voiceless, and to depict more thoughtfully the messiness of our world. In these messy texts, the researcher has become an actor in the story, informants have become coauthors, stories are not necessarily told in a linear fashion, and history, culture, and economics are irrevocably interlinked. According to anthropologist John van Maanen (1995), "such writings often offer a passionate, emotional voice of a positioned and explicitly judgmental fieldworker and thus obliterate the customary and, ordinarily, rather mannerly distinction between the researcher and the researched" (pp. 9–10).

REFLECTION QUESTIONS

1. Why did ethnographic realism become the preferred writing style for pre–World War II ethnographers?

2. What does the term "crisis of representation" mean to you?

3. Have you ever encountered a "messy text?" What did it look like? If not, what do you envision a "messy text" to be?

4. How did the breakup of colonial empires affect ethnographic research?

READING ETHNOGRAPHY

When writing, ethnographers generally engage in a process that begins with a prewriting phase of organizing and planning and moves to drafting and revising. The reporting generally centers around a problem that is addressed by studying "things in their natural setting, attempting to make sense of, or interpret, phenomena in terms of the meanings people bring to them" (Denzin & Lincoln, 1994, p. 2). Evidence is collected in fieldwork and presented as a series of interwoven stories of the ethnographer, the field, the people in the site, and the research process itself. A good ethnography puts the reader in the setting, surrounded by its language, its smells, its sights, and its people, complete with their viewpoints and understandings. As anthropologist James Peacock (1986) wrote, "Ethnography is unlike literature and like science in that it endeavors to describe real people systemically and accurately, but it resembles literature in that it weaves facts into a form that highlights patterns and principles. . . . Ethnography can never describe with complete objectivity, producing a set of facts that are completely true; but through its portrayals and interpretations it can communicate human truths" (pp. 83–84).

What Should a Reader Do?

Let's switch perspectives for a moment, and focus on how to read the text an ethnographer writes. Based on my reading, and bits and pieces I've picked up along the way, I can offer a few tips to make the reading more productive. Reading an article, of course, is different from reading a full ethnographic text, because the article, like a slice of pie, is only one piece of the ethnographic research. For both, focus on the opening statements, the introduction of the article or the preface of the book. Look for information on the research project itself and on the intentions and experience of the author. Your aim here is to simply develop a preliminary understanding of the relationship between this piece and the researcher's broader agenda. Continue reading through the article or book; as you read look for the argument the author is attempting to make. The argument may be specific to the setting, or may have theoretical significance that extends beyond this particular case. Ask yourself the following questions:

- What did the ethnographer research and why?
- What argument is offered, and is adequate evidence, in the form of direct quotes or stories (vignettes, scenarios), for example, presented?
- Where is the ethnographer visible in the ethnography, and does the presence of the researcher intrude on or support the argument?

Jot down or mark key passages and new terms in the ethnography, and make sure you and the author share definitions. As you read, engage the author in a mental conversation, ask questions, pose alternative explanations, clarify the ambiguous, and pay attention to the presence of the author in the text. As anthropologist Nancy Scheper-Hughes (1992) wrote, "the ethnographer has a professional and a moral obligation to get the 'facts' as accurately as possible. This is not even debatable. But all facts are necessarily selected and interpreted from the moment we decide to count one thing, and ignore another, or attend this ritual but not another, so that anthropological understanding is necessarily partial" (p. 23).

Practice Your Reading Skills

Practice your skills as a reader of ethnography by reading the following article. "Connecting and Reconnecting to Work: Low-Income Mothers' Participation in Publicly Funded Training Programs" is drawn from my own ethnographic research (Riemer, 2004) on men and women who moved from welfare recipient to full-time worker. In conducting the research, I collected data in four companies that had collaborated with the state's Department of Public Welfare and local adult education initiatives to hire and train men and women on welfare. The article is a slice of the larger research initiative, and describes one of the four companies, a long-term health care facility named Church Hall.

Read the article, keeping the earlier suggestions in mind. As you are reading, also check for validity by asking the following questions:

- Is there strong agreement between the research question, ethnography as a research mechanism, and the research findings?
- How were the location, sample, setting, and subjects identified?
- How did the author collect data and analyze the data?
- Where is the researcher in the text?
- What does the author conclude, and is adequate evidence provided?

SUMMARY

In this chapter, I introduced ethnography as a research method, discussed ethnographers' beliefs about knowledge, culture, and methodology, and described ethnographers' toolbox of methods. As explained, ethnography, the research methodology of anthropologists, is the study of a particular cultural group or phenomenon. Fieldwork is a fundamental part of that study, and for anthropologists, ethnographic fieldwork involves documenting people's beliefs and practices through observation, interviews, and the review of relevant records and reports.

The goal of ethnographic research is to understand a way of life from the insider's, or *emic*, perspective, and to provide a description that is *etic*, or comprehensible to individuals outside the society. Ethnography, as anthropologist James Spradley (1979) wrote, is a research methodology that helps us understand "how other people see their experience" (p. iv). To accomplish that goal, Spradley continues, "rather than *studying people*, ethnography means *learning from people*" (p. 3).

KEY TERMS

auto-ethnography
Big T theory
code of ethics
coding
confidentiality

crisis of representation
cultural interpretation
emerging themes
emic
ethnographic interviews

ethnographic realism
ethnography
etic
everyday practice
experiential authority
fieldwork
foreshadowed problem
full cycle of activities
grounded theory
informed consent
interdependent relationship
key informants

law of diminishing returns
mid-level theorizing
multiple voices
nonparticipant observer
observation
participant observer
research questions
salvage anthropology
site documents
theory
thick description
triangulate

FURTHER READINGS AND RESOURCES

Suggested Ethnography Article

Riemer, F. (2004). Connecting and reconnecting to work: Low-income mothers' participation, past and present, in publicly funded training programs. In V. Polakow, S. Butler, L. Deprez, & P. Kahn (Eds.), *Shut out: Low-income women and higher education in post welfare America.* Albany, NY: SUNY Press.

Suggested Readings

Becker, G. (1998). *Tricks of the trade: How to think about your research while you're doing it.* Chicago: The University of Chicago Press.

   A particularly clear, concise guide to doing research in a range of settings.

Clifford, J. (n.d.) *The problem of ethnographic representation.* Retrieved April 20, 2004, from http://home.pacbell .net/nicnic/ethnographic.html.

   A concise article that provides a clear overview of the difficulties ethnographers encounter in representing the experiences of the peoples they study.

Fine, M. (1991). *Framing dropouts: Notes on the politics of an urban public high school.* Albany, NY: University of SUNY Press.

   An excellent example of a critical ethnography, this text examines the forces at play in students' dropping out of high school, and the ways that administrators, teachers, and the students themselves understand what it means to drop out of school.

Hall, K. D. (2002). *Lives in translation: Sikh youth as British citizens.* Philadelphia: University of Pennsylvania Press.

   An ethnography that expands the boundaries of the school by revealing the in- and out-of-school experiences of young Sikhs in northern England and the ways they negotiate race, class, and caste inequality.

Nespor, J. (1997). *Tangled up in school: Politics, space, and signs in educational process.* Mahwah, NJ: Erlbaum.

   Based on two years of ethnographic fieldwork in an urban elementary school, this book expands the definition of school by situating it as part of a broader network of parental concerns, school district politics, university and government agendas, and identity politics.

Rabinow, P. (1977). *Reflections on fieldwork in Morocco.* Berkeley: University of California Press.

   A personal account of the experience of fieldwork that reveals the complexities of life in the field.

Spradley, J., & McCurdy, D. W. (1972). *The cultural experience: Ethnography in complex society.* Prospect Heights, IL: Waveland.

A step-by-step guide to conducting ethnographic research that includes ethnographies conducted in a range of familiar settings.

Journals
American Anthropologist

www.aaanet.org/aa/index.htm

Publishes articles that add to, integrate, synthesize, and interpret anthropological knowledge; commentaries and essays on issues of importance to the discipline; and reviews of books, films, sound recordings, and exhibits.

Anthropology & Education Quarterly

www.aaanet.org/cae/AEQ.html

A peer-reviewed journal that publishes scholarship on schooling in social and cultural context and on human learning both inside and outside of schools.

Anthropology Quarterly

www.jstor.org/journals/00035491.html

A peer-reviewed journal that publishes outstanding, original, data-driven articles that advance ethnography and anthropological theory.

Ethnography

www.sagepub.com/journalsProdDesc.nav?prodId = Journal200906

An international, interdisciplinary forum for the ethnographic study of social and cultural change.

Ethnography and Education

www.tandf.co.uk/journals/titles/17457823.asp

An international peer-reviewed journal that publishes articles illuminating educational practices through empirical methodologies, which prioritize the experiences and perspectives of those involved.

Journal of Contemporary Ethnography

www.sagepub.com/journalsProdDesc.nav?prodId = Journal200975

An international and interdisciplinary forum for research using ethnographic methods to examine human behavior in natural settings.

ENDNOTES

1. Emic is from the word "phonemic."
2. Etic is from the word "phonetic."
3. The volume of existing text differs across cultures, and although little text is found in societies that are predominately nonliterate, schools and other social agencies are rich depositories of written text.
4. After Whyte left the field, however, the relationship became more complicated and far less intimate. They fell out of touch, and as Whyte (1996) confessed, "there seemed to be a growing problem between us that led to an estrangement I still do not fully understand" (p. 63). Whyte offered several possibilities for this "estrangement," including Doc's possible embarrassment over Whyte's findings, Doc's resentment

over Whyte's proceeds from the book, or Doc's departure from street corner life to paid production work. Whatever the reason or reasons, the shift from informant to collaborator to distant acquaintance was awkward and somewhat sad, but not uncommon.

5. A few ethnographers (Firestone, 1993; Peacock, 1986; Street, 1984; Whyte, 1994) argue that although their focus may not be typical, some aspects of every case are. As Wolcott (2001) writes, "Each case is unique, yet not so unique that we cannot learn from it and apply its lessons more generally" (p. 175).

CHAPTER

FEMINISM(S): CRITIQUE AND TRANSFORMATION

ROSARY LALIK AND CAROL BRANIGAN FELDERMAN

KEY IDEAS

- Feminist researchers use gender as a unit of analysis.

- A hallmark of feminist research and knowledge development is the use of continual critique as a learning strategy.

- Different groups of feminists have worked for markedly different goals.

- Feminism is often characterized in terms of three waves.

- African American feminists attended to the perspectives and interests of many different racial, social, and economic groups.

- Being oppressed means the absence of choices.

- The concomitant oppressions of racism, sexism, and classism have been construed as a triple jeopardy faced by women of color.

- Binary thinking is thinking that relies on dualisms such as male-female.

- Many feminists have criticized the enterprise of science on numerous grounds.

- The goal of science from a feminist epistemological position is to bring about emancipation for women and for other demeaned groups.

- An Afrocentric feminist epistemology would require scholars to dialogue with common people about their findings.

- Feminist interpretive methods include interrupting efforts to simplify and universalize knowledge.
- Transformation is an essential criterion for feminist research.

FEMINISM IN ACADEMIC AND POPULAR DISCOURSE

We [feminists] . . . must necessarily criticize, question,
reexamine, and explore new possibilities.
—hooks, 1995, p. 277

To begin to understand feminism within society and research one must develop foundational knowledge about what feminism is and how it has evolved. This is essential for many reasons, not the least of which is that although most Western adults have become familiar with the word *feminism*, many misconceptions prevail about what feminism entails and what it purports to achieve. Chief among these may be the misconception that "to be a feminist is to hate men" (Cole, 1995, p. 550); another is that to be a feminist one must put the well-being of women ahead of all other concerns. Such misconceptions interfere with efforts to understand the ways in which feminism has been used to guide knowledge development and inform research and public policy.

The problem of inaccurate or fragmentary knowledge about feminism has been exacerbated because, as a term, feminism has been used by a wide range of individuals and groups to characterize a broad array of issues, and, indeed, the plural form of the term, **feminisms**, is preferred by many proponents. Thus there are more than a few definitions of feminism and, within and among these definitions, there remain wide differences of perspective and approach. Due to this variability, efforts to explicate feminism and feminist methods within research are open to critique, and such critique undoubtedly will be shaped by the orientations toward feminism held by particular critics (Lather, 1991).

In spite of the variability among understandings of feminism, it is possible to look beyond differences and identify significant areas of agreement. Perhaps most important, feminisms cohere in their mutual pursuit of fair treatment and independence for women (Harslanger & Tuana, 2004; Hesse-Biber, 2007; Lewis, 1992). This pursuit has been expressed by feminist researchers in their use of gender as an essential, but not necessarily exclusive, **unit for analysis**. That is, feminist researchers pay attention to gender when designing research questions, gathering and analyzing data, and writing about research.

Another commonality among feminisms is the significance of **continual critique** as a learning strategy. That is, in addition to developing critiques of practices and structures of major social institutions, such as science, feminists direct their critiques at the views and research activities of other feminists, and perhaps most important, at their personal efforts at theory making and research (Gluck & Patai, 1991). It is not uncommon for a feminist to construct a critique of her own research; one example of this is an article in which Lalik and Hinchman (2001) demonstrate how their own research in literacy was limited by their particular positions as white women who were relatively privileged by their positions as professors at major universities in the United States.

Variability Among Feminisms

Feminisms have been informed by various social theories and research traditions, and they hold varying views of an idealized social world (Kenway & Modra, 1992). One method that has been used to highlight differences among feminists has been the categorization of feminists into groups based on the most salient goals they espouse. Thus the term **liberal feminist** has been used to label those within the tradition who work toward a future in which women have access to financial and social benefits and political power equal to those of white, heterosexual, affluent males (Friedan, 2001/1963). **Social feminist** has been used to refer to those who work toward a future in which educational institutions no longer remain complicit in the exploitative processes that limit the life chances of women and other demeaned people (Weiler, 1988). **Radical feminist** has been used for those who work toward replacing what they see as a male-based, white, sexist power structure that they believe is inherently oppressive and irreparable (Dworkin, 2002). **Poststructural feminist** has been used to refer to those who work to analyze the language practices associated with the philosophical tradition of modernity in an effort to clarify the ways that such practices support the unfair treatment of women and other nonmainstream groups (St. Pierre & Pillow, 2000). **Critical postmodern feminist** has been used to refer to those who help girls and women understand how visual and linguistic systems of representation may encourage them to alter themselves in order to attract favorable attention from males, even when the practices they use to do so are unhealthy for them or limit their opportunities to live successful and fulfilling lives (Lalik & Oliver, 2007; Luke & Gore, 1992). It is important to note that the categories of feminism included above are merely illustrative of the many that have come into use. Also important to note is that the categories are derived from the goals of the feminist projects, rather than the research methods used to develop knowledge relevant to each project.

Though categorization of feminisms received considerable attention in the 1980s and 1990s and continues in use, it has lost much of its eminence, and, as a strategy for explication, it has declined considerably for several reasons. Chief among these is that feminists typically eschew categorization, claiming that it tends to obscure important subtleties and distort reality. Further, in recent years distinctions among feminisms have blurred as political orientations of those working in this tradition have become increasingly hybridized through adaptation and critique among feminists (Olesen, 1994). Finally, new versions of feminism continue to emerge throughout the world, thus thwarting the efforts of those who would capture the tradition once and for all.

Waves of Feminism

The term "feminism" came into usage in English in the late nineteenth and early twentieth centuries during the women's suffrage movements in the United States and Europe. This period, culminating in the United States in the passage of the Nineteenth Amendment in 1920, is often called **first-wave feminism**. Next, revived as a social project in the 1960s and achieving its apex in the 1980s as **second-wave feminism**, adherents strove toward achieving women's equality with affluent white males in various settings including educational institutions, the workplace, and other arenas of public power, and the home. Second-wave feminism received considerable attention in the Western media, and for many today it continues to be the commonly understood view of the feminist agenda—one sometimes referred to as liberal feminism. Both first- and second-wave feminism became associated with efforts of largely affluent white women from Britain, France, and the United States, and this fact drew criticism from nonaffluent, nonwhite women who worked across both periods of time to improve conditions for women and others. This criticism, along with the alternative projects it spawned, developed into a more inclusive agenda and an approach to feminism that came to be called **third-wave feminism**. This wave of feminism will be discussed in detail in the following sections of this chapter.

Perhaps best known as feminists are those liberal feminists who examined how women's personal experiences and belief systems, their interactions with men, and their taken-for-granted daily practices in the home and workplace related to larger social and political structures and processes. For example, Friedan (2001/1963) explained how women's belief systems often caused them to focus their lives on activities such as childbearing and homemaking—activities, she argued, that are undervalued in society and ultimately limit women's choices and their potential for achieving economic, social, and political ascendance. Liberal feminists sought political and legal reform as means for achieving equality with males, but they did not advocate altering the basic structure of society. They encouraged women to seek such reform though their individual actions and choices. In their writings and research, liberal feminists addressed a broad array of social issues, including equal pay for equal work, reproductive rights, education, child care, health care, and domestic violence.

African American Feminists Broaden the Conversation

Since the apex of second-wave feminism, the feminist agenda has broadened considerably, as have understandings of what it may mean to be a feminist. Such broadening may be attributed, especially in the United States, to the work and struggle of American black feminists whose efforts emerged from their lived experiences as slaves and their struggle against the institution of slavery (Guy-Sheftall, 1995). These feminists have been credited for broadening the feminist agenda to include "poverty, racism, imperialism, lynching, welfare, economic exploitation, sterilization abuse, decent housing, and a host of other concerns that generations of black women foregrounded" (Stewart, 1995, p. 2).

Though African American women have worked enthusiastically to advance the status of women in the United States, and their efforts can be readily traced to the 1830s when they were working to end the plague of slavery in the United States (Guy-Sheftall, 1995), their use of the word feminism does not appear until the 1970s (Cole, 1995). Distancing themselves from the term feminism, African American feminists have critiqued much of the work conducted by white feminists in the United States as a limited effort by white women from the leisure classes whose interests, they claimed, centered on expanding their relatively privileged position in society. Further, hooks (1995) charged that the feminist project developed by privileged whites showed little opposition to capitalism, classism, and racism, thus maintaining the dominant social values that oppressed other societal groups. In making her case, hooks drew a clear and cogent distinction between **oppression** and forms of **exploitation and discrimination**. "Sexism as a system of domination is institutionalized, but it has never determined in an absolute way the fate of all women in this society. Being oppressed means the absence of choices. It is the primary point of contact between the oppressed and the oppressor. Many women in this society do have choices (as inadequate as they are), therefore exploitation and discrimination are words that more accurately describe the lot of women collectively in the United States. Many women do not join organized resistance against sexism precisely because sexism has not meant an absolute lack of choices" (p. 273).

Black feminists have been highly effective in broadening and deepening feminist perspectives and agendas by introducing and developing the notion of **intersecting oppressions**. Chief among these are racism, sexism, and classism, which these feminists have construed as a **triple jeopardy** for black women grown from "their dual racial and gender identity and their limited access to economic resources" (Stewart, 1995, p. 2). Collins (1991) claimed an essential role for black feminists by asserting that those who experience oppression develop a "special vision" (p. 33); that is, a vision that allows them to access important and often hidden knowledge about social dynamics.

Guy-Sheftall (1995) presents a perspective on feminism derived from the work of black activists, scholars, and creative writers. "I use the term 'feminist' to capture the emancipatory vision and acts of resistance among a diverse group of African American women who attempt in their writings to articulate their understanding of the complex nature of black womanhood, the interlocking nature of the oppressions black women suffer, and the necessity of sustained struggle in their quest for self-definition, the liberation of black people, and gender equality" (p. xiv).

Another barrier separating African American feminists from their more affluent white sisters is that African American women, while recognizing their oppression as women, also "witness countless ways in which their fathers, brothers, sons, lovers—indeed every Black man they know is also victimized by racism" (Cole, 1995, p. 550). These experiences place black feminists in a conflicted situation. They simultaneously express empathy for black men's difficulties as blacks in a white supremacist society, while rejecting the unequal treatment they so often receive from black men in both the private and public realm (Collins, 1991). With respect to their empathy for black men, Cole (1995) explains: "African American women feel a bond with black men which comes from being called the same name, from being denied access to similar opportunities, from so often receiving the poorest of what America has to offer in terms of jobs, education, health care, and housing" (p. 550).

Reminding us how the term feminism may be viewed by many black women and white women who live their lives outside the circles of privilege, hooks (1995) described her experiences participating in feminist groups. "I found that white women adopted a condescending attitude towards me and other nonwhite participants. The condescension they directed at black women was one of the means they employed to remind us that the women's movement was 'theirs'—that we were able to participate because they allowed it, even encouraged it; after all, we were needed to legitimate the process. They did not see us as equals. . . . We could be heard only if our statements echoed the sentiments of the dominant discourse" (pp. 278–279).

The critique of the white feminist agenda so eloquently expressed by hooks, and felt even today (Kim, 2007) by many nondominant women who, in our current context of economic globalization, are aware of gross differences in benefits for different groups of women, led Walker (1983) to develop a counter-discourse that provided a space for the views that the whites in control of the movement apparently ignored or demeaned. Calling these alternative views **womanist**, Walker explains, "womanist is to feminist as purple is to lavender" (cited in Collins, 1991, p. 37). A womanist perspective focuses on connection and concern for all humanity, even while appreciating "autonomous movements of self-determination" (Collins, 1991, p. 38). It prioritizes a commitment to work against those ideologies that support oppression in any form.

Rather than diminishing the importance of feminisms for research, the differences among feminists and the criticisms associated with those differences have led to the development of a collection of feminisms that increasingly take as their agenda the radical transformation of society in the interests of equity and social justice. Thus proponents of feminism see strength in its dynamic character. St. Pierre & Pillow (2000) assert some of the advantages of this indeterminacy. "What kinds of women and what kinds of feminism might we fail to produce if we define 'woman' and 'feminism' once and for all? At any rate, the impulse to regulate and normalize these categories has not been successful. There are many feminisms, and one of the strengths of this proliferating category is that it continues to reinvent itself strategically, shifting and mutating given existing political agendas, power relations, and identity strategies" (p. 8).

Given this appreciation for change and development in feminisms, we can expect new versions to appear as feminists continue to struggle toward what they envision to be social and political transformation; that is, movement toward their ideals of equity and justice.

REFLECTION QUESTIONS

1. Interview several people in your social group about their understandings of feminism and compare their explanations with those described in this chapter.

2. Write a description of yourself in which you reflect on the ways in which your views and activities are consistent and inconsistent with those from feminism(s).

3. Write a vignette to describe a situation in which you or someone you know has been exploited, discriminated against, or oppressed. Use the explanations of these terms developed by hooks to decide whether she would say you have been oppressed. (These distinctions are important because it is common for many people to overuse the words *oppressed* and *oppression*, thus lessening their significance.)

FEMINISM(S) AND THE CRITIQUE OF SCIENCE

To understand the approaches that feminists have taken in their efforts at research and knowledge development, it is important to be informed by the **critique of science** that many feminists have emphasized in their research. Namenwirth (1986) put the critique within a respectful view of science as a human endeavor. "Science is a system of procedures for gathering, verifying, and systematizing information about reality. The knowledge that has been developed in fields such as physics, astronomy, biology through scientific procedures is fascinating, awe inspiring, a tribute to human creativity and perseverance. Applied in technologies, scientific information creates powerful tools for creative use and devastating misuse. In and of itself, none of this should lead us to think of science as inherently masculine. Yet, because science evolved within patriarchal society, it took on a decidedly masculine tone and became burdened and distorted by a pervasive male bias" (p. 19).

Many feminists have criticized science from multiple perspectives. Among these are concerns about (1) women's participation in scientific endeavors, (2) the erasure of knowledge about successful women scientists, (3) the patriarchal nature of science, and (4) the epistemology of science.

Critique Related to Women's Participation in Scientific Endeavors

When addressing questions about participation by women in science, feminist researchers have examined exclusionary practices that made it difficult, if not impossible, for women to gain entry or persist in scientific studies in universities, laboratories, and scientific societies. These lines of inquiry led to uncovering such practices as denying women entry to universities where they might further their study of scientific knowledge; insulting women applicants as part of job-seeking processes at scientific establishments; paying women little or nothing for their work as scientists, even when they distinguished themselves through their contributions; and maintaining inflexible working conditions that interfered with women's continuing responsibilities as primary caregivers for children, the infirm, and elders (Rose, 1986). It is important to note that the dearth of women scientists continues as an issue in contemporary culture in the United States and elsewhere (Lather, 1991).

Critique Related to the Erasure of Knowledge About Successful Women Scientists

The erasure from the history of science of those few women who managed to work and achieve as scientists is another aspect of feminisms' critique of science. Although science remained a function of the private realm of the household during the late 1800s and well into the twentieth century, it was common for "scientific families" (Rose, 1986) to work in laboratories, and it was sometimes possible, under the guidance of a sympathetic male family member, for a woman in the family to work on scientific projects and to excel in that work. Even so, the private context of that work allowed women's accomplishments to be easily erased. When science moved out of homes into the public sphere, even these familial opportunities for women evaporated.

Perhaps more central to this aspect of critique is research by feminists to identify particular women scientists and their important contributions, together with exposure of the ways in which male scientists conspired to diminish and even deny these contributions. We see these phenomena in the case of Rosalind Franklin, whose challenge of the accreditation system of science with respect to DNA led her male contemporaries to "modify their accounts of the history of the discovery of the structure of DNA" (Rose, 1986, p. 63) and the case of Jocelyn Bell, whose leadership on the discovery of quasars led to the conferral of a Nobel prize on her male superior (Rose, 1986, p. 63).

Studies of the accomplishments of extraordinary women in science also uncovered some unique ways in which women conducted their science. Possibly the most salient example of such difference appears in Evelyn Fox Keller's study of Barbara McClintock (1984). This study revealed how the questions McClintock asked and her relationship with the corn plants with which she worked differed markedly from those reported by male contemporaries. In particular, McClintock described her interdependence with the corn plants and related her "feeling for the organism" (Rose, 1986, p. 63) as central to her work. McClintock's language reveals an approach to science that reflects an integration of mind and body—of head and heart—in approaching her research that was generally eschewed by her male contemporaries.

Critique Related to the Patriarchal Nature of Science

In terms of ideology, feminists argue that the claims of science have not merely been neutral or peripheral to the goals of feminisms, but have, in fact, been antithetical to them. Particularly egregious to feminists were the efforts by anthropologists, psychologists, and biologists to explain women's limited access to wealth and political power in terms of biological differences that ostensibly made women unfit for important responsibilities and access to power. Feminist researchers have shown how much of the science conducted in such projects, when examined closely, reveals "weak theory, inadequate and misinterpreted data, poor experiments, and inadmissible extrapolations between observations made on rats or ducks to humans" (Rose, 1986, p. 64). They charged that such poor science was allowed, and at times promoted, simply because it provided a basis for the continued domination of women. "This cavalier approach to the limits of scientific method would not be acceptable in any less ideologically charged task than the legitimation of male domination and female subordination as rooted in biology and, therefore, natural" (Rose, 1986, p. 64).

The domination and subordination of women, uncovered as part of the feminist critique of science, is often attributed to descriptions of the goal of Western science as the domination of nature. Such descriptions appeared in the early writings about science and have been incorporated throughout its development. To counterbalance this theme, feminist researchers and others have explored the possibility of a science that could envision itself as being in harmony with nature. Such an approach is reflected in the writings of Rachel Carson (1962), a biologist whose book *Silent Spring* inspired the ecology movement, even while her work was initially dismissed by much of the mainstream scientific community.

The critique of the ideology of science as patriarchal became widely discussed in society. Although substantiated through the work of feminist researchers and theorists, it also became a focal point for discussion and debate in the public sphere in a wide array of media, in boardrooms, schools, and other institutions, eventually leading to policies and practices that increased the life chances of many women in society. Within the research arena, feminists have raised awareness of **binary thinking**—thinking that relies on dualisms such as male-female, nature-nurture, cognitive-affective, and right brain–left brain—with one term described as positive and the other as deficient in one or more ways. Further they have shown how binary thinking has been used to unfairly inhibit success for women and others by, for example, depicting men as intellectual, decisive, strong, and responsible and women as emotional, indecisive, weak, and unable to shoulder responsibility.

Critique Related to the Epistemology of Science

An **epistemology** is a theory of knowledge that includes "questions about who can be a 'knower'. . . ; what tests beliefs must pass in order to be legitimated as knowledge. . . ; what kinds of things can be known, and so forth" (Harding, 1987, p. 3). Feminists have called into question the justification strategies that underlie the theory of knowledge espoused by many mainstream scientists. For example, Bleier (1986) and other feminists argue that even while many mainstream scientists express a high value for **objectivity** or neutrality as a criterion for the adequacy of the knowledge they produce, the theories, concepts, values, ideologies, and practices of the scientific enterprise reflect the values and attitudes, indeed the worldviews, of the people who have participated in the enterprise—people who have identified predominantly as Western, male, white, middle or upper class, and heterosexual.

Further, feminists have argued that the scientific method is a set of idealized practices and that the life experiences of scientists affect the observations they make, the questions they ask, what they see, and what is hidden from their view or overlooked, how they interpret data, and the language they use in their formal and informal presentations and writings (Bleier, 1986; Harding, 1987). Bleier points to several examples of limited vision among scientists including one rather striking point: "[L]eading microscopists of the 17th and 18th centuries, including the great van Leeuwenhoek, claimed they had seen 'exceedingly minute forms of men with arms, heads and legs complete inside sperm' under the microscope. Their observations were constrained not by the limited resolving power of the microscopes of the time, but rather by the 2,000-year-old concept, dating back to the time of Aristotle, that women, as totally passive beings, contribute nothing to conception but the womb as incubator" (p. 3).

It is important to note, however, that this critique does not hold nonmainstream scientists, including women and people of color, exempt from these limitations. Rather, these critics highlight the intensely human character of science—a perspective that undermines the efforts of many Westerners who argue for the primacy of science as a persistent agent of social progress (Harding, 2006). Pointing out that today most scientists find employment with defense contractors, corporate labs, pharmaceutical companies, and electronic and biotech industries, Harding offers a litany of flaws in scientific endeavor: "The skeptics have focused especially on modern sciences' ties to militarism: on corporate profiteering through appeals to scientific and technological progress . . . on environmental destruction caused by scientific farming, manufacturing, militarism . . . on scientific theories purportedly demonstrating racial or sexual inferiority and on the failure of the transfer of Western sciences and technologies to the developing world to benefit the vast majority of the globe's least-advantaged citizens" (pp. 1–2).

After exposing limitations of widespread acceptance of Western science, Harding uses the feminist strategy of **redefinition of taken-for-granted terms**. That is, she redefines science toward a more inclusive view—one that includes knowledge systems often demeaned or ignored by Westerners: "A knowledge system will be referred to as a science if it is systematic and empirical, regardless of whether it is Western or non-Western, contemporary or ancient, obviously embedded in religious or other cultural beliefs or not apparently so" (p. 10). Further, characteristic of the feminist strategy of **reflexivity**, that is, ongoing critique of one's own statements, Harding reminds readers that her own use of binaries, such as Western–non-Western and first world–third world, are products of imperialism that linger in her usage, even as they oversimplify life and obscure both important distinctions within members of each element of the binary as well as the commonalities across elements of the binary.

Harding's more expansive definition of science highlights the feminist agenda of developing sciences that reflect feminist perspectives. Bleier (1986) clarifies her goal for such sciences by describing an alternative science that would free women from internalized judgments about their biological inferiority—judgments fueled by the workings of mainstream science.

REFLECTION QUESTION

1. Identify a binary composed of two terms often compared to each other, and develop a list of adjectives you associate with each term in the pair. Review your list to determine how the binary may be working to support the unequal distribution of prestige and other rewards and privileges that society has to offer.

POSSIBILITIES FOR A FEMINIST EPISTEMOLOGY

Once alternative approaches to science are construed, the topic of possibilities for a feminist science can be broached. Rose (1986) imagines such a science as one that "transcends dichotomies, insists on the scientific validity of the subjective, on the need to unite cognitive and affective domains; it emphasizes holism, harmony, and complexity rather than reductionism, domination, and linearity. In this, the approach builds on traditions that have always been present in science, though submerged within the dominant culture" (p. 72). Even with the awareness that some of these features of science may already exist in unnoticed corners of the enterprise, Rose's vision for science reveals the extraordinary changes that feminist epistemologists are trying to achieve.

According to Harding (1987), in a feminist epistemology or a feminist theory of what knowledge is and how it can be developed, the **context of discovery** is particularly important. By context of discovery she refers to the questions that are raised and not raised in the pursuit of scientific knowledge. Limiting scientific questions to those raised by a small fraction of society, such as those deriving from white, affluent men's experience, has led to knowledge that conveys both partial and distorted understandings of social life and reality. Feminists argue that women's experiences are a rich and vital resource for identifying research questions, as well as for testing the validity of findings, designing the institutions within which research is conducted and disseminated, and for identifying the individuals who should engage in the process of research. One notable example of the use of women's experiences is seen in the research of psychologist Carol Gilligan (1982), who used the study of women's experiences as a basis for challenging prevailing theories of human development that had largely ignored women.

Such a theory of knowledge or epistemology pluralizes the word *woman* to refer instead to "women's experiences" in clear recognition that there is no single or **essentialized** woman who can well represent the group (Kim, 2007). Rather, women, as well as men, vary along many lines including, for example, race, class, sexuality, physical abilities, life experiences, geographic location, and culture. It is important to note, however, that rather than bemoaning this variability, such an epistemology sees it as a considerable advantage—one that can provide "a rich source of feminist insight" (Harding, 1987, p. 8).

In addition to the source of the questions central to a feminist epistemology is the type of question. Essential are those questions that might lead to the development of more equitable conditions for women and others. Questions could be raised, for example, about factors that sustain inequitable treatment; about ways to change the conditions that sustain a group's undervalued status; and about strategies to win over those individuals or groups who work to maintain inequitable conditions. These are questions that arise from women's political struggles and, rather than demeaning them, a feminist epistemology views them as essential, especially because the goal of science from a feminist epistemological position is to bring about emancipation for women and other demeaned groups.

A feminist epistemology is concerned with people of a particular group studying themselves, as seen in an article by Lalik and Hinchman (2000) in which they examine the limitations in their work teaching beginning and experienced literacy teachers. Alternatively, **studying up**, that is, studying those with more influence or status than the researcher, is seen as essential to such an epistemology. This is a fairly uncommon practice in mainstream social inquiry, where researchers tend to gravitate toward **studying down**; that is, they typically study those outside their group who have less influence than they. Frequently we see university-based researchers studying working-class women, nonwhites, children, and other nonmainstream groups. Although such research may have considerable potential for advancing feminist goals, Harding and others argue that it is insufficient:

> *While employers have often commissioned studies of how to make workers happy with less power and pay, workers have rarely been in a position to undertake or commission studies of anything at all, let alone how to make employers happy with less power and profit. Similarly, psychiatrists have endlessly studied what they regard as women's peculiar mental and behavioral characteristics, but women have only recently begun to study the bizarre mental and behavioral characteristic of psychiatrists. If we want to understand how our daily experience arrives in the forms it does, it makes sense to examine critically the sources of social power. (Harding, 1987, pp. 8–9)*

A feminist epistemology requires the researchers themselves to disclose their particular history and standpoint. Thus research is seen as more credible when researchers report their class, race, culture, as well as their beliefs and assumptions that impinge upon the research. This criterion grows in part from the feminist view that all research is partial and, insofar as it is constrained by the humans conducting the research, **perspectival**, that is, influenced by researcher perspective (Lather, 1991). Without having access to crucial knowledge about those doing the research, any judgment about the credibility of the research is viewed as tenuous. This type of information is understood to increase the quality of the research.

Feminist epistemology supports the notion that men may contribute to the development of feminist knowledge and that those who are members of nondemeaned mainstream groups can contribute knowledge that reflects the tenets of a feminist epistemology. Male researchers may develop knowledge useful to feminists when they have access to settings that bar women. Such settings might include boardrooms, social clubs, sporting activities, and other places where policy making and influence creation ensue. However, even while expecting that males and other oppressor groups might contribute to the development of a feminist epistemology, such an epistemology would simultaneously caution members of any exploited group to carefully examine knowledge produced by members of oppressor groups and avoid uncritically accepting it as knowledge (Scheurich, 1997).

Collins (1995) has developed an approach to science based on what she has called an **Afrocentric feminist epistemology**. As a springboard to articulate this theory of knowledge, Collins has argued that female scholars may know that something is true but be unwilling or unable to legitimate their knowledge claims using conventional criteria for knowledge development. Further, in making a case for the need for an alternative epistemology, Collins highlights the importance of developing an approach to knowledge that recognizes a connection between a researcher and the object of study, sees emotion as a integral part of the research process, relies on values and ethics as the reasons for scientific inquiry and as significant elements in the research process, and questions the use of adversarial debate as a primary strategy for asserting truth.

Afrocentric feminist epistemology combines elements of epistemologies used by blacks as a group with those used by women as a group to "create knowledge that enables them to resist oppression" (Collins, 1995, p. 344). Such an epistemology values lived experience above book knowledge when selecting topics for study and methodological approaches, as suggested in the subtitle of an essay by Elsa Barkley Brown: "How my mother taught me to be a historian in spite of my academic training" (Brown, as cited in Collins, 1995, p. 347). It also values knowledge from lived experience as a basis from which to develop wisdom, as exemplified in the analysis by June Jordon, who used the experience of her mother's suicide to articulate a life commitment to the well-being of women and other oppressed people.

In addition to the essentiality of lived experience, this epistemology requires that scholars act as personal advocates for their work and dialogue with common people about their findings. Such an epistemology may not meet the criteria for adequacy within more dominant epistemologies circulating in universities and other influential arenas. Further efforts to earn legitimacy for this epistemology within these arenas are often seen as fruitless because the knowledge developed there is viewed as largely "antithetical to the best interests of black women" (Collins, 1995, p. 351).

Black feminists and others who articulate and engage in alternative epistemologies often compare their knowledge claims to those arrived at through dominant epistemologies, and they raise questions about what knowledge claims to pass as truth and what processes are reasonable for arriving at truth. In short, they make salient the view that there are multiple epistemologies and none has an exclusive or dominant hold on knowledge development.

FEMINISM(S) AND RESEARCH METHOD AND METHODOLOGY

Drawing on a distinction between **method** and **methodology** in which the former refers to techniques for gathering evidence, and the latter refers to a theory and analysis of how research should be done, Harding (1987) and others have argued that feminisms may be understood as coalescing perspectives, rather than as a research methodology. Feminists embrace a set of understandings, or **perspectives**, that form the context from which they shape their research projects, pose their research questions, select methods of data collection and interpretation, and choose rhetorical strategies for making their research public. Because feminism is not a methodology, feminist researchers have drawn on many different methodologies, often spanning the sometimes celebrated, sometimes decried, divide between quantitative and qualitative study, including those "that traditional androcentric researchers have used" (Harding, 1987, p. 2). Sociology, science, psychology, medicine, and law are areas studied through feminist perspectives and, in each of these fields, considerable differences exist in how the research looks and how it is conducted. One comprehensive source of description of feminist perspectives, methodologies, and methods in the social sciences can be found in the *Handbook of Feminist Research* (Hesse-Biber, 2007). In this volume's chapters, authors explore the meanings of feminisms, and they explain and critique a wide range of approaches to knowledge construction, including but not limited to ethnography, survey research, interviewing, and document analysis.

Rather than attempting to traverse this expansive research territory within which feminist researchers work, we will limit discussion in this chapter to feminist work within the qualitative or **interpretive arena**—those methods within research that confer significance to the study of the experiences of others, particularly nondominant individuals and groups (Lincoln, 1997). We do so for several substantive reasons. Chief among these is that the arena of qualitative research is frequently associated with the feminist goal of transforming society along just and equitable lines by fashioning new ways of doing research. That is, feminists want to change society, and to do so many of them believe that reliance on dominant approaches to meaning making, knowledge construction, and policy making will be doomed to failure because they rely on the established conventions of our patriarchal society—conventions, they argue, that were designed to create and sustain existing practices of exclusion and domination of women and others.

Resisting a Doctrine of Neutrality

Knowledge development is among the central processes taken up by many of those who identify as feminists. Rather than adhering to a doctrine of research neutrality that they see as untenable and distorting, these feminists are consciously aware of their work as knowledge producers and researchers. That is, they typically strive to raise research questions that they believe will produce forms of knowledge that will allow for new ways of living together in the world—ways that counter the many "isms" they see as divisive and often devastatingly harmful. Although such a stance is considered by some to be nonscientific, these feminists see themselves as aligned with efforts of early scientific development during the seventeenth century when, in confronting religious control over knowledge, "the goals of social, political, and educational reform and emancipation" (Bleier, 1986, p. 5) assumed a prominent role and provided an impetus for furthering scientific endeavors. Such knowledge development is crucial in research that strives to inform as well as encourage emancipatory practices.

Although patriarchy and sexism combine to form the central "ism" that informs feminist research projects and against which feminist researchers struggle, their research projects may also include confrontation of a range of other "isms"—including ageism, racism, classism, heterosexism, and other social constructions used to produce difference, justify inequity, and serve as a smokescreen to shield multiple manifestations of abuse and oppression.

Interrupting Efforts to Simplify and Universalize Knowledge

Feminists resist efforts to reduce and simplify in the development of knowledge; they value complexity (Lather, 2000), and they express doubt that knowledge can be developed that will be **universal** or valid across persons, situations, time, and space. St. Pierre and Pillow (2000) describe a feminist suspicion of claims that any knowledge can explain diverse settings, people, and circumstances, and they and others refer to such claims for knowledge, when widely held, as **regimes of truth**, a term they borrow from the French philosopher Michel Foucault (1984). They explain how various kinds of knowledge have become unquestionable and used to support dominant interests at the expense of less powerful groups and individuals. St. Pierre and Pillow (2000) describe many feminists as "suspicious of the emancipatory impulses of humanism that presume we can 'get it right' once and for all. . . . That is not to say that revolution is not possible or desirable but that, often, one regime of truth simply replaces another" (p. 4).

Because feminists object to the development of regimes of truth as all too often lacking in both neutrality and morality, the work of the feminist researcher often focuses on critiquing, and otherwise interrupting taken-for-granted ideologies and practices. One technique that many feminists have used to shape their critiques is a process called **deconstruction**. Deconstruction is an approach to analyzing an argument through a series of moves intended to show the weaknesses in the argument, particularly by revealing contradictions and oversights in the arguments (Gannon & Davies, 2007). The goal of deconstruction is to demystify the realities we create, to fight the tendency for our categories to congeal reality by showing that language is always open to multiple interpretations and continual critique. Feminists have used deconstruction to show how taken-for-granted ways of distinguishing concepts with the use of binaries such as male-female are simply inadequate to describe reality (Gannon & Davies, 2007).

Another technique often demonstrated in feminist critiques is a reflexive retelling of the work being reported. Reflexivity is self-critique infused into the research by the researcher. Borrowed from postmodern ethnographic literature, reflexivity allows feminist researchers to reveal partiality, contradiction, paradox, and other problems and issues that they see in their own research (Stacey, 1991). In an example of reflexivity, Stacey concludes that the ethnography she practiced as a research methodology involves too many ethical problems to be accepted as a fully feminist research methodology. She writes, "while there cannot be a fully feminist ethnography, there can be (indeed there are) ethnographies that are partially feminist, accounts of culture enhanced by the application of feminist perspectives" (1991, p. 117). Even so, feminists continue to be dissatisfied with these partial efforts, and in their research, they work toward more complete expressions of their values.

Studying How Women and Other Marginalized People Experience Life

As mentioned earlier in this chapter, even though Sandra Harding (1987) has advocated studying up, she also encourages researchers to listen carefully to women in order to learn their views and life experiences. Traditionally, little effort had been given to studying the lives and experiences of women and other demeaned people and, in situations where such perspectives became apparent, they were viewed generally as flawed, deficient, or biased. Thus, according to Harding and others, a significant contribution of feminist research has been appreciation, documentation, and explication of the lived experiences of women and other invisible individuals in many different societies. For example, Lalik, Dellinger, and Druggish (2003) explore the lives of Appalachian children and how their teachers incorporate their experiences into the school curriculum. In the study, the researchers make apparent the importance of the children's ideas and stories when these words and stories become a central influence on their own understanding of the research.

Many feminists have argued that the opportunity for invisible individuals to tell their stories and to make sense of their experiences with an attentive and supportive listener is a rewarding and productive experience for respondents—one that makes their voices audible and supports their ability to shape their destinies. Other feminist researchers have designated such opportunities as **bracketed experiences**, or those experiences that temporarily remove a disadvantaged individual from inequitable circumstances, while doing little to change the power dynamics that support inequity. These feminist critics have asked whether such research is not merely the appropriation of a less advantaged individual's life story to accomplish the professional goals of a more advantaged researcher. This inequity, according to critics, is especially deleterious for feminists "because we are among the few who articulate commitments and political priorities—[we] must invoke that better human model of behavior that is as yet nowhere to be found" (Patai, 1991, pp. 138–139).

Because feminists seek an egalitarian approach to research, interviewing is often a two-way process within which both the researcher and respondent raise questions and share information and reciprocal self-disclosure. That is, feminist researchers may conduct lengthy conversations with respondents during which the researchers not only ask respondents to talk about their lives, but also disclose personal information and answer questions that the respondents raise. This interactive process, meant to engender mutuality or sisterhood, is often called **intersubjectivity**.

Although intersubjectivity has been encouraged by many feminist researchers, it has also been critiqued. Reflexively critiquing her own research, Patai (1991) explains problems that grow from the relative psychological and material advantage of the researcher over the respondent. She further argues that the feminist research practice of claiming personal connection with a respondent may be a form of disingenuousness more damaging, perhaps, than "a clear and hierarchical division that definitively separated researcher and researched" (p. 143).

Researching with Intention to Transform Society

Transformation, or cultural, political, social, and economic change toward increased social justice, is seen as an essential and critical criterion for feminist research and ancillary activity. In short, most feminists want material changes to occur. This is true for feminist researchers, as well as for feminists who work in other arenas such as journalism, literature, and politics. Hence many feminists have critiqued research and other efforts within their tradition that appear to neglect transformation. For example, several feminists have been criticized for focusing their attention on the examination of language and the development of a feminist rhetoric, while neglecting the material and political transformation required for alleviating the everyday suffering of women and others (Lykes & Coquillon, 2007). Academic feminists have been criticized as compromising their efforts at transformation in favor of their obligations to the universities in which they work. In critiquing her own research, Patai explains her view of this issue: "As I see it, the problem for us academics, who are already leading privileged existences, resides in the obvious fact that our enjoyment of research and its rewards constantly compromises the ardor with which we promote social transformation" (Patai, 1991, p. 139).

Perhaps one way for feminists to overcome this problem is for us to learn ways to support nonaffluent people in the pursuit of inquiry for themselves and for their own agendas (Oakes & Rogers, 2006). Research by Jeanne Oakes and John Rogers on school inequities demonstrates ways that university faculty collaborated with nonaffluent people by helping them learn strategies for research, knowledge development, and activism. Once learned, these strategies served as resources that were used to shape policy and practice. The university faculty used the interests and concerns of their collaborators as a starting point for inquiry. They characterize their effort as transformative, explaining it as a "commitment to support the interests of the group, and belief in the power of joint action to alter existing circumstances" (Oakes & Rogers, 2006, p. 107). Such collaborative research offers an alternative to the more self-serving approach to research critiqued by Patai.

REFLECTION QUESTION

1. Identify a goal for a research project that would improve conditions for nonprivileged people. Identify new knowledge that is necessary to achieve this goal. Share your plans with others and ask them to help you improve on your ideas.

Example: I want to help impoverished third-world women to be able to support their families financially. I need knowledge about what skills and interests and cares the women have already developed.

SUMMARY

Feminism is a term that has been used to name a wide range of perspectives and projects. Even so, feminists share a commitment to the pursuit of autonomy for women, and feminist researchers use gender as an essential, but not necessarily exclusive, focal point in their work. Though categorization systems have been used to capture the various forms of feminism, distinctions among feminisms have blurred, as feminists have adapted theory and method from each other. Liberal feminists are especially well known in Western society, and their efforts to seek financial, educational, and political equality for women have been well disseminated. However, their attention to the concerns of white affluent women generated critique from African American feminists and others and inspired a broadening of the feminist agenda to include concern for all oppressed people and attention to issues such as poverty, racism, and economic exploitation.

One of the significant contributions of feminisms has been a critique of science that focuses on concerns about women's participation in science; erasure of knowledge about successful women scientists; masculinist ideology in science; and the epistemology proliferated through science. Growing out of this critique, feminists have worked toward alternative epistemologies that focus attention on the types of questions that scientists ask, the persons who are able to raise such questions, the people being studied, and disclosure of important information about the researcher. In addition, feminist scholars have identified and described an Afrocentric feminist epistemology that grows from the experiences of black female scholars.

With respect to method and methodology within the interpretive arena of research, feminist research has become notable for its articulation of the purposes of one's research; the interruption, through strategies such as deconstruction and reflexivity, of efforts to simplify and universalize knowledge; respect for and study of the lived experiences of demeaned and overlooked people; and the use of research as a strategy to promote material change in the interests of social justice and equity for oppressed individuals and groups. Especially characteristic of the work of feminist researchers has been their focused efforts to critique their own research methods and projects.

KEY TERMS

Afrocentric feminist epistemology
binary thinking
bracketed experiences
context of discovery
continual critique
critical postmodern feminist
critique of science
deconstruction
discrimination
epistemology

essentialized
exploitation
feminisms
feminist critique of science
interpretive arena
intersecting oppressions
intersubjectivity
liberal feminist
method
methodology

oppression
perspectival
perspectives
poststructural feminist
radical feminist
redefinition of taken-for-granted terms
regimes of truth
reflexivity
social feminist

studying down
studying up
transformation
triple jeopardy
unit for analysis
universal
waves of feminism: first, second, third
womanist

FURTHER READINGS AND RESOURCES

Suggested Feminist Research Article

Lalik, R., & Hinchman, K. (2000). Power-knowledge formations in literacy teacher education: Exploring the perspectives of two teacher educators. *The Journal of Educational Research*, *93*, 182–191.

A feminist analysis of the practices of two literacy teacher educators who use reflexivity to examine and critique their own teaching.

Suggested Readings

Friedan, B. (2001). *The feminine mystique*. New York: Norton.

A classic and widely read explanation of second-wave feminism often used mistakenly to depict the views of all feminists.

Gluck, S., & Patai, D. (1991). *Women's words: The feminist practice of oral history*. New York: Routledge.

A collection of papers in which feminists critique their own research efforts, particularly those used when interviewing other women and describing the experiences of those women.

Guy-Sheftall, B. (1995). *Words of fire: An anthology of African-American feminist thought*. New York: New Press.

An anthology of the writings of African American journalists, scholars, and activists who inspired a feminist intellectual tradition from the early nineteenth century through the current day. This collection is a must for anyone seeking to develop a comprehensive understanding of feminisms.

Hesse-Biber, S. (Ed.) (2007). *Handbook of feminist research: Theory and practice*. Thousand Oaks: Sage.

A broad collection of papers that describe knowledge-building processes and research tools useful for feminist researchers.

Lincoln, Y. (1997). What constitutes quality in interpretive research? In C. Kinzer, K. Hinchman, & D. Leu (Eds.), *Inquiries in literacy theory and practice* (pp. 54–68). Chicago: The National Reading Conference.

A cutting-edge paper in which Lincoln uses a feminist perspective to outline what she sees as the essential criteria for interpretive research.

Luke, C., & Gore, J. (1992). *Feminisms and critical pedagogy*. New York: Routledge.

A collection of papers written by scholars to examine the intersections and contradictions between feminism and critical theory.

Web Sites and Associations

Association for Feminist Anthropology (AFA)

http://sscl.berkeley.edu/~afaweb

The AFA is part of the American Anthropological Association. They seek to establish an "anthropology of women" and to bring a feminist and gendered anthropology to the discipline. Members include anthropologists, their students, and those with like interests.

Feminist Majority Foundation (FMF)

www.feminist.org

A forum for feminist research. The organization uses research and action to empower women economically, socially, and politically.

CHAPTER

13

USING MULTIPLE METHODS APPROACHES

PAUL A. SCHUTZ, SHARON L. NICHOLS, AND KELLY A. RODGERS

KEY IDEAS

- Research methods are judged by how well they assist problem solving.
- The use of multiple methods allows for greater adaptability.
- Potential benefits of multiple methods research include expansion of understanding and flexible response to unexpected events.
- Triangulation in multiple methods research offers the opportunity to produce convergent and divergent evidence.
- Multiple methods designs can employ concurrent or sequential plans and dominant or balanced methods.
- Sampling in multiple methods research can be random, purposeful, or both.

IN RECENT years there has been an increase in discussions about the nature and use of multiple methods by social science researchers. This interest in **multimethod research** is based to a certain extent on the simple, but insightful, idea that using more than one method during the data collection or analysis phases of a study may be more useful in answering research questions than using a single method. Although the use of multiple methods in a single study is not new, the past decade has seen a growth in the number of discussions on the purposes and nature of multiple methods as a strategic choice in research design and data analysis (Eisenhart, 2005; Howe, 2005; Raudenbush, 2005; Schutz, Chambless, & DeCuir, 2004).

We will begin by defining what we mean by multimethod research and discuss some of the philosophy of science ideas that support this approach. This will be followed by a discussion of the benefits of using more than one method during inquiry. Next, we will talk about some of the research designs that have been used while employing a multimethod approach. Finally, we will summarize the benefits and ways of using multiple methods during the research process.

WHAT IS MULTIMETHOD RESEARCH?

At the most basic level, our view of multimethod research involves the use of more than one approach to data collection or data analysis.[1] However, over time, researchers have not always agreed upon the role and function of research in general or the use of multiple methods in particular. For example, over the past twenty years, there has been a debate centered on the question: What is the fundamental nature of science? In short, should the goal of science be the search for universal "truth" or is science about the search for multiple or relative "truths" (Guba & Lincoln, 1994; House, 1994; Smith & Heshusius, 1986; Tashakkori & Teddlie, 1998)?

One by-product of these debates has been a tendency to create a formalized distinction between, on the one hand, qualitative researchers who are thought to view science as dealing with multiple or relative truths and tend to collect and analyze data as words (for example, an interview) and, on the other hand, quantitative researchers, who are thought to view science as the search for universal truth and who tend to collect and analyze data as numbers (for example, responses to a survey). This polarization of ideology is, in part, what has led some to talk about multimethod research as being a "third" discipline (see Johnson, Onwuegbuzie, & Turner, 2007). As such, once a binary distinction between qualitative approaches and quantitative approaches is legitimized, there is the potential for using multiple methods that involve (1) two or more quantitative approaches, (2) two or more qualitative approaches, or (3) a combination of at least one qualitative and one quantitative method (Schutz, Chambless, & DeCuir, 2004).

Although the labeling of multimethod research as a third discipline has emerged in the research literature, we see this third discipline view of multimethod as an artifact of an imposed binary or dichotomy related to a distinction between qualitative and quantitative research. As such, our view of multiple methods is more consistent with researchers who view research approaches (for example, data collection or data analysis methods) as "tools" that are used in an effort to answer research questions developed to solve problems within a social-historical context (Eisenhart, 2005; House, 1994; Schutz, Chambless, & DeCuir, 2004). From this pragmatic position (that is, **research as a problem-solving process**), the usefulness of research methods is judged by their potential to help solve problems.

Thus, from our pragmatic view, research is seen as a way of investigating and working to solve problems within a social historical context. The researcher's conceptualization of the problem is therefore important in that the research questions that guide the inquiry tend to be developed from the researcher's understanding of the problem. In addition, those research questions are important in that they are used to determine what data collection and analysis methods would be best to answer those questions. When research is thought of as a problem-solving activity, then any method, within moral and ethical constraints (see Crowder, 2004; Howe & Eisenhart, 1990; also see Chapter One for more information), can and should be used. This means that the perceived potential differences between qualitative approaches and quantitative approaches become secondary to the task of solving problems within a social historical context.

REFLECTION QUESTIONS

1. What is multimethod research?

2. From the perspective of this chapter, what comes first—the research questions or the research methods? Why is that the case?

3. What are some current problems in your area for which a multimethod research approach might be useful?

POTENTIAL BENEFITS OF MULTIMETHOD RESEARCH

From our perspective, multimethod research is simply the use of more than one method (tools used for data collection and analysis) during the inquiry process. As with any approach to inquiry, using multiple methods has certain advantages as well as disadvantages compared to single-method approaches. In this section, we focus on its advantages or potential benefits to the researcher. We begin with a description of one of the earlier statements on the use of multiple methods in research inquiry. This is followed by a discussion of a few of the most common potential benefits of multimethod research.

An Early Comment on the Benefits of Multiple Methods Research

In 1959, Campbell and Fiske, in what some believe to be one of the first explicit calls for multiple methods research, talked about the importance of using more than one method to measure any single trait or construct (Teddlie & Tashakkori, 2003). In the social sciences, researchers are tasked with the problem of dealing with phenomena that cannot be seen. Referring to these phenomena as traits or **constructs**, social science researchers try to create tools (for example, surveys) for measuring invisible properties such as delinquency, counselor empathy, or student belonging. In the field of tests and measurement, Campbell and Fiske (1959) argued that it is incumbent upon any researcher to utilize at least two different methods to establish whether the measure of any single construct or trait is valid (that is, measuring what it intends to measure). For example, in order to establish whether a counselor empathy scale is actually measuring something called "counselor empathy," it is critical that the researcher employ two *different* types of measures (for example, a rating scale and observation)—the results of which can be compared and used as corroborating evidence. Here, multiple methods are used to seek "confirmation by independent measurement procedures" (Campbell & Fiske, 1959, p. 81). Schutz, Chambless, and DeCuir (2004) summarized it as follows: "The use of multiple methods in the study of the same phenomenon with the basic purpose being the goal of seeking construct validity through the establishment of both convergent and divergent evidence for the task or test under consideration that confirms expectation" (pp. 276–277).

Since Campbell and Fiske's time, there have appeared in the literature hundreds of studies using multiple methods in their research (Bryman 2006; Greene, Caracelli, & Graham, 1989). And, though some may have used multiple methods to establish measurement-related validity evidence, as described by Campbell and Fiske (1959), many studies have used multiple methods for broader purposes, some of which we describe next. As the field of multiple methods research has grown more prominent in recent years, examinations of these past studies have yielded important information about researchers' goals in adopting multiple methods as well as about their intended and unintended benefits. It is important to note that a line of research that includes multiple methods studies also has benefits in helping to deepen a researcher's understanding of some phenomenon. In this section, we primarily focus on the benefits as they relate to single studies; however, most of these ideas can be broadened to include research agendas or areas of research that incorporate many different types of studies (Schutz, Chambless, & DeCuir, 2004).

Adaptability of Multimethod Research

An important potential benefit of multiple methods research is that it allows for greater adaptability to adjust to planned and unplanned events throughout the research process. Consider that research inquiry generally involves a series of steps that starts with a well-articulated plan of action that is followed by implementation. The planning stage generally entails that the researcher identify (a) the research problem, (b) a research question(s), (c) a literature base associated with that question, (d) a sample, (e) a research design, (f) data collection techniques, and (g) a data analysis approach. Ideally, once the plan is laid out, the research is implemented in the same order: The researcher acquires access to participants for the study, constructs or selects data collection tool(s), engages in the data collection process, and follows up with the data analysis plan. However, at any step in the process, researchers may adjust their plan because of unforeseen events (for example, design must change because the sample changes) or because of emerging ideas (for example, analysis uncovers unexpected variables that lead to new types of analysis). Multimethod research is uniquely suited to adapt to unforeseen events, analyses, and data interpretations that may emerge at any point in the research process.

When used strategically, multimethod research provides avenues for combining data in unique ways to explore phenomena or to test or generate new hypotheses. For example, at the design stage, researchers can plan for the use of qualitative information to assist in identifying certain groups of individuals who will be followed up using a quantitative measure. That is, multiple methods may be used for sampling goals. For example, in a hypothetical study of students' beliefs about their teachers' emotions, we might use interviews in order to identify students who describe (without prompting) unpleasant experiences with their teachers. Once identified, this subgroup may be given a survey of teacher empathy to better understand how their perceptions of teacher empathy may vary (that is, do elementary and secondary students who have had negative experiences with their teachers view teacher empathy differently?). Therefore, researchers can plan for how they will use both types of data based on preformed expectations about how one type of data will support the other.

Similarly, during the data analysis stage, quantitative data analysis may be used to facilitate the interpretation of qualitative data or vice versa (Johnson, Onwuegbuzie, & Turner, 2007; Sieber, 1973). For example, analysis of survey data that suggests some clients find their counselor less empathetic than other clients do may draw researchers' attention to specific themes that arose from qualitative data that maps onto this quantitative finding. Here, qualitative data may be used to elaborate on the how and why questions emerging from the findings that go beyond what would be found from the quantitative data alone. In other words, what perspectives from clients differentiate their views of empathic and nonempathic counselors?

A multiple methods approach is especially useful in assisting with data analysis and interpretation. Multiple methods research provides greater flexibility to the researcher for finding new and interesting ways of understanding a phenomenon. For example, a researcher may collect both quantitative and qualitative data for one purpose, but through the analysis may uncover unexpected outcomes that lead to new ways of combining the data. Suppose a researcher collects data on students' perceptions of student concepts of belonging using both quantitative (a survey) and qualitative approaches (interviews), with the goal of using the data from both sources to develop definitions of student belonging. However, through data analysis, patterns and trends in the quantitative data may lead to different ways of thinking about belonging that can be further explored using the qualitative data (for example, Nichols, 2008). An important benefit is that multiple methods allow for greater flexibility in exploring new ways of thinking about people, constructs, and events and provides a tool for researchers to adapt to emerging problems and questions throughout the entire research process. As Bryman (2006) notes: "The outcomes of multi-strategy research are not always predictable. While a decision about design issues may be made in advance and for good reasons, when the data are generated, surprising findings or unrealized potential in the data may suggest unanticipated consequences of combining them" (p. 99). Thus, the use of multiple methods gives the researcher the potential to deal with many of the unexpected events that might occur during the research process.

Strength and Quality of Inferencing

Studies are largely organized around two general quests: to verify theories, problems, events, and constructs or to generate theory. In many cases, researchers are limited in their ability to make multiple inferences when using only a single tool for data collection or analysis. By contrast, multiple methods research "enables the researcher to simultaneously answer confirmatory and explanatory questions, and therefore verify and generate theory in the same study" (Teddlie & Tashakkori, 2003, p. 15). Therefore, multimethod research enhances a researcher's capacity to make inferences about the nature of the phenomenon being studied. There are some specific examples of the ways in which using multiple methods strengthens researchers' capacities to make different inferences including convergent and divergent triangulation, complementarity, initiation, expansion, and development.

Triangulation is perhaps the most commonly talked about benefit of multiple methods research. Originating from the work of Campbell and Fiske (1959), triangulation is the strategic use of two or more different types of methods to provide validity evidence for the constructs and data interpretations used within a single study. Triangulation can be used in two general ways. First, in the Campbell and Fiske (1959) sense, triangulation provides validity evidence for some measurement tool or device. Here, the focus is explicitly on the measurement device (such as a survey or interview) that is theorized to map onto some underlying construct. For example, we might compare and contrast data gleaned from qualitative and quantitative measures regarding students' beliefs about school belonging in order to provide validity evidence for a measure of student belonging.

A second way of thinking about triangulation relates to the goal of wanting to better understand individuals or situations. Instead of focusing on the measurement tool per se, the goal is to make better sense of people or events. For example, we might use a quantitative measure of students' perceptions of belonging with qualitative observations, and use both types of data to make inferences about the underlying nature of participants' beliefs. This example might address a research question such as, In what ways do students' beliefs map onto student behavior?

Most important, we can think of triangulation as potentially providing either **convergent** or **divergent** evidence. **Convergent triangulation** is the process of using two methods to establish overlapping or confirming evidence of the phenomena being studied. The most important thing to know about convergent triangulation is that it is a process through which the researcher is trying to establish corroborating evidence about people, events, or measurement by using two or more types of methods. That is, do qualitative and quantitative data sources overlap in expected ways?

The following is an example of a hypothetical multiple methods study designed to establish convergent evidence for the counselor empathy construct. Suppose a researcher wanted to understand the role of counselor empathy in therapy. The first step would be to explore the literature to assess the ways in which counselor empathy is theoretically defined. Armed with these definitions, and motivated by the goal of wanting to confirm or deny the adequacy of these definitions, a researcher may conduct a study that employs two types of data collection methods from counselors about their empathy levels. When the data from these two data sources (surveys and interviews) overlap, or converge, then the researcher has provided "convergent" evidence about the phenomenon in question. For example, counselors who consistently say empathy is about respect in both the survey *and* the interview responses provide some evidence that respect is a critical component of empathy. Implications drawn from a study of this nature can be relevant to both (a) measures of counselor empathy, and (b) interpretations about counselors and their empathy.

A very similar process identified by Greene, Caracelli, and Graham (1989) is referred to as **complementarity** (also referred to as **enhancement** by Bryman, 2006). According to Greene, Caracelli, and Graham, complementarity is the process of seeking elaboration, enhancement, illustration, and clarification of the results from one method with the results from another method. In this approach, the researcher could use qualitative data to elaborate on the interpretation gleaned from the quantitative data, or vice versa. This is similar to the process of convergent triangulation in that the researcher employs two types of methods to explore the same construct or phenomenon in a single study. However, in slight contrast to convergent triangulation, complementarity is specifically related to studies that have prior goals and expectations of the ways in which measures, constructs, or people's perceptions will overlap. For example, if a researcher wanted to understand students' perceptions of student sense of belonging, one approach would be to use two types of data collection methods (survey and interview) to assess students' beliefs. If we were engaged in convergent triangulation, the researcher's *intent* would be to examine both types of data to establish where they overlap. That is, the intent would be to establish convergent evidence of the measure (qualitative data confirm what was found in the quantitative data), or of individuals' beliefs (qualitative measure yields same words and thoughts represented in the quantitative measure).

Complementarity goes slightly beyond this goal to include a broader purpose. The researcher may have the goal of wanting to better understand the role or nature of students' perceptions of parental support or of their community as it relates to perceptions of belonging. One multiple method design that could be strategically employed to achieve the goal of complementarity might be a survey of students' beliefs about belonging or an interview that also includes additional questions about parental support or community. Here, the researcher's goal is not just to identify overlapping themes or constructs in the two data sources, but also to elaborate upon the interpretation of the quantitative findings by examining how students respond to the additional interview questions. Hypothetically, the researcher might uncover instances where students with high belongingness scores on the survey (which measures school variables only) also report supportive, nurturing relationships in their communities, whereas those who scored lower may report less-supportive community relationships. Here, data from one method help to expand upon the interpretation of data from another.

Divergent triangulation is the process in which two methods uncover contradictions, paradoxes, or differences in construct meanings and measurements. That is, researchers interested in understanding more fully what a concept *is* are equally interested in understanding what it *is not*. Thus, studies designed with the goal of divergent triangulation are more interested in where constructs, people, or events diverge from one another. Going back to the counselor empathy example, it may be the case that counselors consistently report in the survey that respect is an important part of empathy; however, in the interview, respect may never be mentioned. Results from both data sources provide divergent evidence about counselor empathy. The evidence not only has implications for how empathy is defined and measured, but also provides new insights into counselors' verbal descriptions of what counselor empathy involves.

In general, the process of triangulation is something that can be planned for; however, it may also happen unexpectedly. As Bryman (2006) argues in an analysis of studies employing multiple methods, oftentimes convergent or divergent triangulation occurs spontaneously when "in the course of interpreting the data, an inconsistency between the quantitative and qualitative findings is revealed" (p. 110). He goes on to say, "Similarly, a researcher may employ multi-strategy research with a purpose like 'diversity of views' in mind, but find that the qualitative evidence helps to explain some of the relationships uncovered through an analysis of survey data" (pp. 110–111).

Initiation is a specific type of divergent triangulation that includes studies where paradoxes or contradictions are revealed, sometimes unexpectedly. For example, suppose a researcher was conducting a study around the following research question: Are female counselors more empathic than male counselors? In this example, let's also suppose that the researcher, based on an extensive review of the literature, believes that the study will confirm that indeed female counselors are more empathic than male counselors. The researcher collects two types of data: (a) surveys with male and female counselors on their beliefs about their empathy levels, and (b) interviews with clients about their counselors. Although the survey supports the researcher's hypothesis, the interviews with clients uncover new and largely unexpected information: male counselors display empathy differently from female counselors. Here, the multimethod design yielded unexpected findings that provide some evidence contradictory to what was expected, and this further informs new research questions.

Development is another potential benefit of multimethod research that "seeks to use the results from one method to help develop or inform the other method" (Greene, Caracelli, & Graham, 1989, p. 259). This benefit is perhaps one of the more obviously related to multimethod research because the researcher uses two different methods sequentially (one after the other) with the goal of using the results from the first to inform the use or interpretation of the second. The process of development can be employed at various steps in the research process including sampling, data analysis, and data interpretation. Researchers engage in development when results from a survey inform how a second sample will be selected to participate in an interview. Similarly, development is also used to create instruments—the data collection tool. Clients may participate in an interview study about their perceptions of counselor empathy, the results of which are used to create and implement a new survey with the same sample of clients later.

The final example is **expansion**, which Greene, Caracelli, and Graham (1989) argue "seeks to extend the breadth and range of inquiry by using different methods for different inquiry purposes" (p. 259). Here, the researcher purposely employs several methods at different points in time to analyze various aspects of the phenomenon under question. One of the most common ways expansion is used is in studies that examine program effectiveness. In these studies, program processes are analyzed using qualitative methods, and program outcomes are analyzed using quantitative methods. A researcher may collect qualitative data regarding feelings of student belonging in an elementary school classroom and also collect quantitative test scores related to academic achievement from the students in the classrooms where the qualitative data were collected.

Summary of Benefits

Multiple methods research has many benefits over single method designs. One of the most prominent benefits is that it allows for greater flexibility in study designs, data analysis, and data interpretation. And, though many research designs follow a sequence of steps that map onto a set of expected outcomes, multiple methods research seems particularly well suited for situations where unexpected outcomes emerge and new questions are raised.

In the next section, we explore specific ways to design research studies using multiple methods. Because multiple methods deal with more than one approach to data collection and analysis, it makes sense that there are multiple ways to design how they are used in research studies. As we'll point out, certain designs capitalize on the benefits just described.

REFLECTION QUESTIONS

1. What are some "invisible" constructs that are of interest to you?
   a. Generate a few ideas for how you might measure these constructs.
   b. What types of methods emerge for studying this construct?
2. In what ways is triangulation a potential benefit of multimethod research?
3. Compare and contrast convergent triangulation and complementarity.
4. Compare and contrast divergent triangulation and initiation.
5. Can you think of any other benefits of multiple methods research?

MULTIMETHOD RESEARCH DESIGN

Multimethod research designs typically have two dimensions: *time orientation* and *dominance*. **Time orientation** refers to whether multiple data collection methods will occur *concurrently* or *sequentially* (Onwuegbuzie & Collins, 2007). In **concurrent designs**, both data collection methods occur simultaneously; we can collect survey data at the same time that we conduct interviews. Conversely, data in **sequential designs**, as the name suggests, are collected in some kind of chronological order, such that the findings from the first phase (qualitative versus quantitative), or *strand*, of the study informs the implementation of the second strand (Collins, Onwuegbuzie, & Jiao, 2006). A commonly used sequential multimethod data collection process is to first administer a survey in the quantitative strand and then follow up with qualitative methods, such as interviews, focus groups, or observations.

The second dimension of multimethod research design addresses the dominance of one data strand over another. Is the quantitative strand most dominant, with qualitative data used only to complement, explore, or even provide validity evidence for the findings from the quantitative strand? Or is the qualitative phase posed as the dominant method, with quantitative methods used to complement or support qualitative findings? Or perhaps the qualitative and quantitative data strands are of equal importance in the research design. Unlike the time-orientation dimension, which refers to data collection, the dominance dimension describes the *relationship* between strands, that is, how they serve each other.

Designs

In **qualitative dominant designs**, the researcher is primarily interested in the results gleaned from a qualitative research design, but recognizes that the addition of quantitative data would enhance these findings (Johnson, Onwuegbuzie & Turner, 2007). The inclusion of secondary quantitative data may benefit a predominantly qualitative research design in a variety of ways. Quantitative data can provide additional evidence to support qualitative findings by serving as another strand with which to answer research questions, as in the purpose of triangulation. Suppose we determine through student interviews that students who are involved in campus organizations express greater feelings of belonging than students who are less involved. This finding would be strengthened by quantitative evidence if survey data also suggested a positive relationship between feelings of belonging and amount of campus involvement.

Similarly, in **quantitative dominant designs**, the researcher adopts a predominantly quantitative approach, but supplements the quantitative data with qualitative methods. This design is especially useful because of the potential for qualitative methods to be used for complementarity, or to expand on or add breadth to quantitative results. The addition of a qualitative strand gives the researcher the opportunity to define key terms via interviews with participants or to contextualize the findings. For example, in a study of college students' feelings of belonging, a qualitative strand allows the researcher to learn what meaning "belongingness" has for the participants in the study, as it may be viewed differently among participants. Study participants may even define this construct differently from the researcher. Consequently, such breadth in quantitative dominant designs is particularly useful in interpreting results.

The two basic dimensions of multimethod design, time orientation (concurrent versus sequential) and dominance (dominant designs versus balanced designs), are mixed to produce multimethod research designs with varying degrees of dominance and time orientation. Qualitative-dominant and quantitative-dominant designs can involve either sequential or concurrent data collection. Let's say we want to design a qualitative-dominant study to find out what affects college students' feelings of belongingness. One possibility would be to gather data sequentially. We could start by interviewing students about the different things that make them feel as if they belong to the campus community, such as being involved in campus activities, having friends, and having positive interactions with faculty. A quantitative strand in which students complete a survey instrument on the elements of belongingness might then follow the qualitative strand. This kind of sequential design is especially useful because it allows multiple methods to be used for the purpose of development in that student interviews could be used to inform the development of a survey instrument to be administered in the quantitative strand. Alternately, interview and survey data may be gathered concurrently, using a questionnaire that has already been developed.

Designs that are concurrent and dominant also lend themselves to many multi-method purposes. For example, in **concurrent nested designs**, the nondominant or nested research design (qualitative or quantitative) is used to triangulate, cross-validate, or corroborate the findings of the dominate methodology, whether it is quantitative or qualitative (Creswell, Plano Clark, Gutmann, & Hanson, 2003). In our belongingness study, we can adopt a predominantly quantitative design in which we ask students to rate a variety of statements related to their campus involvement and faculty interactions. Nested in this quantitative approach, we could also select a subset of the student sample to interview. In these interviews, we might ask students to talk about the nature of their interactions with faculty, what types of campus activities they are involved in, and why they engage in these activities. This approach is especially useful for a couple of reasons. First, this approach allows students to describe their faculty interactions and the level of involvement they have with different types of campus activities, which gives us a richer understanding of how these interactions contribute to students' feelings of belonging. Second, findings from the nested qualitative approach might also help to support findings from the dominant quantitative approach. Let's say quantitative findings showed that male students find faculty to be more willing to help than do female students. A nested qualitative approach can provide convergent or divergent evidence for this finding.

A less commonly used type of qualitative- or quantitative-dominant design is the **multilevel multimethod design**. In this design, data are collected at multiple levels and can occur either sequentially or concurrently (Tashakkori & Teddlie, 2003). For example, we might collect qualitative data at the student level about school involvement, social support systems, teacher interaction, and feelings of belonging, and then take a step up a level and collect quantitative data at the teacher level. At the teacher level, we can collect data on such things as teacher involvement with student organizations, and the types of interactions they have with students. Multilevel multimethod designs are also popular in family- and community-based studies. Researchers collect data at the child level using qualitative or quantitative methods, and then go up a level to collect data from parents. Community-based studies often involve data collection at the family level (for example, family size, socioeconomic status, parental involvement, and satisfaction with neighborhood schools and community activities) and then at the community level (for example, utility of community-based programs, achievement of local schools, and tax base for local schools).

The **balanced design** (also called a fully integrated design) represents a true merging of quantitative and qualitative methodologies where there is *no dominance* of one over the other. Rather than one approach supplementing the other, as in the qualitative- and quantitative-dominant designs, a balanced design is one in which quantitative and qualitative methods are equally important, interdependent, reciprocal, and dynamic at all phases of the study (Tashakkori & Teddlie, 2003). In this design, each strand informs and influences the other reciprocally.

Suppose we are interested in using a balanced design to study the discrepancy between teachers' actual empathy and the empathy they display in the classroom in different situations. We might begin by videotaping and coding teachers' observable reactions in particular situations. For example, how do teachers appear to react when students do not seem to be grasping the material or when students do not pay attention during a lesson? From these qualitative data, we can develop a survey in which teachers are asked about their empathy in the classroom situations observed in the videotape. If there is a discrepancy between teachers' self-reported empathy and their observed empathy in the classroom, it might be useful for the researchers to view the videotape with teachers, who could then explain in greater detail what they were feeling at each critical moment. This additional qualitative segment would allow teachers to clarify their interpretation of the critical moment and make it easier for researchers to identify classroom interactions that may trigger differential actual and expressed teacher empathy. This design would be considered balanced because the qualitative and quantitative strands are interdependent and influence each other in a reciprocal fashion.

Sampling Schemes

The sampling methods to which you have likely been introduced in other chapters in this book are also used in multimethod research. Sampling methods (also called sampling schemes) are typically tied to the study design utilized, with quantitative designs lending themselves to **random sampling methods**, and qualitative designs are more likely to be associated with **purposeful sampling methods**. However, Onwuegbuzie and Collins (2007) suggest that sampling methods should be tied to the type of generalization to be made, rather than to whether the study is quantitative, qualitative, or multimethod. Quantitative designs involve generalizing based upon statistical results, and qualitative designs involve generalization based upon analyses of qualitative data (for example, interviews and observations).[2] By thinking of the relationship between research design and sampling method in this way, we allow room for many design-sampling combinations, such as one that involves random sampling in a qualitative study. We can, for example, use a random sample of teachers within a district in a qualitative study to investigate emotional responses in classroom situations. Conversely, we can purposefully sample new teachers in a district for a quantitative study of teachers' overall mental health.

There are two general classes of sampling schemes: **random sampling** and **purposeful sampling**. In keeping with the importance of the sampling scheme reflecting the goals of the data generalization, the purpose of *random sampling* is to garner as many representatives from a population as are needed to make inferences or generalizations about that population. In the study about teacher empathy, the pool of all teachers represents the population under study. If we were interested in the ways that teachers demonstrate empathy, we would want a random sample of teachers. Random sampling increases the likelihood that we draw a sample of teachers with a variety of attributes, such as length of service, gender, age, district, grade level taught, and variance on the constructs under investigation.

In *purposeful sampling* the idea is to draw a specific sample from a population that will allow a researcher to examine a phenomenon most effectively. In the example above, if we were specifically interested in teacher empathy in the early years of teaching, a purposive sample would be only teachers who have fewer than five years of service. Our sample might vary greatly on other characteristics, such as gender, age, or grade level taught, but would be purposively chosen because of the teachers' length of service. We might add other restrictions as well, such as including only teachers for whom teaching is their first career (as opposed to having come to teaching after being in some other profession).

Multimethod Sampling

Mixed or **multimethod sampling** involves the use of both random and purposeful sampling techniques within a single, often multimethod, study (Kemper, Stringfield, & Teddlie, 2003). Onwuegbuzie and Collins (2007) describe a typology that includes two major considerations for multimethod sampling designs: time orientation and the relationship between the qualitative and quantitative samples. Sampling may occur concurrently or sequentially, and the data strands may be arranged in several ways: parallel, identical, nested, or multilevel.

Parallel samples consist of different participants drawn from the same population. From the population of college students, we would either randomly or purposefully choose students to participate in *either* the qualitative or quantitative phases of the study, but not both.

Identical sampling designs use the same participants in both the qualitative and quantitative strand. Let's say that we have managed to pull a sample of one hundred college students for our sense of belonging study. In an identical sampling design, all one hundred students would participate in both the qualitative and quantitative phases of the study. As you might expect, this kind of sampling design can be problematic, given the different standards related to quantitative and qualitative data collection goals. Quantitative research typically warrants a sample that is sufficiently large to allow us to make statistical inferences. By contrast, qualitative data is better suited for small samples because of the time, money, and labor involved in its collection and analysis. Thus, identical sampling requires a sample size that strategically balances the affordances and constraints of both approaches.

An alternative to identical sampling is to nest a smaller sample within a larger sample. In **nested designs**, participants in the second strand are a subset of the first strand. Let's say we have collected quantitative data on sense of belonging from all one hundred of our student participants and the results indicate that high-achieving students expressed a stronger overall sense of belonging. Within this sample of one hundred students, we can purposefully sample twenty high-achieving students to participate in interviews or focus group sessions. Alternately, we could *randomly* choose a subset of twenty students from our initial pool of one hundred. This subset will have participated in both phases of the study.

Finally, sampling may occur on multiple levels. As in multilevel research design, participants are chosen from different levels, and thus from different populations. Let's say that we are interested in students' ideal student-faculty relationship. We could design a qualitative-dominant study in which students participate in focus groups to discuss different aspects of faculty-student interactions. We would pull a random sample of students with a variety of characteristics, such as year in school, gender, ethnic or racial background, academic achievement, and campus involvement. Qualitative results might suggest that high-achieving students express frequent and more positive feelings toward interacting with faculty, but lower-achieving students appear ambivalent towards faculty interaction and do not interact as much. Perhaps we are particularly interested in how interactions differ between faculty and high-achieving and low-achieving students. We can investigate this specific relationship quantitatively by surveying a faculty sample to lend support to the qualitative finding. In this way, we have maintained the qualitative dominance of the study while using quantitative methods to substantiate a specific finding in the qualitative phase by sampling from a different population (both students and faculty).

Research Design Conclusion

Multimethod studies may be designed in a variety of ways, each design meshing and ordering quantitative and qualitative methods in a different way. The research design employed is dependent upon the purpose of the study. Studies implemented for the purpose of triangulation may lend themselves to concurrent nested designs, while studies carried out for the purpose of development might be best addressed through a balanced or fully integrated design wherein quantitative and qualitative methods inform each other reciprocally and equally. Similarly, selected sampling schemes (*random* versus *purposeful*) should be based upon the type of generalization to be made from the data; whether it is a *statistical* generalization or an *analytical* generalization via qualitative methods. Taken together, our purpose for using multiple methods, the designs that result from the purpose, and the method and types of samples we draw all contribute to allow us to answer the research questions that guide the study.

REFLECTION QUESTIONS

1. Suppose we wanted to better understand how to motivate students in school. One research question might be: What is the role of teacher questions in motivating students?

    a. Generate qualitative and quantitative strategies for measuring student motivation.

    b. Generate qualitative and quantitative strategies for measuring teacher question asking.

    c. What are some benefits of using multimethods in your study? Explain.

2. Select a topic of interest to you in your discipline. What research question(s) might lend themselves to exploration using multimethods inquiry?

SUMMARY

We see research as a problem-solving task. From that pragmatic perspective, the use of different methods or methodologies in a single study reflects an approach that focuses on using the best available tools to help solve problems within social-historical contexts. Social problems related to issues such as racism, classism, and sexism, for example, are complex, multidimensional, and require multiple perspectives to understand and work towards solutions. Thus, as suggested by Denzin (1978), "each method implies a different line of action toward reality—and hence each will reveal different aspects of it, much as a kaleidoscope, depending on the angle at which it is held, will reveal different colors and configurations of objects to the viewer. Methods are like a kaleidoscope: depending on how they are approached, held, and acted toward, different observations will be revealed" (p. 90). As such, the question regarding the use of different methods is not "Can we use these different methods in the same study?" but rather "How can we use these different methods to help solve problems?"

KEY TERMS

balanced designs
complementarity benefit
concurrent design
concurrent nested designs
constructs
convergent triangulation
development benefit
divergent triangulation
enhancement benefit
expansion benefit
identical sampling
initiation benefit

multilevel multimethod design
multimethod research
multimethod sampling
nested designs
parallel sampling methods
purposeful sampling
qualitative dominant designs
quantitative dominant designs
random sampling methods
research as problem solving
sequential design

FURTHER READINGS AND RESOURCES

Suggested Multimethods Articles

Daley, C. E., & Onwuegbuzie, A. J. (2004). Attributions toward violence of male juvenile delinquents: A concurrent mixed-methodological analysis. *The Journal of Social Psychology*, *144*, 549–570.

Hicks-Coolick, A., Burnside-Eaton, P., & Peters, A. (2003). Homeless children: Needs and services. *Child & Youth Care Forum*, *32*(4), 197–210.

Nichols, S. L. (2008). An exploration of students' belongingness beliefs in one middle school. *Journal of Experimental Education*, *76*(2), 145–169.

Suggested Readings

Bryman, A. (2006). Integrating quantitative and qualitative research: How is it done? *Qualitative Research*, *6*, 97–113.
    The author describes how researchers are actually using multiple methods in their research.

Eisenhart, M. (2005). Hammers and saws for the improvement of educational research. *Educational Theory*, *55*, 244–261.
    The author discusses the need and importance of using multimethod approaches to improve the research process.

Raudenbush, S. W. (2005). Learning from attempts to improve schooling: The contribution of methodological diversity. *Educational Researcher*, *34* 25–31.

From a slightly different perspective, the author argues for the need and importance of using multimethod to improve the research process.

Schutz, P. A., Chambless, C. B., & DeCuir, J. T. (2004). Multimethods research. In K. B. deMarrais & S. D. Lapan (Eds.), *Research methods in the social sciences: Frameworks for knowing and doing* (pp.267–281). Hillsdale, NJ: Erlbaum.

These authors describe their worldviews and use them to characterize why, from a philosophy perspective, using multiple methods is useful in helping to solve problems within a social-historical context.

Journals and Web Sites

The following resources are focused specifically on using mixed or multiple methods for research.

Journal of Mixed Methods Research John W. Creswell and Abbas Tashakkori (Eds.), issued quarterly by Sage Publications. ISBN 1558–6898.

Mixed Methods Research—Special Interest Group (SIG) of the American Educational Research Association

http://personal.bgsu.edu/~earleym/MIXEDMETHODS

ENDNOTES

1. A variety of terms is used in the literature for research that combines use of qualitative and quantitative methods in a single study. They include terms such as "multimethod," "multiple method," "mixed methods," and "multiple strategy." See Johnson, Onwuegbuzie, and Turner (2007) for a discussion of those different terminologies. In this chapter we will use "multimethod" or "multiple methods."

2. We acknowledge that for some researchers, making generalizations, statistical or analytical, is not considered part of the inquiry process. In those situations, the researchers generally use purposeful sampling with the goal of finding information-rich cases that yield insights or in-depth understanding of the target phenomenon.

Note: Special thanks go to Ji Hong, Rebecca Lynn, Jeremy Sullivan, and the editors, Stephen D. Lapan and MaryLynn T. Quartaroli, for their comments on earlier versions of this chapter. Their comments were very useful and the chapter is better because of their time and effort.

CHAPTER

QUALITATIVE DATA ANALYSIS

MARYLYNN T. QUARTAROLI

KEY IDEAS

- Analyzing qualitative data enables researchers to find patterns and meanings in texts, photographs, and other artifacts.

- The analysis of qualitative data usually begins during the data collection process, not after.

- Qualitative data analysis is an iterative, cyclic process.

- Qualitative data analysis is both reading- and writing-intensive.

- Coding is a central data analysis technique that is used to reveal the patterns and themes in qualitative data.

- Creating representations of the qualitative data as texts and graphic images is a useful analysis strategy.

- Thorough descriptions, analyses, and interpretations of qualitative data can be restricted by word limits in publications such as journals.

IN CHAPTER Six (on quantitative data analysis), I discussed various techniques that researchers use to analyze numerical data representing such diverse topics as the distribution of females and males in university classrooms, test scores, student ratings of university professors, the relationship between female obesity and criminal behavior, and the crimes committed by middle school students who participated in the D.A.R.E. program.

The results of these analyses of quantitative data allow researchers to describe patterns of *what is* or *is likely to be:* typical conditions (such as the number of females in classrooms, test scores in different classrooms, student ratings of professors, relationship between female obesity and criminal behavior) and the implications of these patterns for predicting impacts or results to large populations (such as the effectiveness of the D.A.R.E. program in reducing juvenile crime).

But if researchers want to know *why* or *how* variables or conditions are related or the *meaning* that participants attribute to events, situations, or ratings, they must turn to other sources of data. The following research questions would require that behaviors and thinking processes be more explicitly revealed:

- What is it like to be an underrepresented gender or ethnicity in physics classes?

- Why do clients (or students) perceive their counselors (or professors) as caring?

- How does the professional practice of teachers (or counselors or probation officers) change after attending staff development training?

As described in the chapters on ethnography (Chapter Eleven), case study, (Chapter Nine), evaluation (Chapter Ten), historical (Chapter Eight), and multiple methods research (Chapter Thirteen), researchers can explore these diverse types of research questions in many ways. They might include open-ended questions on questionnaires (for example, "How would you describe the relationship you have with your counselor?"); make observations in the natural settings (in classrooms, offices, or juvenile detention centers); review the archives of written or image documents (newspapers, laws, policy statements, drawings, or diaries); interview key participants or informants (teachers, counselors, clients, students, parents, or inmates); or collect and describe artifacts (tools, jewelry, or other physical objects). The results of these data collection techniques are in the form of words or pictures, rather than numbers. So, how do researchers make sense of this kind of data? The answer is not quite as straightforward as it was for quantitative data. In this chapter, I will describe the process from an insider's perspective as a data analyst. You will need to use your imagination to become my co-researcher and data analyst, for the best way to learn about qualitative data analysis is to do it.

WORDS, WORDS, WORDS—NOW WHAT?

To a researcher who collects **qualitative data**, all those words, pictures, and artifacts are rich sources of information. **Analysis of qualitative data** involves reducing the many words, images, or artifacts that are collected during research projects into a "more manageable form . . . to tell a story about the people or group that is the focus of their research" (LeCompte & Schensul, 1999, p. 2). But at this point, the researcher is not finished; an interpretation of the story is needed to make the results meaningful to both the participants in the study and the readers of the report. As in quantitative data analysis, **interpretation** goes beyond presenting results to determining what the results say about the people, groups, or programs, and to attaching "meaning or significance to the patterns, themes, and connections that the researcher identified during analysis; why they have come to exist; and indicating what implications they might have for future actions" (p. 5).

Suppose a counselor wants to understand her clients' initial values and beliefs about counseling. She asks all new clients to complete a questionnaire that includes the following open-ended questions:

- Why did you decide to seek counseling?
- What three characteristics do you think a good counselor must possess?

As you might expect, responses to the questions will vary widely. For the first, clients might write, "I need help handling my grief," or "My family (or friends) thought it would help me," or "The judge (or my spouse) made me come." The second question might result in a lengthy list of different characteristics, such as empathetic, caring, organized, insightful, encouraging, analytical, problem solver, supportive, objective, and so on. Now what does the counselor do with this information?

First of all, it is important to distinguish between two general approaches to handling this kind of qualitative data. In her study, the counselor might choose to convert the collected qualitative data into quantitative data. She will tabulate all the responses she received from all her new clients in a certain period of time (say, twelve months), counting the number of instances that clients choose to come on their own, are encouraged to come by others, or are forced to come by some outside authority. Similarly, she can count the number of times clients list each of these characteristics. Using this approach, she essentially substitutes numerical values (as frequency counts) for types of responses that she then analyzes statistically, as discussed in the quantitative data analysis chapter, to reveal the typical patterns and variety of responses.

The counselor might also wish to examine the qualitative data in its original form (how each individual client answered these questions) and context (the situation of each client) so that she can consider how to approach her work with particular clients as well as how her professional practice addresses the needs of a diverse clientele. Therefore, she must utilize other processes for analyzing, summarizing, and interpreting the meanings of the responses. Further, she might want to consider these responses in relation to the observations she makes of each client and the types of interactions that she has with each client during counseling sessions. To do this, she will employ a different approach, leaving the data in its original form and analyzing it using the techniques described in the next sections.

Organizing the Data

In studies that rely primarily on quantitative data, such as experimental (Chapter Three), nonexperimental (Chapter Four), survey (Chapter Five), and meta-analysis

(Chapter Seven), the researchers begin their analyses *after* all the data have been collected. They compile the data into spreadsheets or databases and then proceed with the statistical analysis procedures described in Chapter Six. In most cases, the computer programs available for conducting the analyses make short work of this step of the research process.

But as you might imagine when you read the chapters on ethnography, case study, evaluation, and other approaches that gather qualitative data, researchers who use these approaches must analyze large volumes of text, possibly including multiple files full of observation notes, transcripts of interviews, and copies of documents such as letters, handbooks, journals, Web sites, or grant proposals. These are all examples of **texts**, meaning any published or unpublished document containing written words or symbols that represent concepts or ideas. An example of a response to one question during an interview with a graduate student in her final semester of coursework before student teaching is provided in Exhibit 14.1. This study focuses on the development of appropriate professional behaviors, attitudes, and values (also called dispositions) in undergraduate and graduate pre-service teachers; the prompt for this response is, "Describe how your behavior in this class models the appropriate professional dispositions of a teacher." I will use this response to demonstrate some of the analysis techniques in subsequent sections; in your role as a coanalyst, you should also be thinking about how you would apply these strategies to the same text.

EXHIBIT 14.1.   Sample Pre-service Teacher Interview Response

I feel that I am generally prepared for class and punctual, although not always. This is something I could work on. However, I always attend courses (unless there is a valid reason not to) and am honest in my contributions and respect my instructor and peers.

I believe that all students, no matter their ethnic or cultural background, can learn; this is the most important factor for creating successful education programs and I intend to work tirelessly toward creating more sensitivity in our system. Within this classroom, I treat individuals from all backgrounds and abilities with the same high regard. I've always been respectful of others' well-being and always try to extend a helping hand when needed for any form of support.

I always listen to feedback and take it very seriously. If this were not the case I would be failing my duties as a student and as a future teacher. We must always seek to improve ourselves. In this class I have read my instructor's feedback carefully and ask for help when needed. I listened to my peers in our groups and took their insights to heart.

Although I believe myself to be an attentive listener and an individual who pays close attention to the nonverbal cues of a person's well-being, I also believe that one has never mastered the skill of communicating effectively. We will always be learning how to interact with others through the many interactions we encounter. Some of my interactions were more effective than others in this class. I find that I still need to be more sensitive to the differing personalities I am surrounded by. I do not always trust those around me to have valuable insights. This is wrong of me.

As is evident from the length of this response to only one interview question, it would be a truly overwhelming task to postpone analysis until after *all* the qualitative data for a research project are collected (for example, until all the interviews were completed with all participants and all the classroom observations were transcribed). More important, while doing the data analysis, we researchers might find that we need some data that we did not collect; it is very expensive in terms of both time and money to stop our analysis and go back into the field to collect additional data. While analyzing the above example, we might find that this interviewee used the concept of "communicating effectively" to mean something different from other interviewees. If this becomes apparent only after all data collection is complete, the interviewees may no longer be available to provide clarification, having dispersed to begin their new teaching positions across the country. This limits our analysis to just what we originally collected and perhaps limits our understanding of effective communication as a professional disposition.

To overcome these two challenges, researchers typically begin the analysis of qualitative data at the beginning of data collection. Gay, Mills, and Airasian (2006) list the following steps in the collection-analysis process:

- Gather data
- Examine the data
- Compare the new data to prior data
- Identify new data to gather

This is an ongoing, **iterative** cycle, repeating over and over until the researchers are satisfied that they have explored the problems or issues in a complete and thorough manner. During each cycle of data collection-analysis, the researchers are asking themselves such questions as "What else do we want to know about that participant's feelings? What new ideas have we found in this round of data collection? Is this a new concept or is it the same as one we found before? Are we finding any negative evidence that contradicts our emerging understanding? If not, where and how should we look for this?" In our example, the interviewee said that she does not trust others to have valuable insights. As co-researchers, you and I would want to look at the responses of other interviewees to see if this is a persistent pattern and if it is supported or contradicted by the behaviors of the pre-service teachers in the study.

As a project continues, researchers must organize and label their data so that they know what each file or document represents, as well as when, from whom, and where it was collected. Separate labels might be used for field notes, interviews, journal entries, newspaper articles, and so on. Some researchers also find it helpful to develop a table of contents or index as files accumulate to facilitate locating particular texts, especially if the volume of data is quite large. Making multiple copies of data and storing these in different locations (whether in hard copy or electronically as computer files) is an important safety procedure to prevent data loss. Having multiple copies also allows the researchers to make notes or underline important sections while preserving the original document as it was first collected. The use of computers has greatly simplified the task of storing, organizing, and retrieving documents from folders and files, as long as these are backed up onto other computers, servers, flash or jump drives, CDs, or DVDs; it is tragic to lose data because a computer crashed.

Describing the Data

Early in the data collection-analysis process, researchers find it useful to thoroughly describe the participants, the research setting, and the topic or issue under study. The purpose of these descriptions is to paint "a verbal picture of the context, processes, and the world as viewed from the participants' perspective" (Gay, Mills, & Airasian, 2006, p. 470). These descriptions allow readers to understand the context of the research in more detail: who was involved, what was the location, what cultural beliefs and values are important, and what typically happened there. These descriptions also lead the researchers to begin the process of identifying the important characteristics and key concepts represented in the data. In describing the interviewee for the Exhibit 14.1 response above, I wrote the following introduction:

> The respondent is a graduate student, returning to school after spending two years living and teaching English in France. She is seeking a master's degree in bilingual and multicultural education, along with a state teaching certificate; she is scheduled to student teach during the next semester. Her undergraduate degree is in French. She is in her late 20s and is very goal-oriented, more so than the typical pre-service teacher. Her academic work reflects a gifted and conscientious student. She asks many informed questions in class, engages other students and her teacher in thoughtful conversations, and is aware that she could dominate classroom discussion so she says that she intentionally refrains until others have had the opportunity to provide input and ask questions in class.

From this description, you can identify some dispositions that the respondent exhibits: maturity, focused, thoughtful, and studious, to name a few. What other dispositions would you say are evident here? By including this description in a written report, our readers would already begin to understand the perspective of one of the participants in this study. The readers would also expect that the dispositions exhibited by the pre-service teacher's behavior might be reflections of her interview responses.

REFLECTION QUESTIONS

1. In your discipline, what are some potentially useful sources of qualitative data?
2. In what circumstances might it be useful for you as a practitioner to collect and analyze your own qualitative data? How would you organize and manage this data?

Coding the Data

A primary activity involved in analyzing qualitative data is to assign codes to items or sections of the texts or images. A **code** is a word or phrase applied to an item or section of text as a label for categorizing, sorting, compiling, organizing, and comparing data. These codes are developed and applied by researchers as a way to summarize a large set of qualitative data, similar to how descriptive statistics are used to summarize quantitative data. Exhibit 14.2 shows the sample response again, with my initial coding.

EXHIBIT 14.2.	**Coded Sample Pre-service Teacher Interview Response**
Organized Self-critical	I feel that I am generally <u>prepared for class and punctual,</u> <u>although not always. This is something I could work on</u>. However, I always attend courses (unless there is a valid reason
Honest; respectful	not to) and am <u>honest</u> in my contributions and <u>respect</u> my instructor and peers.
Open-minded	I believe that <u>all students, no matter their ethnic or cultural</u> <u>background can learn</u>; this is the most important factor for creating successful education programs and I
Goal-oriented	<u>intend to work tirelessly</u> toward creating more sensitivity in our system. Within this classroom, I treat individuals from all
Respectful Respectful Helpful	backgrounds and abilities with the <u>same high regard</u>. I've always been <u>respectful</u> of others well-being and always try to <u>extend a helping hand</u> when needed for any form of support.
Reflective	I always <u>listen to feedback and take it very seriously</u>. If this were not the case I would be failing my duties as a student and as a
High expectations	future teacher. <u>We must always seek to improve ourselves</u>. In this class I have read my instructor's feedback carefully and
Open-minded	<u>ask for help</u> when needed. <u>I listened to my peers in our groups</u> <u>and took their insights to heart</u>.
	Although I believe myself to be an attentive listener and an individual who pays close attention to the non-verbal cues of a
Self-critical Lifelong learner	person's well-being, I also believe that <u>one has never mastered</u> <u>the skill of communicating effectively</u>. We will <u>always be learning</u> how to interact with others through the many interactions we
Self-critical Insensitive Distrustful	encounter. <u>Some of my interactions were more effective than</u> <u>others</u> in this class. I find that <u>I still need to be more sensitive</u> to the differing personalities I am surrounded by. I do <u>not always</u> <u>trust those</u> around me to have valuable insights.
Judgmental	<u>This is wrong of me</u>.

The codes must be **operational**; that is, the codes have observable boundaries that answer the question, "An X [name of code] looks like this" (LeCompte & Schensul, 1999, p. 57), and are distinctly different from other codes. The names of codes tend to be close to what they describe. In some cases, I used the respondent's actual words (for example, honest, respectful); in others, I coded the response with a more general label for this kind of statement made (for example, self-critical, open-minded, reflective).

As you read through the example, perhaps you saw other items that you would also highlight or code. What were those? Perhaps you questioned why I labeled two different parts of the text with the same code.

There are two primary approaches to coding; in our example I used a **bottom-up coding** approach. I did not have a set or list of codes prior to beginning the analysis. Rather, I began by reading and rereading the data, letting the codes or labels emerge directly from the words or images in the text. Developing a set of initial codes that identify the properties and dimensions of concepts revealed in the data is also called **open coding** (Strauss & Corbin, 1998). In one study, there may be thirty, forty, or many more initial codes.

Another approach to initial coding is to have a list of codes in hand before beginning the coding; this is called **top-down coding** (LeCompte & Schensul, 1999). When I review the previous research literature or conceptual framework, I might find a list of codes that another researcher used. I might adapt, or modify, a code list from a published work on the same topic. Or, I might adopt a published generic coding scheme. For example, the Human Relations Area Files (HRAF, available at www.yale.edu/hraf) are a compilation of eighty-eight major codes, with subcodes, used by anthropologists and other social scientists, representing the components of cultural, social, economic, and political life (Murdock, 1971). The major code categories group together concepts such as social relationships, religion, political organization, health, arts, education, and so on. For example, within "social relationships" major codes include individuation and mobility, social stratification, interpersonal relations, family, kinship, and gender roles and issues. These are divided into subcodes; for "interpersonal relations" one subcode addresses ethics, which is further subdivided into smaller categories such as cultural norms, personality, or professional practice. By using the same codes, researchers facilitate making comparisons across different studies, sites, and cultures. Although this does provide a structure to the coding process, some researchers find this structure to be too limiting and not as sensitive to the important differences and variability of research sites, questions, and participants.

In either approach (bottom-up or top-down), initial coding must be considered provisional, subject to modification as analysis continues. What is important to remember here is that there is not one "right" way to code qualitative data, nor is coding complete with only one reading of the data. The quantity and complexity of qualitative data require multiple readings and reexamination of the codes. Are some labels too broad (such as "self-critical" in our example, perhaps) and do they need to be subdivided? Do we need to combine any of the codes into a single category? These are the types of questions that researchers must continuously ask themselves as the analysis progresses through all the qualitative data collected. If we change or add to the coding scheme as we read through other documents, we will need to return to the first ones that we coded to see if we need to recode some items. We are constantly comparing the codes to each other and also checking to see that the codes are being consistently used to mark the same concepts, behaviors, or values. This process is sometimes called **constant comparison**.

Initial coding is only the first step in analyzing qualitative data. Now that we have a list of codes for our data, we must begin to look for patterns. In Exhibit 14.2, we had the following thirteen codes: *organized; self-critical; honest; respectful; open-minded; goal-oriented; helpful; reflective; high expectations; lifelong learner; insensitive; distrustful; judgmental.* As you read through this list, are there some that seem to naturally go together into a larger category? Are there others that are not really related to the focus of the study? For example, we could group together both "high expectations" and "organized" into a code called *professional conduct.* Other labels might be *positive relationship with others,* which might include "helpful, respectful, open-minded, and honest;" *negative relationships with others* might include "insensitive, distrustful, and judgmental;" *personal growth* might include "self-critical, goal-oriented, reflective, and lifelong learner."

No matter which approach was used for initial coding, an analyst will continue as we did to reduce the large number of initial codes into larger groups in order to identify patterns, a process known as **axial coding** (Strauss & Corbin, 1998) or **focused coding** (Lofland & Lofland, 1995). This is done by collapsing categories or combining some codes into overarching ideas, as we just did, or by subdividing or elaborating others. In other words, the codes themselves are then coded. The researcher is answering questions about the codes, such as "Where do these codes usually occur, what characteristics do codes have in common, how else are the codes related to each other, and what are the results if I link one code to another?" Answering these questions helps the researcher find relationships and patterns between concepts, events, and persons, as discussed in the next section.

How Patterns Emerge

So, how do we begin looking for patterns? The question response example provided represents only a very small piece of a much larger data set, so it will be somewhat difficult to identify larger patterns here. Combining the positive and negative relationships with others might result in a pattern called *interpersonal relationships.* At this point, I would not combine the other two codes (personal growth and professional conduct); I would wait to see what other codes emerge from our other data sources. How did I make these decisions?

There are several different strategies that help with the decisions. I identified codes or categories that might be alternative forms of essentially the same concept or idea (in this case, interpersonal relationships); this pattern emerged because of similarity. Margaret LeCompte and Jean Schensul (1999) suggest some additional strategies. One common way to identify patterns is to look for repeated occurrences. "When a particular unit, theme, or idea appears over and over in the data, then researchers can feel fairly certain that a pattern may exist" (p. 99). Thus, frequency can reveal a pattern.

Sometimes the participants will tell the researcher about an existing pattern. This strategy is called declaration. For example, a pre-service teacher might say, "I think the most important aspects of professional conduct are dressing appropriately, using correct language, being prepared, being punctual and ready to teach, maintaining your composure, and honesty." Most of these are examples of "professional behaviors." Then it is the researcher's job, our job, to look for additional data that confirm or refute that pattern.

Although somewhat more difficult to detect, but very important, researchers should also look for what is *missing* that might be expected to be present; this is a pattern resulting from omission. In our student teacher study, what if we find no mention in any of our data sources of protecting the privacy of student personal information and academic performance? Is valuing the legal and ethical rights of students a disposition of importance for pre-service teachers? This is an important pattern to notice.

Another important strategy for identifying patterns is to look for co-occurrence. The researcher looks to see which items, events, responses, or kinds of people appear at the same time or in the same place. Similarly, what repeated practices, behaviors, or events can be identified as commonly occurring sequences? These also represent patterns that are important to consider.

The researcher also identifies patterns by looking to see if different data sources (interviews, observations, documents) have the same kinds of codes or themes. In other words, do the types of responses, items, events, or themes in different data sources corroborate each other? In our study, did we find that all the respondents' stated dispositions match with the observations that we made of them in the classroom? We would specifically look for this pattern.

Finally, the researcher must consider if the patterns that are emerging appear to be congruent with prior hypotheses. Prior to beginning a study and collecting data, most researchers read other studies and theoretical articles; these inform their work and often create ideas about what patterns *should* exist. It is up to the researcher to look for both confirming and disconfirming evidence. If none of our data sources mentioned appropriate and correct language, for example, but the goals of the pre-service education program and the research literature indicate that this is a critical component in becoming a professional, we would include this omission in our discussion of the data.

You are probably getting the impression that the analysis of qualitative data requires reading and rereading through all those pages of data. You're right! Whether analysts choose to do this by using printed copies of the notes, documents, and transcripts or by using various computer qualitative data analysis software programs (such as Atlas-ti, Hyperresearch, NVivo 7, or QDA Miner; Web links are provided at end of this chapter), it is a recurring and lengthy process. Often, much of this process is not completely described in written reports; as a reader of research, you will need to look carefully to determine how the authors organized their data, selected the codes to be used, and searched for patterns. Qualitative data analysis also requires lots of writing, in addition to repetitive reading, as described in the next section.

 REFLECTION QUESTIONS

1. What codes would you use to analyze the sample pre-service teacher interview response? Why did you select those codes? How would you define those codes so that they represent separate and distinct categories?

2. For a problem or issue in your field of study, what codes might be useful to have in hand before researchers begin to analyze qualitative data?

REPRESENTING THE FINDINGS

The process of qualitative data analysis is also writing intensive. In addition to developing lists of codes, as described in the previous section, analysts must also document the processes used in creating and changing codes, and in identifying patterns in the data. You can call this process "writing as thinking on the page." In your past educational experiences you may have discovered that when you have to explain an idea or an argument on paper, you actually make your thought processes visible on the page, leading to more careful and refined work. This is what qualitative data analysts do all the time. In fact, sometimes the written documentation of their emerging thinking also becomes a data source for additional analysis. How is writing a part of qualitative data analysis? The following are several strategies used by analysts. The inclusion of one or more of these strategies in written reports can also help readers understand how deeply and thoroughly the researchers analyzed the data.

Writing Memos

Writing a memo allows the analyst to define and explain the relationships between codes or elaborate on the coding categories (Lofland & Lofland, 1995). Sometimes memos are very short, only a sentence or two, to define the boundaries of the codes; for example, what I meant by "self-critical" in our example is a phrase that indicates the respondent believes she has done poorly in the past or could do better in the future. Would this be how you define the concept? As data analysis continues into the more advanced stage of axial coding, memos can also explain how codes are sorted and integrated.

Creating Vignettes

Some qualitative data analysts also find it helpful to organize their data into **vignettes** (LeCompte & Schensul, 1999). "A vignette is a short dramatic description, some of which typify, creating a composite of all the people or events studied; others dramatize a person, act, event, or activity so as to catch the attention of the reader; and still others summarize a biography, event, or other phenomenon" (p. 181). As you might expect from this definition, writing the vignette is a way of revealing or showing the patterns or themes that are emerging from the data. Researchers often use these vignettes in written reports to introduce the topic or to engage the reader in the study. The description of the pre-service teacher interviewee could be used as a vignette, especially if we expanded it to include some critical action and unique quotations or behaviors.

Developing Metaphors

In a classic study of the procedures and documents necessary for university faculty to obtain tenure, Frank Lutz (1986) used the metaphor of witchcraft, with its inherent rituals, rites, charms, and fetishes to describe the process. Just as witches are apprenticed over time into advanced understandings of the correct way to perform rituals, rites, and charms, so too are new faculty initiated into the acceptable behaviors, publications, and institutional procedures in their departments in order to advance to tenured status.

The use of this metaphor both engages the reader in the study and helps the reader understand a process that is not familiar to most people. LeCompte and Schensul (1999) also point out the value of an organizing metaphor, linking a familiar image with the more unfamiliar phenomenon that is being studied. This both helps the analyst organize the findings and draws the reader into the finished report.

Creating Diagrams or Displays

"When in doubt, draw a picture!" (LeCompte & Schensul, 1999, p. 195). When words are confusing and relationships are complex, nothing helps make sense of the data as effectively as a diagram or display. Graphic organizers, charts, tables, time lines, flowcharts, pictures, and diagrams can be helpful throughout a research project, especially during data analysis. You might think that these are strictly in the domain of quantitative data analysts, but researchers working with concepts and ideas often find it beneficial to produce concept maps showing the relationships. Many of these representations can be included in the written reports to assist the readers in understanding the researcher's findings.

Building Theory

If the analyst has used the techniques described above, an overarching theme emerges; this is known as the **central** (or **core**) **category** (Strauss & Corbin, 1998). It represents the big idea of the findings of a research study. All other major categories in the data logically and consistently relate to it. The theme should also explain the variation of alternative or contradictory cases. Sometimes, it is helpful to think of this category as the "elevator version" of the research findings; it answers the question, "What did your research show?" in the amount of time that two people can share an elevator ride. As you read research articles, look to see if the authors clearly state this big idea.

Once the central category is developed, the researcher refines the theory by "reviewing the scheme for internal consistency and for gaps in logic, filling in poorly developed categories and trimming excess ones, and validating the scheme" (Strauss & Corbin, 1998, p. 156). A word of caution is necessary here. In this context, the word "validating" does not mean the same thing as the concept of "validity" as discussed in the chapters describing approaches focusing on quantitative data, such as experimental (Chapter Three), nonexperimental (Chapter Four), or survey (Chapter Five). To validate theory developed from qualitative data, the researcher compares the theory and the raw data, asking questions such as, "Does it explain most cases? Do the participants in the study recognize themselves? Is the variation or discrepancy due to process or temporal considerations (for example, does it go a different direction or take a different amount of time to get there)?"

Not all qualitative data analysis is conducted with the express purpose of developing theory. But if the value of qualitative data is to answer questions about *why* and *how* variables or conditions are related and *what meaning* is there, then developing theory is what needs to be done. Theory goes beyond a simple description of patterns to answer these questions about the patterns. Better yet, theory should also be significant (not in terms of statistical significance), providing important insights or implications of the research for understanding the research problem, issues, or topic.

Data Analysis Is Iterative

Although the above description seems to imply a linear process for analyzing qualitative data, let me repeat—in reality, the process is iterative, repeating or recurring many times throughout the analysis. Data are subjected to analysis throughout the research project and may be coded, categorized, and interpreted many times before the final written report appears, in order to ensure that the researchers are letting the interpretation emerge from the data, rather than imposing their own biases on the data. To do this, researchers must be open-minded and think flexibly throughout the qualitative data analysis process. Lofland and Lofland (1995) caution analysts to "withhold judgment about the final shape of an analysis as long as it is possible, in a practical way, to do so" (p. 203). One commonly used strategy is **constant comparison** (Glaser & Strauss, 1967); during analysis, researchers ask questions such as "How is this instance of X similar to or different from previous instances?" or "How is X in this setting similar to or different from X in another setting?" to determine how each new item relates to previously examined data. Thinking in extremes or opposites also helps to identify the boundaries of a code or interpretation, by determining what would always be classified as X, and what never would be. Looking for what's missing and for contradictory evidence is equally important.

As it was for quantitative data analysis, further study, either by taking one or more courses, or by working your way through some of the cited and recommended texts at the end of this chapter, is required for developing a deeper understanding of the techniques used for qualitative data analysis. But as a reader of research, there are clues you can look for in the written reports to help you assess the quality of the analysis, described in the next section.

 REFLECTION QUESTIONS

1. In your discipline, what are some metaphors that would be useful to explain practitioners' work?

2. Why is thinking flexibly important during qualitative data analysis? What might limit a researcher's ability to be open-minded? How could you determine if the authors of research reports were open-minded?

EVALUATING REPORTS WITH QUALITATIVE DATA

Just as collecting qualitative data results in a large quantity of text, so too does preparing the written reports for these studies. Unfortunately, journals impose word-count limits on articles that are accepted for publication. Often, the result is that researchers who primarily use qualitative data are faced with a critical problem: How to describe the data analysis process, present the findings, and interpret these findings within the space limitation of the journal. For many, the answer lies in publishing book-length works.

You probably noticed that many of the suggested readings in the chapters on historical, ethnographic, and feminist research are books, rather than journal articles.

As a reader of journal articles, you will need to look carefully and sometimes read between the lines to evaluate how well the researchers analyzed the qualitative data and reported their findings. Important topics that should be discussed in the articles include an explanation of how the researchers gathered, organized, and analyzed the data. How were codes selected? Did they use a bottom-up coding strategy, with codes emerging directly from the data? If preexisting codes were used, how were these generated? Some reports will also include the list of codes used; if a list is not included, is it clear how the themes emerged? Did the authors describe any changes to these codes that occurred during the study? Did the authors demonstrate an open-minded approach to data analysis by looking for what is not there, by constantly comparing the codes and interpretations throughout the research process, by looking for extreme or opposite examples? Did the authors reveal how their own positions and biases affected the research study and their data analysis? Are the patterns and themes reported consistent with the codes that were used? All of the questions that researchers must ask themselves during the analysis process are also questions readers of these research articles would like to have answered.

In most cases, you as a reader should be given the opportunity to see for yourself their analysis and interpretation process. There should be sufficient raw data (such as direct quotations from interviews, observation notes, photos, and so on) included in the report to illustrate how the findings and interpretations arose. Although these passages will not usually have the coding included, they should be representative of the patterns and themes that the researchers found in the data. Ideally, the authors should have about equal amounts of data description (or examples), analysis, and interpretation in the final report (Strauss & Corbin, 1998).

In summary, these are the questions you should be able to answer to evaluate the reports:

- Are the sources of the data clearly explained?
- Do the data come from a variety of sources?
- Are there examples of the interview questions, documents, and images used?
- Is more than one type of data analyzed?
- Is the process of data analysis thoroughly explained?
- Are the codes, categories, or labels used for concepts appropriate?
- Does there seem to be a balance between description, analysis, and interpretation?
- Is the analysis consistent with the data presented?
- Are enough data provided (for example, samples of quotations or images) so that you can begin to see for yourself the patterns and themes?
- Are rival explanations or negative findings addressed in the analysis and interpretation?
- Are the researchers' biases addressed in the process of data analysis and reporting?

Reread the suggested article from one of the previous chapters that emphasize the collection of qualitative data, such as historical (Chapter Eight), case study (Chapter Nine), evaluation (Chapter Ten), ethnography (Chapter Eleven), or feminist research (Chapter Twelve). Carefully examine the "Methodology" or "Study Design" and subsequent sections of the report to answer these questions.

SUMMARY

Qualitative data analysis is a time-consuming, labor-intensive task; it is also rewarding in revealing why, how, or what meanings are given to events, situations, behaviors, or opinions. The researcher is the primary tool both for collecting and processing the data. Researchers do not wait until after all the data are collected to begin the analysis; instead, they use the data analysis process to refine their data collection methods while conducting the study. Reading, coding, rereading, and recoding the data numerous times helps the researchers identify patterns or themes, which are used to answer important questions about the problems, processes, or issues under study. Readers expect the authors of these research reports to be very clear about how the analyses were conducted.

KEY TERMS

analysis of qualitative data
axial coding
bottom-up coding
central (core) category
code
constant comparison
focused coding
interpretation (of qualitative data)

iterative
open coding
operational
qualitative data
texts
top-down coding
vignettes

FURTHER READINGS AND RESOURCES

Suggested Readings

The following texts represent the classic works on analyzing qualitative data. All are fairly approachable, with many examples provided.

Corbin, J., & Strauss, A. (2007). *Basics of qualitative research: Techniques and procedures for developing grounded theory* (3rd ed.). Thousand Oaks, CA: Sage.

LeCompte, M. D., & Schensul, J. J. (1999). *Analyzing and interpreting ethnographic data: Ethnographer's toolkit* (Vol. 5). Walnut Creek, CA: AltaMira.

Lofland, J., Lofland, L. H., Snow, D., & Anderson, L. (2005). *Analyzing social settings: A guide to qualitative observation and analysis* (4th ed.). Belmont, CA: Wadsworth.

Web Sites

The Research Room: Online Guide to Social Science Research

www.class.uh.edu/sociology/researchroom

This is a University of Houston reference source for information and resources on social science research, both qualitative and quantitative.

The Qualitative Report: An Online Journal Dedicated to Qualitative Research Since 1990

www.nova.edu/ssss/QR

In addition to publishing current qualitative research in multiple disciplines, the site has links to many, many resources and articles about qualitative research design, data analysis, and evaluating published qualitative studies.

Human Relations Area Files: Cultural Materials for Education and Research

www.yale.edu/hraf

The Human Relations Area Files, Inc. (HRAF) is an internationally recognized organization in the field of cultural anthropology. The mission of HRAF is to encourage and facilitate worldwide comparative studies of human behavior, society, and culture.

Data Analysis Computer Programs

There are many programs available, both as shareware and proprietary. Commonly used ones, with links to the Web sites, are provided here:

Atlas-ti: www.atlasti.com

Hyperresearch: www.researchware.com

NVivo 7: www.qsrinternational.com/products_nvivo.aspx

QDA Miner: www.provalisresearch.com

CHAPTER

APPLYING RESEARCH METHODS TO PROFESSIONAL PRACTICE

DAVID HOPKINS AND ELPIDA AHTARIDOU

KEY IDEAS

- Action research is an approach to research that includes systematic reflection upon one's craft.

- Reflective practice can become a vehicle for professional emancipation and autonomy.

- Professional emancipation and autonomy refer to a practitioner's ability to improve his or her own practice confidently.

- Professional judgments are based on evidence gathered from action research.

THIS CHAPTER aims to assist professionals who wish to undertake research with the purpose of improving their practice. Conducting research, in the sense that we refer to it here, is an act undertaken by professionals to enhance their own or a colleague's practice, to test the assumptions of theories in practice, or as a means of evaluating and implementing organizational priorities. So, when we refer to action research of a practitioner as a researcher, we are not envisioning scores of professionals assuming a research role and carrying out research projects to the exclusion of their practice. Our vision is of practitioners who have extended their role to include systematic reflection upon their craft with the aim of improving it and becoming "autonomous in professional judgment" (Stenhouse, 1984, p. 69).

Engaging with action research can become a vehicle for professional emancipation and autonomy. Our aim is to assist those practitioners who wish to research their own practice, and toward this end, in this chapter we will explore:

▣ The history of action research

▣ Different models of action research

▣ Ways in which research projects can be identified and initiated

▣ Ways of gathering data

▣ Ways of interpreting and analyzing the data gathered from research

WHAT IS ACTION RESEARCH?

Action research combines a substantive act with a research procedure; it is action disciplined by inquiry, a personal attempt at understanding while engaging in a process of improvement and reform.

Here are three definitions of action research. The first is by Dave Ebbutt (1985, cited in Hopkins, 2002, p. 43), who not only gives a definition of his own, but also quotes from Kemmis. He writes that action research "is about the systematic study of attempts to improve educational practice by groups of participants by means of their own practical actions and by means of their own reflection upon the effects of those actions. Put simply, action research is the way groups of people can organize the conditions under which they can learn from their own experience. Action research is trying out an idea in practice with a view to improving or changing something, trying to have a real effect on the situation."

The second is from John Elliott (1991): "Action research might be defined as *'the study of a social situation with a view to improving the quality of action within it'*. It aims to feed practical judgment in concrete situations, and the validity of the 'theories' or hypotheses it generates depends not so much on 'scientific' tests of truth, as on their usefulness in helping people to act more intelligently and skillfully. In action-research 'theories' are not validated independently and then applied to practice. They are validated through practice" (p. 69).

The third is from McNiff (2002): "Action research is a term which refers to a practical way of looking at your own work to check that it is as you would like it to be. Because action research is done by you, the practitioner, it is often referred to as practitioner based research; and because it involves you thinking about and reflecting on your work, it can also be called a form of self-reflective practice" (p. 12).

The development of the idea of action research is generally attributed to Kurt Lewin (1948), who in the immediate post–World War II period used it as a methodology for intervening in and researching the major social problems of the day. Lewin maintained that through action research advances in theory and needed social changes might simultaneously be achieved. Action research, according to Lewin (see Table 15.1), "consisted in analysis, fact-finding, conceptualization, planning execution, more fact-finding or evaluation; and then a repetition of this whole circle of activities; indeed a spiral of such cycles" (quoted in Kemmis, 1988, p. 13).

REFLECTION QUESTION

1. At this point, how might you apply Lewin's definition of reflection to any work you do?

More recently, action research has been seen as a methodology through which the aspirations of critical theory might be realized. Critical theory builds on the work of Marx, Freud, and the traditions of the Frankfurt School of philosophy, in particular the writings of Jurgen Habermas. Unfortunately, the outstanding characteristic of critical theory is its unintelligibility! This is a great pity as well as a paradox, because the central purpose of critical theory is emancipation—enabling people to take control and direction over their own lives. There are now, however, a number of books that admirably "translate" critical theory and explore its educational implications. In one of them, our colleague at Cambridge, the late Rex Gibson, describes the central characteristic of critical theory as follows:

> ***Critical theory*** *acknowledges the sense of frustration and powerlessness that many feel as they see their personal destinies out of their control, and in the hands of (often unknown) others. . . . Critical theory attempts to reveal those factors which prevent groups and individuals taking control of, or even influencing, those decisions which*

TABLE 15.1. **Lewin's Action Research Model**

Fact finding	Searching for ideas to begin reflection process
Conceptualizing	Deciding on the focus of the action research plan
Action planning	Making the plan to include observation plan
Implementation	Engaging in the activity and making observations
Evaluation	Using observations to determine effectiveness of implementation
Problem analysis	Using results to begin fact-finding process cycle once again

crucially affect their lives. . . . In the exploration of the nature and limits of power, authority and freedom, critical theory claims to afford insight into how greater degrees of autonomy could be available. . . . This characteristic marks out critical theory's true distinctiveness: its claim to be emancipatory. *Not only does it provide enlightenment (deeper awareness of your true interests); more than that (indeed, because of that), it can set you free. Unlike scientific theory, it claims to provide guidance as to what to do. (Gibson, 1986, pp. 5–6)*

If this all sounds too good to be true, Gibson goes on to warn us, "There are clearly immense problems attaching to a theory which not only argues that it reveals the world more clearly, but also asserts that it can be used to change the world, to liberate from inequalities and unfair restrictions" (Gibson, 1986, p. 6).

Obviously, neither critical theory nor action research is a panacea, and they should not be regarded as such. However, there are practical applications that do provide a rationale and method for professionals who wish to take more control of their professional (and personal) lives.

Even from this brief description, it can be seen how the method of action research, with its twin emphases on committed action and reflection, is particularly suited to putting into practice such an emancipatory philosophy.

MODELS OF ACTION RESEARCH

The combination of the action and the research components has a powerful appeal for professionals. In this section we will discuss some additional models of action research. Some of these models have been developed particularly for teacher-researchers but can be applied to other practices and contexts. For example, lawyers, business leaders, counselors, and even agency supervisors should be able to use these guidelines.

Kemmis Model

The Stephen **Kemmis model** of action research is of interest. This model is found in *The Action Research Planner* (Kemmis & McTaggart, 1988), where they summarize this approach to action research in the model shown in Figure 15.1. The reader should take note of the cyclical nature of this diagram, moving from planning to action, to observing and reflecting, and then back to revised planning.

Elliott Model

John Elliott was quick to take up Kemmis's schema of the action research cycle or spiral and he, too, produced a similar but more elaborate model. Elliott, as seen in Figure 15.2, summarizes Kemmis's approach and then outlines his elaborations.

Although I think Kemmis' model is an excellent basis for starting to think about what action research involves, it can allow those who use it to assume that "The General Idea" can be fixed in advance, that "Reconnaissance" is merely fact-finding and that

"Implementation" is a fairly straightforward process. But I would argue that "The General Idea" should be allowed to shift. "Reconnaissance" should involve analysis as well as fact-finding, and should constantly recur in the spiral of activities, rather than occur only at the beginning. "Implementation" of an action-step is not always easy, and one should not proceed to evaluate the effects of an action until one has monitored the extent to which it has been implemented. (Elliott, 1991, p. 70)

As this model suggests, identifying initial ideas for reflection is only one portion of the planning stage. Elliott characterizes the entire process in action research as much more complicated than Kemmis implies.

REFLECTION QUESTION

1. Examine the Kemmis and Elliott models. Which makes the most sense to you? Why?

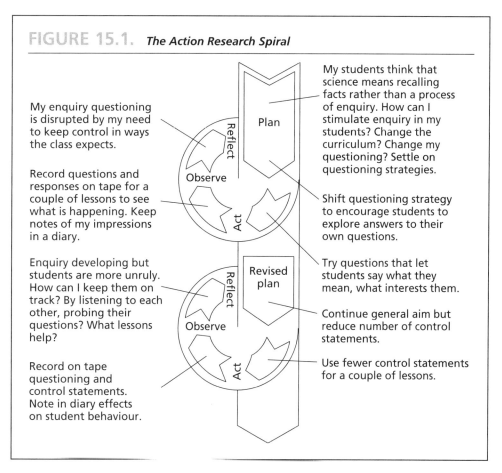

FIGURE 15.1. *The Action Research Spiral*

My students think that science means recalling facts rather than a process of enquiry. How can I stimulate enquiry in my students? Change the curriculum? Change my questioning? Settle on questioning strategies.

My enquiry questioning is disrupted by my need to keep control in ways the class expects.

Plan

Reflect

Observe

Act

Shift questioning strategy to encourage students to explore answers to their own questions.

Record questions and responses on tape for a couple of lessons to see what is happening. Keep notes of my impressions in a diary.

Try questions that let students say what they mean, what interests them.

Enquiry developing but students are more unruly. How can I keep them on track? By listening to each other, probing their questions? What lessons help?

Revised plan

Reflect

Observe

Act

Continue general aim but reduce number of control statements.

Record on tape questioning and control statements. Note in diary effects on student behaviour.

Use fewer control statements for a couple of lessons.

Source: Kemmis & McTaggart, 1988, p. 14.

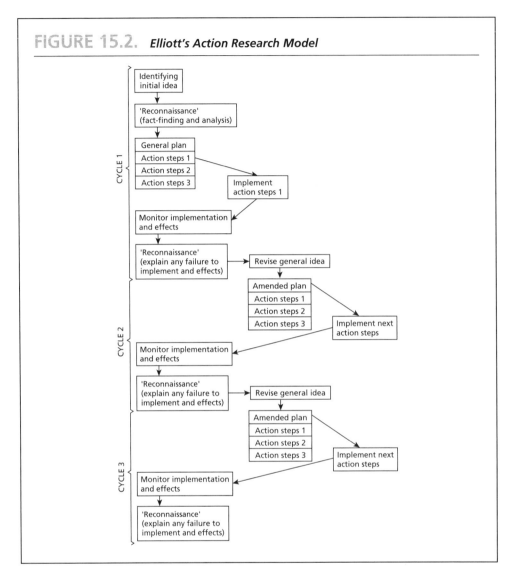

FIGURE 15.2. *Elliott's Action Research Model*

Source: Elliott, 1991, p. 71.

Ebbutt Model

Dave Ebbutt (1985), a colleague of Elliott, provides us with another variation on Kemmis's model and makes these comments about it. "I would argue that it is not the case that Kemmis equates reconnaissance with fact finding only. The Kemmis diagram . . . clearly shows reconnaissance to comprise discussing, negotiating, exploring opportunities, assessing possibilities and examining constraints. In short there are elements of analysis in the Kemmis notion of reconnaissance. Nevertheless I suggest that the thrust of Elliott's three underlined statements is an attempt on the part of a person experienced in directing action research projects to recapture some of the 'messyness' of the action-research cycle which the Kemmis version tends to gloss" (p. 164).

But Ebbutt (1985) claims that the spiral is not the most useful metaphor (see Figure 15.3). Instead, he suggests that the most "appropriate way to conceive of the process of action research is to think of it as comprising a series of successive cycles, each incorporating the possibility for the feedback of information within and between cycles" (p. 164).

A number of other similar models have recently been developed, most of which build on Lewin's original idea or Kemmis's interpretation of it. For example, James McKernan (1996) suggests a "time process" model (see Figure 15.4), which emphasizes the importance of not allowing an action research "problem" to become too rigidly fixed in time, and of rational problem solving and democratic ownership by the community of researchers.

REFLECTION QUESTIONS

1. Comparing all of the models from Kemmis to McKernan, what do they all have in common?

2. Which model do you prefer of all of these? Why?

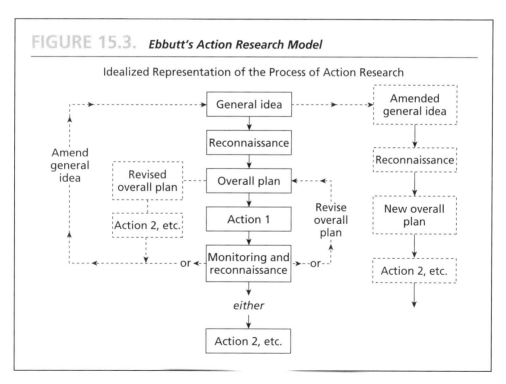

FIGURE 15.3. *Ebbutt's Action Research Model*

Idealized Representation of the Process of Action Research

Source: Ebbutt, 1985, p. 166.

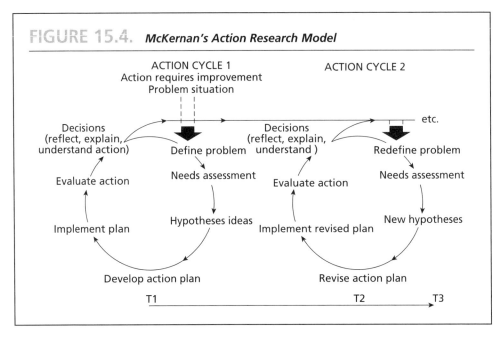

FIGURE 15.4. *McKernan's Action Research Model*

Source: McKernan, 1996, p. 29.

We have briefly discussed the history of action research and explored several models that one could use to conduct a research project. We now turn our attention to the way that the research project can be initiated and the methods that practitioner-researchers could employ in order to carry out their research.

METHODS OF ACTION RESEARCH

Action research does not necessarily start with the setting of precise hypotheses. As Kemmis and McTaggart (1988, p. 18) point out in their seminal book *The Action Research Planner:*

You do not have to begin with a "problem." All you need is a general idea that something might be improved. Your general idea may stem from a promising new idea or the recognition that existing practice falls short of aspiration. In either case you must centre attention on:

- *What is happening now?*
- *In what sense is this problematic?*
- *What can I do about it?*

    General starting points will look like

- *I would like to improve the . . .*
- *Some people are unhappy about . . .*
- *What can I do to change the situation?*

■ *I am perplexed by . . .*

■ *. . . is a source of irritation. What can I do about it?*

■ *I have an idea I would like to try out in my class.*

■ *How can the experience of . . . be applied to . . . ?*

■ *Just what do I do with respect to . . . ?*

(Kemmis & McTaggart, 1988, p. 18)

Developing a Focus

Ideas that come to mind are more likely to relate to practical and immediate concerns, but they may also relate to organizational or personal priorities. It is worth taking a few minutes to jot down these ideas. Do not worry about how well they are formed; at this stage it is more important to generate a list of topics from which one can work. Having produced a list, the next step is to evaluate the usefulness, viability, or importance of the individual issue. The following guidelines can be of use:

1. Do not tackle issues that you cannot do anything about. For example, it may be impossible in the short or medium term to alter the data-gathering systems in your organization. Because you cannot do anything about it, either avoid the issue or rephrase it in a more solvable form.

2. Only take on, at least initially, small-scale and relatively limited issues. There are several reasons for this. It is important to build on success, and a small-scale project satisfactorily completed in a short space of time is reinforcing and encouraging. It is also very easy to underestimate the scale and amount of time a project will take. It is very discouraging to have found after the initial flush of enthusiasm that you have bitten off more than you can chew.

3. Choose an issue that is important to you or to your customers, or one that you have to be involved with anyway in the course of your normal everyday activities. The topic that you focus on needs to be intrinsically motivating. If not, then again, after the initial flush of enthusiasm and when the difficulties begin to build up, you will find that your motivation will begin to evaporate.

4. As far as possible try to work collaboratively on the focus of your research. Professional partnerships are a powerful form of staff development and personal support. They are also a way of reducing the isolation in which some practitioners work.

5. Make connections between your research work and your organization's development plan, priorities, or aims. Although there need not be a direct relationship, it is important to relate one's individual professional inquiry to the direction in which the organization is moving.

Practitioner Reflection in Action

The action researcher or reflective practitioner might follow the logic presented by Kemmis and McTaggart (1988) of planning, acting, observing, and reflecting. A therapist, for instance, could choose to engage in some form of reflective practice by *planning* to learn more about his role during group counseling. An area of interest might be his verbal behavior that either encourages or inhibits patients' expressions of thoughts or feelings. Using an audio recording of one group session (*acting*), the therapist could make notes (*observing*) about what he said that could be placed into the encouragement and inhibiting categories, then *reflect* on these findings in his next cycle of planning (revised planning) in an attempt to reduce his inhibiting statements while increasing supportive verbal behavior.

In another example, a college professor might use this reflective practice model to sharpen her instructional effectiveness by requesting students in the course to anonymously complete a questionnaire about the clarity and usefulness of assignments. These questionnaire results could be summarized and discussed with the students to produce an improved plan for assigning homework. To repeat the cycle, a questionnaire could be administered again in a month or so followed by the same summary, discussion, and potential changes.

In each example, the process is repeated only as needed, followed by a change in focus or topic of study. The therapist may decide to examine his verbal skills during individual sessions and the professor may shift focus to the examination of her communication ability during instruction.

REFLECTION QUESTIONS

1. Now that you have seen an example of reflective planning, how might the instructor for this course conduct action research?

2. In your own professional practice, what might be appropriate topics for action research?

Data Collection Methods

There is a range of **data collection** methods that practitioners can use, some of which are illustrated in this section. Researchers should ensure that the method(s) they employ are fit for the purpose, respond to the needs of the project, and are suited to the time frame allocated for completing it.

Observation   Observation plays a crucial role not only in action research, but also more generally in supporting professional growth. It seems to be the pivotal activity that links together reflection for the individual and collaborative inquiry for pairs or groups of professionals. It also encourages the development of a language for talking about one's practice and provides a means for working on developmental priorities for the staff as a whole. There are four methods of undertaking observation: **open**, **focused**, **structured**, and **systematic** observation, which we describe next. The descriptions refer specifically to classroom research but could be adjusted for use by practitioners in other professions.

Open observation. In this approach, the practitioner-researcher (observer) literally uses a blank sheet of paper to record a particular practice. The observer either notes down key points about the situation or uses a personal form of shorthand for making a verbatim recording of transactions. The aim is usually to enable subsequent recon-struction of the particular situation. A variation of this approach is to decide to record only those events that fit into certain broad categories or under certain headings, as in the therapist example above. Figure 15.5 shows how open observation can be used in classroom research.

A problem with this approach is that it is often unfocused and can lead to premature judgments. The best way to handle this approach is to make open recording as factual as possible and postpone interpretation until a discussion after the particular practice.

Focused observation. In this approach two or more professionals decide on a particular area they are going to observe. However, in many cases, after defining the focus of the observation, practitioners often feel at a loss as to exactly what to look at or for. In classroom research, for example, if they decide to focus on questioning techniques, they may not know the concepts of higher-order and lower-order questions. In another situation, they may have decided to look at "praise" in their classrooms, but after more reflection they may have some difficulty in describing all the different possible forms of praise.

Practitioners should not forget, however, that all the forms or summaries of research they may decide to use when conducting a focused observation can be of help as long as they are subject to their own judgment. Problems arise when the checklist controls the focus of the observation, or encourages the observer to become too subjective. It should also go without saying that such "prompts" should be negotiated and agreed on beforehand. If the use of criteria is implied in the observation, they should be negotiated, shared, and understood by all those involved.

Structured observation. Information can also be collected by using either a tally system or a diagram. This approach is what we call **structured observation**. With a tally system, an observer puts down a tally *every time* a particular event occurs, such as every time the teacher asks a question or gives praise. The resulting record is factual

---

FIGURE 15.5.   *Example of Open Observation*

The observer should aim to record factual and descriptive information.

Teaching Skills

(i) Presentation	
(ii) Indirect teaching	
(iii) Direct teaching	
(iv) Voice	
(v) Questioning strategies	
(vi) Feedback	
(vii) Subject matter	
(viii) Expectations	

Source: Bollington & Bradley, 1990, p. 31.

rather than judgmental. The aim of a *diagram* is to produce a record of what happens in the classroom. It records in diagrammatic form a series of classroom interactions. This approach lends itself to a factual or a descriptive record. It should be noted that all of these approaches can fit a wide range of concerns. They can focus on aspects of the teacher's work, pupil-teacher interaction, or the work of one or more pupils.

Below is an example of a structured observation developed by teachers who were interested in gathering data on questioning techniques. Figure 15.6 shows *question distribution*. The circles represent pupils. When they answer a question it is tallied in their circle. At the end of the lesson the observer is able to identify how many questions each student has answered. Blank circles indicate pupils who have not answered a question.

Field Notes **Field notes** are written records of observations, reflections, and reactions to problems during fieldwork. Ideally, they should be written as soon as possible, but can be based on impressionistic jottings made during the investigation of the practice. Field notes can be issue-oriented insofar as the observations focus on a particular aspect of one's practice and constitute an ongoing record; they also can reflect general impressions of the practice, its climate, or incidental events. They can also be used

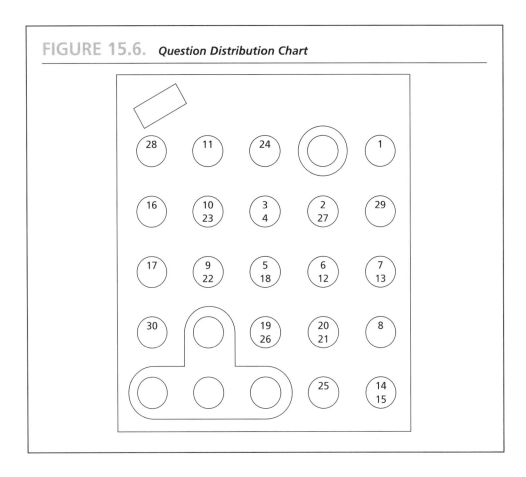

FIGURE 15.6. *Question Distribution Chart*

to provide case study material of a particular patient, child, staff member, or others. This information should be descriptive rather than speculative, so that a broad picture amenable to interpretation can be constructed.

Audio Recording   Audiotape recording is one of the most popular research methods. **Transcripts**, the written records of your recordings, are excellent in providing very specific and accurate evidence of a limited aspect of your practice, or of a particular interaction. Also, simply playing back tapes of one's practice can be very illuminating and can provide useful starting points for further investigation. However, playing back tapes or making transcripts can be very time-consuming and expensive. Practitioner-researchers should not forget that the use of the tape recorder requires some technical knowledge—for example, ensuring that the microphone is picking up what is intended. Often, research participants find the presence of a tape recorder disturbing and have to be introduced to the technique. Researchers should always gain consent, either verbal or written, from all the participants before recording. In this way the researchers ensure that participants' rights are not violated (see Chapter One).

Interviews   Interviewing is a very popular research method of data collection. Interviews can prove very time-consuming, but individual interviews are often very productive sources of information for a participant observer who wants to verify observations previously made. Interestingly, like other researchers, we increasingly find group interviews with three or four interviewees the most productive. Far from inhibiting each other, the individuals "spark" themselves and each other into sensitive and perceptive discussion. We also find it helpful to tape-record a summary of the discussion at the end of the interview. This enables interviewees to correct or amplify our interpretation and provides us with a brief and succinct account of the interview that can easily be transcribed.

Walker and Adelman (cited in Hopkins, 2002, pp. 109–110) make a number of helpful points about effective interviewing.

1. Be a sympathetic, interested, and attentive listener, without taking an active conservative role.

2. Be neutral with respect to subject matter. Do not express your own opinions on the subjects being discussed, and be especially careful not to betray feelings of surprise or disapproval towards the interviewee(s).

3. Your own sense of ease is also important. If you feel hesitant or hurried, the interviewees will sense this feeling and behave accordingly.

4. Interviewees may also be fearful that they will expose an attitude or idea that you do not think is correct. You can offer them reassurance along the lines of "Your opinions are important to me. All I want to know is what you think—this isn't a test and there isn't any one answer to the questions I want to ask."

5. Specifically we suggest that you:
   a. Phrase questions similarly each time.
   b. Keep the outline of interview questions before you.

  c. Be prepared to reword a question if it is not understood or if the answer is vague and too general. Sometimes it is hard not to imply an answer to the question in the process of rewording it.

Videotape Recording and Digital Photography   The videotape recorder and digital photography allow researchers to observe many facets of their practice quickly, and provide accurate information for diagnosis. After the overall diagnosis, the researcher may wish to use a different method to examine specific aspects of her or his practice. If an observer can be used to operate the videotape recorder or the digital camera, then more attention can be paid to specific practice episodes (identified beforehand).

Questionnaires   **Questionnaires** are documents that contain a set of questions and are designed to elicit specific information about aspects of one's practice. They are a quick and simple way of obtaining broad and rich information. It is important, however, to pay particular attention to the wording of the questionnaire so that it is easily understood by its audience. Also, ensure that questions are phrased in a neutral way to avoid leading respondents to a particular answer.

When your respondents are children, ensure that the questionnaire is relatively unsophisticated in its question structure. Condense the usual five-point scale to two or three responses, keep the questions simple, and use the basic "what did you like best," "what did you like least," and "what would you do differently" type of open-ended question. With younger children it is often more profitable to use a happy face as the criterion response to questions, as in Figure 15.7.

Case Study   The **case study** is a relatively formal analysis of an aspect of a single instant or event. For example, a counselor may wish to produce case studies of some patients or teachers for a university course he or she is taking. This approach should not be confused with **case study research** outlined in Chapter Nine. Here, we refer to the idea as the study of individuals. These situations aside, it is unlikely that practitioners will devote time to producing a formal case report of their research efforts every time they undertake a project.

The techniques described above are open-ended insofar as they are used most effectively for diagnostic purposes. Although these techniques have been described individually, it is important to realize that they can and are most often used eclectically and in combination.

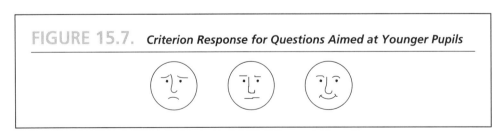

FIGURE 15.7.   *Criterion Response for Questions Aimed at Younger Pupils*

Source: Hopkins, 2002, p. 118.

1. Which data collection approach fits best for action research in either this class or with your own situation?

2. What problems do you foresee in using some of the approaches described above?

A FRAMEWORK FOR DATA ANALYSIS

Making sense of social situations has long been the task of sociologists and it is from their (and anthropologists') methodological canons that much avant-garde work on educational evaluation was initially drawn. This research tradition provides a framework within which to consider practitioner-based research.

Two of the classic statements on sociological fieldwork were made by Becker (1958) and Glaser and Strauss (1967). Examining their work, we were able to identify basic similarities in their approaches to the analysis of field data. Each envisages the analytical process as having four distinct generic stages: (a) **data collection** and the initial generation of categories, (b) **validation** of categories, (c) **interpretation** of categories, and (d) **action**. These various stages represent standard practice for the analysis of qualitative field data and can be used by practitioners to analyze data emerging from their own research efforts. We discuss each of these stages in turn.

Data Collection

In the research process, the first step is collecting data. Having collected the data, a substage follows immediately or coexists with the collection of data—the generation of a number of hypotheses and of constructs or categories that begin to explain what is happening in the classroom. These hypotheses not only reflect the data but also are an interpretation of them. At this stage, the more ideas one has, the better. The richer and more creative our thoughts, the more likely it is that the research will result in a coherent and complete interpretation of the problem. It is in the following stage that we begin to evaluate the hypotheses, therefore initially one should be as creative and as suggestive as possible.

Validation

The second stage in the process concerns the validation of the hypotheses. There are a number of techniques for establishing the **validity** of a category or hypothesis. We will discuss two of these techniques, starting with triangulation, as it is probably the most well known.

In general, the idea of **triangulation** refers to checking to see whether information from different sources or different data collection techniques corresponds or is parallel. The technique of triangulation was popularized by John Elliott and Clem Adelman (1976) during their work with the Ford Teaching Project. It involves contrasting the perceptions of one actor in a specific situation against those of other actors in the same situation. By doing this, an initial subjective observation or perception is fleshed out and given a degree of authenticity.

However, triangulation is not always an easy process to engage in. Initially, it may be threatening for a practitioner to involve his customers in the evaluation of his own practice, or it may prove difficult to obtain the services of a peer to act as a participant observer. Practitioners with the personal openness and interest in their practice needed to initiate such research will eventually overcome these difficulties. Incidentally, we believe that it is important for the practitioner to involve customers in the research process as soon as personal confidence allows.

Another well-known technique is **saturation**. Becker (1958) and Glaser and Strauss (1967) point to a similar process; Becker refers to "the check on the frequency and distribution of phenomenon" (p. 653) and Glaser and Strauss to *saturation*, a situation where "no additional data are being found . . . [to] develop properties of the category" (p. 67). When applied to the research situation, this implies that the hypothesis or category generated from observation is tested repeatedly against the data in an attempt to modify or falsify it.

It is difficult and perhaps reckless to suggest a frequency that ensures the validity of a category, for that will vary from case to case, but during this process a number of predictable events can occur. First, if on repeated testing, the category is found wanting, it is then discarded. Second, the category may have been conceptualized crudely and, through repeated observation, the concept is modified, refined, and amplified. Third, although the process of falsification is never complete, there comes a time when repeated observation leads neither to refutation nor amplification and only serves to support the hypothesis. At this point, when the utility of observation decreases, saturation can be said to have occurred and the hypothesis has been validated.

Interpretation

The third stage in the research process is **interpretation**. This involves taking a validated hypothesis and fitting it into a frame of reference that gives it meaning. For the researcher, this means taking a hypothesis and relating it either to theory, the norms of accepted practice, or the practitioner's own intuition as to what comprises good practice. This allows the researcher to give meaning to a particular observation or series of observations that can lead profitably to action. In doing this, the researcher is creating meaning out of hitherto discrete observations and constructs.

Action

As mentioned earlier, the final step that we have identified in the process of analyzing data through our examination of the work of Becker (1958) and Glaser and Strauss (1967) is action. Having created meaning out of the research data, the researcher is in a position to plan for future action. Building on the evidence gathered during the research, the practitioner is able to plan realistic strategies which are themselves monitored by research procedures.

It is important to add that although the four stages of research are described here in a linear fashion, they are far more interactive than that. In fact, the whole process is a very dynamic one. There are two aspects of this "dynamism" that we want to mention in particular.

1. *The data collection and analysis processes are ongoing.* In the initial phase, one analyzes the questionnaire or interview results, and then uses the analyzed data from a number of different sources to generate the categories or hypotheses. Having done that, one validates them in the second phase and then returns to phase one to collect more data.

2. *The whole process is interactive.* Miles and Huberman (1994, pp. 21–22) describe the interactive model of data analysis as follows:

> *Data reduction:* **Data reduction** refers to the process of selecting, focusing, simplifying, abstracting, and transforming the "raw" data that appear in written-up field notes. As data collection proceeds, there are further episodes of data reduction (doing summaries, coding, teasing out themes, making clusters, making partitions, writing memos). And the data reduction or transforming process continues after fieldwork, until a final report is complete.

> *Data display:* The second major flow of analysis activity is **data display**. We define a "display" as an organized assembly of information that permits conclusion drawing and action taking. Looking at displays helps us to understand what is happening and to do something—further analysis or action—based on that understanding.

> *Conclusion drawing and verification:* The third stream of analytic activity is **conclusion drawing** and **verification**. From the start of data collection, the researcher is beginning to decide what things mean, noting regularities, patterns, explanations, possible configurations, causal flows, and propositions. The competent researcher holds these conclusions lightly, maintaining openness and skepticism, but the conclusions are still there, inchoate and vague at first, then increasingly explicit and grounded.

REFLECTION QUESTIONS

1. Going back to the guidelines for action research and reflective practice, how would you apply these data analysis methods in one of the models?

2. Where in a reflective practice model do you use validation and verification?

SUMMARY

In this chapter we have examined the processes that researchers have to follow, and presented a series of methods and techniques that they can use in their research efforts. In particular we have explored the different ways one can identify and initiate her or his research project, illustrated a variety of data collection methods, and provided a framework for data analysis. It is not necessary that the above processes be followed in a linear fashion; they can be interactive and researchers should feel free to engage in these processes in their own preferred way.

However, what we hope to have achieved, apart from illustrating the processes and methods involved in practitioner research, is to have motivated practitioners to engage in research and improve their practice. The practitioner-researcher image is a powerful one. It embodies a number of characteristics that reflect on the individual practitioner's capacity to be, in Stenhouse's phrase, "autonomous in professional judgment" (1984, p. 69). A major factor in this is the ability to think systematically and critically about what one is doing and to collaborate with one's colleagues within an institution, and beyond. Central to this activity is the systematic reflection on the experience of one's practice, to understand it, and to create meaning out of that understanding. By becoming self-conscious, collaborative, and critical about their practice, practitioners develop more power over their professional lives, extend their repertoire of practices, and are better able to create environments that are responsive to the most idealistic vision one could have. Although lip service is often paid to this idea, we live in a system that tends to limit individual initiative by encouraging conformity and control. We deserve better than that.

KEY TERMS

action

action research

action research models

case study

case study research

conclusion drawing and verification

critical theory

data collection

data display

data reduction

documents

field notes

focused observation

interpretation

open observation

questionnaires

saturation

structured observation

systematic observation

transcripts

triangulation

validation

validity

FURTHER READINGS AND RESOURCES

Suggested Action Research Article

Anguiano, P. (2001). A first-year teacher's plan to reduce misbehavior in the classroom. *Teaching Exceptional Children, 33*, 52–55.

Suggested Readings

Bell, J. (2005). *Doing your research project* (4th ed.). Buckingham, England: Open University Press.

This is probably one of the most accessible books on conducting research. This source is highly recommended to students and novice researchers. Topics cover how one can get started with her or his research; how to do literature reviews; the use of different methods of data collection and analysis; and how data can be reported.

Cohen, L., Manion, L., & Morrison, K. (2007). *Research methods in education* (6th ed.). London: Routledge/Falmer.

Although aimed toward specifically supporting research in educational settings, this book contains detailed and helpful advice on research methods useful to all novice and experienced practitioners in all fields. This text is now on its sixth edition and very rightly so.

Hopkins, D. (forthcoming). *A teacher's guide to classroom research* (4th ed.). Maidenhead, England: McGraw Hill/Open University Press.

This book is an excellent introduction to action research for teachers as well as practitioners in other fields who wish to improve their own and their organization's practice. This best-selling practical guide has been highly praised for its accessible language and easy-to-follow structure. It is focused on practice and contains the history and the theoretical debates on action research; practical examples; reviews different models of action research; and details methods of collecting, analyzing, and reporting data.

McNiff, J., & Whitehead, J. (2006). *All you need to know about action research.* London: Sage.

This is also an excellent introduction to action research. It is a well-written and easy-to-follow source for anyone interested in conducting action research.

Associations and Web Sites
British Educational Research Association (BERA)

www.bera.ac.uk

BERA aims to promote a vital research culture in education and maintains a number of online resources helpful to all action researchers.

Center for Action Research in Professional Practice (CARPP)

www.bath.ac.uk/carpp

CARPP is associated with Judi Marshall, Peter Reason, and Jack Whitehead at the University of Bath, United Kingdom, and maintains several sources on action research. Of particular help for any novice and experienced practitioner is Whitehead's Web page, Action Research Net (http://people.bath.ac.uk/edsajw).

Action Research—Special Interest Group #2 of American Educational Research Association

www.aera.net/Default.aspx?menu_id = 368&id = 4718

This group's goal is to involve teachers, administrators, researchers, and community members in dialogue about action research that examines educational practice and encourages educational reform and professional development.

Online Resources for Action Research across the Disciplines

www.emtech.net/actionresearch.htm

www.goshen.edu/soan/soan96p.html

CHAPTER

16

RESEARCH, POLICY, AND PRACTICE: THE GREAT DISCONNECT

DAVID C. BERLINER

KEY IDEAS

- Simple models of how research affects practice are inadequate.

- Basic research rarely informs a practitioner about what to do in concrete situations.

- Teachers' professionalism can be undermined when research is used to prescribe what teachers should do in their classrooms.

- Conceptions about what constitutes the act of teaching are relatively fixed, making it difficult to change teaching behavior.

- Changing teachers' roles often makes classroom management more difficult.

- Teachers' need for order may outweigh their need to be innovative.

- Classroom contexts are remarkably varied and complex, thus limiting generalizations from research about appropriate teacher behavior.

- Decentralized educational systems, such as those in the United States, make it easier for teaching fads to take hold.

- Treating educational research as a design science or field of engineering may be more fruitful than regarding it as basic social science research.

ONCE UPON a time, early in my career, when the world seemed quite a bit simpler than it really is, I believed that my research, and that done by my fellow educational psychologists, would influence what happens in America's classrooms and in teacher education. I believed in the model of research that famous researchers often espoused. They discussed a linear process linking **basic** (theoretical) **research** to **applied** (practical) **research**, that connected research to the improvement of practice. The model espoused made it seem that if we researchers generated the data, then the application of scientific findings to the solution of problems in the real world was inevitable.

ORIGINS OF FAITH AND APOSTASY IN RESEARCH AS A GUIDE TO PRACTICE

Many educational researchers inherited their faith in easily affecting practice from the "father" of educational psychology, Edward L. Thorndike. Upon the founding of the *Journal of Educational Psychology* in 1910, Thorndike penned an opening essay, saying:

> *A complete science of psychology would tell every fact about everyone's intellect and character and behavior, would tell the cause of every change in human nature, would tell the result which every educational force . . . would have. It would aid us to use human beings for the world's welfare with the same surety of the result that we now have when we use falling bodies or chemical elements. In proportion as we get such a science we shall become masters of our own souls as we now are masters of heat and light. Progress toward such a science is being made. (p. 6)*

Thorndike and most scientists of his day thought that the world would be made better year after year, as scientific research replaced fad, fashion, and hunch, as evidence drove out ignorance, much as Jesus drove out the moneychangers from the temple. A complete science, Thorndike thought, would dictate the nature of appropriate practice. With great assurance he predicted that in only a few short decades *all* of educations' problems would be solved through research. But Thorndike eschewed going to schools and watching how instruction actually takes place (Berliner, 2006a), thus it is no wonder that Thorndike was so very wrong.

However, Thorndike's views met with opposition, even back then, when it seemed that science would cure all of mankind's ills. There were always those who believed that a science of education or instruction could be achieved, and that it was desirable to do so, but they were less sure that such a science would strongly influence classroom instruction. For example, William James, another founder of educational psychology, in one of his most quoted yet least influential statements, said, "[Y]ou make a great, a very great mistake, if you think that psychology, being the science of the mind's laws, is something from which you can deduce definite programmes and schemes and methods of instruction for immediate school-room use. Psychology is a science, and teaching is an art;

and sciences never generate arts directly out of themselves. An intermediate inventive mind must make that application, by using its originality" (James, 1899/1983, p. 15).

James recognized that psychologists and other social scientists could not tell educators precisely what to do amid the complexity of the world that they face:

A science only lays down lines within which the rules of the art must fall, laws which the follower of the art must not transgress; but what particular thing he shall positively do within those lines is left exclusively to his own genius. . . . To know psychology, therefore, is absolutely no guarantee that we shall be good teachers. To advance that result we must have an additional endowment altogether, a happy tact and ingenuity to tell us what definite things to say and do when that pupil is before us. That ingenuity in meeting . . . the pupil, that tact for the concrete situation, . . . are things to which psychology cannot help us in the least. (James, 1899/1983, pp. 15–16)

Yet another of the early founders of the scientific tradition in education, John Dewey, noted in a major speech that those promoting a scientific approach to education needed to recognize that the teacher

lives in a social sphere—he is a member and an organ of a social life. His aims are social aims. . . . Whatever he as a teacher effectively does, he does as a person; and he does with and towards persons. His methods, like his aims, . . . are practical, are social, are ethical, are anything you please—save merely psychical. In comparison with this, the material and the data, the standpoint and the methods of psychology, are abstract. . . . I do not think there is danger of going too far in asserting the social and the teleological nature of the work of the teacher; or in asserting the abstract and partial character of the mechanism into which the psychologist . . . transmutes the play of vital values. (Dewey, 1900, p. 117)

Dewey saw that the abstract world of the researcher, and the partial characterization or simplification of the classroom that researchers necessarily create to study phenomena, along with the intensely social world that teachers inhabit, made it difficult for scientific knowledge to influence teachers' classroom practices. In that same speech, Dewey's apostasy to the simple faith about how things happen ("basic research → applied research → changed practice") was seen to be something even more profound than mere skepticism. He wondered, as well, whether it was ethical to have the educational psychologist on the one side, acting as a legislator of behavior, and the classroom teacher on the other side, following the orders from the scientist as an obedient child might. He wondered about the influential role most people wanted teachers to play in our society, and whether that could ever happen if the scientist were to dictate the behavior of teachers. "Can the teacher ever receive 'obligatory prescriptions'? Can he receive from another a statement of the means by which he is to reach his ends, and not become hopelessly servile in his attitude?" (Dewey, 1900, p. 110).

Dewey's caution of a century ago has not been heeded in the current educational climate in which our federal and state governments force certain kinds of "evidence-based" teaching practices upon teachers and demand that they comply, regardless of their professional opinions and experience. For example, in the last few years we have seen various government agencies require teachers to use the controversial program known as Reading First. Government agencies have demanded that English language learners be educated through Structured English Immersion. And governments have required high-stakes testing to improve learning. Thorndike would not have minded such authoritarian policies for teachers were the science behind these initiatives solid, which it is not. But James and Dewey would have seen problems in dictating to teachers even if the science were more solid than it is. They simply did not believe that it was possible to succeed with a system of instruction-through-fiat. Even with strong data to back up the demands for certain kinds of classroom behavior, they would have been suspicious. They saw a much greater disconnect between research and practice than did Thorndike and those who followed his simple line of reasoning. James and Dewey understood that the world of research and the world of practice were only loosely coupled, like the educational system itself.

I was once a simple thinker about these issues, firmly in Thorndike's camp. But I eventually learned that research data do not provide the surety that I believed such data possessed. I learned that practice is amazingly more complex than I first understood it to be, filled with variables not easily captured in one's research, all of which are interacting with each other simultaneously (Berliner, 2002). I learned that practitioners are, by and large, doing remarkably well in the complex world they inhabit and that the student achievement for which they are held responsible is determined by many forces that operate outside of the school (Berliner, 2006b; Berliner & Biddle, 1995). And I learned that policy and politics have more power than research to change practice—even, sometimes, for the worse (Edelman, 1988; Smith, 2004). This chapter explores my changing opinions and the reasons for them. To foreshadow the conclusion of this chapter, the Great Disconnect between research, policy, and practice may be inevitable.

REFLECTION QUESTIONS

1. How do you think research influences practice?
2. Who makes the best case above for the effects of science?

EXAMPLES OF THE PROBLEM

Consider the following examples of the relationship between research, policy, and practice.

Case 1

The capacity of a teaching method known as **reciprocal teaching** to improve reading comprehension is not in doubt. But there is also a twenty-five-year history of this well-documented method finding little or no foothold in the world of practice. Reciprocal teaching refers to an instructional activity that takes place in the form of a dialogue between teachers and students regarding segments of text. The dialogue is structured by the use of four cognitive strategies: summarizing, question generating, clarifying, and predicting. The teacher and students take turns assuming the role of teacher in leading this dialogue. The goal is to teach students how to make meaning from text. This research was first described by Palincsar (1982), elaborated on by her a few years later (1986), and also described in an influential journal article by Palincsar and Brown (1984). The work was stunning in claiming that through a relatively simple-to-learn set of procedures, over a relatively short period of time, and for not much cost, teachers and other adults could dramatically influence the comprehension of children in the middle school age range. By the mid-1990s the research community had looked closely at this remarkable work and done what scientific communities always should do: they replicated and extended the original work.

Rosenshine and Meister (1994) performed a **meta-analysis** (see Chapter Seven) of sixteen studies of reciprocal teaching that followed the original work. A meta-analysis allows the different studies to be combined so that a set of similar studies can be evaluated as a whole. When standardized tests were used to see if reciprocal teaching works as claimed, the meta-analysts found an effect size of .32. That is, the students who had the reciprocal teaching, compared to students that did not, were scoring about a third of a standard deviation higher, roughly 13 percentile ranks higher. On the tests that were made by the various researchers to assess learning, tests that were tied more to the curriculum that students had been practicing with, the effect size was .88, almost a full standard deviation higher. This translates into an advantage for the students who received training in reciprocal teaching of about 31 percentile ranks over those who did not receive such training.

In a wide variety of settings, reciprocal teaching has been found to work similarly to how it was described in the original studies. Clearly, for classroom teachers, this is a research finding with power; this technique can dramatically increase student comprehension of text among students with reading comprehension problems. But here is the conundrum: Reciprocal teaching is not used by the vast majority of teachers and, worse, has not even been heard about by the vast majority of teachers. Powerful, practical, and replicated research too often seems not to reach the classroom teacher. There is some kind of disconnect.

Case 2

I doubt if there is any better-established finding in the science of education than that which demonstrates the folly of retaining students in grade. Reading the literature in this area over many years provides strong and verifiable warrants for action by practitioners. The data reveal that if you had two similar children who were behind the same amount in what they had learned, the child who goes ahead with his or her age mates profits more than the one who stays back (Holmes & Matthews, 1984). These positive effects show up in measures of their academic achievement and their attitude toward school. The research suggests that there is a much more successful policy than retaining the child in grade, but unfortunately it often goes by the name of "social promotion." This policy has many negative connotations associated with it, making it sound as if low achieving students were being promoted for just showing up in school.

Nevertheless, negative connotations or not, the data strongly suggest that for a child not keeping up with his or her classmates the proper course of action in almost every case is that the child should be promoted to the next grade along with his age mates, *and* extra resources should be allocated to help the struggling child (that is, tutoring, after-school programs, counseling, and so on). The data set supporting this recommendation to practitioners, administrators, school boards and teachers is large, and highly (though not perfectly) consistent (Brophy, 2002; Shepard & Smith, 1989; Smith & Shepard, 1988). Furthermore, it is now well established that the odds of dropping out of school go up considerably if a child is retained in grade once, and they rise much higher if retained in grade more than once (Brophy, 2002). But to the scientific community's complete dismay, two recent presidents, Congress, and state legislatures across the country have endorsed polices that will result in about 10 percent of public school students age sixteen through nineteen being left back at least once in their K–12 years (National Center for Educational Statistics, 2006). Research informs us that this was the wrong decision for almost all of the five million American students retained in grade, over one-third of whom have already dropped out of school! Even more ironic, George W. Bush, with the bipartisan support of most members of Congress, signed in 2002 an educational bill that mentions scientific educational research and evidence-based decisions in education at least a hundred times. And with no hint of hypocrisy, that same bill has been used to advocate against promotion for students who are behind in their work, with the legislation used to point out the preferability of retention in grade. Because of this bill we can expect that the *wrong* decisions about retention will be made hundreds of thousands of times per year. So we have policy and practice ignoring research, harming most of the children who are retained and their families, increasing the American dropout rate, and affecting the poor, minorities, and males at many times the rate of white or female students. There is obviously a disconnect between research, policy, and practice here as well.

Case 3

Homework debates rage regularly in the United States and Canada. Is homework, in general, good for students? If you give homework, how much might be recommended at particular ages? Should homework require parental support? Although the debates occur at school board meetings and among parents and teachers, these debates are not usually informed by a remarkable set of studies that help us to reach some very reasonable conclusions. Harris Cooper (2007) has studied research on homework for a number of years. His advice is authoritative and often unheeded. Literally, he has reviewed hundreds of studies, and with these he conducted a meta-analysis on those that met minimum standards of quality. Cooper's recommendations have been adopted by the National Parent Teacher Association and the National Education Association and resulted in similar research and policy guidance in Canada (Rushowy, 2008). Cooper found that homework seems to have little positive effects on achievement much before junior high and only seems genuinely beneficial at the high school level. The recommendation is that homework for children in grades K–2, *were it wanted*, should not exceed 10–20 minutes each day. Older children, in grades 3–6, seem able to handle up to 30–60 minutes a day total, *were that wanted*. Although there are reasons to assign homework, such as developing habits of home study and responsibility for one's own work, the effects of those homework assignments on achievement for students in the

K–6 grades are likely to be undetectable! Cooper has noted often that if politicians, educators, and parents expect homework for young children to result in big gains in test scores, they will be disappointed. In fact, Cooper notes that too much time spent in homework can lead to boredom with schoolwork, as most activities remain interesting to most people only for so long. And homework can prevent access by our youth to leisure activities or community service that also teach important life skills. Furthermore, parents can find themselves getting too involved in homework, and while doing so they can confuse children by using different instructional techniques from the teacher.

Such writers as Alfie Kohn (2006) would go further than Cooper, persuasively arguing for a ban on most homework. But neither Cooper nor Kohn is listened to by politicians and administrators, particularly those fighting to have test scores rise in schools that are failing under the **No Child Left Behind Act**, a United States law requiring all children to pass standardized exams. Research does not matter. Opinion is much more powerful. I once gave some "facts" about a particular educational issue to a politician, demonstrating, quite convincingly I thought, that he had the wrong approach to the issue. He responded to me by saying "David, don't you know that facts are negotiable, but perceptions are rock solid!" So in the case of homework, when unwarranted and unjustified perceptions, opinions, or beliefs are combined with a mild kind of sadistic, punishment mentality that is held by many older citizens toward our youth, inappropriate policies are the predictable result.

Case 4

The eminent researcher David Cohen (1990) studied a mathematics teacher who said with excitement that research changed her ways of thinking about mathematics and her classroom practice. Mrs. Oublier noted how innovative her class was compared to when she began her teaching—her kids were more comfortable, her teaching was more flexible, group work was exciting, and she now taught for understanding—all the result of professional development associated with California's "new mathematics" curriculum. Here, at last, was success of the simple research-to-practice model described by so many. But on deeper analysis all was not so simple.

When Cohen observed her class, there certainly was evidence that children were working in groups. There were mathematics materials in use, as suggested by research, and these concrete manifestations of mathematical ideas and principles were incorporated into the lessons. But when he observed Mrs. O's class over a lengthy period of time, Cohen found something quite different from what Mrs. Oublier thought was happening. He says:

> [S]he filled the new social reorganization of discourse with old discourse processes. The new organization opened up lots of new opportunities for small group work, but she organized the discourse in ways that effectively blocked realization of those opportunities. (p. 321)
>
> [Although her] class was spatially and socially organized for . . . cooperative learn-ing, [the] class was conducted in a highly structured and classically teacher-centered fashion. The chief instructional group was the whole class. The discourse . . . consisted either of dyadic exchanges between the teacher and one student or of whole-group

activities, many of which involved choral responses to teacher questions. No student ever spoke to another about mathematical ideas as a part of the public discourse. Nor were conversations between students ever encouraged by the teacher. Indeed, Mrs. O specifically discouraged students from speaking with each other, in her efforts to keep the class orderly and quiet. (p. 320)

[D]iscourse in Mrs. O's class tended to discourage students from reflecting on mathematical ideas, or from sharing puzzles with the class. There are few opportunities for students to initiate discussion, explore ideas or even ask questions. Their attention was focused instead on successfully managing a prescribed, highly structured set of activities.... Even if the students' minds were... privately full of bright ideas and puzzling mathematical problems, the discourse organization effectively barred them from the public arena of the class. (p. 322)

Cohen noted that we should not be too harsh on Mrs. O. She and others who try to adopt research to their classrooms, to change how they think and act, are really special beings, but they "cannot simply shed their old ideas and practices, like a shabby coat, and slip on something new. Their inherited ideas and practices are what teachers and students know, even as they begin to know something else.... [A]s they reach out to embrace or invent a new instruction, they reach with their old professional selves, including all the ideas and practices comprised therein. The past is their path to the future. Some sort of mixed practice, and many confusions, therefore seem inevitable" (p. 323).

The findings of the historian Larry Cuban (1993, 2007) make this same point: *Plus ça change, plus c'est la même chose* (the more things change, the more they stay the same). Cuban noted that constancy, not change, has been the discernable pattern when studying teachers over a hundred years. He likens classrooms to the bottom of the sea during a storm. The surface of the sea may be all roiled up with foam and froth in the midst of storm after storm, but just a few feet down, the bottom of the sea is calm, rarely changing very much, however long the storm blows. Teachers seem much the same, as research and policy roil the surface. Life in classrooms appears to be remarkably stable, as illustrated by the four cases described above.

 REFLECTION QUESTIONS

1. Which of the research findings above do you find the hardest to believe and why?
2. Are any of the findings a good match with your own beliefs?

WHY THE DISCONNECT?

There appear to be many reasons for the disconnect between research and practice. A brief look at some of these follows.

The Privacy Problem

Cohen and Spillane (1992) wondered why U.S. teachers are not as easily guided to new forms of practice as teachers in some other countries. They note that, "The classroom doors behind which teachers labor are no thicker here than elsewhere, but teachers in the United States receive fewer strong and consistent messages about content and pedagogy. Hence, they and their students have found it relatively easy to pursue their own preferences once the doors have closed behind them" (p. 23).

Thus, the privacy of American teaching, once described as the second most private act adults engage in with another, affords teachers the luxury of doing what they do in the ways they always have. It is always difficult to get people to change, as any psychotherapist will attest. And when left alone, as teachers often are, their need to change is not particularly urgent if they think they are doing pretty well, doing things the way they always have done with their students.

The Changed Roles Problem

Cohen and Spillane (1992) also note that most of the current reform efforts, with origins in modern **constructivist theories** of learning, ask teachers and their students to make dramatic, not small, changes in the roles that they play. This too could explain why such reforms leave classroom life relatively unchanged. Cohen and Spillane, citing numerous examples, say:

> *Even if teachers knew all that they needed, the reforms propose that students become active, engaged, and collaborative. If so, classroom roles would have to change radically. Teachers would have to rely on students to produce much more instruction, and students would have to think and act in ways they rarely do. Teachers would have to become coaches or conductors and abandon more familiar and didactic roles in which they "tell knowledge" to students. Researchers have studied only a few efforts at such change, but they report unusual difficulty, for teachers must manage very complex interactions about very complex ideas in rapid-fire fashion. The uncertainties of teaching multiply phenomenally, as does teachers' vulnerability. (pp. 30–31)*

REFLECTION QUESTION

1. How would you argue that "privacy" and "changed roles" explain the disconnect between research and practice?

The Problem of Complexity in Classrooms and Other Social Settings

Lee J. Cronbach, with whom I was lucky enough to work, eventually decided that social science research (and the educational and psychological research that was a part of social science research) was extremely hard to do well. He realized that in doing such research many variables, some knowable and controllable, many neither knowable nor controllable, simultaneously interact. The complexity of these interactions makes solid scientific generalizations from the social sciences, across time and across settings, hard to come by. This suggests, as well, that research guides for practice must be very tentative. Science simply cannot deal with all the complexities of practice occurring in different locales and across different decades. Cronbach (1975) says:

Our troubles do not arise because human events are in principle unlawful; man and his creations are part of the natural world. The trouble, as I see it, is that we cannot store up generalizations and constructs for ultimate assembly into a network. (p. 123, emphasis in original)

Instead of making generalization the ruling consideration of our research, I suggest that we reverse our priorities. An observer collecting data in one particular situation is in a position to appraise a practice or proposition in that setting, observing effects in context. In trying to describe and account for what happened, he will give attention to whatever variables were controlled, but he will give equally careful attention to uncontrolled conditions, to personal characteristics, and to events that occurred during treatment and measurement. As he goes from situation to situation, his first task is to describe and interpret the effect anew in each locale, perhaps taking into account factors unique to that locale or series of events. (pp. 124–125)

Intensive local observation goes beyond discipline to an open-eyed, open-minded appreciation of the surprises nature deposits in the investigative net. This kind of interpretation is historical more than scientific. (p. 125)

The special task of the social scientist in each generation is to pin down the contemporary facts. Beyond that he shares with the humanistic scholar and the artist in the effort to gain insight into contemporary relationships, and to align the culture's view of man with present realities. To know man as he is is no mean aspiration. (p. 126)

This extensive quotation from a measurement specialist, often thought of as one of the most hard-nosed scientists of the twentieth century, argues a number of points. First, that education is complex, and therefore variables are interacting in ways we cannot really understand. Second, that observation and making sense of local conditions by sympathetic observers is probably better feedback for practitioners than is reference to a traditional research finding in an educational research journal. Finally, that it is no small achievement to understand practitioners in the contexts in which they work, be they teachers or air traffic controllers.

It was the complexity of educational settings that made Cronbach a nonbeliever in the simple research-to-practice model that existed in the early and middle of the twentieth century. And by the end of that century it was understood that the complexity of the tasks teachers faced produced severe limits on what researchers might ever say to practitioners that would improve their instruction.

REFLECTION QUESTION

1. What makes teaching and classrooms so complex?

The Problem of Science When It Delves into the Arts

As Cronbach noted, the social scientist has much in common with the artist and humanistic scholar—perhaps, Cronbach might opine, even more than they do with the physical scientist. Elliot Eisner always took this view as well. Like Dewey, Eisner worried about the democratic element: Can teachers ever act like origins if they are treated like pawns? But he also thought of teaching as much more of an art than a science. Using the arts to think about the jobs that teachers do, Eisner said (1983): "Teachers are more like orchestra conductors than technicians. They need rules of thumb and educational imagination, not scientific prescriptions" (p. 5). Perhaps this misunderstanding about art and science as articulated by Cronbach and Eisner provides another reason that prescriptions about instruction derived from educational research are so often ignored by practitioners.

Eisner, with his colleague, Tom Barone, helped to develop and promote arts-based education (Barone & Eisner, 2006). They try through the arts to capture more of the aesthetic qualities that characterize classrooms and to tell the stories of their research through media other than the traditional journal article, using theater, story, dance, and drawing instead. Arts-based research in classrooms and other educational settings has, like qualitative research in general, a kind of authenticity about it. Similar to qualitative research, arts-based research focuses on the particular, rather than the general; thus, arts-based research sometimes appears to the practitioner to have more legitimacy than they are willing to credit to traditional quantitative social science research. Although not as widely used as other qualitative forms of inquiry, practitioners often perceive this kind of research as having fidelity, and so arts-based research may have a slightly better chance to influence classroom life than traditional quantitative research.

REFLECTION QUESTION

1. When you think of teachers, can you think of other metaphors in addition to the conductor?

The Problem of Quality in Research

Mary Kennedy (1997) has been one of the most thoughtful writers about the great disconnect. She gives many reasons for that state of affairs, one of which is the problem of quality in research. She notes that researchers have a habit of criticizing each other's work, arguing in particular over the proper or the improper design of studies and methods of statistical analysis. The famous Campbell and Stanley chapter on research design in 1963 argued that there were "true" experiments, and thus for the practice community, everything else, which were the majority of the inquiries in education, must be interpreted as less than "true" experiments: untrustworthy either as research or as guides to practice. Campbell and Stanley (1963) saw the experiment as "the only means for settling disputes regarding educational practice, as the only way of verifying educational improvements, and as the only way of establishing a cumulative tradition in which improvements can be introduced without the danger of a faddish discard of old wisdom in favor of inferior novelties" (p. 2).

Campbell and Stanley elaborated on the many threats to the validity of studies, and the problems with the generalizability of studies across ecological settings, making it appear to those outside the research field that the quality of most educational research is poor. The internal arguments by statisticians and other scholars over methodology then become an excuse for ignoring educational research—or perhaps because of the squabbling, ignoring research appears to be a reasonable response to such ambiguity about quality. The internal squabbles in the field seem to make the research insufficiently persuasive or authoritative to the practitioner, despite the fact that arguing over methodology is precisely what one would expect of an active scientific community. I know of no scientific field of inquiry that is complacent about its methods of inquiry and satisfied with the quality of its research. To argue about such things is to do science. Such arguments should never be an excuse to ignore the current research that a science has to offer.

The Problem of Relevance

Mary Kennedy (1997) points out that it really was not until Philip Jackson's important book *Life in Classrooms* (1968) that the focus of educational psychologists began to switch to studying real teachers in their real world. Learning researchers understood that instructional psychology, which was booming by the mid-1980s, was about human learning in educational contexts, and that was a far cry from the earlier laboratory studies of learning with animal subjects. Instructional psychology not only held more promise to influence practice, but the applied research was influencing basic understandings about learning (Resnick, 1981). The simple model of basic research leading to applied research that might affect practice switched direction, with applied research in school contexts beginning to influence basic ideas about human learning.

Toward the end of the twentieth century, learning in real-world contexts began to be studied more earnestly (Greeno, Collins, & Resnick, 1996), but sadly, such research still appears not to be affecting practice very much. The relevance of the insights by psychologists or other researchers still seems to miss the mark. Changes in practice attributable to research are hard to document, even though educational researchers are now more than ever wedded to conducting their studies in real-world contexts, and using more qualitative than quantitative methods. Because of changes in where and how research is done, perhaps, over time, the problem of relevance will be overcome. But I doubt it.

As Kennedy notes, in many classes the need for order is highest on the list of teacher needs, as teachers usually face twenty-five or more students at a time. Furthermore, in many of those same classes the students would prefer to be elsewhere, doing little of the teacher's assigned work, which many students see as dreary and unconnected to their lives. Thus classroom life is about managing a good deal of uncertainty, and that is not fertile ground for implementing research-based practices. Some of the research produced by scholars in education can adequately, if not poignantly, describe the complexity and uncertainty that characterize classroom life (for example, Doyle, 1986; Jackson, 1968), but describing classrooms better, as the researchers have learned to do, is far different from actually influencing practice in those classrooms.

REFLECTION QUESTION

1. Why might you trust or mistrust research describing classrooms?

The Problem of Accessibility to Ideas by Practitioners

Kennedy (1997) notes that accessibility has been the most common belief about why research does not influence practice. But there is now a long history of trying to ensure that research be accessible to practitioners, and it still seems not to affect classroom life very much. For example, in the 1960s the U.S. federal government created research and development (R&D) laboratories and charged them with disseminating research, a model like that used to improve agriculture. Many of these R&D centers have been working on school improvement for forty years by publishing pamphlets and policy briefs, providing professional development, and holding conferences about educational research that could make a difference in classrooms. These regional centers for dissemination of research have been augmented by the federal government's promotion and funding of technical assistant centers (TACs), so that even more personnel can provide the expertise needed to change practice in desired ways. The R&D laboratories and TACs, as well as a huge (multimillion-dollar) professional development industry, are designed to play the role that William James thought was necessary, namely, the development of intermediate inventive minds to stand between the basic researchers and those in practice. But the R&D laboratories and TACs still do not have great effects on practice. The complexity of life in classrooms pushes back against the ideas and technologies put forward by researchers and their spokespersons about what might improve practice.

It appears not to be true that a lack of accessibility to research is a major reason given when explaining the big disconnect between research and practice. All the work done by R&D laboratories, TACs, and through university courses and the providers of professional development, has apparently increased *knowledge* about research more than it has changed practice. Recent research revealed, surprisingly, that educational research is better known by school principals in both Australia and the United States than was heretofore appreciated (Biddle & Saha, 2002). But *knowing about* and *implementing* research are quite different processes. Although many school leaders knew about cooperative learning and a dozen other innovative teaching practices, such knowledge seems not to lead to implementation of those findings systematically in classrooms.

The Problems of Stability and Instability in the Education System

Kennedy (1997) also notes that the problem of research failing to influence practice much may not be the fault of the research community but the fault of the practice community. The remarkable stability of classroom life has been documented by Cuban (1993, 2007). Part of this is attributable to the long apprenticeship of observation (Lortie, 1975) that teachers undergo. Unlike other professions, teachers spend at least twelve years observing how teaching takes place, and so it should not be surprising that their norms for teacher behavior are rather entrenched, and thus hard to change.

It is also true that teachers depend on students for their jobs as well as for their emotional fulfillment. By changing their teaching behavior, by adding uncertainty into classroom life, teachers endanger the relationship with students that is based on order and certainty. Ramping up the requirements for performance, for example, something urged by politicians and parents all the time, means that some students may become management problems, and classroom control will be lost. Spending more time in test preparation means that students become bored more quickly in school and thus become behavior problems. Teachers need to negotiate these tensions. Some comfortable balance is needed between teacher behavior and student acquiescence to teacher authority, and that kind of need may produce remarkable stability in classroom life: a desire for stability that is almost impermeable to change.

Kennedy notes, however, that from another viewpoint, it is the excessive instability of classrooms that works against changes of the type we are interested in effecting. The lack of centralization of the U.S. educational enterprise, with fifty different states and about fifteen thousand local educational systems, makes political influence at the local level nearly impossible. This can be seen in the relatively wide variety of textbooks in use, all with different philosophies behind them. Math can be taught in some places using a variety of everyday problems, taught in other places with strong reliance on materials, and in still other places as memory and drill oriented.

The decentralization of the American educational system, and the constant yearning for magic bullets that will fix what is perceived to ail schools in different locales, also result in excessive fads in schools, adding to the instability of the system. Thus educational systems see Madeline Hunter's techniques for conducting lessons come and go; or they see discovery learning come and go; or they try cooperative learning one year but abandon it the next; or homework is increased under one superintendent and cut by another; and so forth. (Also see the case of Ms. Oublier discussed earlier.) As Kennedy notes:

> So we have a system that can be characterized by a lack of agreed-on goals, a lack of shared guiding principles, no central authority to settle disputes, decentralized decision-making, a continual stream of new fads and fancies, limited evidence to support or refute any particular idea, textbooks that manage conflicts by including all possible ideas and giving no serious attention to any of them, and reforms that are running at cross-purposes to each other.
>
> These two views of the education system as large, cumbersome, and unchanging on the one hand, and as disorganized and driven by fads on the other, are not incompatible. Most [educational] fads and fancies are more observable in rhetoric than in practice . . . and those that do influence practice tend to alter its more superficial features rather than altering the fundamental character of teaching and learning. (Kennedy, 1997, p. 8)

REFLECTION QUESTION

1. What would be the effects of making all schools uniform and centralized?

The difficulty of getting research to affect practice, the great disconnect that is the subject of this chapter, is related to a host of problems that contribute to the bad reputation of educational research (Kaestle, 1993; Lagemann, 2000). The difficulties inherent in the educational system include the privacy of teaching, so that changes in practice need not be attempted, if the changes are not of sufficient interest to the teachers. Change also appears to be hard when there is the need, as there sometimes is, for dramatic alterations in role enactment for teachers and students. The problem of the complexity of classroom life also becomes a barrier for the researcher whose relatively simple social science methods may not be able to capture the complexity of school life. These problems are compounded by the fact that some of teaching is surely much more of an art than a science, and the ways of perceiving and knowing in these two traditions are quite different.

Complexity of classroom life and the methodological debates of researchers as they try to deal with such complexity often result in practitioners' negative perceptions of the quality of the research that is being produced. The perceived relevance of the research to practitioners, along with its presumed inaccessibility, adds to the list of problems that work against research influencing practice often, or to a significant degree. And finally, the twin factors of excessive stability and excessive instability in parts of the educational system work against research having much effect on practice. There is, however, evidence that research has an effect on practitioner discussions of practice (for example, Biddle & Saha, 2002), but stability rather than change continues to characterize life in classrooms.

It is important to note that the United States is not alone in its problems regarding research's influence on practitioner life. Pessimistic views about the influence of research on practice are echoed across the Atlantic by two of Europe's leading educational scholars (Weinert & De Corte, 1996). They say: "After 100 years of systematic research in the fields of education and educational psychology, there is, in the early 1990s, still no agreement about whether, how, and under what conditions research can improve educational practice. Although research and educational practice have changed substantially since the beginning of the twentieth century, the question of how science can actually contribute to the solution of real educational problems continues to be controversial" (p. 249).

In part, I think the entrenched stability of teaching is due to the nature of teacher reasoning in classrooms. It is becoming apparent that practitioners do not often use the formal methods of scientific reasoning and proof to make sense of their world. It is, instead, the method of practical argument that is used, a much more contextualized and pragmatic form of reasoning that may not be "scientific" but is highly functional for survival and success amid the complexity that was noted earlier. This is the case argued by Fenstermacher and Richardson (1993, 1994), and it is worth considering this as a major reason for the practice community's imperviousness to what is offered by the research community.

HOW MIGHT THINGS CHANGE?

Although there are many reasons for pessimism, there are still ways to think about research and practice that might change these disconnected worlds. First to be recommended is the research method called "design experiment" (Schoenfeld, 2006). **Design experiments** are more like the kind of tinkering an inventor does than they are like either applied or basic research. They are an inquiry into how things can be manipulated or how they get done in live classrooms, within their real-world complexity. Edison and

Ford are more the models for the design experiment than are Einstein or Pasteur. The goal is to make ideas that *might* be good, that *might* work, actually work in the midst of the booming, buzzing world that characterizes life in schools. Design experiments require extensive time in classrooms observing and tinkering to find the solutions, say, to getting reciprocal teaching into classroom life.

One other form of research that might change practice is called teacher research or **action research** (Cochran-Smith & Donnell, 2006; see Chapter Fifteen). This is where teachers engage in inquiry at a local level to change existing practices that are problematic, or to start a program they think might work and monitor its effects at the local level. The design experiment and teacher research are research methods that hold promise for thinking that, one day, research and practice can be better connected. But I am not sure that is likely!

Research may be classified along two dimensions (Stokes, 1997): Whether it is primarily a quest for new, basic knowledge, or whether it is primarily a quest for knowledge that is useful. Although it is not always easy to categorize the intentions of the research or the researcher, this simple analysis can provide a two-by-two matrix for analyzing research goals (see Table 16.1).

Three cells are of interest. The **pure research** cell, where there is only the quest for knowledge and no concern for usefulness, is where theoretical physics or astronomy would be located. This is where almost all the animal studies of learning would be classified as well as the thousands of studies published in educational research journals that examine basic processes of learning and instruction in classrooms, laboratories, and child-care centers, and on computers. These studies are typically not intended to be immediately useful to classroom teachers.

Pasteur's quadrant is different. In this quadrant the goal of the researcher is a conscious attempt to be useful while also developing scientific knowledge of the kind that is generalizable, contributing to the discipline in which the work is done. Named after the great scientist Louis Pasteur, whose work on the development of vaccinations and the germ theory (usefulness) also revolutionized basic research in microbiology (creation of generalizations in the field of biology). The now common process of pasteurization is the outcome of some of this scientist's work. Educational research, such as that surrounding reciprocal teaching, is often of this same type. Reciprocal teaching was a search for a useful technique to help students in the middle grades who had comprehension difficulties, *and* the research contributed to an understanding of text

TABLE 16.1. **Types of Research Goals**

| | | **Is This an Inquiry Primarily About Usefulness?** | |
		No	Yes
Is This a Quest Primarily to Generate New Knowledge?	Yes	*Pure research.* Albert Einstein, Nils Bohr, for example.	*Pasteur's quadrant.* Use inspired basic research.
	No	*[Empty cell]*	*Edison's quadrant.* Invention more than science.

comprehension processes through scaffolding, a contribution to basic scientific knowledge, as well. The work on homework and retention in grade, described earlier, can also be classified most easily in Pasteur's quadrant. This is because it is policy research, designed certainly to be useful, but designed as well to illuminate public policies. Policies are created out of the values and beliefs about how people and governments ought to act, and those beliefs are often widely held or they could not be easily enacted. Thus policies function for individuals or nations in a way similar to the function of scientific theories in the physical and behavioral sciences. Policy research, therefore, is intended to be useful *and* often to be **generalizable**, to affect the ways people frame certain issues that are of wide public interest.

The cell that is called **Edison's quadrant** describes research that is not intended to be generalizable at all. It is about the invention or tryout of ways to do things that seem desirable. Thomas Edison, Henry Ford, the Wright brothers, Steve Jobs, and the founders of Google made few contributions to science, but they took scientific ideas and from them they made things that work. They tinkered and they carefully studied the effects of that tinkering. They made knowledge that already existed into something useful. This is where I would classify much of the research called design experiments, and where I would classify much of the research called teacher research. Design research and teacher research are often attempts to engage in useful forms of scholarship, often of the particular, rarely with a concern for the generalizable, though that need not be excluded. But this is an engineering style of research and development. It is certainly not anti-science, but it is much more about using the principles of science to make things work. Bridges and churches were built long before engineers understood the properties of building materials and the geologic formations in which those structures were built. Masons, architects, and engineers tinkered and modeled, and they did trial runs until they could build the structures they wanted, long before the researchers could explain why some structures were better than others.

It is the tinkering by teachers and researchers, and the study of their craft by the teachers themselves, that seems to me the most likely to pay off in improved education. If those in the research community can learn to do more design experiments in real-world settings, and join teacher-researchers to produce knowledge about how things work in real-world classrooms, the great disconnect might become a much smaller disconnect. Educational research would end up being less a field of traditional scientific research, and much more a field of engineering, invention, and design. It might be that concentrating on working in Edison's quadrant instead of Pasteur's can provide education with bigger payoffs. The teachers of Alberta, Canada, for example, engaged in a massive province-wide effort to conduct their own research and they have done so with amazingly positive results (Alberta Initiative for School Improvement, n.d.). They picked their problems based on local needs. They learned to think a bit more systematically about those problems than they might ordinarily have done in order to write proposals to obtain funding by the province. They conducted their own research and evaluations of the programs they designed. Their engineering and tinkering were remarkably successful (Alberta Initiative for School Improvement, n.d.).

I think educational research might gain a better reputation if it could help those working in Pasteur's quadrant, and in the more basic areas of research, to apply their scientific findings to classroom life through a corps of engineers and inventors. These individuals would act as the intermediate inventive minds that William James predicted over a hundred years ago that we would need to bridge the gap between research and practice. But note what is important in this view of the great or little disconnect between research and practice: it still champions more and better research of the kind that is both basic and use oriented.

My views of what might be needed to better connect research and practice are not a plea to stop funding other forms of research, as tinkering, innovation, design, and the profession of engineering require well-warranted scientific knowledge as an underpinning. Design experiments and teacher research need to be supported for their ecological fit as much as we need to support research of a more traditional kind for its generative power. In the end, we want knowledge of three kinds—knowledge for its own sake, knowledge for its usefulness, and knowledge about how to make things work well in the settings we want to improve.

REFLECTION QUESTIONS

1. How do design experiments work?
2. What examples can you think of using this approach?
3. How would you explain action research in your own words?

SUMMARY

Educational science began just over a hundred years ago with great hopes that basic research on learning and instruction would improve teaching and student achievement. For some individual teachers and schools, educational research has made a difference in what has been accomplished. But for most of these years there has been a disconnect between the research and practice communities. A number of case studies demonstrate that the abstract and simplified research from educational scientists does not easily cross over to the concrete and complex world of practice. Thus, constancy in education is the norm.

Among the reasons that educational practitioners do not use educational research is the fact that teaching is often a private activity. With few observers of teachers actually in the act of teaching,

there is little pressure for teachers to engage in the changes recommended by research. In addition, changing teacher behavior based on research findings may add uncertainty to classroom life, and that is uncomfortable for both teachers and students, particularly as teachers have a strong need to keep order. And the complexity of life in classrooms means that educational research may only be able to provide practitioners rules of thumb—not rules of practice. The assumption that classrooms might run better if we had a prescriptive science may simply be wrong. Other talents for successful management of classrooms may be needed. This suggests that qualitative and arts-based research, rather than quantitative basic research, may be more compatible with the realities of life in classrooms than the majority of the research community now believes to be true.

Educational research also suffers from a public relations problem. Its quality is not perceived to be high, and it seems to be inaccessible to practitioners. But closer examination suggests that neither of these beliefs is true. It is true, however, that there is a tendency toward excessive stability in some parts of the educational system and excessive instability in other parts of the educational system. These two characteristics make it difficult to move research into practice. It may be possible for the current unhappy situation to change only if educational research becomes more like the fields of design or engineering, that is, solving local problems by engaging in action research or design experiments to make educational environments function the best they can. Ultimately three kinds of research are needed to improve practice: research that is basic, unrelated to need; research that is applied, oriented toward usefulness; and research about how to make things actually work in the settings we want to improve. The latter form of research requires engineering of the first order. Were more of such research to be done, the great disconnect between research and practice might be substantially reduced.

KEY TERMS

action research
applied research
basic research
constructivist theories
design experiments
Edison's quadrant
generalizable

meta-analysis
No Child Left Behind Act
Pasteur's quadrant
policy research
pure research
reciprocal teaching

REFERENCES

Adair, J. G. (2001). Ethics of psychological research new policies: Continuing issues; new concerns. *Canadian Psychology*, *42*, 25–37.

Agar, M. (1980). *The professional stranger: An informal introduction to ethnography.* New York: Academic Press.

Alberta Initiative for School Improvement (AISI). (n.d.). Home page. Retrieved January 30, 2008, from http://education.alberta.ca/admin/aisi.aspx.

American Anthropological Association. (1998). Code of ethics of the American Anthropological Association. Retrieved September 30, 2007, from www.aaanet.org/committees/ethics/ethcode.htm.

American Educational Research Association. (2000). *Ethical standards of the AERA.* Retrieved September 30, 2007, from www.aera.net/uploadedFiles/About_AERA/Ethical_Standards/EthicalStandards.pdf.

American Evaluation Association. (2003). *Guiding principles for evaluators.* Retrieved December 17, 2007, from www.eval.org/Publications/GuidingPrinciples.asp.

American Psychiatric Association. (2000). *Diagnostic and statistical manual of mental disorders: Text revision* (4th ed.). Washington, DC: American Psychiatric Association.

American Psychological Association. (2002). *The ethical principles of psychologists and code of conduct. American Psychologist*, *57*, 1060–1073. Retrieved October 13, 2007, from www.apa.org/ethics/code2002.html.

American Psychological Association. (2006). Evidence-based practice in psychology. *American Psychologist*, *61*, 271–285.

Anastasi, A., & Urbina, S. (1997). *Psychological testing* (7th ed.). Upper Saddle River, NJ: Prentice Hall.

Andrews, R., & Harlen, W. (2006). Issues in synthesizing research in education. *Educational Research*, *18*, 287–299.

Armfield, S.W.J. (2007). *A descriptive case study of teaching and learning in an innovative middle school program.* Unpublished doctoral dissertation, Northern Arizona University, Flagstaff, Arizona.

Asad, T. (1973). *Anthropology and the colonial encounter.* New York: Humanities Press.

Babbie, E. (2001). *The practice of social research* (9th ed.). Belmont, CA: Wadsworth.

Bangert-Drowns, R. L., & Rudner, L. M. (1991). Meta-analysis in educational research. *Practical Assessment, Research & Evaluation*, *2*(8). Retrieved March 14, 2008, from http://PAREonline.net/getvn.asp?v = 2&n = 8.

Barone, T., & Eisner, E. (2006). Arts-based educational research. In J. L. Green, G. Camilli, & P. B. Elmore (Eds.), *Handbook of complementary methods in education research* (pp. 95–109). Mahwah, NJ: Erlbaum.

Baumrind, D. (1964). Some thoughts on ethics of research: After reading Milgram's "Behavioral Study of Obedience." *American Psychologist*, *19*, 421–423.

Becker, H. (1958). Problems of inference and proof in participant observation. *American Sociological Review*, *23*, 652–60.

Becker, H. S., Greer, B., Hughes, E. C., & Strauss, A. L. (1961). *Boys in white: Student culture in medical school.* Chicago: University of Chicago Press.

Becker, H. S., Greer, B., Hughes, E. C., & Strauss, A. L. (1992). *Boys in white: Student culture in medical school.* New Brunswick, NJ: Transaction Publishers.

Behar, R. (2003). *Translated woman: Crossing the border with Esperanza's story* (10th ed.). Boston: Beacon.

Benjamin, J. R. (2007). *A student's guide to history.* Boston: Bedford/St. Martin's.

Berends, M. (2006). Survey research methods in educational research. In J. Green, G. Camilli, & P. Elmore (Eds.), *Handbook of complementary methods for research in education* (pp. 521–538). Mahwah, NJ: Erlbaum.

Bergin, A. E. (1962). The effect of dissonant persuasive communication upon changes in a self-referring attitude. *Journal of Personality*, *30*, 423–438.

Berliner, D. C. (2002). Educational research: The hardest science of them all. *Educational Researcher*, *31*(8), 18–20.

Berliner, D. C. (2006a). Educational psychology: Searching for essence throughout a century of influence. In P. Alexander & P. Winne (Eds.), *Handbook of educational psychology* (2nd ed., pp. 3–27). Mahwah, NJ: Erlbaum.

Berliner, D. C. (2006b). Our impoverished view of educational reform. *Teachers College Record*, *108*, 949–995.

316 References

Berliner, D. C., & Biddle, B. J. (1995). *The manufactured crisis.* New York: Addison-Wesley.

Berri, D. J., Schmidt, M. B., & Brook, S. L. (2006). *The wages of wins: Taking measure of the many myths in modern sport.* Stanford, CA: Stanford University Press.

Biddle, B. J., & Saha, L. J. (2002). *The untested accusation: Principals, research knowledge, and policy making in schools.* Westport, CT: Ablex.

Bleier, R. (1986). *Feminist approaches to science.* New York: Pergamon Press.

Bollington, R., & Bradley, H. (1990). *Training for appraisal: A set of distance learning materials.* Cambridge, England: University of Cambridge Institute of Education.

Borge, C. (2007). *Basic instincts: The science of evil.* Retrieved September 30, 2007, from http://abcnews.go.com/Primetime/Story?id = 2765416&page = 1.

Bourgois, P. I. (1995). *In search of respect: Selling crack in El Barrio.* Cambridge, England: Cambridge University Press.

Broad, W. J. (1982). Harvard delays in reporting fraud. *Science, 215,* 478–482.

Bröder, A. (1998). Deception can be acceptable. *American Psychologist, 53,* 805–806.

Brophy, J. (2002). Social promotion. In J. Guthrie (Ed.), *Encyclopedia of education* (2nd ed., Vol. *6*, pp. 2262–2265). New York: Macmillan.

Bruner, E.M.M. (2004). *Culture on tour: Ethnographies of travel.* Chicago: University of Chicago Press.

Bryman, A. (2006). Integrating quantitative and qualitative research: How is it done? *Qualitative Research, 6,* 97–113.

Campbell, D. T., & Fiske, D. W. (1959). Convergent and discriminant validation by the multitrait-multimethod matrix. *Psychological Bulletin, 56,* 81–105.

Campbell, D. T., & Stanley, J. C. (1963). Experimental and quasi-experimental designs for research on teaching. In N. L. Gage (Ed.), *Handbook of research on teaching* (pp. 171–246). Chicago: Rand McNally.

Campbell, D., Sanderson, R. E., & Laverty, S. G. (1964). Characteristics of a conditioned response in human subjects during extinction trials following a single traumatic conditioning trial. *Journal of Abnormal and Social Psychology, 68,* 627–639.

Carlini-Marlatt, B. (2005, December). Grandparents in custodial care of their grandchildren: A literature review. Report for Mentor UK Foundation, London. Retrieved March 14, 2008, from www.mentorfoundation.org/uploads/UK_Grandparents_Lit_Review.pdf.

Carson, R. (1962). *Silent spring.* Boston: Houghton Mifflin.

Cassady, J. C. (2001). The stability of undergraduate students' cognitive test anxiety levels. *Practical Assessment, Research, & Evaluation, 7*(20). Retrieved October 4, 2007, from http://PAREonline.net/getvn.asp?v=7&n=20.

Chambliss, D. F., & Schutt, R. K. (2003). *Making sense of the social world: Methods of investigation.* Thousand Oaks, CA: Sage.

Clifford, J. (1983). On ethnographic authority. *Representations, 2,* 118–146.

Clifford, J. (1988). *The predicament of culture: Twentieth-century ethnography, literature, and art.* Cambridge, MA: Harvard University Press.

Cochran-Smith, M., & Donnell, K. (2006). Practitioner inquiry: Blurring the boundaries or research and practice. In J. L. Green, G. Camilli, & P. B. Elmore (Eds.), *Handbook of complementary methods in education research* (pp. 503–518). Mahwah, NJ: Erlbaum.

Cohen, D. K. (1990). A revolution in one classroom: The case of Mrs. Oublier. *Educational Evaluation and Policy Analysis, 12,* 311–329. Retrieved February 1, 2008, from www.jstor.org/pss/1164355.

Cohen, D. K., & Spillane, J. P. (1992). Policy and practice: The relations between governance and instruction. *Review of Research in Education, 18,* 3–49. Retrieved January 10, 2008, from www.jstor.org/pss/1167296.

Cole, J. (1995). Epilogue. In B. Guy-Sheftall (Ed.), *Words of fire: An anthology of African-American feminist thought* (pp. 549–551). New York: The New Press.

Coleman, S., &. Simpson, B. (1998). *Discovering anthropology: A resource guide for teachers and students.* Durham, England: Royal Anthropological Institute.

Collins, K.M.T., Onwuegbuzie, A. J., & Jiao, Q. G. (2006). Prevalence of mixed-methods sampling designs in social science research. *Evaluation and Research in Education, 19,* 83–101.

Collins, P. (1991). *Black feminist thought: Knowledge, consciousness, and the politics of empowerment.* New York: Routledge.

Collins, P. (1995). The social construction of black feminist thought. In B. Guy-Sheftall (Ed.), *Words of fire: An anthology of African-American feminist thought* (pp. 337–357). New York: The New Press.

Consumers Union. (2007). *Consumer reports.* Yonkers, NY: Consumers Union of U.S.

Cooper, H. (2007). *The battle over homework: Common ground for administrators, teachers, and parents* (3rd ed.). Thousand Oaks, CA: Corwin Press.

Crapanzano, V. (1977). On the writing of ethnography. *Dialectical Anthropology*, *2*, 69–73.

Creswell, J. W., Plano Clark, V. L., Gutmann, M. L., & Hanson, W. E. (2003). Advanced mixed methods research designs. In A. Tashakkori & C. Teddlie (Eds.), *Handbook of mixed methods in social and behavioral research* (pp. 209–240). Thousand Oaks, CA: Sage.

Cronbach, L. J. (1975). Beyond the two disciplines of scientific psychology. *American Psychologist*, *30*, 116–127.

Crowder, K. (2004). Being vulnerable and being ethical with/in research. In K. B. deMarrais & S. D. Lapan (Eds.), *Foundations for research: Methods of inquiry in education and the social sciences* (pp. 13–30). Mahwah, NJ: Erlbaum.

Cuban, L. (1993). *How teachers taught: Constancy and change in American classrooms. 1890–1990* (2nd ed.). New York: Longman.

Cuban, L. (2007). Hugging the middle: Teaching in an era of testing and accountability. *Education Policy Analysis Archives*, *15*(1). Retrieved January 15, 2008, from http://epaa.asu.edu/epaa/v15n1/.

de Certeau, M. (2002). *The practice of everyday life.* Berkeley: University of California Press.

Denzin, N. K. (1978). *The research act: An introduction to sociological actions.* New York: McGraw-Hill.

Denzin, N. K., & Lincoln, Y. S. (Eds.) (1994). *Handbook of qualitative research.* Thousand Oaks, CA: Sage.

Dewey, J. (1900). Psychology and social practice. *Psychological Review*, *7*, 105–124.

Diamond, J. (1999). *Guns, germs and steel: The fates of human societies.* New York: Norton.

Dillman, D. A. (1978). *Mail and telephone surveys: The total design method.* New York: Wiley.

Doherty, T. (1988). *Teenagers and teenpics: The juvenilization of American movies in the 1950s.* Boston: Unwin Hyman.

Doyle, W. (1986). Classroom organization and management. In M. C. Wittrock (Ed.), *Handbook of research on teaching* (3rd ed., pp. 392–431). New York: Macmillan.

Dumont, J.-P. (1978). *The headman and I.* Austin: University of Texas Press.

Dworkin, A. (2002). *The political memoir of a feminist militant.* New York: Perseus Books.

Earle, A. M. (1899/1993). *Child life in colonial days.* Stockbridge, MA: Berkshire House.

Ebbutt, D. (1985). Educational action research: Some general concerns and specific quibbles. In R. Burgess (Ed.), *Issues in educational research* (pp. 152–176). Lewes, England: Falmer Press.

Edelman, M. (1988). *Constructing the political spectacle.* Chicago: University of Chicago Press.

Eisenhart, M. (2005). Hammers and saws for the improvement of educational research. *Educational Theory*, *55*, 244–261.

Eisner, E. (1983). The art and craft of teaching. *Educational Leadership*, *40*(4), 4–13. Retrieved January 15, 2008, from www.ascd.org/ASCD/pdf/journals/ed_lead/el_198301_eisner.pdf.

Ellen, R. F. (Ed.). (1984). *Ethnographic research: A guide to general conduct.* New York: Academic Press.

Elliott, J. (1991). *Action research for educational change.* Buckingham, England: Open University Press.

Elliott, J., & Adelman, C. (1976). *Innovation at the classroom level: A case study of the Ford Teaching Project, Unit 28.* Open University Course E 203: Curriculum Design and Development. Milton Keynes, England: Open University Educational Enterprises.

Emerson, R. W. (1837). An oration delivered before the Phi Beta Kappa Society at Cambridge, August 31. Retrieved December 19, 2007, from www.emersoncentral.com/amscholar.htm.

Family Educational Rights and Privacy Act, 20 U.S.C. § 1232g; 34 CFR Part 99. (1974).

Fenstermacher, G. D., & Richardson, V. (1993). The elicitation and reconstruction of practical arguments in teaching. *Journal of Curriculum Studies*, *25*, 101–114.

Fenstermacher, G. D., & Richardson, V. (1994). Promoting confusion in educational psychology: How is it done? *Educational Psychologist*, *29*, 49–55.

Fetterman, D. M. (1989). *Ethnography: Step by step.* Newbury Park, CA: Sage.

Fetterman, D. M. (1997). *Ethnography: Step by step* (2nd ed.). Newbury Park, CA: Sage.

Firestone, W. (1993). Alternative arguments for generalizing from data as applied to qualitative research. *Educational Researcher*, *22*(4), 16–23.

Fisher, C. B. (2002). Participant consultation: Ethical insights into parental permission and confidentiality procedures for policy relevant research with youth. In R. M. Lerner, F. Jacobs, & D. Werlieb (Eds.), *Handbook of applied developmental science* (Vol. *4*, pp. 371–396). Thousand Oaks, CA: Sage.

Fisher, C. B., Hoagwood, K., Boyce, C., Duster, T., Frank, D. A., Grisso, T., Levine, R. J., et al. (2002). Research ethics for mental health science involving ethnic minority children and youths. *American Psychologist*, *57*, 1024–1040.

Foley, D. E. (1990). *Learning capitalist culture: Deep in the heart of Texas*. Philadelphia: University of Pennsylvania Press.

Foucault, M. (1984). What is enlightenment? In P. Rabinow (Ed.), *The Foucault reader* (pp. 32–50). New York: Pantheon Books.

Fowler, F. J. (1993). *Survey research methods* (2nd ed.). Newbury Park, CA: Sage.

Fowler, F. J. (2002). *Survey research methods* (3rd ed., Vol. *1*). Thousand Oaks, CA: Sage.

Fraser, S., & Gerstle, G. (Eds.). (1990). *The rise and fall of the New Deal order, 1930–1980*. Princeton, NJ: Princeton University Press.

Freimuth, V., Quinn, S. C., Thomas, S. B., Cole, G., Zook, E., & Duncan, T. (2001). African Americans' views on research and the Tuskegee Syphilis Study. *Social Science and Medicine, 52*, 797–808.

Friedan, B. (2001). *The feminine mystique*. New York: Norton (Original work published 1963).

Gall, M. D., Gall, J. P., & Borg, W. R. (2003). *Educational research: An introduction* (7th ed.). Boston: Allyn & Bacon.

Gamble, V. (1977). Under the shadow of Tuskegee: African Americans and health care. *American Journal of Public Health, 87*, 1773–1778.

Gannon, S., & Davies, B. (2007). Postmodern, poststructural, and critical theories. In S. Hesse-Biber (Ed.), *Handbook of feminist research: Theory and practice* (pp. 71–106). Thousand Oaks, CA: Sage.

Garan, E. (2001). Beyond the smoke and mirrors: A critique of the National Reading Panel Report on phonics. *Phi Delta Kappan, 82*, 500–506.

Gay, L. R., Mills, G., & Airasian, P. W. (2006). *Educational research: Competencies for analysis and applications* (8th ed.). Upper Saddle River, NJ: Pearson Prentice Hall.

Geertz, C. (1965). *The social history of an Indonesian town*. Cambridge, MA: MIT Press.

Geertz, C. (1973). *The interpretation of cultures*. New York: Basic Books.

Gemmell, C., Moran, R., Crowley, J., & Courtney, R. (1999). *Literature review on the relation between drug use, impaired driving, and traffic accidents*. (CT.97.EP.14) Lisbon: EMCDDA.

Gibson, R. (1986). *Critical theory and education*. London: Hodder and Stoughton.

Gilligan, C. (1982). *In a different voice: Psychological theory and women's development*. Cambridge, MA: Harvard University Press.

Glaser, B., & Strauss, A. L. (1967). *The discovery of grounded theory: Strategies for qualitative research*. Chicago: Aldine.

Glass, G. V (1976). Primary, secondary, and meta-analysis of research. *Educational Researcher, 5*(10), 3–8.

Glass, G. V (1978). Integrating findings: The meta-analysis of research. *Review of Research in Education, 5*, 351–379.

Gluck, S., & Patai, D. (1991). *Women's words: The feminist practice of oral history*. New York: Routledge.

Goffman, E. (1961). *Asylums: Essays on the social situation of mental patients and other inmates*. Peterborough, England: Anchor Books.

Green, B., Johnson, C., & Adams, A. (2001). Writing narrative literature reviews for peer-reviewed journals: Secrets of the trade. *Journal of Sports Chiropractic & Rehabilitation, 15*(1), 5–19.

Greene, J. C., Caracelli, V. J., & Graham, W. F. (1989). Toward a conceptual framework for mixed-method evaluation designs. *Educational Evaluation and Policy Analysis, 11*, 255–274.

Greeno, J. G., Collins, A. M., & Resnick, L. (1996). Cognition and learning. In D. C. Berliner & R. C. Calfee (Eds.), *The handbook of educational psychology* (pp. 2–46). New York: Macmillan.

Griffin, P., & Ouellett, M. (2003). From silence to safety and beyond: Historical trends in addressing lesbian, gay, bisexual, transgender issues in K–12 schools. *Equity & Excellence in Education, 36*, 106–114.

Groves, R. M., Fowler, F. J., Couper, M. P., Lepkowski, J. M., Singer, E., & Tourangeau, R. (2004). *Survey methodology*. New York: Wiley.

Guba, E. G., & Lincoln, Y. S. (1994). Competing paradigms in qualitative methods. In N. Denzin & Y. Lincoln (Eds.), *Handbook of qualitative research* (pp. 105–117). Thousand Oaks, CA: Sage.

Guy-Sheftall, B. (1995). *Words of fire: An anthology of African-American feminist thought*. New York: The New Press.

Halpern, L. R., & Dodson, T. B. (2006). A predictive model to identify women with injuries related to intimate partner violence. *Journal of the American Dental Association, 137*, 604–609.

Harding, S. (1987). *Feminism and methodology: Social science issues*. Bloomington: Indiana University Press.

Harding, S. (2006). *Science and social inequality: Feminist and postcolonial issues*. Chicago: University of Illinois Press.

Hargreaves, D. (1996). Teaching as a research-based profession: Possibilities and prospects. Teacher Training Agency Annual Lecture. London: Teacher Training Agency.

Hargreaves, D. (1998). A new partnership of stakeholders and a national strategy for research in education. In J. Rudduck & D. McIntyre (Eds.), *Challenges for educational research* (pp. 114–138). London: Paul Chapman.

Harslanger, S., & Tuana, N. (2004). Topics in feminism. In *Stanford encyclopedia of philosophy*. Retrieved October 10, 2007, from http://plato.stanford.edu/entries/feminism-topics/.

Hayano, D. M. (1982). *Poker faces: The life and work of professional card players.* Berkeley: University of California Press.

Hedges, L. V., & Olkin, I. (1985). *Statistical methods for meta-analysis.* New York: Academic Press.

Heise, M. (2004). Criminal case complexity: An empirical perspective. *Journal of Empirical Legal Studies, 1*, 331–369.

Hesse-Biber, S. (Ed.) (2007). *Handbook of feminist research: Theory and practice.* Thousand Oaks, CA: Sage.

Higley, A. M., & Morin, K. H. (2004). Behavioral responses of substance-exposed newborns: a retrospective study. *Applied Nursing Research, 17*, 32–40.

Holden, C. (1987). NIMH finds a case of serious misconduct. *Science, 235*, 1566–1567.

Holland, D., & Eisenhart, M. A. (1990). *Educated in romance: Women, achievement, and college culture.* Chicago: University of Chicago Press.

Holmes, T. M., &. Matthews, K. M. (1984). The effects of non-promotion on elementary and junior high school pupils. *Review of Educational Research, 54*, 225–236.

hooks, b. (1995). Black women: Shaping feminist theory. In B. Guy-Sheftall (Ed.), *Words of fire: An anthology of African-American feminist thought* (pp. 270–282). New York: The New Press.

Hopkins, D. (2002). *A teacher's guide to classroom research* (3rd ed.). Maidenhead, England: McGraw-Hill/Open University Press.

House, E. R. (1994). Integrating the quantitative and qualitative. In C. S. Reichardt & S. F. Rallis (Eds.). *The qualitative-quantitative debate: New perspectives* (pp. 13–22). San Francisco: Jossey-Bass.

Howe, E., & Eisenhart, M. (1990). Standards for qualitative (and quantitative) research: A prolegomenon. *Educational Researcher, 19*(4), 2–9.

Howe, K. R. (2005). The question of education science: Experimentism versus experimentalism. *Educational Theory, 55*, 307–321.

Hox, J. J. (1997). From theoretical concept to survey question. In L. Lyberg, et al. (Eds.), *Survey measurement and process quality* (pp. 47–69). New York: Wiley.

Humphreys, L. (1975). *The tearoom trade: Impersonal sex in public places.* Hawthorn, NY: Aldine de Gruyter.

Institute of Medicine. (2001). *Crossing the quality chasm: A new health system for the 21st century.* Washington, DC: National Academies Press.

Jackson, P. W. (1968). *Life in classrooms.* New York: Holt, Rinehart and Winston.

James, W. (1899/1983). *Talks to teachers on psychology and to students on some of life's ideals.* Cambridge, MA: Harvard University Press.

Johnson, B. (2001). Toward a new classification of nonexperimental quantitative research. *Educational Researcher, 30*(2), 3–13.

Johnson, R. B., Onwuegbuzie, A. J., & Turner, L. A. (2007). Toward a definition of mixed methods research. *Journal of Mixed Methods Research, 1*(2), 112–133.

Kaestle, C. F. (1993). The awful reputation of education research. *Educational Researcher, 22*(1), 23, 26–31.

Kaestle, C. F., & Vinovskis, M. (1980). *Education and social change in nineteenth-century Massachusetts.* Cambridge, MA: Cambridge University Press.

Karras, R. M. (2003). *From boys to men: Formations of masculinity in late medieval Europe.* Philadelphia: University of Pennsylvania Press.

Katz, M. B. (1968). *The irony of early school reform: Educational innovation in mid-nineteenth century Massachusetts.* Cambridge, MA: Harvard University Press.

Keene, J. D. (2003). *Doughboys, the Great War, and the remaking of America.* Baltimore, MD: The Johns Hopkins University Press.

Keller, E. F. (1984). *A feeling for the organism: The life and work of Barbara McClintock.* New York: Henry Holt.

Kemmis, S. (1988). Action research in retrospect and prospect. In S. Kemmis & R. McTaggart (Eds.), *The action research reader* (pp. 27–39). Victoria, Australia: Deakin University Press.

Kemmis, S., & McTaggart, R. (1988). *The action research planner* (3rd ed.). Victoria, Australia: Deakin University Press.

Kemper, E., Stringfield, S., & Teddlie, C. (2003). Mixed methods sampling strategies in social science research. In A. Tashakkori & C. Teddlie (Eds.), Handbook of mixed methods in social and behavioral research (pp. 273–296). Thousand Oaks, CA: Sage.

Kennedy, M. (1997). The connection between research and practice. *Educational Researcher, 26*(7), 4–12.

Kenway, J., & Modra, H. (1992). Feminist pedagogy and emancipatory possibilities. In C. Luke & J. Gore (Eds.), *Feminisms and critical pedagogy* (pp. 138–166). New York: Routledge.

Kerber, C. S. (2005). *Problem and pathological gambling.* Salem, OR: Oregon Department of Human Services.

Kerlinger, F. N., & Lee, H. B. (2000). *Foundations of behavioral research.* Orlando, FL: Harcourt Brace.

Kim, H. (2007). The politics of border crossings: Black, postcolonial, and transnational feminist perspectives. In S. Hesse-Biber (Ed.), *Handbook of feminist research* (pp. 107–122). Thousand Oaks, CA: Sage.

Kimmel, A. J. (1998). In defense of deception. *American Psychologist, 53*, 803–805.

Kirk, R. E. (1995). *Experimental design: Procedures for the behavioral sciences* (3rd ed.). Pacific Grove, CA: Brooks/Cole.

Kluckhorn, C., & Leighton, D. (1947). *The Navaho.* Cambridge, MA: Harvard University Press.

Kohn, A. (2006). *The homework myth: Why our kids get too much of a bad thing.* Cambridge, MA: Da Capo Books.

Koocher, G. P., & Keith-Spiegel, P. (1998). *Ethics in psychology: Professional standards and cases* (2nd ed.). New York: Oxford University Press.

Korn, J. H. (1998). The reality of deception. *American Psychologist, 53*, 805.

Laden, F., Neas, L. M., Tolbert, P. E., Holmes, M. D., Hankinson, S. E., Spiegelman, D., et al. (2000). Electric blanket use and breast cancer in the Nurses' Health Study. *American Journal of Epidemiology, 152*, 41–49.

Lafollette, M. C. (1992). *Stealing into print: Fraud, plagiarism, and misconduct in scientific publications.* Berkeley: University of California Press.

Lagemann, E. C. (2000). *An elusive science: The troubling history of education research.* Chicago: University of Chicago Press.

Lalik, R., & Hinchman, K. (2000). Power-knowledge formations in literacy teacher education: Exploring the perspectives of two teacher educators. *The Journal of Educational Research, 93*, 182–191.

Lalik, R., & Hinchman, K. (2001). Critical issues: Examining constructions of race in literacy research: Beyond silence and other oppressions of White liberalism. *The Journal of Literacy Research, 33*, 529–561.

Lalik, R., & Oliver, K. (2007). Differences and tensions in implementing a pedagogy of critical literacy with adolescent girls. *Reading in Research Quarterly, 42*, 46–69.

Lalik, R., Dellinger, L., & Druggish, R. (2003). Fostering collaboration between home and school through curriculum development: Perspectives of three Appalachian children. In A. Willis, G. Garcia, R. Barrera, & V. Harris (Eds.), *Multicultural issues in literacy research and practice* (pp. 69–100). Mahwah, NJ: Erlbaum.

Lapan, S. D. (2004). Evaluation studies. In K. deMarrias & S. D. Lapan (Eds.), *Foundations for research: Methods of inquiry in education and the social sciences.* Mahwah, NJ: Erlbaum.

Lapan, S. D., & Hays, P. A. (2004) Collaborating for change. In K. T. Henson (Ed.), *Curriculum planning: Integrating multiculturalism, constructivism, and education reform* (3rd ed., pp. 263–267). Longrove, IL: Waveland Press.

Lareau, A. (2000). *Home advantage: Social class and parental intervention in elementary education.* Lanham, MD: Rowman and Littlefield.

Lather, P. (1991). *Getting smart: Feminist research and pedagogy with/in the postmodern.* New York: Routledge.

Lather, P. (2000). Drawing the line at angels: Working the ruins of feminist ethnography. In E. St. Pierre & W. Pillow (Eds.), *Working the ruins: Feminist poststructural theory and methods in education* (pp. 284–311). New York: Routledge.

Lather, P., & Smithies, C. (1997). *Troubling the angels: Women living with HIV/AIDS.* Boulder, CO: Westview Press.

LeCompte, M. D., Preissle, J., & Tesch, R. (1993). *Ethnography and qualitative design in educational research* (2nd ed.). San Diego, CA: Academic Press.

LeCompte, M. D., & Schensul, J. J. (1999). *Analyzing and interpreting ethnographic data: Ethnographer's toolkit* (Vol. 5). Walnut Creek, CA: AltaMira Press.

Levin, H. M., Glass, G. V, & Meister, G. R. (1987). Cost-effectiveness of computer aided instruction. *Evaluation Review, 11*, 50–72.

Lewin, K. (1948). *Resolving social conflicts: Selected papers on group dynamics.* New York: Harper Row.

Lewis, M. (1992). Interrupting patriarchy: Politics, resistance and transformation in the feminist classroom. In C. Luke & J. Gore (Eds.), *Feminisms and critical pedagogy* (pp. 167–191). New York: Routledge.

Lincoln, Y. (1997). What constitutes quality in interpretive research? In C. Kinzer, K., Hinchman, & D. Leu (Eds.), *Inquiries in literacy theory and practice* (pp. 54–68). Chicago: The National Reading Conference.

Lodico, M. G., Spaulding, D. T., & Voegtle, K. H. (2006). *Methods in educational research: From theory to practice.* San Francisco: Jossey-Bass.

Lofland, J., & Lofland, L. H. (1995). *Analyzing social settings: A guide to qualitative observation and analysis* (3rd ed.). Belmont, CA: Wadsworth.

Lortie, D. (1975). *Schoolteacher.* Chicago: University of Chicago Press.

Luke, C., & Gore, J. (1992). *Feminisms and critical pedagogy.* New York: Routledge.

Lutz, F. (1986). Witches and witchfinding in educational organizations. *Educational Administration Quarterly, 22,* 49–67.

Lykes, M., & Coquillon, E. (2007). Participatory and action research and feminisms: Towards transformative praxis. In S. Hesse-Biber (Ed.), *Handbook of feminist research: Theory and practice* (pp. 227–326). Thousand Oaks, CA: Sage.

Mabry, L., & Ettinger, L. (1999). Supporting community-oriented educational change: Case and analysis. *Education Policy Analysis Archives, 7*(14). Retrieved March 15, 2008, from http://epaa.asu.edu/epaa/v7n14.html.

Malinowski, B. (1922). *Argonauts of the Western Pacific.* Long Grove, IL: Waveland Press.

Mangione, T. W. (1995). *Mail surveys: Improving the quality.* Thousand Oaks, CA: Sage.

Marcus, G. E. (1998). *Ethnography through thick and thin.* Princeton, NJ: Princeton University Press.

Marcus, G. E., & Cushman, D. (1982). Ethnographies as texts. *Annual Review of Anthropology, 11,* 25–69.

Marcus, G. E., &. Fischer, M. J. (1999). *Anthropology as cultural critique: An experimental moment in the human sciences* (2nd ed.). Chicago: University of Chicago Press.

Markus, M. L. (1983). Power, politics, and MIS implementation. *Communications of the ACM, 26,* 430–444.

Mayo Foundation for Medical Education and Research. (2007). *Seasonal affective disorder (SAD).* Retrieved October 9, 2007, from http://mayoclinic.com/health/seasonal-affective-disorder/DS00195.

McCulloch, G., & Richardson, W. (2000). *Historical research in educational settings.* Berkshire, England, and Philadelphia: Open University Press.

McFadden, A. C. (1999). College students' use of the Internet. *Education Policy Analysis Archives, 7*(6). Retrieved March 15, 2008, from http://epaa.asu.edu/epaa/v7n6.html.

McKernan, J. (1996). *Curriculum action research: A handbook of methods and resources for the reflective practitioner* (2nd ed.). London: RoutledgeFalmer.

McMillan, J. H. (2004). *Educational research* (4th ed.). Boston: Allyn & Bacon.

McNiff, J. (2002) *Action research for professional development: Concise advice for new action researchers* (3rd ed.). Retrieved September 12, 2007, from www.jeanmcniff.com.

Mead, M. (1928). *Coming of age in America.* New York: Morrow.

Mehta, R., & Sivadas, E. (1995). Comparing response rates and response content mail versus electronic mail surveys. *Journal of the Market Research Society, 37,* 429–439.

Meyers, R. J., Miller, W. R., Smith, J. E., & Tonigan, J. S. (2002). A randomized trial of two methods for engaging treatment-refusing drug users through concerned significant others. *Journal of Consulting and Clinical Psychology, 70,* 1182–1185.

Miles, M., & Huberman, M. (1994). *Qualitative data analysis: A sourcebook of new methods.* Beverly Hills, CA: Sage.

Milgram, S. (1974). *Obedience to authority: An experimental view.* New York: Harper and Row.

Miller, C. (2003). Ethical guidelines in research. In J. C. Thomas & H. Hersen (Eds.), *Understanding research in clinical and counseling psychology* (pp. 271–293). Mahwah, NJ: Erlbaum.

Monaghan, E. J. (1989). Literacy instruction and gender in colonial New England. In C. Davidson (Ed.), *Reading in America: Literature and social history* (pp. 53–80). Baltimore, MD: The Johns Hopkins University Press.

Murdock, G. P. (1971). *Outline of cultural materials* (4th rev. ed., 5th printing, with modifications). New Haven, CT: Human Relations Area Files.

Myers, M. D. (1994). A disaster for everyone to see: An interpretive analysis of a failed IS project. *Accounting, Management, and Information Technologies, 4,* 185–201.

Namenwirth, M. (1986). Science seen through a feminist prism. In R. Bleier (Ed.), *Feminist approaches to science* (pp. 18–41). New York: Pergamon Press.

Nardi, P. M. (2006). *Doing survey research: A guide to quantitative methods.* New York: Allyn & Bacon.

Nash, J. (1979). *We eat the mines and the mines eat us: Dependency and exploitation in Bolivian tin mines.* New York: Columbia University Press.

National Cancer Institute. (2008). *New treatment significantly improves long-term outlook for breast cancer survivors.* Retrieved February 25, 2008, from www.cancer.gov/newscenter/pressreleases/letrozole.

National Center for Education Statistics. (2006). *The condition of education 2006.* (U.S. Department of Education, NCES Report # 2006–071). Washington, DC: U.S. Government Printing Office. Retrieved January 10, 2008, from http://nces.ed.gov/programs/coe/2006/pdf/25_2006.pdf.

National Center for Education Statistics. (1988). *National Education Longitudinal Study of 1988* (NELS:88). Retrieved October 1, 2007, from http://nces.ed.gov/surveys/nels88/.

National Commission for the Protection of Human Subjects of Biomedical and Behavioral Research. (1979). *The Belmont Report: Ethical principles and guidelines for the protection of human subjects of research* (GPO 887–809). Washington, DC: U.S. Government Printing Office.

National Reading Panel. (2000). *Teaching children to read: An evidence-based assessment of the scientific research literature on reading and its implications for reading instruction.* Washington, DC: National Reading Panel.

Nesbary, D. K. (2000). *Survey research and the World Wide Web.* Boston: Allyn & Bacon.

Nichols, S. L. (2008). An exploration of students' belongingness beliefs in one middle school. *Journal of Experimental Education, 76*, 145–169.

Nurses' Health Study. Channing Laboratory, Brigham and Women's Hospital, Harvard Medical School. Publications available from the Nurses' Health Study Web site, http://www.channing.harvard.edu/nhs/publications/index.shtml.

Oakes, J., & Rogers, J. (2006). *Learning power: Organizing for education and justice.* New York: Teachers College Press.

Office of Human Subjects Research. (1991). *Guidelines for the conduct of research involving human subjects at the National Institutes of Health.* Retrieved Sept. 30, 2007, http://ohsr.od.nih.gov/guidelines/index.html.

Olesen, V. (1994). Feminisms and models of qualitative research. In N. Denzin & Y. Lincoln (Eds.), *Handbook of qualitative research* (pp. 158–174). London: Sage.

Onwuegbuzie, A. J., & Collins, K.M.T. (2007). A typology of mixed methods sampling designs in social science research. *The Qualitative Report, 12*, 281–316.

Ortmann, A., & Hertwig, R. (1997). Is deception acceptable? *American Psychologist, 52*, 746–747.

Ortner, S. B. (1978). *Sherpas through their rituals.* Cambridge, England: Cambridge University Press.

Ortner, S. B. (1984). Theory in anthropology since the sixties. *Comparative Studies in Society and History, 26*, 126–165.

Pagano, R. R. (2001). *Understanding statistics in the behavioral sciences* (6th ed.). Belmont, CA: Wadsworth.

Palincsar, A. S. (1982). *Improving the reading comprehension of junior high students through tile reciprocal teaching of comprehension-monitoring strategies.* Unpublished doctoral dissertation, University of Illinois at Urbana-Champaign.

Palincsar, A. S. (1986). The role of dialogue in providing scaffolded instruction. *Educational Psychologist, 21*, 73–98.

Palincsar, A. S., & Brown, A. L. (1984). Reciprocal teaching of comprehension-fostering and comprehension-monitoring activities. *Cognition and Instruction, 2*, 117–175.

Patai, D. (1991). U. S. academics and third world women: Is ethical research possible? In S. Gluck & D. Patai (Eds.), *Women's words: The feminist practice of oral history* (pp. 137–153). New York: Routledge.

Peacock, J. L. (1986). *Anthropological lens: Harsh light, soft focus.* Cambridge, England: Cambridge University Press.

Pedhazur, E. J., & Schmelkin, L. P. (1991) *Measurement, design, and analysis: An integrated Approach.* Hillsdale, NJ: Erlbaum.

Perlmann, J. (1988). *Ethnic differences: Schooling and social structure among the Irish, Italians, Jews and Blacks in an American city, 1880–1935.* Cambridge, England: Cambridge University Press, 1988.

Perrone, K. M., Webb, L. K., & Jackson, Z. V. (2007). Relationships between parental attachment, work and family roles, and life satisfaction. *The Career Development Quarterly, 55*, 237–248.

Peshkin, A. (1978). *Growing up American: Schooling and the survival of community.* Prospect Heights, IL: Waveland Press.

Peshkin, A. (1986). *God's choice: The total world of a fundamentalist Christian school.* Chicago: University of Chicago Press.

Powell, P. J. (2005). *The effects of grade retention: Life histories of adults who were retained as children.* Unpublished doctoral dissertation, Northern Arizona University, Flagstaff, Arizona.

Protection of Pupil Rights Amendment, 20 U.S.C. § 1232h; 34 CFR Part 98 (1974).

Rabinow, P. (1977). *Reflections on fieldwork in Morocco.* Berkeley: University of California Press.

Rampolla, M. L. (2004). *A pocket guide to writing in history* (4th ed). Boston: Bedford/St. Martin's.

Raudenbush S. W. (2005). Learning from attempts to improve schooling: The contribution of methodological diversity. *Educational Researcher, 34*(5), 25–31.

Ravitch, D., & Vinovskis, M. (1995). *Learning from the past: What history teaches us about school reform.* Baltimore, MD: The Johns Hopkins University Press.

Reed-Danahay, D. (1997). *Auto/ethnography: Rewriting the self and the social.* New York: Berg.

Resnick, L. B. (1981). Instructional psychology. In M. R. Rosenzweig & L. W. Porter (Eds.), *Annual review of psychology* (Vol. *32*, pp. 659–704). Palo Alto, CA: Annual Reviews.

Riemer, F. (2001). *Working at the margins: Moving off welfare in America.* Albany: State University of New York Press.

Riemer, F. (2004). Connecting and reconnecting to work: Low-income mothers' participation, past and present, in publicly funded training programs. In V. Polakow, S. Butler, L. Deprez, & P. Kahn (Eds.), *Shut out: Low-income women and higher education in post-welfare America* (pp. 97–114). Albany, NY: SUNY Press.

Robinson, D. H., Levin, J. R., Thomas, G. D., Pituch, K. A., & Vaughn, S. (2007). The incidence of "causal" statements in teaching-and-learning research journals. *American Educational Research Journal, 44*, 400–413.

Rohan, K. J., Roecklein, K. A., Lindsey, K. T., Johnson, L. G., Lippy, R. D., Lacy, T. J., & Barton, F. B. (2007). A randomized controlled trial of cognitive-behavioral therapy, light therapy, and their combination for seasonal affective disorder. *Journal of Consulting and Clinical Psychology, 75*, 489–500.

Rose, H. (1986). Beyond masculinist realities: A feminist epistemology for the sciences. In R. Bleier (Ed.), *Feminist approaches to science* (pp. 57–76). New York: Pergamon Press.

Rose, L. C., & Gallup, A. M. (2007). The 39th annual Phi Delta Kappa/Gallup Poll of the public's attitudes toward the public schools. *Phi Delta Kappan, 89*, 33–48.

Rosenshine, B., & Meister, C. (1994). Reciprocal teaching: A review of the research. *Review of Educational Research, 64*, 479–530. Retrieved February 1, 2008, from www.jstor.org/pss/1170585.

Rottinghaus, P. J., Coon, K. L., Gaffey, A. R., & Zytowski, D. G. (2007). Thirty-year stability and predictive validity of vocational interests. *Journal of Career Assessment, 15*, 5–22.

Roznowski, M., Reith, J., & Hong, S. (2000). A further look at youth intellectual giftedness and its correlates: Values, interests, performance, and behavior. *Intelligence, 28*, 87–113.

Rushowy, K. (2008, February 9). Homework a homewrecker: Report. *Toronto Star.* Retrieved February 9, 2008, from www.thestar.com/article/302001.

Sabbe, E., & Aelterman, A. (2007). Gender in teaching: A literature review. *Teachers and Teaching, 13*, 521–538.

Said, E. (1979). *Orientalism.* New York: Random House.

Salant, P., & Dillman, D. A. (1994). *How to conduct your own survey.* New York: Wiley.

Schatzman, L., &. Strauss, A. L. (1973). *Field research: Strategies for a natural sociology.* Englewood Cliffs, NJ: Prentice-Hall.

Scheper-Hughes, N. (1992). *Death without weeping—the violence of everyday life in Brazil.* Berkeley: University of California Press.

Scheurich, J. (1997). *Research method in the postmodern.* London: Falmer Press.

Schoenfeld, A. (2006). Design experiments. In J. L. Green, G. Camilli, G. & P. B. Elmore (Eds.), *Complementary methods for research in education* (3rd ed., pp. 193–205). Washington DC: American Educational Research Association.

Schutz, P. A., Chambless, C. B., & DeCuir, J. T. (2004). Multimethods research. In K. B. deMarrais & S. D. Lapan (Eds.), *Foundations for research: Methods of inquiry in education and the social sciences* (pp. 267–281). Mahwah, NJ: Erlbaum.

Scriven, M. S. (1991). *Evaluation thesaurus* (4th ed.). Newbury Park, CA: Sage.

Shadish, W. R., Cook, T. D., & Campbell, D. T. (2002). *Experimental and quasi-experimental designs for generalized causal inference.* Boston: Houghton Mifflin.

Shepard, L. A., & Smith, M. L. (1989). *Flunking grades: Research and policies on grade retention.* New York: Falmer Press.

Shouksmith, G., Pajo, K., & Jepsen, A. (1990). Construction of a multidimensional scale of job satisfaction. *Psychological Reports, 67*, 355–364

Sieber, J. E. (1992). Planning ethically responsible research: A guide for students and internal review boards. *Applied Social Research Methods Series* (Vol. 31). Newbury Park, CA: Sage.

Sieber, J. E. (1994). Will the new code help researchers be more ethical? *Professional Psychology Research and Practice*, *25*, 369–365.

Sieber, J. E. (1996). Typically unexamined communication processes in research. In B. H. Stanley, J. E. Sieber, & G. B. Melton (Eds.), *Research ethics: A psychological approach* (pp. 73–104). Lincoln: University of Nebraska Press.

Sieber, S. D. (1973). The integration of fieldwork and survey methods. *The American Journal of Sociology*, *78*, 1335–1359.

Simon, A., & Boyer, G. (Eds.). (1973). *Mirrors for behavior III: An anthology of observation instruments.* Wyncotte, PA: Research for Better Schools.

Simons, H. (1977). Case-studies of innovation. In D. Hamilton, B. MacDonald, C. King, D. Jenkins, & M. Parlett (Eds.), *Beyond the numbers game: A reader in educational evaluation* (pp. 178–180). Berkeley, CA: McCutchan.

Simsek, Z., & Veiga, J. F. (2001). A primer on Internet organizational surveys. *Organizational Research Methods, 4*, 218–235.

Slater M., Antley A., Davison A., Swapp D., Guger C., Barker, C., et al. (2006). A virtual reprise of the Stanley Milgram obedience experiments. *PLoS ONE*, *1*(1). Retrieved September 30, 2007, from www.plosone.org/article/fetchArticle.action?articleURI = info:doi/10.1371/journal.pone.0000039.

Slavin, R. E. (1986). Best-evidence synthesis: An alternative to meta-analytic and traditional reviews. *Educational Researcher*, *15*(9), 5–11.

Smith, E. R., & Tyler, R. W. (1942). *Appraising and recording student progress.* New York: Harper.

Smith, J. K., & Heshusius, L. (1986). Closing down the conversation: The end of the quantitative-qualitative debate among educational researchers. *Educational Researcher*, *15*(1), 4–12.

Smith, M. L. (2004). *Political spectacle and the fate of American schools.* New York: Routledge.

Smith, M. L., Glass, G. V, & Miller, T. I. (1980). *The benefits of psychotherapy.* Baltimore, MD: The Johns Hopkins University Press.

Smith, M. L., & Shepard, L. A. (1988). Kindergarten readiness and retention: A qualitative study of teachers' beliefs and practices. *American Educational Research Journal*, *25*, 307–333.

Spector, P. E. (1985). Measurement of human service staff satisfaction: Development of the Job Satisfaction Survey. *American Journal of Community Psychology*, *13*, 693–713.

Spies, R. A., & Plake, B. S. (Eds.). (2005). *The sixteenth mental measurements yearbook.* Lincoln: University of Nebraska Press.

Spradley, J. P. (1979). *The ethnographic interview.* New York: Holt, Rinehart, and Winston.

St. Pierre, E., & Pillow, W. (2000) Introduction: Inquiry among the ruins. In E. St. Pierre, & W. Pillow (Eds.), *Working the ruins: Feminist poststructural theory and methods in education* (pp. 1–24). New York: Routledge.

Stacey, J. (1991). Can there be a feminist ethnography? In S. Gluck & D. Patai (Eds.), *Women's words: The feminist practice of oral history* (pp. 111–119). New York: Routledge.

Stake, R. E. (1967). Countenance of educational evaluation. *Teachers College Record*, *68*, 523–540.

Stake, R. E. (1995). *The art of case study research.* Thousand Oaks, CA: Sage.

Stake, R. E. (2005). Qualitative case studies. In N. K. Denzin & Y. S. Lincoln (Eds.), *Sage handbook of qualitative research* (3rd ed., pp. 443–466). Thousand Oaks, CA: Sage.

Stake, R. E., & Schwandt, T. A. (2006). On discerning quality in evaluation. In I. F. Shaw, J. C. Greene, & M. M. Mark (Eds.), *The Sage handbook of evaluation* (pp. 404–418). Thousand Oaks, CA: Sage.

Stake, R. E., & Trumbull, D. J. (1982). Naturalistic generalizations. *Review Journal of Philosophy and Social Science*, *7*, 1–12.

Stenhouse, L. (1984). Artistry and teaching: The teacher as focus of research and development. In D. Hopkins & M. Wideen (Eds.), *Alternative perspectives on school improvement* (pp. 67–76). Lewes, England: Falmer Press.

Stewart, M. (1995). Introduction. In B. Guy-Sheftall (Ed.), *Words of fire: An anthology of African-American feminist thought* (pp. 26–33). New York: The New Press.

Stokes, D. E. (1997). *Pasteur's quadrant: Basic science and technological innovation.* Washington, DC: The Brookings Institute.

Strauss, A. L., & Corbin, J. (1998). *Basics of qualitative research: Techniques and procedures for developing grounded theory* (2nd ed.). Thousand Oaks, CA: Sage.

Street, B. (1984). *Literacy in theory and practice.* New York: Cambridge University Press.

Tashakkori, A., & Teddlie, C. (1998). *Mixed methodology: Combining qualitative and quantitative approaches.* Thousand Oaks, CA: Sage.

Tashakkori, A., & Teddlie, C. (2003). *Handbook of mixed methods in social and behavioral research.* Thousand Oaks, CA: Sage.

Teddlie, C., & Tashakkori, A. (2003). Major issues and controversies in the use of mixed methods in the social and behavioral sciences. In A. Tashakkori & C. Teddlie (Eds.), *Handbook of mixed methods in social and behavioral research* (pp. 3–50). Thousand Oaks, CA: Sage.

Thorndike, E. L. (1910). The contribution of psychology to education. *Journal of Educational Psychology*, *1*, 5–12.

Torraco, R. (2005). Writing intergrative literature reviews: Guidelines and examples. *Human Development Review*, *4*, 356–367.

Tourangeau, R., Rips, L. J., & Rasinski, K. (2000). *The psychology of survey response.* Cambridge, England: Cambridge University Press.

Trochim, W. M. (2005). *Research methods: The concise knowledge base.* Cincinnati, OH: Atomic Dog.

Tyack, D., & Cuban, L. (1995). *Tinkering toward utopia: A century of public school reform.* Cambridge, MA: Harvard University Press.

Tyler, R. W., Lapan, S. D., Moore, J. C., Rivers, L. W., & Skibo, D. B. (1978). *The Florida accountability program: An evaluation of its educational soundness and implementation.* Washington, DC: National Education Association.

Ulrich, L. T. (1991). *A midwife's tale: The life of Martha Ballard, based on her diary*, 1785–1812. New York: Vintage Books.

United States Department of Education. (2003, December 9). *Identifying and implementing educational practices supported by rigorous evidence: A user friendly guide.* Retrieved October 4, 2007, from www.ed.gov/rschstat/research/pubs/rigorousevid/index.html.

United States National Institutes of Health. (2007). *Resource information.* Retrieved January 3, 2008, from http://clinicaltrials.gov/.

van Maanen, J. (1995). *Representation in ethnography.* Thousand Oaks, CA: Sage.

Vittengl, J. R., Clark, L. A., Dunn, T. W., & Jarrett, R. B. (2007). Reducing relapse and recurrence in unipolar depression: A comparative meta-analysis of cognitive-behavioral therapy's effects. *Journal of Consulting and Clinical Psychology*, *75*, 475–488.

Walker, A. (1983). *In search of our mothers' gardens: Womanist prose.* New York: Harcourt Brace Jovanovich.

Walker, R., & Adelman, C. (1990). *A guide to classroom observation.* London: Routledge.

Washington, H. A. (2007). *Medical apartheid: The dark history of medical experimentation on black Americans from colonial times to the present.* New York: Doubleday.

Waxman, H., Connell, M., & Gray, J. (2002). *Meta-analysis: Effects of educational technology on student outcomes.* Naperville, IL: North Central Regional Educational Laboratory.

Waxman, H., Lin, M., & Michko, G. (2003). *Meta-analysis of the effectiveness of teaching and learning with technology on student outcomes.* Naperville, IL: North Central Regional Educational Laboratory.

Weiler, K. (1988). *Women teaching for change: Gender, class and power.* New York: Bergin & Garvey.

Weinert, F. E., & De Corte, E. (1996). Translating research into practice. In E. De Corte & F. E. Weinert (Eds). *International encyclopedia of developmental and instructional psychology* (pp. 43–50). Oxford, England: Elsevier.

White, K. R. (1982). The relation between socioeconomic status and academic achievement. *Psychological Bulletin* *91*, 461–481.

Whyte, W. F. (1981). *Street corner society* (3rd ed.). Chicago: University of Chicago Press.

Whyte, W. F. (1994). *Participant observer: An autobiography.* New York: Cornell University Press.

Whyte, W. F. (1996). On the evolution of street corner society. In A. Lareau & J. Shultz, *Journeys through ethnography: Realistic accounts of fieldwork* (pp. 9–74). Boulder, CO: Westview Press.

Williams, E. (1944). *Capitalism and slavery.* Chapel Hill: University of North Carolina Press.

Willis, P. (1977). *Learning to labour.* London: Routledge & Kegan Paul.

Wolcott, H. F. (1967/2003). *A Kwakiutl village and school.* Walnut Creek, CA: AltaMira Press.

Wolcott, H. F. (1978). *The man in the principal's office: An ethnography.* Prospect Heights, IL: Waveland Press.

Wolcott, H. F. (1999). *Ethnography: A way of seeing.* Walnut Creek, CA: AltaMira Press.

Wolcott, H. F. (2001). *The art of fieldwork.* Walnut Creek, CA: AltaMira Press.

Yammarino, F. J., Skinner, S. J., & Childers, T. L. (1991). Understanding mail survey response behavior: A meta-analysis. *Public Opinion Quarterly*, *55*, 613 639.

Yin, R. K. (2003). *Case study research: Design and methods* (3rd ed.). Thousand Oaks, CA: Sage.

Zimbardo, P. G. (1972). The pathology of imprisonment. *Society*, 6(4), 6–8.

Zimbardo, P. G., Maslach, C., & Haney, C. (2000). Reflections on the Stanford Prison Experiment: Genesis, transformations, consequences. In T. Bass. (Ed.), *Obedience to authority: Current perspectives on the Milgram paradigm* (pp. 193–238). Mahwah, NJ: Erlbaum.

Zwick, R., & Green, J. G. (2007). New perspectives on the correlation of SAT scores, high school grades, and socioeconomic factors. *Journal of Educational Measurement*, *44*, 23–45.

Index

Subject Index

P

p value, 126, 127
panel study, 67
parallel samples, 255
parameters, 20, 21, 29–30, 88
participant observers, 169, 207
participants: anonymity of, 12, 96–98; autonomy of, 2, 4; beneficence toward, 4; coercion of, 8; confidentiality of, 12, 96–98, 211; deception of, 2, 7–11, 49–50; disagreement of, 85; in experimental research, 40; families and children as, 8–9, 12, 253, 288; feedback from, 194; identification of, 192, 210, 303; minorities as, 14; privacy of, 7; relationship to researchers (*See* relationships); rewards to, 9, 90; rights of, 2, 4, 9–10; risks to, 4–13, 210; self awareness of, 10, 11; understanding of research goals, 86. *See also* sampling
Pasteur's quadrant, 310
patterns in data, types of, 267–268
Pearson *r*, 123, 127
peer-reviewed, 21
percentiles, 120–121, 135
personnel evaluation, 184
perspectival research, 233–234
perspective of researchers, 158
perspectives, multiple, 235
Phi Delta Kappa/Gallup Poll of the Public's Attitudes, 66, 81
philosophies of history, 159
pilot research, 43, 87–88. *See also* pretest, value of
plagiarism, 14
pluralism, 212–213
Pocket Guide to Writing in History, A (Rampolla), 162, 164
policy: evaluation of, 184; and historical research, 150; relationship of, to research, 298–309
political history, 161
population, 44
population parameters, 88
population validity, 53
populations: general *versus* specific, 67; hypothetical, 142
positive correlations, 123
positively skewed data, 110
postmodernism, 159, 216. *See also* critical postmodern feminism
poststructural feminism, 225
Practice of Everyday Life, The (Certeau), 215
Practice of Social Research, The (Babbie), 99
practice *versus* research, 298–302
practitioners, relevance of research to, 307. *See also* policy
predictive nonexperimental research, 65–66, 70
predictive validity, 46
predictor variables, 65, 71
presentism, 146
pretest, value of, 51, 55. *See also* pilot research

Pretreatment Expectations Survey, 40
primary sources of data, 151–156
prioritization. *See* scope
privacy of participants, 7. *See also* anonymity of participants; confidentiality
privacy of teaching, 303
probabilistic techniques, 142
probability level. *See p* value
probability sampling, 192–193
Problem and Pathological Gambling (Kerber), 22
Problem of Ethnographic Representation, The (Clifford), 219
problem-solving process, role of research in, 245
procedural irregularities, 46
Professional Psychology Research and Practice, 17
program antecedents, 185
program evaluations, 168; bias in, 194–195; communication during, 197; criteria of, 182–185, 188–189; data analysis in, 182–183; definition of, 182; design of, 182–183, 187–188, 190–193, 197–198; dissemination of findings from, 182–183, 186, 193, 199; ethical issues in, 195–196; evaluation of, 194–199; examples of, 182; history of, 186–187; purposes of, 185–186, 188, 199; research questions in, 182–183, 189; resources related to, 200–201; stakeholders in, 183, 188–189, 197; types of, 183–186; validity in, 198–199. *See also* case study research
program outcomes, 185
progressive philosophy of history, 159
prospective nonexperimental research, 66–70
Protection of Pupil Rights Amendment, 5, 8–9
protocol, interview, 190–191
protocol, research, 42
providential philosophy, 159
psychology, 9, 140–141, 297
psychotherapy, 140–141
public records, 153
publishing, 13–14. *See also* dissemination of findings; writing
pure research, 310
purpose of research, 38–39, 148–150. *See also* usefulness of research
purposeful sampling, 45, 47, 90–91, 177, 192, 254
purposive sampling, 45, 53, 177, 192

Q

QDA Miner, 268
qualitative analysis, 266, 271; use of software in, 267–268
qualitative data: analysis of, 260–268, 273–274; co-occurrence in, 268; describing, 270; omission in, 268; patterns in, 267–268; types of, 104, 247, 255, 260–262. *See also* qualitative research
qualitative dominant design, 252
Qualitative Report, The, 274
qualitative research: and the arts, 305; and case study research, 169; coding of data in, 260–261, 264–267;

University of North Carolina at Chapel Hill, 33

usefulness of research: case studies, 167, 177–178; feminist research, 235–236; literature reviews, 21; meta-analyses, 143; nonexperimental research, 65–66; program evaluations, 199; relationship to practice, 290–291, 296–298, 310–312; and validity, 52–54

utilitarian approach, 2, 9–10

utilitarian view of risk, 7

V

validation, 270; in action research, 289. *See also* triangulation

validity: in case study research, 178; in ethnographic research, 218; in experimental research, 49; external, 52–54; internal, 47–50, 52, 54; in interviews, 154; in literature reviews, 25–26, 29–31; in multimethod research, 246; in observations, 191; in program evaluation, 198–199; *versus* reliability, 45, 62; in survey research, 84, 87; types of, 46–50, 52–54, 53. *See also* quality in research; reliability; triangulation

value of research. *See* usefulness of research

values of data, 105

variability: measures of, 45, 117–120, 122; in meta-analyses, 135

variables: attribute, 60, 71, 81, 160; categorical, 61, 112–114; confounding, 73; criterion, 71; definition of, 61–64, 83, 123; dependent, 37, 40, 71, 83–84, 126; extraneous, 37, 47–50; independent, 37, 39, 71, 84; intervening, 55; lurking, 73–74; manipulation of, 37, 60; measurement of, 83, 155, 182–183, 190–192; in nonexperimental research, 71; predictor, 65, 71

variance, analysis of, 127

verb tense, 214

verification, 291

video recordings, 288

vignettes in qualitative research, 269

W

waves of feminism, 225–226

Wayback Machine, 144

Web-based surveys, 95–96

Whiggish interpretation of history, 159

Wikipedia, 144

Wilcoxon matched-pairs signed ranks test, 127

womanism movement, 228

women. *See* gender

women in science, 229–231, 237–238

Women's Words (Gluck and Patai), 240

Words of Fire (Guy-Sheftall), 240

World Health Organization, 185

World History Association, 162

World Wide Web, 133, 144

writing: bias in, 26; ethnographic findings, 214–216; of executive summaries, 193; of literature reviews, 27–31; narrative techniques in, 214–215; plagiarism and, 14; of qualitative data reports, 269, 271; of research questions, 64; style choices in, 31, 151, 214, 217; of survey questions, 64, 84–86, 88; value of clarity in, 27–28, 31, 73, 193, 277, 307

Z

z scores, 121–122